D1110683

TAJ MAHAL
DELHI & JAIPUR

MARGOT BIGG

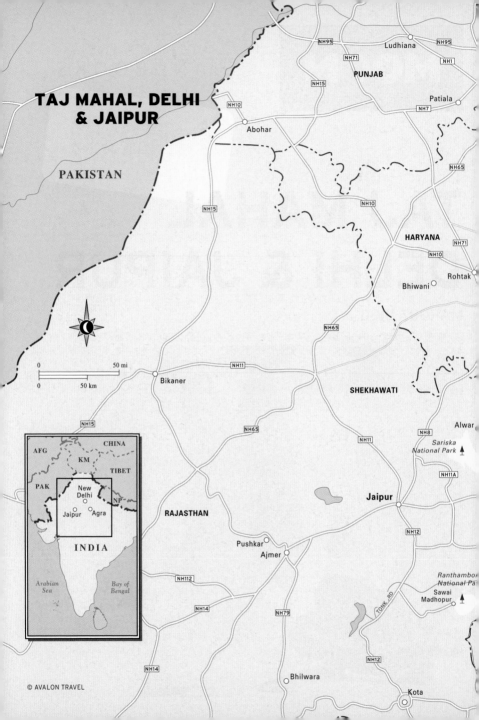

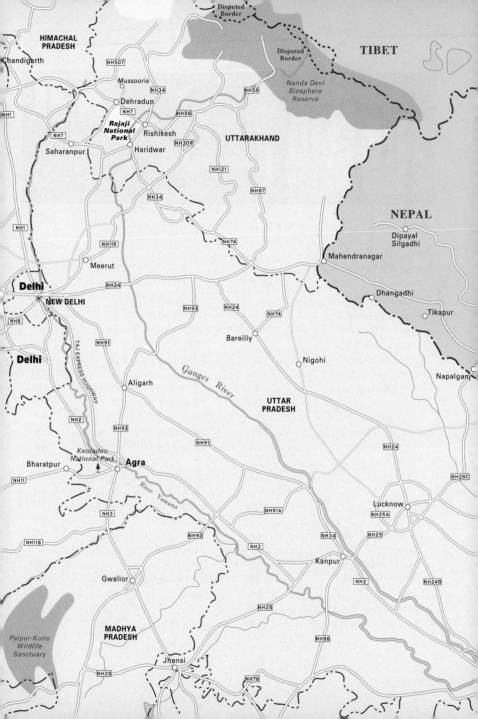

Contents

Discover Taj Mahal, Delhi & Jaipur

With its shimmering white marble domes and perfect symmetry, the Taj Mahal is among the most stunning marvels on the planet as well as the world's most magnificent emblem of love. Photos cannot do justice to this architectural masterpiece. A stroll along the reflecting pool that cuts through the lush grounds of this breathtaking mausoleum transports you back to a time when bejeweled royalty feasted on richly spiced delicacies and terraced fountains flowed with rose water.

In an ideal world, everyone would get the chance to see India at least once. This intense country is like nowhere else on earth. You could spend lifetimes exploring its extraordinary landscapes, architecture, and cultural traditions. The North Indian cities of Delhi, Jaipur, and Agra, home of the Taj Mahal, are collectively known as India's Golden Triangle. Even a brief visit to this region will give you a good feel for the country's regal past, not to mention plenty of amazing memories of your own.

Stepping onto the streets of Jaipur is like jumping into the pages of an illustrated fairy tale. Elephant processions, grandiose forts, chivalrous men with mustaches that stretch extravagantly, and starbursts of color contrast against the starkness of the golden desert.

The vibrant gateway city of Delhi can seem hectic to the first-time

visitor, particularly because it's constantly thronging with people. That said, once you get into the groove of things, you will discover that this sprawling metropolis is one of the most history-rich spots on the planet. Stroll through Old Delhi, where hole-in-the wall stores crowned with colorful hand-painted signboards are set against a backdrop of sky-piercing sandstone mosques and forts that date back centuries. Drive down Central and South Delhi's broad leafy avenues alongside luxury cars and the odd oxcart, past 500-year-old tombs and Raj-era buildings that blend neoclassical architecture with Indian aesthetics.

India's liveliness, color, and contrasts strike visitors almost immediately. However, most leave with a much deeper impression of India, one that's illustrated by the stories of the people they meet and the adventures they have. Whatever your Indian experience ends up being, it's sure to have a lasting impact on the way you see our world and its people.

Planning Your Trip

▶ WHERE TO GO

Delhi

India's capital, Delhi, is an increasingly cosmopolitan city with great shopping, exceptional restaurants, and some of India's most interesting historical sights. Here you'll be able to explore the ruins of well-preserved Lodi and Mughal-era tombs, admire the grandeur of the colonial buildings and monuments in Lutyens's Delhi, stroll through verdant old gardens, and seek solace at some of India's most impressive temples—all in the same day. In the evening you can attend an event in one of Central Delhi's many cultural centers (there's always plenty to choose from) or dance the night away at one of the city's many live music venues.

Agra and the Taj Mahal

Agra is home to the Taj Mahal, arguably the greatest ode to love in architectural history, and so much more. This easy-to-navigate city was built primarily by the Mughals, who invaded India in the 16th century and brought with them mind-bogglingly intricate architecture and a passion for beauty. Admire the well-preserved tombs in Agra, and don't forget to pay a visit to the city's sprawling fort. The whole area around Agra is filled with interesting sights, from the abandoned city at Fatehpur Sikri to the Tomb of Akbar the Great in the nearby town of Sikandra.

IF YOU HAVE . . .

- **THREE DAYS:** Spend two days in **Delhi** and one day in **Agra,** where you can visit the **Taj Mahal.**
- **ONE WEEK:** Add **Jaipur** and **Pushkar** or **Ranthambore National Park.**
- **TWO WEEKS:** Add **Keoladeo National Park,** the **Shekhawati Region, Rishikesh,** and **Mussoorie.**

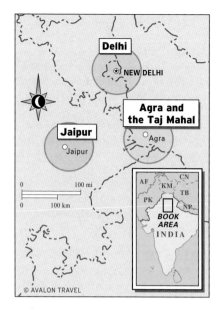

Map labels: Delhi, NEW DELHI, Agra and the Taj Mahal, Jaipur, Jaipur, Agra, 0 100 mi, 0 100 km, AF, CN, KM, TB, PK, NP, BOOK AREA, INDIA, © AVALON TRAVEL

Jaipur

Deep in the desert of Rajasthan, the royal city of Jaipur is chock-full of enchanting old palaces, stunning forts, and beautiful heritage hotels. Jaipur's old town, dubbed the Pink City for its salmon-hued walls, is a charming conglomeration of historic royal structures and lively handicraft markets. A short drive away, Amber, Jaipur's ancient predecessor, is home to a series of imposing forts and stunning gardens set against the backdrop of the rugged Aravalli mountain range. Taking an elephant ride to the top of Amber Fort is one of the highlights of many a visitor's trip to this dazzling city.

Excursions Around the Taj Mahal, Delhi & Jaipur

There are plenty of interesting spots near Delhi, Jaipur, and Agra, and if you have the time, an excursion or two is definitely in order. North of Delhi, Rishikesh is considered the yoga capital of the world and provides a fascinating glimpse into the Hindu belief system. Near Rishikesh, the old colonial hill station of Mussoorie is a perfect place to escape the heat of the Indo-Gangetic Plain. Rajasthan's Shekhawati region is filled with beautiful old homes covered in gorgeous frescoes, and farther south, the incredibly photogenic holy town of Pushkar hosts the world's largest camel fair every autumn. Outdoorsy types won't want to miss one of Rajasthan's national parks: Keoladeo National Park is heaven for bird-watchers, and if you're lucky, you may spot a tiger in Sariska Tiger Reserve or Ranthambore National Park.

▶ WHEN TO GO

India's high season runs October–March, as this is the time of year when temperatures are coolest. October–November is the most festive time to be in India, especially in the days leading up to Diwali, the annual Hindu festival of light. January can get remarkably cold and foggy. If you want to avoid crowds, September and April are still good times to visit, although both months can get a bit hot.

Monsoon season runs late-June–August, and this helps reduce temperatures a bit. Note that some national parks close during the summer and monsoon seasons. During the off-season you can usually haggle for heavy discounts, particularly in Agra and Jaipur. Delhi, on the other hand, welcomes visitors year-round (it is a capital city, after all), and room rates here are pretty consistent throughout the year.

▶ BEFORE YOU GO

Passports and Visas

You need a passport and a visa to enter India. Citizens of most countries, including the United States, the United Kingdom, Canada, and Australia, have to obtain a visa ahead of time from their local Indian consulate or embassy.

Vaccinations

It's a good idea to get vaccinated against hepatitis A and B, polio, and typhoid before you head to India. Also make sure you are up-to-date on routine vaccinations against illnesses such as tetanus. Some people also take malaria prophylactics—discuss this and all other pretravel vaccination questions with your doctor well in advance of your trip.

Transportation

Most visitors to northern India fly into Delhi's Indira Gandhi International Airport. The airport at Jaipur is primarily for domestic flights, although there are a couple of international flights to Jaipur from the Middle East. Agra also has an airport with flights only to Delhi.

Getting around the Golden Triangle is fairly straightforward, and there are plenty of regular buses and trains among the three major cities. Many people choose to book a car with a driver for the journey. All three options can be arranged in advance through a travel agent or once you arrive in India.

What to Take

Don't forget to bring mosquito repellent, sunscreen, and an electrical adapter (the type designed for use in continental Europe work well). Loose-fitting cotton clothing is appropriate for both men and women and

Frescoes adorn the walls in Rajasthan's Shekhawati region.

Shekhawati fresco

a small shrine to the Hindu god Shiva

will keep you shaded yet cool. Both men and women need to cover their legs and shoulders before entering many of India's religious sites, so make sure to bring a pair of long trousers or a long skirt. Winters can get surprisingly cold in this region, so remember to pack sweaters if you are visiting between December and February.

Explore Taj Mahal, Delhi & Jaipur

► THE BEST OF INDIA'S GOLDEN TRIANGLE

Delhi, Agra, and Jaipur collectively make up what is known as India's Golden Triangle, and all three cities are home to a number of incredible sights, including the magnificent Taj Mahal. To really get a feel for these cities and a few key excursions nearby, it's ideal to spend about 10-14 days on the circuit, taking the time to visit the sights at a relaxed pace. However, it is possible to hit the key sights in all three cities in less time. The fastest trains take two hours to travel between Agra and Delhi (it's about four hours by road). Jaipur is 4-5 hours by train and road from both Agra (to the east) and Delhi (to the north).

Ranthambore National Park, near the town of Sawai Madhopur, is 2-3 hours by road or train from Jaipur. From Agra, driving takes 3-4 hours, and the train takes 4-6 hours.

Ajmer, the town with the nearest railway station to Pushkar, is 2-3 hours by train from Jaipur or about 6.5 hours from Delhi if you take the fast *Shatabdi* train. Haridwar, the major railway town for Rishikesh, is 4-5 hours by train from Delhi.

The day-by-day itinerary below begins and ends in Delhi and provides suggestions for visiting all the major destinations in India's Golden Triangle in two weeks. Depending on your schedule, you can use these recommendations to plan a trip that's shorter or longer while taking in the many enchanting sights of this fascinating region.

The Taj Mahal is the world's most magnificent symbol of undying love.

sunset over Pushkar

Delhi

DAYS 1-3

If you only have a few days in India, or if you've come for work and don't have much free time, you might want to stick just to Delhi, with a day trip to the Taj Mahal. Use your first day to explore the sights in Central Delhi. Grab some breakfast at Connaught Place and then head to the Jantar Mantar to check out the unusual astronomical instruments on display. Next, join the scores of Sikhs paying obeisance at the magnificent Gurudwara Bangla Sahib just down the road. From here, take an autorickshaw or taxi to the Lodi Gardens and visit the Lodi-era monuments in this verdant park. A short jaunt down the road takes you to Khan Market, a great place to do a bit of shopping and grab a bite to eat. Spend your afternoon exploring the UNESCO World Heritage Site of Humayun's Tomb before making your way to the Nizamuddin Dargah—if you're here on a Thursday, you may even catch a lively

Qawwali (Sufi devotional music) session. Otherwise, you can head to the India Habitat Centre or the India International Centre for an evening music or dance performance.

Spend Day 2 in Old Delhi. Start your morning off bright and early with a visit to the Lal Qila (Red Fort), the seat of Mughal emperor Shahjahan after he shifted his capital to what is now Old Delhi and named it Shahjahanabad. After your visit, head across the street to the Sri Digambar Jain Lal Mandir and its adjoining bird hospital. You'll probably have worked up an appetite by now, so make your way down Chandni Chowk and get lunch at Karim's, an Old Delhi institution famous for its kebabs. Spend your afternoon browsing the charming little shops in the Chandni Chowk area before making your way to the Jama Masjid, India's largest mosque. If you have time left over, make your way to Raj Ghat, a memorial to Mahatma Gandhi, and the nearby National Gandhi Museum. Alternatively, you can head north to

DELHI CHIC

If you're looking for luxury on your Indian holiday, Delhi will not disappoint. The capital is home to a fine selection of places to sleep, dine, and dance, ranging from elegant hotels to trendy nightclubs. Here are a few favorites.

RESTAURANTS

- For a fine-dining experience without frills (or silverware), head straight to **Bukhara** in the ITC Maurya Hotel. This cozy restaurant specializes in dishes from the Northwest Frontier region between Pakistan and Afghanistan and gets a steady stream of celebrity clientele.

- Tucked away in South Delhi's Garden of the Five Senses, **Magique** is arguably the most romantic dining spot in town. This garden restaurant specializes in seafood and continental dishes and has an excellent wine list.

NIGHTLIFE

- The recently opened Delhi branch of Mumbai club **blueFROG** is the best place in town to check out Indian and international bands and DJs. This contemporary pub and restaurant has plenty of dining space and a large dance floor.

- Delhi's best-heeled tend to spend a lot of time at **Smokehouse Grill** in Greater Kailash Part II. The ambiance is social, and most nights DJs spin pop and commercial house.

- Popular with expats, **TLR** is the most established venue in Delhi's trendy Hauz Khas Village. It regularly hosts energetic dance nights, open-mike sessions, and the occasional themed party.

HOTELS

- One of the newest five-star hotels to open in town, Lodi Road's **Aman New Delhi** is a luxurious, discreet hotel with minimalist interiors and amazing views of Central Delhi. The spa is superb.

- Near Connaught Place, **The Imperial** is a classic hotel with old-fashioned interiors, genial staff, and excellent dining. The hotel's pool is one of the largest in Delhi.

- South Delhi's **The Manor Hotel** is tucked at the end of a verdant upscale residential neighborhood. This boutique hotel is one of the quietest places to stay in the city, although it occasionally holds low-key Indo-electronic music events on-site.

the Majnu-ka-Tilla area and wander the little streets of this predominantly Tibetan enclave.

Use Day 3 to visit the sights in South Delhi. Start your morning at the Qutb Minar Complex, one of the oldest and most fascinating of Delhi's archaeological sites (and home to India's tallest, and most iconic, tower). From here, head north to the bohemian Hauz Khas Village to visit a couple of contemporary art galleries and the deer at the sprawling Deer Park before ordering lunch at one of the many delicious cafés. Spend the afternoon visiting the temples in the southeast part of town, starting with the historic Kalkaji Mandir and then making your way to the Baha'i Lotus

Temple and the ISKCON Temple complex. If you can, try to make it to the Garden of the Five Senses in time for sunset; it's the perfect place to unwind after a hard day's sightseeing.

Agra and the Taj Mahal
DAY 4
SHATABDI EXPRESS TRAIN FROM NEW DELHI: 2 HOURS; DRIVING TIME: 4 HOURS

Get up bright and early and head straight to the Taj Mahal. If you are going by taxi, you may want to leave in the middle of the night to arrive by dawn (leave four hours before sunrise). If you are taking the train,

ARCHITECTURAL MARVELS

Hawa Mahal, Jaipur

North India is home to a vast array of architectural treasures, many of which fuse a variety of influences, both domestic and imported. Agra's famed **Taj Mahal,** with its gargantuan onion-dome roof, its glistening white marble inlaid with semiprecious stones, and the perfect symmetry of its construction, is arguably the most spectacular of them all. It's no surprise that this bedazzling tribute to romantic love is among the New Seven Wonders of the World.

Near the Taj Mahal, **Agra Fort** is yet another architectural masterpiece. It was built primarily of red sandstone, although there are also plenty of white marble structures inside its walls. Many of the buildings are prime examples of the convergence of Hindu and Islamic styles of architecture and silently illustrate the way the meeting of the two philosophies shaped the culture of the region for centuries to come. Just outside Agra, the now abandoned city of **Fatehpur Sikri** is filled with magnificent Mughal-era architectural treasures. The most stunning sight is the massive **Buland Darwaza,** believed to be the largest entryway in the world. The red sandstone gate sits atop a perilously steep flight of stairs and features intricate black and white marble inlay work.

As India's capital, it is only natural that Delhi is home to many fascinating architectural wonders. It has an amazing selection of Lodi-era tombs; those found in the city's verdant **Lodi Gardens** are among the city's most spectacular. The 16th-century **Humayun's Tomb** is considered the first major example of Mughal architecture. The highly ornamental architecture and adornment of Old Delhi's **Lal Qila** (Red Fort) borrows from Indian, Persian, and Western European schools of design to create a style that was unique to the era of architecture-obsessed Shahjahan (who also commissioned the Taj Mahal).

Delhi also has its fair share of more recent architecture. One notable example is the **Baha'i House of Worship,** known colloquially as the Lotus Temple, built to emulate the sacred flower from which it takes its nickname; it features 27 marble-coated "leaves." The more recent temple at the **Swaminarayan Akshardham Complex** is made of intricately carved pink sandstone and is supported by 10-meter-high pillars.

Much of the architecture of Jaipur incorporates Rajput, Islamic, and British elements. The pink-sandstone **Hawa Mahal** is among the city's iconic structures and features nearly 1,000 tiny latticed windows in an arrangement often likened to a beehive. The windows are positioned in such a way that breezes can pass through, cooling the building's interior. Jaipur's water palace, or **Jal Mahal,** is yet another of the city's stunners, blending Rajput and Mughal architecture with a few Bengal-style elements. It sits right in the middle of Man Sagar Lake and can only be accessed by boat. The 19th-century **Albert Hall** was modeled after the Victoria and Albert Museum in London and is among the world's finest examples of Indo-Saracenic architecture, a style that blends Indian and Mughal styles with the neo-Gothic architecture that was all the rage in Victorian England.

a woman preparing opium water in Rajasthan

flower sellers at Pushkar Lake

try to get tickets on the 6:15 A.M. *Shatabdi Express,* which gets you into Agra at 8:12 A.M. Give yourself the entire morning to explore the Taj Mahal—you may only want to stay a couple of hours, but it's good to have a bit of extra time in case of long lines. Spend the afternoon exploring Agra Fort and the ruins of Chini-ka-Rauza. If you're doing a day trip from Delhi by car, you'll want to leave Agra by about 4 P.M. to get back to Delhi around 8 P.M. (any earlier and you'll hit rush-hour traffic in Delhi). If you don't mind ending up back in Delhi a bit later, you may wish to stop for an hour at Akbar's Tomb in Sikandra or at the holy towns of Mathura and Vrindavan; Both are on the way back to Delhi.

If you're taking the train back to Delhi or spending the night in Agra, end your day with a stroll in the Taj Nature Walk. You'll have time before catching the evening *Shatabdi Express* train, which leaves Agra at 8:30 P.M. and reaches Delhi at 10:30 P.M. Dinner is served on the train.

Fatehpur Sikri
DAY 5
BUS FROM IGDAH BUS STAND OR TAXI: 1 HOUR

The next morning, leave Agra and head to Fatehpur Sikri, a UNESCO World Heritage Site that was the capital of the Mughal Empire under Akbar. This 16th-century ghost town is home to some beautiful red sandstone architecture, including the stunning *Buland Darwaza,* purported to be the largest gateway in the world. If you've got a car, you can stop by the tombs of Mariam and Akbar in Sikandra on your way back. Alternatively, head back to Agra and catch an autorickshaw from Igdah Bus Stand to the tombs.

Ranthambore National Park
DAYS 6-7
TRAIN OR TAXI TO SAWAI MADHOPUR: 3-4 HOURS

Spend the morning in Agra visiting any sites you may have missed, or do a bit of shopping. In the afternoon, head toward Sawai Madhopur for Ranthambore National Park. You'll arrive in the evening, when there's not much to do, so check into your hotel and get an early night's sleep for the next morning's safari.

Wake up before sunrise and go on a tiger-sighting safari. Don't miss the stunning Ranthambore Fort on your way out. Head for Jaipur by 2 p.m. and spend the evening wandering the markets of the Pink City.

Jaipur
DAYS 8-10
TAXI OR TRAIN FROM SAWAI MADHOPUR: 2-3 HOURS;
TRAIN OR TAXI FROM AGRA: 3-4 HOURS
Start your first full day in Jaipur with an elephant ride up to the top of Amber Fort, and spend 2-3 hours exploring here. Next, head west on Amber Road and over to the Jal Mahal, a beautiful, recently restored water palace in the middle of Amber's Man Sagar

Lake. Go back to Jaipur for lunch and spend your afternoon visiting the Hawa Mahal, Jaipur's stunning Palace of Wind that is built to stay cool inside even on the hottest days. Then head to Jaipur's Jantar Mantar, a fascinating outdoor collection of astronomical instruments ranging from enormous sundials to tools that can measure the latitude and longitude of constellations.

Spend the morning of Day 9 wandering through the many galleries of the City Palace. Don't miss the interesting historical displays inside the Chandra Mahal, the current residence of Jaipur's royal family. In the afternoon, head to the Albert Hall Museum, a stunning example of Indo-Saracenic architecture. The museum has a wide assortment of artifacts in its collection, including an Egyptian mummy. Next, head to the Birla Mandir, south of the Albert Hall. This temple is one of Jaipur's newest, but its beautiful stained-glass windows and high-domed white-marble architecture more than make up for its relative youth.

a free-roaming bull at Pushkar's Jagnnath Ghat

FOCUS ON WELLNESS

India is a wonderful place to focus on health and relaxation. In the Himalayan foothills, the holy city of **Rishikesh** is filled with **ashrams** and **yoga centers,** and yogis of all experience levels flock here every year to attend the city's **International Yoga Festival.** A 30-minute drive uphill from Rishikesh is the magnificent **Ananda in the Himalayas,** one of the top spa resorts on the planet. Guests come here to detox, lose weight, or just get a bit of rest and relaxation while taking advantage of Ananda's many **therapeutic ayurvedic offerings.**

North India's cities also have plenty to offer the health-conscious visitor. A day at Delhi's **Aman Spa** is the perfect way to wind down a trip to India, and an exfoliating visit to their hammam, or **Turkish bath,** is not to be missed. Agra also has a number of excellent spas and is home to the flagship location of the award-winning **Kaya Kalp,** a sprawling spa that's beautifully adorned with Mughal-inspired art and deep-red curlicue designs. There are also branches in Delhi and Jaipur.

On Day 10, make your way to either Pushkar or Rishikesh, where you'll get a feel for life in India beyond the big cities.

Pushkar or Rishikesh
DAYS 11-13

If you have time for only one more excursion, choose between Pushkar and Rishikesh. You can reach Pushkar from Jaipur by road (4 hours) or by taking a train to Ajmer (3-4 hours) and then heading to Pushkar from by bus or taxi (30 minutes). If you're headed to Rishikesh, you may want to stop in Delhi overnight, especially if you are going by car (9-11 hours). There's a 4 A.M. train to Haridwar called the *Uttaranchal Express,* which reaches Haridwar just before 5 P.M. However, your best bet is the overnight *Haridwar Mail* train (13 hours), which leaves Jaipur at 11:15 P.M. and arrives in Haridwar the next day at around noon. From Haridwar, Rishikesh is about an hour by road.

Pushkar

If you arrive in Pushkar during the day, you'll have plenty of time to wander about town and soak in the atmosphere. Don't miss the beautiful sunset view over Pushkar Lake. Before you

sleep, remember to set your alarm for an hour before sunrise. That way you can get up early and take a hike to the Savitri Temple, high on a hilltop overlooking Pushkar, to watch the sun come up.

After your hike, head down into town for breakfast, and visit the famous Jagatpita Shri Brahma Temple. Spend the rest of the morning wandering through town, taking photos, or shopping. You can also use this time to take a camel ride through town or a drum lesson at the International Nagara Drums Music School with the world-renowned *nagara* drum maestro Nathu Lal Solanki.

On your third day in Pushkar, spend the morning shopping and visiting the Old Rangji Temple. If you are returning to Delhi by train, check out of your hotel and head to the nearby city of Ajmer by noon. Stop at Ajmer's railway station cloakroom (left-luggage office), where you can leave your luggage safely for a small fee, and head to the famous Dargah Sharif, a sacred Sufi shrine, and the Nasiyan Jain Temple, home to an intricate sculpture depicting scenes from Jain mythology. Take the *Shatabdi Express* train to Delhi, which leaves Ajmer at 3:50 P.M. and reaches the capital just before 11 P.M. If you're driving, you'll want to leave Ajmer by about 2 P.M. in order to beat the heavy evening truck traffic that piles up most nights on National Highway 8 just before Delhi.

Rishikesh

Assuming you arrive in Rishikesh in the early afternoon on Day 11, you'll have a bit of time to wander around town. Pay a visit to the 13-story Trayambakeshwar Temple near Laxman Jhula, which provides some excellent views of the Ganges River from its top floor. Then head downstream to the Swargashram area, home to many of Rishikesh's famed ashrams. Don't miss the evening *aarti* ceremony on the riverside ghat of the Parmarth Niketan Ashram. Every night at sunset, the ghat fills with pilgrims, visitors, and young students from the ashram who chant Sanskrit mantras and release offerings in the form of hundreds of tiny leaf boats filled with flowers and candles.

The next day, get up in time for an early morning yoga class at one of the dozens of ashrams and yoga centers in town. After breakfast, take a stroll past Swargashram to the now defunct Maharishi Mahesh Yogi Ashram, also known as the Beatles Ashram in honor of its most famous guests. Parts of this run-down old complex have been overtaken by foliage, but it's still a superb spot to explore. You can then head upstream and across the Ram Jhula suspension bridge to the Divine Life Society, which was founded by Swami Sivananda in the 1930s. In the afternoon, take a shared autorickshaw to Rishikesh's city center and ask to be dropped at Triveni Ghat, the most significant bathing ghat in Rishikesh. This is believed to be the confluence point of the Ganges, the Yamuna, and the mythical Saraswati Rivers. The Bharat Mata Mandir, originally built in the 12th century then destroyed and rebuilt later, is near the ghat.

an optometrist's sign in Bharatpur

Deep fried *kachoris*, a Rajasthani specialty snack

If you have the time, spend your last day in Rishikesh taking advantage of the excellent rafting trips on the Ganges River. You can opt for a 26-kilometer half-day circuit or a full-day 35-kilometer trip. Just make sure you have time to get to the train station in Haridwar, one hour away, in time for the 6:13 P.M. *Dehradun Shatabdi* train, which will get you back to Delhi by 11 P.M.

Return to Delhi
DAY 14

Most international flights leave Delhi in the morning, but if you're lucky enough to have an afternoon flight, you can use your morning to squeeze in a bit of last-minute shopping at central Delhi's many handicraft emporiums, or go on a relaxing walk through the city's Lodi Gardens.

▶ CALL OF THE WILD

The Golden Triangle is home to some of India's most spectacular national parks, some of which are also home to wild tigers. If you're more interested in Mother Nature than in monuments, Northern India won't disappoint.

Ranthambore National Park

This beautiful park is home to a large old fort, a beautiful variety of wispy trees, and all types of birds and animals. If you're lucky, you may just spot a tiger, but even if you don't see one, you'll likely get an up-close look at some of the other wild beasts that live in this beautiful reserve, such as sloth bears, hyenas, antelopes, and a number of varieties of wild cats. Many people, especially wildlife photographers, try to up their chances of seeing a tiger by going on both morning and afternoon safaris.

a serene tiger in Ranthambore National Park

FAMILY ADVENTURES

an astronomical instrument at Jantar Mantar observatory in Jaipur

Children are welcome almost everywhere in India, and there's enough going on in most towns and cities to keep the young entertained. Delhi's **Garden of Five Senses** is a clean spot with a lot of room to run around and plenty of interesting installations to explore. The **Sulabh International Museum of Toilets** is as educational as it is amusing. Children may also enjoy a visit to Old Delhi's **Bird Hospital** at the Shri Digambar Jain Lal Mandir, a temporary home for hundreds of local birds suffering from injuries and illness.

Jaipur's **Amber Fort** is a definite hit with kids, as it is the prime spot in North India to go on an elephant ride. The **Jantar Mantar,** with its gigantic astronomy tools, is another interesting spot to explore, and some children may enjoy the **Bhagwani Bhai Sakseria Doll Museum,** home to a huge collection of dolls

from around the world, each dressed in its region's traditional garb.

A visit to Agra's **Taj Mahal** is also a special treat for little ones, and older children might find the well-narrated audio guides entertaining. Akbar's Tomb in Sikandra is also a hit with youngsters, not so much because of the tomb itself but because of the large number of deer and gentle langur monkeys that live here year round.

Children are also likely to get a kick out of Rajasthan's national parks, particularly **Ranthambore,** where you can go on a jeep safari and, if you're lucky, spot a tiger in the wild. **Keoladeo National Park** is also a lot of fun, and on cool days you can rent a bicycle and pedal along the wide stretch of road that cuts through the park, stopping to take pictures of the beautiful migratory birds that visit the park at various times of year.

elephants in front of Oberoi Vanyavilas, near Ranthambore National Park

Hanuman langurs at Pushkar Lake

Keoladeo National Park

Home to hundreds of species of migratory birds as well as cows, snakes, and a diverse variety of flora, Keoladeo National Park is an excellent place for bird lovers to visit in any season. Try to visit the park in the early morning so you can hear the songs of the many avian species. Don't forget to stop by the Visitor Interpretation Centre to learn more about migratory birds and North India's ecosystem.

Sariska Tiger Reserve

This national park in the heart of Rajasthan is home to an array of birds and mammals as well as a few rarely seen tigers. Go on an early morning safari and keep your eyes peeled for wild boars, striped hyenas, and jungle cats, including the elusive caracals, beautiful lynx-like felines with pointy ears. If you come after the monsoon season (late June-Aug.), you'll likely notice the stunning fiery-red flowers of Sariska's many dhak trees.

Mussoorie

The old hill station of Mussoorie is known for cool temperatures, lush pine forests, and excellent walking trails. Make sure you take a stroll or horseback ride down Mussoorie's Camel's Back Road, breathing in the fresh air generated by the town's surrounding forest. You can also walk up to the suburb of Landour and keep going until you reach the summit of Lal Tibba (Red Hill), one of the region's most stunning viewpoints. A short drive from Mussoorie, Kempty Falls is pretty commercialized, so you may prefer to head straight to the office of the Himalayan Adventure Institute and inquire about the outdoor activities they have to offer.

Agra

Agra has a number of gardens, although most of these are designed using the *char bagh* system, which puts more emphasis on fountains than on greenery. The best place to feel at one with nature while taking in some great views of the Taj Mahal is the Taj Nature Walk, home to a large variety of plants and birds.

Delhi

Nature lovers in Delhi won't want to miss Deer Park, which provides a peaceful sanctuary to dozens of deer in South Delhi. Central Delhi's Lodi Gardens is a good place to get familiar with the region's flora and fauna by studying the large illustrated information boards that are displayed just inside the park's Lodi Road entrance.

▶ SPIRITUAL SOJOURN

Divinity plays a role in even the most mundane aspects of day-to-day life in India, and this spiritually rich land has been attracting seekers for generations. The following is a list of some of the most significant spiritual sites in and around Delhi, Jaipur, and Agra.

Delhi

India's capital is home to numerous holy sites for people of all faiths. The shrine of Nizamuddin Auliya, Nizamuddin Dargah, is an important site for Sufis, and even the nondevout are likely to find the evening Qawwali (devotional music) performances moving. The Sikh temple, or *gurudwara,* of Bangla Sahib is another significant holy spot in Delhi, and the water that comes from its large outdoor tank is considered holy. The Hindu goddess Kali is extoled at South Delhi's Kalkaji Mandir, and for centuries people have been making offerings to this terrific manifestation of female divinity at this very spot. The large ISKCON Temple nearby is the Delhi base for the ISKCON organization (a.k.a. the Hare Krishnas). Just behind this temple is the Baha'i House of

Follow the spiritual trail in Pushkar.

Worship, also called the Lotus Temple, a beautiful, silent place of worship and quiet reflection that is open to all.

Agra

Agra is better known for tombs and archaeological sites than for places of worship, although there are a great number of mosques and temples. The holiest spot for Sufis in the area is arguably the Dargah of Salim Chisti at the Jama Masjid in Fatehpur Sikri. The twin towns of Mathura and Vrindavan, north of Agra, are significant to devotees of Krishna, who is said to have grown up here. The Banke Bihari Mandir is Vrindavan's most famous temple.

Jaipur

Jaipur is more known for its royalty than its religion, although the city is home to a couple of significant spiritual sites. Amber Fort's Sheela Mata Temple is an important stop for Hindu visitors to the palace, as it is believed that the goddess idol kept here was found after a local king located it in a prophetic dream. Galtaji is another important site that houses a number of temples, including one dedicated to the sun god Surya, as well as tanks containing holy water.

Rishikesh and Haridwar

On the banks of the Ganges River, Rishikesh and Haridwar are among India's holiest cities. Evening *aartis* (prayer ceremonies) are held along the banks of the Ganges in both cities, when hundreds of tiny candle-containing boats are floated across the waters. Both cities are home to hundreds of temples, including famous ones such as Haridwar's hilltop Mansa Devi Mandir as well as Neelkanth Mahadev, a forest temple dedicated to Shiva at the end of an 13-kilometer trekking path from Rishikesh.

Pushkar and Ajmer

Pushkar is one of India's holiest towns and is considered by some to be the earthly abode of Brahma, the creator in the Hindu trinity. The city is full of temples, and most of its residents are of the Brahman, or priestly, caste. Pushkar is most famous for the Jagatpita Shri Brahma Temple, one of the only Brahma temples in the world. It sits on the banks of Pushkar Lake, which attracts pilgrims from across the Hindu world who come to bathe in its holy waters.

Ajmer's Dargah Sharif is the shrine of the founder of the Chishti order of Sufism and is probably India's holiest spot for South Asian Muslims.

DELHI

Delhi has a reputation of being a noisy, chaotic, and somewhat unruly city, and there is some truth to this stereotype. Indeed, Delhi has all the bustle of a capital city with the added chaos of India thrown in for good measure. The city has a population of more than 16 million, and the streets and markets are almost always at least somewhat crowded. It's also loud: really loud. Delhi's drivers love honking their horns (you'll find this in other parts of India too), and this is generally not out of aggression so much as the inevitable boredom that arises in the city's incessant traffic jams. However, it's also a beautiful green city filled with stately tree-lined boulevards, quiet parks, trendy cafés, and some of the most incredible archaeological sites in the world. In fact, you'll find that the travelers who complain the most about India's capital have often seen very little of the city beyond the admittedly hectic Old Delhi and the grimy backpacker enclave of Paharganj.

Delhi is also the most culturally rich city in the country and is home to a great number of cultural centers, art galleries, media outfits, publishers, and top-notch educational institutes. On any given evening, you'll have a great number of activities and events to choose from, and you'll never go hungry in this city of foodies—Delhi has an amazing culinary scene. The shopping is fantastic and generally quite affordable, and the nightlife is getting better by the day. Most of all, Delhi has an incredible

HIGHLIGHTS

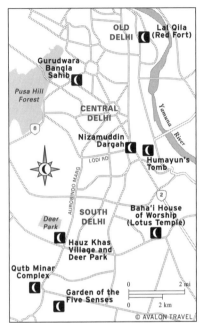

◖ Lal Qila (Red Fort): At the heart of Old Delhi, this enormous 17th-century fort was once the seat of the Mughal Empire (page 30).

◖ Gurudwara Bangla Sahib: Behold the beauty of this historic Sikh *gurudwara* (page 34).

◖ Nizamuddin Dargah: This shrine of Sufi saint Nizamudin Auliya gets particularly animated on Thursday evenings, when traditional Qawwali performances are staged (page 39).

◖ Humayun's Tomb: The tomb of Humayun, the second Mughal emperor, exemplifies early Muhgal architectural aesthetics (page 39).

◖ Baha'i House of Worship (Lotus Temple): This serene lotus-shaped temple is for adherents of the Baha'i faith or anyone seeking solace (page 41).

◖ Garden of the Five Senses: An enchanting garden specially designed to stimulate the five senses, adorned with statues, installations, and plants (page 43).

◖ Hauz Khas Village and Deer Park: Bourgeois bohemia prevails at this charming South Delhi arts and fashion village (page 44).

◖ Qutb Minar Complex: This amazing collection of towers, tombs, and architectural oddities is one of the oldest archaeological sites in Delhi (page 45).

LOOK FOR ◖ TO FIND RECOMMENDED SIGHTS, ACTIVITIES, DINING, AND LODGING.

selection of important historical sights and tourist attractions, and the government has gone to great lengths to keep the city's cultural heritage well preserved, even as the great capital city becomes increasingly globalized.

HISTORY

Archaeologists believe that Delhi has been inhabited for at least three millennia. It is thought to be the location of Indraprastha, a city mentioned in the ancient text the *Mahabharata* as the capital of the Pandava people, as evidenced by excavation work done at Central Delhi's Purana Qila, the likely site of the ancient city.

Delhi city was officially founded in 736, when Anangpal of the Tomar clan, who claimed to be descendants of the Pandavas, set up a city called Lal Kot at the present-day Qutb Minar complex. By the end of the 12th century, the city was taken over by Prithviraj III of the short-lived Chauhan Dynasty, and then taken over by Muhammad of Ghor, who ruled until his death in 1206. For the next 320 years, Delhi was ruled by a succession of Turkic clans before finally succumbing to Babur, the founder of the Mughal Empire, at the First Battle of Panipat in 1526.

Delhi remained under Mughal rule well

into the 19th century, with the exception of a few years when it was taken over from Babur's son Humayun by Sher Shah Suri, founder of the short-lived Sur Dynasty; Humayun later regained control over Delhi in 1555, only to die the next year. In the mid-18th century, the Maratha rulers from the south took control of Delhi, indirectly ruling its people via the de facto Mughal emperor. However, in 1803 the British East India Company defeated the Marathas at the Battle of Delhi of the Second Anglo-Maratha War, effectively taking over Delhi's indirect rule. A Mughal emperor remained on the throne until the 1857 Indian Rebellion (a.k.a. the Sepoy Mutiny), during which the East India Company exiled the last Mughal emperor (Bahadur Shah II) to Rangoon and transferred its power to the British crown. Calcutta was declared India's capital, which it remained until 1911, when King George V of England, emperor of British India, declared that Delhi would once again be capital. He commissioned architect Edwin Lutyens to design the city of New Delhi, and the part of Central Delhi characterized by its well-planned leafy avenues is known as Lutyens' Delhi to this day.

The 20th century was one of great change for the capital. After Independence, India was divided from Pakistan and what is now Bangladesh. The states of Punjab and Bengal were split in half along the Radcliffe Line, a culturally arbitrary yet incredibly significant border named for the British lawyer who had never been to India yet was charged with chalking out the Republic's new frontiers in all of five weeks. This division, known as Partition, led to a great number of Hindu and Sikh Punjabis fleeing Pakistan, and many Muslim Punjabis escaping west to Pakistan. Millions of people were displaced during this time, many having to flee their homes overnight. Those who didn't die en route had to start over with nothing in their new homes. Many of them headed to what

was then known as Western Pakistan ended up settling in Lahore; those coming into India came in great numbers to Delhi, and much of South Delhi was built up as a result of this mass immigration. Delhi consequently has a huge Punjabi population (as well as a sizeable number of Bengali people, most of whom live in the leafy Chittaranjan Park neighborhood, not far from the landmark Lotus Temple). As the capital, the city has also seen waves of immigration from around the country, and pretty much every community in India is represented. In the 1960s, many Tibetans fled the Chinese occupation of their homeland and settled in India, and these days the capital is home to a sizable number of second- and third-generation Tibetans. India's economic boom over the past couple of decades has also led to an influx of expatriates, and it's no longer uncommon to meet people from around the world who have made this diverse city their adopted home.

PLANNING YOUR TIME

It's unfortunate that so many people see Delhi as simply a stopping-off point for exploring other destinations, especially considering how rich the city is in history and culture. If you have the time, you should attempt to spend at least three or four days here, and while realistically this isn't enough time to visit all of Delhi's sights, it's enough time to visit a handful and take advantage of the city's exceptional shopping. You can easily spend a full day in Old Delhi alone, and as it's arguably the most chaotic part of town, you may want to do it all at once. You can cover Central Delhi's main attractions on your second day, and save a third day for South Delhi and a bit of shopping. Just one thing to keep in mind when planning your itinerary: Delhi's traffic is notoriously bad, so leave plenty of time in your schedule for delays, and try to avoid traveling at peak rush hour times.

Central Delhi is arguably the most

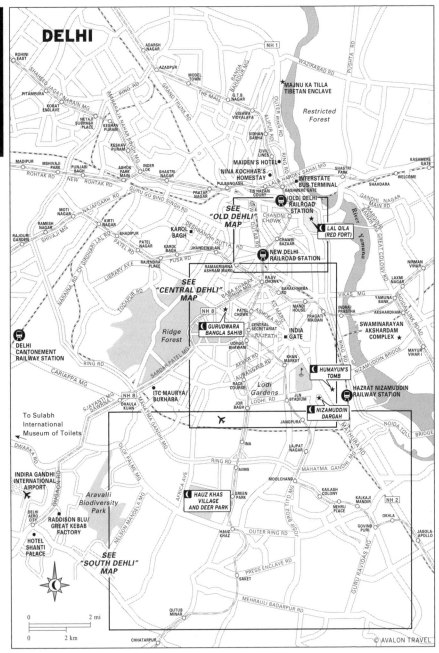

convenient spot to stay in town due to its proximity to many major sights. This part of town also has the best access to the Metro, as it's where many of the major lines converge. However, many visitors prefer the calm of South Delhi, where many of the city's most charming independent hotels are located. Some people prefer the rustic feel of staying in Old Delhi, but there's not much in terms of restaurants, and the shopping options are more geared toward local residents.

SAFETY AND SCAMS

Contrary to popular belief, Delhi is actually a very safe city for foreign visitors. Your main concerns are likely to be related to health. It's not unheard of for visitors, especially those who are gung-ho about eating street food, to succumb to the notorious "Delhi belly." The air quality here is also not great (although it has improved dramatically over the past decade), and asthma sufferers may have trouble breathing.

Like any large capital city, there's plenty of crime in Delhi. However, violent crime directed at foreigners is rare. That said, it's still a good idea to be vigilant of your surroundings and your belongings. Sexual harassment and groping are fairly common—if anybody touches you in a way that makes you feel uncomfortable, tell them to stop immediately, and don't smile while doing it. If someone gropes you, feel free to slap him. In crowded areas, meaning most of Delhi, keep track of your wallet, camera, and phone at all times, and don't keep any valuables within easy reach of potential thieves.

There are a few common scams to be aware of. The most common is fake international tourist bureaus. Here's how it works: You're at New Delhi Railway Station about to board a train. A man approaches you and says he's an Indian Railways employee and asks to see your ticket. When you show him your ticket, he claims it's either fake or invalid and you will need to buy a new one from the international ticketing counter. He will then lead you out of the train station and across the street to a travel agent with a sign claiming that they are the "official international tourist bureau." The only international tourist ticketing office in all of Delhi is *inside* the New Delhi Railway Station on the first floor, near the Paharganj entrance. Also note that the only people you need to show your ticket to are uniformed police officers who sometimes screen baggage at the station entrance, and uniformed trainmasters.

The most frightening scam in Delhi takes place primarily in Paharganj and involves hypnosis, coercion, and mind control. You may be approached by a turbaned man who will want to demonstrate his psychic powers to you. He'll show you an old class photo and ask you to choose one person from it and concentrate on that person. Then he'll tell you, correctly, who you were thinking of. Next, he'll guess your favorite color, details about your father, and all kinds of other strange things. After that, he'll invite you to tea, and soon you'll find yourself walking to the ATM and pulling out a large donation for him. It's difficult to say how this scam works, but while I've personally never fallen for it, I have seen plenty of foreigners marching trancelike to a Paharganj ATM with one of these tricksters in tow.

Most scams in Delhi involve overcharging for services. Budget guesthouses may tack on breakfasts that were never ordered or fees that were never disclosed—this rarely happens at nicer places. Another scam often spoken about and rarely witnessed is the old poo-on-the-shoe trick. You'll be walking along when suddenly a bit of animal dung splats squarely on your shoes. A shoeshine boy will run up and start scrubbing off the muck without even asking, and then demand an exorbitant price for the service.

ORIENTATION

Delhi is an enormous, sprawling city, and crossing from one end to the other can take hours.

The city is divided into Old Delhi, North Delhi, East Delhi, West Delhi, Central Delhi, and South Delhi. The suburban "satellite cities" of Gurgaon and Noida are also often considered part of greater Delhi (also known as the National Capital Region, or NCR), although both cities have their own administration. Fortunately, most of the sights are located in South, Central, and Old Delhi, and these are the three parts of town where visitors will spend most, if not all, of their time. These three areas also have the best food and accommodations options in town, and there's very little reason to stay elsewhere.

Old Delhi has the most Mughal-era sights and is more or less synonymous with Shahjahanabad, the 17th-century city built by Mughal emperor Shahjahan of Taj Mahal fame. This area is best known for its old houses and mosques, lively markets, and street food. It's also one of the louder and dirtier parts of town, and most visitors prefer to come for a day and then return to their hotels in Central or South Delhi.

Much of Central Delhi was designed under British rule by well-known architect Edwin Lutyens. This gives it a bit more of a colonial—and somewhat European—feel, and the area is characterized by long tree-flanked boulevards, regal government buildings and palaces, and chic shopping districts, such as Connaught Place and Khan Market. It's also home to a number of Lodi and Mughal-era tombs.

South Delhi is a bit more of a hodgepodge, with everything from modern temples to crumbling ruins. This part of town began to develop rapidly after Independence, and today it's one of the trendier parts of Delhi, especially among the middle and upper echelons of society. Here you'll find all the typical signs of globalization (McDonald's, shopping malls), as well as some of the best shopping and dining options in the city.

One of the best ways to get around Delhi is by Metro. This system of underground and aboveground train stations covers a good deal of the city, and it is expected to expand its reach considerably within the next 5-10 years. Currently only some sights, restaurants, and hotels are within walking distance of a Metro station. Listings without a corresponding station are too far to walk. That said, you can save a lot of money by taking the Metro to the nearest station and then catching an auto or cycle rickshaw to your destination.

Sights

Delhi has tons of sights, most of which are either religious or historical (although some, such as Old Delhi's Jama Masjid, are a combination of both). The most popular sight in Old Delhi is the Lal Qila, or Red Fort, which many people visit in the morning, seeing other nearby sights in the afternoon. Central Delhi has a wider variety of sights, ranging from landmarks such as India Gate to crumbling old tombs. It's also home to many of the city's best-known museums. South Delhi is home to many interesting religious sites, including the Kalkaji Mandir and the string of temples on Chhatarpur Mandir Road. There are few major sights in North Delhi and East Delhi, save the Majnu Ka Tilla Tibetan enclave and the Swaminarayan Akshardham Complex, respectively.

OLD DELHI
C Lal Qila (Red Fort)
The Lal Qila (sunrise-sunset Tues.-Sun., Rs. 250 foreigners, Rs. 10 Indians, video Rs. 25; sound and light show Rs. 80 adults,

CAPITAL OF CULTURE

© MARGOT BIGG

The India Habitat Centre hosts cultural events almost every day.

Delhi is not only the capital of India but also the capital of the country's cultural life. Nowhere else in in the country will you find such a diverse array of regular cultural events and performances, and there are usually plenty of events to choose from every night of the week.

IF YOU WANT TO . . .

- **Catch a play:** Head to one of the many theaters in the Mandi House area of central Delhi, the capital's undisputed theater district.

- **Browse modern art:** A large number of the city's finest modern art galleries are clustered in South Delhi's Hauz Khas Village.

- **Take in a classical music recital:** Both the India Habitat Centre (IHC) and the India International Centre (IIC) have regular music performances and are within a few minutes of each other in the south-central Lodi Road area.

Rs. 30 children), or Red Fort, was built by Emperor Shahjahan after he shifted his base from Agra to Delhi and established the city of Shahjahanabad. Construction on this red sandstone citadel began on April 16, 1639, and the project was finished exactly nine years later on April 16, 1648. The massive octagonal fort sits on 50 hectares and is surrounded by 2.4 kilometers of walls as well as a moat that once connected to the Yamuna River. In other words, it's a huge place that merits at least a two-hour visit.

Entering through the **Lahore Gate,** you'll pass through the **Chhatta Chowk,** a roofed arcade full of two-story apartments that have been converted into shops. The next building is the Naubat Khana, a house of drums where music was once played five times a day. This

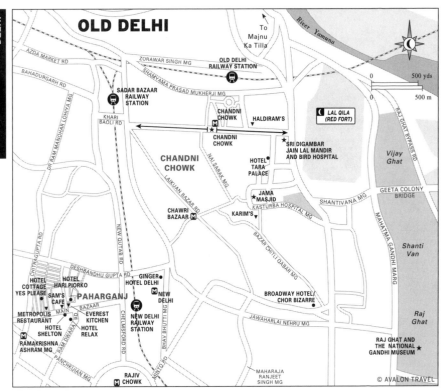

three-story structure features carved designs that were once painted in gold.

The next building is the **Diwan-i-Aam** (Hall of Public Audiences), which was once decorated with gilded stucco. This was where both the emperor and the prime minister received the public (the prime minister even had his own marble dais to stand on, complete with inlaid precious stone). A series of panels on the back wall depicts flowers and birds in stone inlay, as well as Orpheus with his lute; they are believed to have been crafted by Florentine jeweler Austin de Bordeaux. These panels were transferred to the Victoria and Albert Museum in London but were returned in 1903 at the insistence of Lord Curzon, India's Viceroy at the time.

Facing the Yamuna River, on the south side of the fort's wall, the **Mumtaz Mahal** is believed to have been built by Shahjahan's queen, Arjumand Banu Begum. Today, it is a museum of Mughal history featuring art, armory, manuscripts, and astronomy tools spread over six themed galleries. North of the museum are the **Rang Mahal** (Palace of Color) and the **Khas Mahal** (Private Palace). The former contains six apartments, including two Sheesh Mahal (Mirror Palace) rooms, which are decorated with small fragments of mirrors arranged to create a beautiful display at night with reflected candlelight. The Khas Mahal comprises three rooms used for praying, sleeping, and dressing.

The **Diwan-i-Khas** (Hall of Private Audiences) sits just beyond the Khas Mahal and features aisles of decorated arches and a wooden ceiling that was painted in 1911 and topped with *chhatris* (canopies) on each of its four corners. Just beyond the Diwan-i-Khas is the **Hammam,** or bathhouse, which features marble inlaid floors. There are three rooms, and the center room features a large basin. The western room, from where the heating was supplied, was where people would go to take hot steam baths, and the eastern room, used for changing, has three fountains that once spouted rose water. Just west of the Hammam is the small **Moti Masjid** (Pearl Mosque), which was used by Aurangzeb. Note the small black marble outlines of prayer rugs that decorate the walls of the prayer hall. On the roof of the structure are three domes that are believed to have formerly been plated with copper.

Sri Digambar Jain Lal Mandir and Bird Hospital

At the east end of Chandni Chowk, just a few paces from the Red Fort, is the red sandstone Sri Digambar Jain Lal Mandir and Bird Hospital (Chandni Chowk, Metro: Chandni Chowk, tel. 11/3290-9216, 10 A.M.-5 P.M. daily, free). The Lal Mandir is dedicated to Parshvanath, the 23rd Tirthankara (enlightened ascetic) of the Jain faith, and was built in 1628, making it one of Delhi's oldest temples. The Lal Mandir is best known for its Bird Hospital, which has been treating sick and injured birds since 1956. The hospital admits upward of 60 birds a day, and contrary to popular belief, the strictly vegetarian Jain veterinarians and attendants here do not turn away birds of prey.

Jama Masjid

India's largest mosque, the Jama Masjid (between Chowri Bazaar Rd. and Meena Bazaar Rd., Metro: Chandni Chowk, 7 A.M.-noon and 1:30-6:30 P.M. daily, free, camera Rs. 200) was built by Shahjahan from 1650 to 1656 at a cost

© RAJAT DEEP RANA

Gurudwara Bangla Sahib is an important place of pilgrimage for Sikhs.

of around one million rupees. The red sandstone and white marble mosque was extensively used by the emperor and other royalty, and there's a terrace above the eastern gateway that was originally reserved primarily for the nobility. The two minarets here stand 40 meters tall and are worth a visit if you're not afraid of heights or stairs, but disappointingly, women are not allowed to visit them without a male companion. On the western side, a large prayer hall has a beautiful 11-arch facade and is capped with three black and striped marble domes. The main courtyard here is nearly 100 square meters and can accommodate up to 20,000 people.

Raj Ghat and the National Gandhi Museum

On the banks of the Yamuna River, Raj Ghat (MG Rd., sunrise-sunset daily, free) marks the spot where Mahatma Gandhi was cremated on January 31, 1948, the day after he was assassinated. A memorial in the form of a black marble platform has been placed here with "Hey Ram" (allegedly, though debatably, Gandhi's last words) written in Devanagari, the Hindi script, on its side. The memorial is regularly decorated with fresh flowers, and there's an eternal flame. The memorial itself is not much to see, and most visitors just stop by for a few minutes to pay their respects, but the surrounding grassy knolls are good for stroll.

Just across the main road from Raj Ghat is the National Gandhi Museum (opposite Raj Ghat, tel. 11/2331-1793, www.gandhimuseum. org, 10 A.M.-5 P.M. Tues.-Sun., free), which houses a large collection of art and artifacts related to Gandhi and the freedom movement, ranging from old documents to audiovisual recordings of the Mahatma. They also have a library and a small collection of books for sale, including some hard-to-find titles.

CENTRAL DELHI
Gandhi Smriti

The last home of Mahatma Gandhi, where he was assassinated on January 30, 1948, was turned into a museum in the 1980s and dubbed Gandhi Smriti (Birla House, 5 Tees January Lane, tel. 11/2301-2843, http://gandhismriti. gov.in, 10 A.M.-5 P.M. Tues.-Sun., free). The museum is filled with old photographs of the Mahatma as well as a few personal effects and lots of miniature scenes depicting various significant events in Gandhi's life. The museum is divided into three sections that deal with keeping Gandhi's memory alive, explaining his values, and illustrating the emphasis he placed on serving others.

◖ Gurudwara Bangla Sahib

Delhi's best-known *gurudwara* (Sikh place of worship), the Gurudwara Bangla Sahib (Ashok Rd., Metro: Patel Chowk, tel. 11/2336-5486, 24 hours daily, free) was originally a bungalow belonging to Raja Jai Singh of the Mughal Empire. Guru Har Krishan, the eighth guru of Sikhism, stayed here during a trip to Delhi in the 17th century. During his residency, the Guru helped smallpox victims from this house, although he later ended up dying of that disease. Raja Jai Singh then built a small tank over the bungalow's well, and these days, the devout come to take holy water, which is referred to as *amrit* (nectar) and is believed to have healing powers.

The bungalow was later transformed into a *gurudwara,* and today the complex also houses a school and a hospital as well as an art gallery devoted to spiritual and historical art and a library full of books on Sikh history and faith, both of which are open to visitors. As per Sikh tradition, the *gurudwara* also houses a volunteer-run *langar* (community kitchen) where people of all faiths and backgrounds are invited to eat communally for free (of course, those

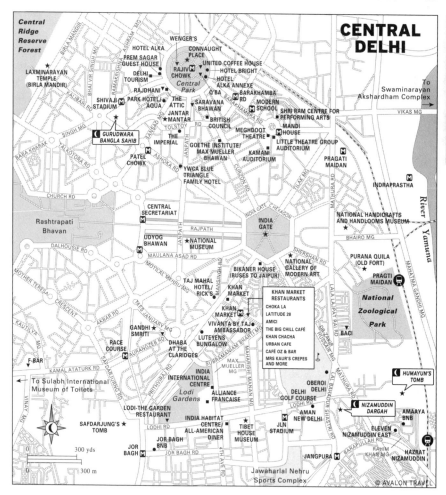

CENTRAL DELHI

Central Ridge Reserve Forest

To Swaminarayan Akshardham Complex

LAXMINARAYAN TEMPLE (BIRLA MANDIR)

WENGER'S
HOTEL ALKA
PREM SAGAR GUEST HOUSE
CONNAUGHT PLACE
UNITED COFFEE HOUSE
DELHI TOURISM
RAJIV CHOWK
HOTEL BRIGHT
HOTEL ALKA ANNEXE
RAJDHANI
Central Park
BARAKHAMBA RD
Q'BA
SHIVAJI STADIUM
PARK HOTEL/ AQUA
THE ATTIC
SARAVANA BHAVAN
MODERN SCHOOL
SHRI RAM CENTRE FOR PERFORMING ARTS
JANTAR MANTAR
BRITISH COUNCIL
MANDI HOUSE
GURUDWARA BANGLA SAHIB
THE IMPERIAL
MEGHDOOT THEATRE
LITTLE THEATRE GROUP AUDITORIUM
PATEL CHOWK
GOETHE INSTITUTE/ MAX MUELLER BHAVAN
KAMANI AUDITORIUM
PRAGATI MAIDAN
YWCA BLUE TRIANGLE FAMILY HOTEL
INDRAPRASTHA
CHURCH RD
INDIA GATE
CENTRAL SECRETARIAT
RAJPATH
NATIONAL HANDICRAFTS AND HANDLOOMS MUSEUM
Rashtrapati Bhavan
UDYOG BHAWAN
NATIONAL MUSEUM
BHAIRO MG
PURANA QILA (OLD FORT)
DALHOUSIE RD
MAULANA ASAD RD
BIKANER HOUSE (BUSES TO JAIPUR)
NATIONAL GALLERY OF MODERN ART
PRAGTI MAIDAN
National Zoological Park
TAJ MAHAL HOTEL/ RICK'S
KHAN MARKET
GANDHI SMRITI
KHAN MARKET
VIVANTA BY TAJ AMBASSADOR
LUTEYENS BUNGALOW
RACE COURSE
F-BAR
DHABA AT THE CLARIDGES
To Sulabh International Museum of Toilets
INDIA INTERNATIONAL CENTRE
Lodi Gardens
ALLIANCE FRANCAISE
HUMAYUN'S TOMB
LODI-THE GARDEN RESTAURANT
DELHI GOLF COURSE
NIZAMUDDIN DARGAH
SAFDARJUNG'S TOMB
INDIA HABITAT CENTRE/ ALL-AMERICAN DINER
TIBET HOUSE MUSEUM
AMAN NEW DELHI
OBEROI DELHI
BACI
AMAAYA BNB
JOR BAGH BNB
JLN STADIUM
ELEVEN NIZAMUDDIN EAST
JOR BAGH
JOR BAGH RD
JANGPURA
HAZRAT NIZAMUDDIN
Jawaharlal Nehru Sports Complex
River Yamuna
300 yds
300 m

KHAN MARKET RESTAURANTS

CHOKA LA
LATITUDE 28
AMICI
THE BIG CHILL CAFÉ
KHAN CHACHA
URBAN CAFE
CAFÉ OZ & BAR
MRS KAUR'S CREPES AND MORE

© AVALON TRAVEL

who can always donate or help out with food preparation and serving).

The massive white-marble *gurudwara* acts as a place of solace for both Sikh and non-Sikh visitors alike, and the mood feels calmer and more orderly than most other sights in Delhi. Adding to the ambience is the meditative chants from the Guru Granth Sahib, the Sikh holy book, which devotees read out melodically from the *gurudwara's* sanctum. Out of respect for the sanctity of the sight and Sikh tradition, men and women alike should remove their shoes and cover their heads before entering the complex.

India Gate

Although its real name is the "All India War Memorial Arch," everybody refers to this 42-meter-high freestanding arch simply as India Gate. The arch commemorates the service of the 90,000 Indian soldiers who lost their lives in World War I. The names of the 13,516 Indian and British

© RAJAT DEEP RANA

Central Delhi's India Gate

foreigners, Rs. 5 Indians, video Rs. 25) is still worth a visit if you are in the Connaught Place area. The Jantar Mantar was built by Maharaja Sawai Jai Singh II of Jaipur in 1724 and is the first of five similar sights the king built across the northern plains. It is essentially a collection of oversize tools used to make astrological measurements, including the heart-shaped Samrat Yantra (Supreme Instrument) sundial and the Mishra Yantra (Mixed Instrument), a four-in-one calculation tool that has a number of functions, including determining the entry of the sun into Cancer and finding meridians in four spots (two in Europe, one in Japan, and one in the Pacific Ocean). Unfortunately, the instruments fall in the shadow of the tall buildings of nearby Connaught Place and are thus of little astronomical use today. There's also a small temple dedicated to the god Bhairava on the site, which is also believed to have been built by Sawai Jai Singh II.

soldiers who died fighting in the Third Anglo-Afghan War and on the treacherous Northwest Frontier (in present-day Pakistan) are engraved on the archway. There's also an ever-burning Amar Jawan Jyoti (Flame of the Eternal Soldier), which commemorates the tomb of the Unknown Soldier. Despite the fact that India Gate represents some rather somber events in history, it actually feels more like a party spot most of the time, especially in the evenings when families flock here to eat ice cream and play on the monument's large lawns. There's also a small artificial lake with pedal boats for hire, although on hot days local boys descend on the lake to roughhouse and get a bit of relief from the heat.

Jantar Mantar

Although it's not nearly as impressive as its sibling in Jaipur, Delhi's Jantar Mantar (Parliament St., Connaught Place, Metro: Patel Chowk, sunrise-sunset Tues.-Sun., Rs. 100

Laxminarayan Temple (Birla Mandir)

One of the many temples built by the Birla family of industrialists, the Laxminarayan Temple (near Gole Market, Mandir Marg, Metro: Ramakrishna Ashram Marg, 6 A.M.-10 P.M. daily, free) was inaugurated by Gandhi in 1939, who requested that it be open to people of all castes and religions (many Indian temples restrict foreigners, non-Hindus, or "low-caste" people from entry). This three-story temple is built in the North Indian Nagura style, with its signature conical rooftop. The temple houses idols of Lakshmi, goddess of wealth, and her consort, Narayan, an avatar of Vishnu, as well as shrines to a smattering of other deities, including the Buddha. The temple is surrounded by a small park that has a number of colorful plaster animals large enough for children to climb on. Note that photography is not allowed inside the complex, but there's a special section for foreign visitors at the entrance with secure lockers and a shoe area.

Worshippers chant at Nizamuddin Dargah.

Lodi Gardens

The beautiful 36-hectare Lodi Gardens (Lodhi Rd., just east of Aurobindo Marg, Metro: Jor Bagh, sunrise-sunset daily, free) is popular with joggers, dog walkers, and young couples and is one of Delhi's best-maintained green areas. There are a variety of birds and trees, and it's popular with picnickers and Frisbee players. It's also home to four tombs. The first of these is the 15th century mausoleum of Muhammad Shah, an octagonal tomb crowned with a large central dome. There's a total of eight graves in this tomb. The second tomb is the Bara Gumbad, and the identity of the person interred here is unknown, although he is believed to have been an officer under Sikandar Lodi's reign. A 15th-century mosque adjoins the tomb. North of the Bara Gumbad, the double-storied Shish Gumbad looks a lot like the Bara Gumbad and contains several graves, although once again, nobody knows whose graves they are. At the northwestern corner of the gardens lies the tomb of Sikandar Lodi himself, which is surrounded by a square garden enclosed in high walls.

National Gallery of Modern Art

Delhi's government-run National Gallery of Modern Art (Jaipur House, C-Hexagon, India Gate, http://ngmaindia.gov.in, 10 A.M.-5 P.M. Tues.-Sun., Rs. 150 foreigners, Rs. 10 Indians) houses a collection of paintings and sculptures from 1850 onward. The museum was inaugurated in 1954 at Jaipur House, the former residence of the Maharaja of Jaipur. Along with the permanent collection of primarily Indian works, the museum also hosts special exhibitions year-round and occasionally screens films and organizes cultural events. There's also a library and a small gift shop selling postcards and print reproductions of some of the museum's more celebrated pieces.

DELHI

National Handicrafts and Handlooms Museum

Designed to resemble a rural village, the National Handicrafts and Handlooms Museum (Pragati Maidan, Bhairon Rd., Metro: Pragati Maidan, tel. 11/2337-1887, www.nationalhandicraftsmuseum.nic.in, 10 A.M.-5 P.M. Tues.-Sun., Rs. 150 foreigners, Rs. 10 Indians) houses collections of ethnic and folk art, ritual art, sculpture, and textiles. The government-run museum also doubles as a research center for scholars of the traditional arts. The rest of us can enjoy the on-site craft demonstrations, including pottery and hand weaving, just in front of the museum. The gift shop is fabulous and stocks a wide selection of high-quality souvenirs as well as art supplies ranging from pottery tools to locally inspired paint-by-number kits.

National Museum

Delhi's best-known museum, the National Museum (tel. 11/2301-9272, www.nationalmuseumindia.gov.in, 10 A.M.-5 P.M. Tues.-Sun., Rs. 300 foreigners, includes audio tour, Rs. 10 Indians, camera Rs. 20) is home to some 200,000 separate artifacts and works of art from around the world, some of which are believed to be 5,000 years old. The museum has large collections of artifacts from the Harappan Civilization, armory, miniature paintings, coins, textiles, and musical instruments. There is also a selection of artifacts from India's culturally distinct northeastern states, including costumes, masks, and tools used in everyday life. There's a large wooden chariot here from South India that weighs almost 2,300 kilograms.

National Rail Museum

If you're into trains, don't miss the National Rail Museum (Rao Tula Marg, Chanakyapuri, tel. 11/2688-1816, 9:30 A.M.-5:30 P.M.

© RAJAT DEEP RANA

Humayan's Tomb is the earliest major example of Mughal architecture in Delhi.

Tues.-Sun., Rs. 20 adults, Rs. 10 children, video Rs. 100). This museum has everything from model trains (including one of India's first train) to documents that help illustrate the history of India's railroads as well as old railcars, a fire engine, old equipment, and exhibits illustrating how trains work. There is even a working train on the museum grounds, the *Joy Express*, which gives visitors the chance to experience a short train ride.

Nizamuddin Dargah

Nizamuddin Dargah (Mathura Rd., Nizamuddin West, 24 hours daily, free) is the marble, lattice-screened *dargah* (shrine) of Nizamuddin Auliya, a famous Sufi saint of the Chishti order who lived in Delhi in the 13th and 14th centuries. It is a holy place for Muslims, and there's always a stream of visitors. The present structure was built in 1563 and is essentially a square chamber surrounded by

Safdarjung's Tomb

verandas. Although the *dargah* is the main attraction, it's equally fun to simply wander the tiny lanes in Nizamuddin West, the highly traditional, predominantly Muslim neighborhood around the shrine. The area seems like it could have been plucked from another century, especially if you compare this part of Nizamuddin to the ultraposh neighborhoods surrounding it.

Most people try to plan their visit for Thursday evenings around sunset, when a lively session of Qawwali, a form of Sufi devotional music that was popularized in the West by Pakistani musician Nusrat Fateh Ali Khan, is held. Qawwali has its roots in the Sema musical tradition of Persia that came to India in the 11th century and was developed into a distinct art form in the 13th century by Amir Khusro, a devotee of Nizamuddin. Note that it can get really crowded and stuffy here during Qawwali performances, so turn up early to find a patch of floor and bring a fan and plenty of water unless you're visiting in the dead of winter. You'll also need to leave your shoes at a repository near the entrance to the shrine. Head coverings are not required, but most women prefer to use them as a mark of respect. Male devotees often don a *taqiyah*, or skull cap, available at many of the stalls that flank the walkway to the shrine.

Humayun's Tomb

Set on the grounds of a well-manicured Mughal garden, Humayun's Tomb (Mathura Rd., Nizamuddin East, sunrise-sunset Tues.-Sun., Rs. 250 foreigners, Rs. 10 Indians, video Rs. 25) is the final resting place of Humayun, son of Babur, founder of the Mughal Empire. The tomb, now a UNESCO World Heritage Site, was commissioned by Humayun's widow in the 1570s or 1580s and is considered the first major example of true Mughal architecture. It is also the oldest double-domed structure in India. Along with Humayun, two of his wives and a number of other Mughal rulers are buried in the dank interior of the tomb.

© MARGOT BIGG

THE UNKNOWN TOMBS OF GREEN PARK

Delhi's leafy Green Park neighborhood is home to a few old tombs that are rarely visited by travelers, probably because little is known about their history. These include Bagh-i-Alam Ka Gumbad, a square tomb built in the Lodi style in 1501 A.D. Just up the road from Hauz Khas Village is a small collection of Lodi Tombs; although there is little information as to when they were built or who is buried in them, they are often referred to as the tombs of Dadi and Poti (grandmother and granddaughter). There are plenty of other tombs in the neighborhood, most of which are in the middle of quiet residential streets; again, little is known about their history.

The last Mughal emperor, Bahadur Shah II, was captured here by a British lieutenant during the 1857 Indian Rebellion. The tomb itself is interesting (although it is a bit dark inside), and the raised platform it sits on affords good views of Delhi, but the real highlight of this sight is the sprawling gardens complete with pretty fountains.

The same compound is also home to a number of other tombs. To the southeast of the main building sits a double-domed square tomb known as the Barber's Tomb, although nobody really knows who is buried here. The same applies to the blue-domed Nila Gumbad, which, unusually, does not have a double dome. There is debate on when this tomb was built and who is buried here; some believe it may even predate Humayun's mausoleum. The Arab Sarai adjoining the southwestern corner of Humayun's Tomb is believed to have been built to house 300 mullahs (priests) brought from Mecca by Humayun's widow. Others believe it was simply the house of the craftsmen who built the tomb.

Purana Qila

The Purana Qila (Mathura Rd. and Bhairon Marg, Metro: Pragati Maidan, sunrise-sunset Tues.-Sun., Rs. 100 foreigners, Rs. 5 Indians, video Rs. 25, sound and light show Rs. 80 adults, Rs. 40 children), or Old Fort, sits on a mound that is believed to contain the ruins of the ancient city of Indraprastha. Part of the site has been excavated, and the subsequent archaeological findings—Painted Grey Ware pottery from the first millennium B.C.—seem to support this theory. The site was also once the location of the city of Dinpanah, built by Humayun and destroyed by Sher Shah Suri, founder of the brief Sur Empire and a major rival of the Mughals, who then built a citadel here. It is believed that Sher Shah was unable to finish the project, and Humayun ended up finishing it. Interesting features of the fort include the Qal'a-i-Kuhna-Masjid, a beautiful mosque featuring marble and stone inlay and plenty of high arches and oriel windows. The mosque mixes elements popular in Lodi and Mughal design and is considered significant in that it marks the transition between the two architectural styles. South of the mosque is the Sher Manda, a two-story tower crowned with an octagonal pavilion. It is believed to have been used as a recreational place by Sher Shah and as a library by Humayun. Humayun died here, after falling down the stairs and cracking his head.

Safdarjung's Tomb

Safdarjung was the viceroy of Awadh under Mughal emperor Muhammad Shah. His tomb (Aurobindo Marg and Lodhi Rd., Metro: Jor Bagh, sunrise–sunset Tues.-Sun., Rs. 100 foreigners, Rs. 5 Indians, video Rs. 25), dating from 1754, is the youngest of Delhi's enclosed garden tombs, and its layout is based on the much grander Humayun's Tomb. Its 28-square-meter garden is built in the *char bagh* (four-quarter) style popular in Mughal

The Baha'i House of Worship is often called the Lotus Temple.

gardens, although unfortunately it hasn't been very well maintained and is somewhat muddy or dusty, depending on whether you visit in the wet or dry season. A reflecting pool, now empty, leads up to the structure. The interior of the tomb looks like a Jell-O mold and has beautiful carved floral designs on the ceiling. Interestingly, the red stone and marble used to build the tomb was removed from the mausoleum of Khan-i-Khana, near Humayun's Tomb.

Tibet House Museum

Anyone interested in Tibetan history and culture will not want to miss the Tibet House Museum (1 Institutional Area, Lodhi Rd., tel. 11/2461-1515, http://tibethousenewdelhi.org, 9:30 A.M.-5:30 P.M. Mon.-Fri., Rs. 10). Tibet House was established by the Dalai Lama in 1965 in order to preserve the cultural heritage of his people after their country was occupied by the Chinese; India is home to their government in exile. The museum houses one of

the world's finest collections of *thangkas* (devotional scroll paintings of religious themes) as well as art, costumes, and ritual artifacts. Tibet House also hosts a range of educational activities, including discourses on dharma and music workshops.

SOUTH DELHI
Baha'i House of Worship (Lotus Temple)

Often referred to as the Lotus Temple due to its lotus shape (check it out in satellite images if you get a chance), the Baha'i House of Worship (Kalkaji, Metro: Nehru Place, Kalkaji Mandir, tel. 11/2647-0526, www.bahaihouseofworship. in, 9 A.M.-7 P.M. Tues.-Sun., free) is a peaceful place for prayer and reflection for people of all faiths. It's worth a visit not just for its tranquil ambiance but also for its architectural impressiveness. This beautiful temple was built in the 1980s based on blueprints drawn up by Persian Canadian architect Fariborz Sahba.

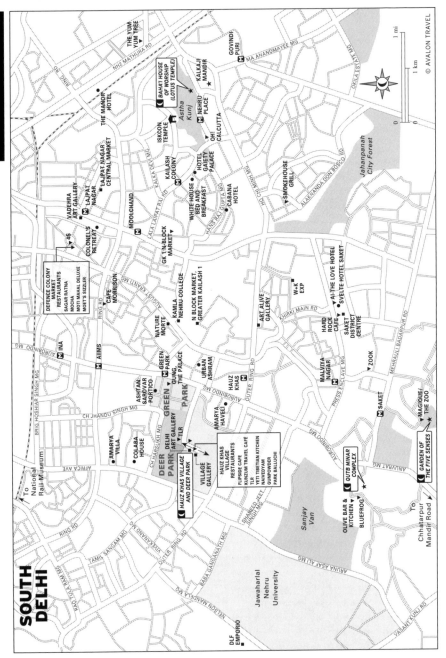

SOUTH DELHI

Sahba traveled across India to draw inspiration for the temple, and he took both Indian symbolism and India's climate into account when developing the concept for the structure. The idea was to craft the temple in the form of a lotus, a symbol of divinity in many eastern religions. Although the temple's architecture is most stunning when seen from the outside, it's also quite impressive from within. The furnishings are on the plain side, but the lotus-shaped skylight at the pinnacle of the temple's ceiling is worth craning your neck to see.

Almost 3.5 million people visit the site every year, and while it's usually a bit crowded, only a select number of people are allowed in the temple's main prayer hall at any given time, and the staff does an incredible job at managing logistics. You must remove your shoes before entering the temple and maintain complete silence. The only time people speak inside is during the five-minute prayer services (10 A.M.,

noon, 3 P.M., and 5 P.M. daily). Photography is not allowed inside the prayer hall.

Chhatarpur Mandir Road

Those interested in temple architecture and Hinduism won't want to miss a visit to the temple-flanked stretch of Chhatarpur Mandir Road between MG Road and the Chattarpur Mandir (Metro: Chattarpur), also known as Gadaipur Mandi Road. Approaching from the Chhatarpur Metro station on MG Road, you'll notice that the first 500 meters or so of this road is lined with amazing temples and ashrams, including the most famous sight, the Shri Adhya Katyani Shakti Peeth Mandir (commonly referred to as the Chattarpur Mandir). This massive white marble temple was built in the 1970s and blends northern and southern Indian architectural styles. Although images of a number of gods and goddesses appear, the primary deity is Katyayani, an avatar of the goddess Durga. If you visit in the evenings during the nine-night festival of Navratri (Sept.-Oct.), the entire street is decorated with tiny multicolored lights.

◀ Garden of the Five Senses

The beautiful Garden of the Five Senses (Said-ul-Ajaib, Mehrauli-Badarpur Rd., tel. 11/2953-6401, 9 A.M.-7 P.M. daily Apr.-Sept., 9 A.M.-6 P.M. daily Oct.-Mar., Rs. 20 adults, Rs. 10 children) occupies an eight-hectare site and is run by Delhi's tourism department. The park is laid out to stimulate the five senses, hence its name, and the flowers and installations are arranged to create a full sensory experience. There are a number of small boutiques as well as a few world-class alfresco restaurants.

The property is split into a number of small gardens, including the Khas Bagh, a model Mughal garden featuring fountains that are gorgeously lit at night by fiber-optic lights. The color gardens feature a number of blooming perennials alongside cacti and other unusual

© RAJAT DEEP RANA

a whimsical tree of bells in the Garden of the Five Senses

DELHI

plants. The entire garden is sprinkled with beautiful sculptures, and there's a large amphitheater that regularly hosts plays and concerts. Delhi's Garden Tourism Festival is held here every February.

◖ Hauz Khas Village and Deer Park

One of the most popular hangout spots for expats and artsy Delhiites, Hauz Khas Village (off Aurobindo Marg, just north of Outer Ring Rd., most shops 11 A.M.-7 or 8 P.M. daily), often abbreviated HKV (Delhiites love abbreviations), is worth a visit not only for its many good restaurants and trendy independent boutiques but also for the Lodi-era monuments in the adjoining Deer Park. Although the village has been undergoing gentrification for many years, there has been a real surge in the area's development lately, and dozens of restaurants have set up in the last few years.

Deer Park gets its name from a large caged-in area that doubles as a deer sanctuary. Some of the deer are astonishingly comfortable with humans, and although it's against the rules, plenty of visitors like to offer the animals grass and other treats through the gates. A popular drum circle is held near the gates every two weeks, usually on Saturday.

At the other end of the park is a collection of monuments next to an enormous tank that was built by Alauddin Khilji (1296-1316) to collect water for his nearby city of Siri. The tank later dried up but was restored by Feroz Shah in the latter part of the 14th century. Feroz Shah also set up a madrassa (religious college) here, the mazelike ruins of which are popular with college students to this day. The ruler's tomb, which blends Indian and Islamic structural features, is also located in the complex, and he is buried here along with his son and grandson.

ISKCON Temple

The Delhi base of the International Society for Krishna Consciousness (ISKCON), also known as the Hare Krishnas, the ISKCON Temple (Sant Nagar, east of Kailash, tel. 11/2623-5133, www.iskcondelhi.com, 4:30 A.M.-1 P.M. and 4:15-9 P.M. daily, free) is an interesting spot to learn more about the life of Lord Krishna and ISKCON's mission. The temple was built in the 1990s by acclaimed Indian architect Achyut P. Kanvinde and opened to the public in 1998. It's dedicated to Radha and Krishna (although iconography of other deities, as well as ISKCON's founder, Swami Prabhupada, can also be found). There are a couple of small shops on the temple grounds that stock books, religious memorabilia, and CDs of devotional music. The temple's delicious vegetarian restaurant, Govinda's, is reason enough to visit.

Kalkaji Mandir

Not far from the Lotus and ISKCON Temples, the Kalkaji Mandir (Kalkaji Flyover, Outer Ring Rd., Metro: Kalkaji Mandir, 4 A.M.-3 P.M.

© RAJAT DEEP RANA

the ISKCON Temple in South Delhi

Priests bless devotees at Kalkaji Mandir.

and 4 P.M.-midnight daily, free) is dedicated to the goddess Kali. A temple is believed to have stood here since the third century B.C., although the current structure dates from the 18th century. The temple is very popular with devotees and travelers, so you may have to wait in long lines and deal with a bit of pushing and shoving. The covered pathway leading up to the temple is flanked with stalls selling sweets and flowers as offerings, and it is customary to present something to the goddess when you enter. Interestingly, the temple is not run by a single priest or clan but by different families who take over the duties of temple maintenance and performing *pujas* (rituals) here on a monthly rotational basis.

◖ Qutb Minar Complex

Among Delhi's most iconic sites, the towering Qutb Minar (west of Aurobindo Marg, Mehrauli, Metro: Qutb Minar, sunrise-sunset Tues.-Sun., Rs. 250 foreigners, Rs. 10 Indians, video Rs. 25) is one of Delhi's oldest historic sites. It stretches 72.5 meters into the sky, has 379 steps, and is the highest tower in India. Construction of the Qutb commenced at the end of the 12th century under the reign of Qutb-ud-din Aibak, and it is believed to have been built either as a tower of victory or as a high spot from which people could be called to prayer at the nearby **Quwwatu'l-Islam Mosque.** This mosque was built between 1192 and 1198, and is the oldest extant mosque in India after the pre-sultanate monuments in Kutch, Gujarat. The mosque features a beautifully carved screen featuring geometric patterns and Islamic inscriptions.

Just next to the mosque stands the 7.2-meter-high **Iron Pillar,** believed to date back to the Gupta Dynasty in the late 4th century due to its Sanskrit inscriptions in the Gupta script; it is thought to have been brought to the complex from elsewhere. A third tower, the unfinished Alai Minar, also stands on the complex. It was

© RAJAT DEEP RANA

the innovative Sulabh International Museum of Toilets

© MARGOT BIGG

built by Alauddin Khilji, who had planned for it to be double the size of the Qutb Minar. He had also doubled the size of the mosque, so it's assumed he wanted his tower to be proportionate. Unfortunately, he died before it could be completed, and nobody bothered to carry on where he'd left off.

Another interesting feature of the complex is the **Alai Darwaza,** a domed pavilion with interiors that are a few degrees cooler than the outside temperature (that means a lot in Delhi's summer months). The gateway is made of red sandstone and is one of India's earliest examples of strictly Islamic architecture. Just beyond the Alai Darwaza sits the slightly run-down tomb of an imam from Turkestan by the name of Zamin. This tiny octagonal tomb was built in the 16th century and features beautiful, perforated screens and a large sandstone dome. Like the Alai Darwaza, the temperatures inside are remarkably cool.

You'll definitely want to block out at least

an hour to explore the grounds. The complex is spacious, the gardens are kept in great shape, and there's a lot of open space to move around, so it never feels too crowded. It's also fairly close to the airport, and the low-flying aircraft passing over the towering Qutb Minar make for some great photo ops.

Sulabh International Museum of Toilets

Consistently nominated as one of the world's strangest museums, the Sulabh International Museum of Toilets (Sulabh Bhawan, Mahavir Enclave, Palam Dabri Marg, tel. 11/2503-6122, www.sulabhtoiletmuseum.org, 10 A.M.-5 P.M. Mon.-Sat., free) is as fascinating as it is unusual. The small museum hall is packed with latrines and urinals from around the world along with information about the history of the toilet and advances in sanitation practices over the years. It may sound gimmicky, but the goal is actually to raise awareness about the often overlooked need for adequate sanitation.

The museum is run by the Sulabh International Service Organization, a nonprofit that helps provide much-needed sanitation services and waste recycling technology to India's most needy. The people at Sulabh are experts at converting human excreta into biogas and extracting contaminants from urine, essentially converting it to water that can be safely used for irrigation. The staff is very friendly and eager to assist visitors, and it's easy to get someone to explain how the toilets and related waste conversion processes work. Ask to see the staff kitchen—the stove they use runs entirely on biogas sourced from human waste.

NORTH DELHI
Majnu Ka Tilla Tibetan Enclave

The small Tibetan enclave of Majnu Ka Tilla (near the Majnu Ka Tilla Gurudwara, Mahatma Gandhi Rd., Metro: Vidhan Sabha) is primarily home to Tibetan people who were no longer able to stay in their native land after the Chinese invaded. It's a popular alternative to Paharganj among the backpacker set, but it's quite far from town, and the quality of accommodations is not good enough to get a recommendation in this book. The colony, however, is worth a visit if you're interested in Tibetan culture, and there are plenty of shops and eateries selling Tibetan (and, ironically, Chinese) products and food. The main square is home to the local Tibetan monastery, which features a massive prayer wheel on its stoop as well as

a number of smaller wheels flanking its sides. Devotees customarily circumambulate the building in the clockwise direction, spinning each wheel as they pass by.

EAST DELHI
Swaminarayan Akshardham Complex

Delhi's newest major attraction, the Swaminarayan Akshardham Complex (Gurjar Samrat Mir Bhoj Marg and Noida Link Rd., Metro: Akshardham, tel. 11/2201-6688, www.akshardham.com, 9:30 A.M.-6:30 P.M. Mon.-Sat., free) officially opened in 2005 and is named after Bhagwan Swaminarayan, founder of the Swaminarayan sect of Hinduism. At the center of the complex sits a 33-meter-tall, intricately carved temple dedicated to Swaminarayan made entirely of pink sandstone (6,000 tons of it, no less). The temple features beautifully carved screens, bas-reliefs, and pillars, including four that, at 10 meters, are the tallest in the country. Other popular attractions on the site include the fabulously cheesy audio-animatronics show (think a higher-tech version of a robotics show, like the Pirates of the Caribbean ride at Disneyland). *Mystic India,* a film that retells the fascinating true-life story of an 11-year-old yogi who traveled across the country in search of spiritual truth, is also screened. The complex is home to several other exhibits and experiences, including sound and light shows, interactive fiber-optic installations, and displays of scenes from some of India's greatest epic tales.

Entertainment and Events

Delhi is a fairly festive place, and there's usually something going on, be it a religious festival, a fashion week, a convention, or an international sporting event. It also has a lively arts scene, arguably unparalleled anywhere else in the country, and lovers of the fine and performing arts will find plenty going on. Delhi also has a growing nightlife scene, and on most nights you'll be able to choose from a number of places to go out dancing.

NIGHTLIFE

Delhi's nightlife scene is growing, and a number of new and successful bars and nightclubs open every year. Most are required to close by 1 A.M., although club owners often find ways of getting special permission to go on until the wee hours. The official drinking age in clubs and bars is 25, although this is rarely enforced. Most have dress codes, and men without close-toed shoes may be denied entry. Others prohibit stag (single-male) entry, so call ahead to check, or make sure you have a woman for every man in your group.

The most popular types of music among Delhi's youth are the ubiquitous Bollywood film songs, followed by Punjabi bhangra music. Rock music is a close third, and India has a thriving homegrown rock music scene. If you're interested in electronic dance music, it's a good idea to check what's going on ahead of time. Club listings can be found in the Nightlife section of *Time Out* magazine. Also note that things change really fast in the capital, and today's hot club may be shut down permanently tomorrow (the city's bureaucratic Excise Commission, responsible for issuing alcohol licenses, doesn't help things much). The venues listed below are pretty well established and are likely to be around for many years to come.

Nicknamed "the press club" for its popularity with Delhi journalists, **4S** (A-26 Defence Colony Market, tel. 11/4166-4314, noon-midnight daily, no cover) is Delhi's most beloved dive bar, partially because the 50-percent-off happy hour at this already cheap bar lasts until 10 P.M. 4S is what is known in India as a resto-bar, and they serve up a great selection of deep-fried Chinese snacks, which taste great after a few beers. The doorman, with his long mustache and perpetual smile, makes the place feel incredibly welcoming, whether you're a first-time customer or a tipsy regular.

One of the newest clubs in Delhi, **blueFROG** (The Kila, Seven Style Mile, opposite Qutb Minar, Mehrauli, tel. 11/2664-5298, www.bluefrog.co.in, 8 A.M.-1 A.M. Tues.-Sun., cover after 8 P.M. Sat., after 9 P.M. Sun.-Fri., charge varies) opened at the end of 2011 and has already become a popular place to dance the night away. Modeled after its flagship club in Mumbai, Delhi's blueFROG offers modern interiors and a great selection of cocktails. They regularly host bands and DJs from across India and abroad.

Rock is not dead at **Café Morrison** (E-12 South Extension II Market, tel. 9810/261-442, www.cafemorrison.com, noon-1 A.M. daily); in fact, it's celebrated with verve at this multistory bar decorated with rock posters. Café Morrison is popular with college students, who come to get drunk and listen to *Smells Like Teen Spirit* at full blast. If that doesn't sound like your idea of a, um, rocking time, you can always hang out on the top floor, which regularly hosts DJs.

The fashionable **F-Bar** (The Ashok, 50, Chanakyapuri, tel. 11/2611-1119, www.fbardelhi.com, 24 hours daily, from Rs. 2,000, couples only) is good for people-watching, throwing away vast amounts of money, and general ostentation. The cover charge is expensive, and the main draw of this little place is that it never closes (although the DJs do eventually go home). F-Bar occasionally host some amazing major artists from India and abroad, which attract a good crowd of happy, dancing people.

Ever heard of tinnitus, that unceasing ringing in your ears that's often caused by operating loud machinery without ear protection? If not, you'll know all about it after a visit to **Hard Rock Café** (M-110, Multiplex Bldg., 1st Fl., DLF Place, Saket District Centre, tel. 11/4715-8888, www.hardrock.com, noon-1 A.M. daily, cover charge for some performance nights), where the decibels are pushed up far beyond reasonable limits. The Delhi branch of this international institution hosts some great bands every once in a while. The rest of the time, they blast really loud rock music. Like all venues in Delhi, it's nonsmoking, although they do have an unventilated aquarium-like smoking room. The burgers and ice cream sundaes are delicious.

Connaught Place's **Q'ba** (Radial No 7, E Block, Connaught Place, tel. 11/4517-3333, noon-1 A.M. daily, no cover) is a spacious, reasonably-priced bar-restaurant right in the middle of town. It's more a drinking spot than a place to dance, although they occasionally host events, and it's popular with the after-work crowd.

Rick's (Taj Mahal Hotel, 1 Mansingh Rd., tel. 11/6651-3246, 12:30 P.M.-1 A.M. Sun.-Thurs., 12:30 P.M.-2 A.M. Fri.-Sat., no cover) is a small, quite chic hotel bar that attracts a fun-loving set of big spenders. It's cozy, and the music is not played at full blast, although it's still loud enough to get down on the small dance floor.

Delhi's wealthy over-30 set flock to **Smokehouse Grill** (2 VIPPS Center, LSC Masjid Moth, Greater Kailash II, tel. 11/4143-5531, http://smokehousegrill.in, 7:30 P.M.-1 A.M. daily, no cover most nights). This double-story restaurant serves excellent cocktails, and there's usually a DJ playing commercial house music. It's a friendly place, and

most of the guests are on the social side. Note that the dress code is strictly enforced.

An expat favorite, **TLR** (31 Hauz Khas Village, Metro: Green Park, tel. 11/4608-0533, www.tlrcafe.com, 11 A.M.-midnight daily, no cover) hosts regular open mike and themed dance music events, where everything from animal masks to sparkly pom-poms are distributed to the audience. It's a convivial place with frequent specials on beer (often two-for-one). They also serve food, and the dress code is a bit more casual than many other places in Delhi.

In the enchanting Garden of the Five Senses, **The Zoo** (Garden of Five Senses, Said-Ul-Ajaib, Mehrauli, tel. 11/6557-6198, 7 P.M.-1 A.M. daily, no cover most nights) is a popular nightspot featuring primarily electronic music DJs. There's a small dance floor indoors, but guests tend to congregate in the enclosed outdoor area, where it's a bit easier to have a conversation. There's rarely a cover charge, and there is usually no problem for single men to gain entry; nice shoes are a must.

Part hookah bar, part restaurant, **Zook** (No. 3 PVR Anupam Complex, Saket, tel. 11/4105-7482, noon-1 A.M. daily, no cover most nights) hosts some interesting events, including reggae parties put on by Delhi's Reggae Rajahs as well as drum-and-bass and dubstep nights by local sound system BASSFoundation. The interiors are modern and incorporate light wood with colorful posters, including a corny pointillist version of the iconic shirtless photo of Jim Morrison.

THE ARTS
Art Galleries

Although it has only been around for a bit over a decade, South Delhi's **Art Alive Gallery** (S-221 Panchsheel Marg, tel. 11/4163-9000, www.artalivegallery.com, 11 A.M.-7 P.M. Mon.-Sat.) has made a tremendous contribution to India's art scene. This gallery focuses on contemporary Indian art and is active in promoting Indian art on the international scene. There's a second branch in the nearby city of Gurgaon.

Delhi Art Gallery (11 Hauz Khas Village, tel. 11/4600-5300, http://delhiartgallery.com, 11 A.M. to 7 P.M. Mon.-Sat.) has a huge collection of pieces from Indian modernists. Appraisal and authentication services are also offered, and the knowledgeable staff can help those who are new to buying art or are unfamiliar with Indian art.

Named for the French term for still life, **Nature Morte** (A-1, opposite Kamla Nehru College, Niti Bagh, tel. 11/4174-0215, www.na-turemorte.com, 10 A.M.-6 P.M. Mon.-Sat.) exhibits a variety of modern art from established artists. This basement gallery is run by Peter Negi, one of India's best-known curators. There are additional branches in Gurgaon and Berlin.

One of the best-known and most respected galleries in the capital, **Vadehra Art Gallery** (D-40 Defence Colony, Metro: Lajpat Nagar, tel. 11/2462-2545, http://vadehraart.com, 10:30 A.M.-7 P.M. Mon.-Sat.) has exhibited work from India's best-known modern artists. The gallery is home to the Foundation for Indian Contemporary Art and even has its own publishing branch.

It has been over 20 years since **Village Gallery** (14 Hauz Khas Village, Metro: Green Park, tel. 11/2685-3860, http://thevillagegal-lery.co.in, 2:30-7 P.M. Mon.-Sat.) first opened its doors in South Delhi's artsy Hauz Khas Village. The gallery continues to exhibit art from established and up-and-coming Indian artists to this day.

The official Delhi gallery of Oregon advertising behemoth Wieden+Kennedy (the people who coined the phrase "Just Do It" for Nike), **W+K Exp** (B-10 DDA Complex, Sheikh Sarai Phase I, Metro: Malviya Nagar, tel. 11/4600-9595, www.wkdelhiblog.com, 10 A.M.-7 P.M. Mon.-Sat.) hosts rotating exhibitions from Indian and international artists.

Cinemas

There are literally hundreds of cinemas in Delhi,

ranging from dinky little places that screen the same old Bollywood film week after week to ultramodern multiplexes. **Regal Cinema** (Connaught Place, tel. 11/2336-2245, Metro: Rajiv Chowk) is Connaught Place's best-known movie hall, although it's not as nice as some of the newer venues. PVR Cinemas (various locations, www.pvrcinemas.com) operate the vast majority of Delhi's newer high-quality cinemas and consistently screens English-language films. Other cinema companies include Satyam Cineplexes (various locations, www.satyamcin-eplexes.com) and M2K Cinemas (various locations, www.m2kcinemas.com).

Cultural Centers

The main focus of the **Alliance Française** (72 Lodhi Estate, Connaught Place, tel. 11/5101-2091, http://delhi.afindia.org, 9 A.M.-6 P.M. Mon.-Sat.), the French cultural center, is imparting French language skills on those who care to learn, but it also hosts a wide range of cultural events and lectures, usually with a French touch. There's also a small theater and an art gallery.

The Attic (36 Regal Bldg., Connaught Place, Metro: Rajiv Chowk, tel. 11/2374-6050, http://theatticdelhi.org, open only for events) was set up with the goal of preserving and showcasing textiles and heirlooms, but they do much more. This Connaught Place gallery hosts regular talks, recitals, and concerts on a wide range of topics and by a diverse group of performers.

Painted to look like a black-and-white cow, the **British Council** (17 Kasturba Gandhi Marg, Connaught Place, Metro: Barakhamba Rd., tel. 11/2371-1401, www.britishcouncil. org, 9 A.M.-5 P.M. Mon.-Fri.) sponsors a wide range of cultural activities aimed at strengthening the Indo-British relationship. Events are occasionally held in the courtyard.

Germany's cultural center, the **Goethe Institute/Max Mueller Bhawan** (3 Kasturba Gandhi Marg, Connaught Place, Metro:

Barakhamba Rd., tel. 11/2332-9506, www. goethe.de/newdelhi, 9:30 A.M.-6 P.M. Mon.-Fri.) plays host to a great number of cultural events on its spacious lawns and in its indoor performance area. Performers, especially electronic musicians, are regularly brought from Germany.

The massive **India Habitat Centre** (Lodhi Rd, Lodhi Estate, Lodhi Colony, tel. 11/2468-2001, http://indiahabitat.org, 8 A.M.-9 P.M. daily) holds a wide variety of musical performances, art exhibitions, lectures, and film screenings. A number of government and nongovernmental organizations also have branches here.

Just up the road from the Habitat Centre, the **India International Centre** (40 Lodhi Rd., Max Mueller Marg, Connaught Place, tel. 11/2461-9431, http://iicdelhi.nic.in, 10 A.M.-5 P.M. daily) hosts similar events, ranging from classical music performances to talks from some of India's finest scholars.

Theaters and Auditoriums

Plays are staged at one of the many theaters in Central Delhi's Mandi House area. You can see plays performed in both English and Hindi. Prices vary depending on the performance, but ticket prices usually range from Rs.100-500. Theaters include the National School of Drama's **Abhimanch Auditorium** (1 Bhagwan Das Rd., Pragati Maidan, Metro: Mandi House, tel. 11/2338-2821, www.nsd.gov.in), **Kamani Auditorium** (1 Copernicus Marg, Connaught Place, Metro: Mandi House, tel. 11/4350-3351, www.kamaniauditorium.org), **The Little Theatre Group Auditorium** (Copernicus Marg, near Barakhamba Rd., Metro: Mandi House, tel. 11/2338-9713), **Meghdoot Theatre** (Rabindra Bhawan, Copernicus Marg, Mandi House, Metro: Mandi House, tel. 11/2338-7241), and the **Shri Ram Centre for Performing Arts** (4 Safdar Hashmi Marg, Metro: Mandi House, tel. 11/2371-4307, www.shriramcenterart.org), which has its own repertory company. Call

ahead or check local papers for showtimes and ticket prices.

FESTIVALS AND EVENTS
Bharat Rang Mahotsav

The largest theater festival in Delhi, the National School of Drama's two-week-long Bharat Rang Mahotsav (www.nsdtheatrefest.com) in January stages dozens of performances in a variety of genres, performed by both local and international theater companies.

Republic Day

Republic Day (www.republicday.nic.in), January 26, is the national holiday that commemorates the Republic of India's constitution. It is observed across India, but nowhere are the celebrations more fervent than in Delhi. In the morning a large parade moves along Rajpath in Central Delhi, featuring floats, military marchers, and even elephant processions.

Garden Tourism Festival

This government-run outdoor garden festival in February takes place at the beautiful Garden of the Five Senses and features gardening demonstrations, lectures on horticulture, a plant and flower market, cultural performances, a bonsai exhibition, and a flower show.

Monsoon Festival

The Monsoon Festival (http://themonsoonfestival.com) is an arts festival is held in honor of the refreshing annual monsoon. It features a wide selection of activities, including art exhibitions, theatrical performances, handicrafts markets, and lectures.

Osian's Cinefan Festival of Asian and Arab Cinema

The Cinefan Festival (www.cinefan.osians.com) is staged in July at multiple venues and celebrates the best in cinema from across Asia and the Arab world with screenings, discussion panels, and film awards.

International Mango Festival

Really more of a convention than a bona fide festival, July's International Mango Festival is dedicated to India's best-loved fruit and features exhibitions, tastings, and cooking demonstrations as well as the opportunity to sample dozens of varieties of this succulent fruit and related products.

Delhi Book Fair

The annual Delhi Book Fair (www.delhibookfair.in), held in August-September, is primarily aimed at people in the publishing industry, but it always ends up attracting nonindustry folk who flock here to check out the latest titles on offer and to pick up discounted books.

Delhi Photo Festival

Held in October in odd-numbered years, the Delhi Photo Festival (www.delhiphotofestival.com) features a wide range of activities, including hands-on photography workshops, lectures, contests, and, naturally, photography exhibitions.

Delhi International Arts Festival

The enormous Delhi International Arts Festival (www.diaf.in) takes place over a couple of weeks in November and is spread over multiple venues around town. The organizers take a comprehensive view of what an arts festival should be, so along with traditional visual and performing arts, the best of literature, film, and even culinary arts are featured.

Qutb Festival

Set against the backdrop of the iconic Qutb Minar, this five-day music festival, held in November or December, features performances from top Indian musicians, ranging from classical artists to popular Hindi film singers.

Shopping

If someone were to hold a contest for India's best shopping city, Delhi would easily win. The capital is filled with shopping options for every budget, from ultralow-cost open-air markets to fancy malls specializing in prêt-à-porter from France and Italy's top designers. It's a great place to buy handicrafts, and while Delhi doesn't have much of a crafts tradition of its own, you can pick up bits and pieces from around the country.

SHOPPING DISTRICTS

There are plenty of good spots to shop in Delhi, some better than others. The most established is Central Delhi's **Connaught Place** (Metro: Rajiv Chowk, most shops Mon.-Sat.), the commercial center of New Delhi and home to a great number of shops selling toys, books, clothing, and housewares. Also in Central Delhi, **Khan Market** (Metro: Khan Market, most shops Mon.-Sat.) is popular with rich Delhiites and embassy staff. It also has one of the highest concentrations of great restaurants in town.

In South Delhi, **Greater Kailash I** (east of Josip Broz Tito Marg, between Lala Lajpat Rai Path and Outer Ring Rd.) is a hugely popular shopping and residential area and is usually referred to simply as "GK." While the M-Block Market here focuses more on Western clothes, appliances, and other items that are not likely to be of much interest to visitors, the N-Block Market just down the road has lots of lovely upscale Indian clothing boutiques as well as a number of slick home furnishings shops. The ultratrendy **Hauz Khas Village** (off Aurobindo Marg, just north of Outer Ring Rd.) is

© RAJAT DEEP RANA

South Delhi's trendy Hauz Khas Village

chock-full of cute little independent clothing boutiques, antiques dealers, and art galleries, but gentrification is making it difficult for some artists to sustain their workshops. Many are moving to the much more bohemian village of **Shahpurjat** just down the road, and this is the place to go for bargain bespoke pieces from up-and-coming young designers.

The epicenter of Old Delhi's commercial activity, the never-boring and usually chaotic **Chandni Chowk** (west of Lal Qila, between Netaji Subhash Rd. and GB Rd., most shops 10 A.M.-8 P.M. Mon.-Sat.) is Delhi's most famous market and a popular place to pick up jewelry, textiles, and *itar* (essential oil). It's also a good place to buy spices, but to be completely honest, the reputable supermarket brands (such as MDH) are generally just as good and are easier to get through customs than unlabeled bulk items.

The market was established in the 17th century by Emperor Shahjahan in what was then the walled city of city of Shahjahanabad. Chandni Chowk is Hindi for Moonlight Square; there was once a canal here positioned to reflect moonlight.

HANDICRAFTS

India has some amazing handicraft items, including beautiful shawls and papier-mâché pieces from Kashmir, silk saris from Varanasi, and mirrored bedspreads from Rajasthan. All of this can be found under one roof at the government-run **Cottage Industries** (Jawahar Vyapar Bhavan, Janpath, Metro: Rajiv Chowk, tel. 11/2332-0439, http://cottageemporium.in, 10 A.M.-7 P.M. daily). This huge showroom sells items from around the country at fixed prices, and although the items are slightly pricier than they might be if you got into a bargaining match with a local vendor, you can be sure of the quality.

Another government-run initiative aimed at promoting regional handicrafts, the **State**

Emporia Complex (Baba Kharak Rd., Patel Chowk, Metro: Shivaji Stadium, 11 A.M.-7 P.M. Mon.-Sat.) has shops run by the tourism departments of the various states. You'll find a wide range of handicraft items, mostly housewares, arts, and textiles from around the country. Just pick your state of choice and start shopping. You can also find products from around India at the government-run crafts village **Dilli Haat** (Auobindo Marg and Ring Rd., 10:30 A.M.-9 P.M. daily, Rs. 20 adults, Rs. 10 children).

BOUTIQUES

The Delhi outlet of a well-respected Jaipur jewelry shop, **Amarpali** (39-39A Khan Market, Metro: Khan Market, tel. 11/4175-2024, www.amrapalijewels.com, 10:30 A.M.-7:30 P.M. Mon.-Sat., noon-5 P.M. Sun.) features a huge assortment of primarily silver jewelry designs, ranging from traditional Rajashtani enamel pieces to ultracontemporary designs.

For beautiful block-printed women's wear and upholstery, head straight to **Anokhi** (32 Khan Market, Metro: Khan Market, tel. 11/2460-3423, www.anokhi.com, 10 A.M.-8 P.M. daily). This Jaipur institution is a big hit in Delhi, selling a large range of Indian women's wear as well as dresses, duvet covers, and super-soft cotton pajamas, all made of fine hand-block printed cottons. There's also a branch in Greater Kailash I (N-16 N-Block Market, Greater Kailash I, Metro: Kailash Colony, tel. 11/2923-1500, www.anokhi.com, 10 A.M.-8 P.M. daily).

Flouncy skirts and subtly bejeweled kurtas (tunics) abound at **Cottons** (N-11 Greater Kailash I, Metro: Kailash Colony, tel. 11/4163-5108, 10:30 A.M.-7 P.M. daily). This women's wear shop specializes in ethnic apparel with modern cuts, and it is a great place to pick up the beautiful long scarves, called *dupattas,* that you'll often see Indian women draping around their shoulders.

If you'd like to pick up a few pieces of

traditional Indian clothing but don't want anything too shiny or brightly colored, **Fab India** (B-28 Upper Ground Fl., Inner Circle, Connaught Place, Metro: Rajiv Chowk, tel. 11/4151-3371, www.fabindia.com, 11 A.M.-8 P.M. daily) is your best bet. This shop specializes in tunics for men and women made from hand-dyed natural fabrics. They also have a good array of skirts, blouses, stoles, *salwars* (loose trousers) and *churidars* (trousers tapered at the ankles) as well as home furnishings and organic spices. Fab India has branches around India, including one in Greater Kailash (N-14 Greater Kailash I, Metro: Kailash Colony, tel. 11/2923-2183, 10 A.M.-8 P.M. daily) and Khan Market (Middle Lane, above Shop 20-21, Khan Market, Metro: Khan Market, tel. 11/4368-3100, 10 A.M.-8 P.M. daily).

One of the best interior design shops in India, **Good Earth** (9 Khan Market, Metro: Khan Market, tel. 11/2464-7175, www.goodearth.in, 11 A.M.-8:30 P.M. daily) stocks a beautiful array of everything from candles to cutlery, including many designs that blend classical Indian aesthetics with contemporary functionality. There's a small selection of beautiful linen dresses on the second floor.

For high-quality leather goods at a fraction of what you would pay back home, check out **Hidesign** (N-10 Greater Kailash I, Metro: Kailash Colony, tel. 11/2923-6034, http://hidesign.com, 10:30 A.M.-8:30 P.M. daily). The Pondicherry-based company is India's best-known producer of leatherwear, and their products—handbags, wallets, and attaché cases—are sold in department stores around the world. The designs are contemporary and on par with what you might find in Italy. There are outlets across India, including one at Khan Market (49-A Khan Market, Metro: Khan Market, tel. 11/2461-5314, 10 A.M.-8 P.M. daily).

For unique souvenirs, check out **Khazana India** (50-A Haus Khas Village, Metro: Green Park, tel. 11/6469-0579, 10:30 A.M.-8 P.M.

daily). This small shop is a perfect place to pick up old advertising posters, magnets, and other aging Indian curios. It also stocks very cool antique candy tins, adorned with images of Indian deities.

Nappa Dori (HKV) (Shop 4, Hauz Khas Village, Metro: Green Park, tel. 9810/400-778, www.nappadori.com, 11:30 A.M.-7:30 P.M. Tues.-Sun.) stocks colorful trunks with stands so that they can double as tables, journals, handbags, billfolds, and toiletry cases featuring sepia-toned scenes from India's past. There's a second showroom a few doors down showcasing additional Nappa Dori items as well as pretty cushion covers and other soft furnishings by local designer Shruti Reddy.

Looking for a gift for someone back home and not sure what to get? **Purple Jungle** (16 Ground Fl., Hauz Khas Village, Metro: Green Park, tel. 11/2653-8182, http://purple-jungle.com, 11 A.M.-7 P.M. daily) just may be the shop you've been searching for. This tiny boutique specializes in brightly colored purses, toiletry cases, cushions, and other gift items made from up-cycled educational posters from India. Additional stock is kept in the studio-warehouse a few doors down—feel free to ask to visit it if you don't find the perfect gift in the main showroom.

BOOKSTORES

A Khan Market favorite, **Bahri Sons** (opposite Main Gate, Khan Market, Metro: Khan Market, tel. 11/2469-4610, www.booksatbahri.com, 10 A.M.-2 P.M. and 2:30-7:30 P.M. Mon.-Sat.) has been selling books to Delhiites for over half a century. They stock a huge variety of fiction titles as well as hundreds of magazines from India and abroad.

You can pick up excellent coffee-table books on India at **Full Circle** (N-16 Greater Kailash I, Metro: Kailash Colony, tel. 11/2924-5643, www.fullcirclebooks.in, 9:30 A.M.-8:30 P.M. daily). Although the art book section is the main

draw, there is also a great selection of children's lit, spiritual books, and Indian fiction. There are other branches around Delhi, including one at Khan Market (Shop 23, 1st and 2nd Fl., Middle Lane, Khan Market, Metro: Khan Market, tel. 11/2465-5641, 9:30 A.M.-8:30 P.M. daily).

No book lover should miss **Yodakin Bookstore** (2 Hauz Khas Village, Metro: Green Park, tel. 11/4178-7201, www.yodakin.com, 11 A.M.-8 P.M. Mon. and Wed.-Sat., 2-8 P.M. Tues., noon-8 P.M. Sun.), a cozy shop specializing in books from independent publishers with plenty of titles that you won't find elsewhere. There's also a large selection of art and design periodicals as well as a small collection of music and films.

MUSICAL INSTRUMENTS

If you'd like to pick up a classical Indian instrument, your two best bets are South Delhi's **Bharat Music House** (B-113 Lajpat Nagar I, Metro: Lajpat Nagar, tel. 11/2981-0212, www.bharatmusichouse.com, 11:30 A.M.-7:30 P.M. Tues.-Sun.) and Connaught Place's **Rikhi Ram** (G-8 Marina Arcade, Connaught Circus, Connaught Place, Metro: Rajiv Chowk, tel. 11/2332-7685, www.rikhiram.com, 12:30-8 P.M. Mon.-Sat.). Both manufacture a wide array of Indian instruments—Rikhi Ram even has miniature versions—and can help you figure out a way to ship instruments home if you don't want to carry them as luggage.

SHOPPING MALLS

Delhi has tons of shopping malls, most of which have a lot of stores similar to what you might find back home. One of the oldest is **Ansal Plaza** (August Kranti Marg, between Ring Rd. and Siri Fort Rd., shop hours vary, mall 11 A.M.-10:30 P.M. daily) in South Delhi. There's a big cluster of malls in South Delhi's Saket neighborhood in a strip known as **Saket District Centre** (Press Enclave Marg, east of Lal Bahadur Shastri Marg, shop hours vary, malls 10 A.M.-11 P.M. daily). The malls, including **Select Citywalk, DLF Place,** and **Metropolitan Mall,** are home to a huge number of cinemas, restaurants, department stores, and chain boutiques. Few visitors to Delhi find any real reason to visit these malls, which stock items that can be found in most of the Western world at more or less the same prices. Popular shops include Zara, FCUK, Levi's, and Adidas. Designer brands such as Gucci, Jimmy Choo, and Louis Vuitton can be found at **DLF Emporio** (4 Nelson Mandela Marg, Vasant Kunj, shop hours vary, mall 11 A.M.-1 A.M. daily), but because of high import taxes, these items will cost you far more than they would in your home country. The biggest mall in India, **Ambience Mall,** is just outside Delhi in the satellite city of Gurgaon. It features hundreds of shops, a huge food court with a play area, a bowling alley, and a brewery. Gurgaon is home to scores of other malls, all of which stock more or less the same things, namely sportswear, Indian clothes, and shoes. The majority of these malls can be found on Gurgaon's MG Road, accessible via the IFFCO Chowk or MG Road Metro stations.

OUTDOOR MARKETS

Delhi has tons of excellent outdoor markets. For kitchenware and Indian clothes—especially saris—head to busy **Lajpat Nagar Central Market** (Metro: Lajpat Nagar, most shops 10 A.M.-8 P.M. Tues.-Sun.). The market is one of the most congested shopping areas in South Delhi, and entire sections focus on kitchenware, saris, fabric, and shoes. This is also a great place to buy bangles; whole shops are devoted to these beautiful bracelets.

Karol Bagh Market (Pusa Rd. and Arya Samaj Rd., most shops 10 A.M.-8 P.M. Tues.-Sun.) is a bit more convenient if you're coming from Paharganj or Connaught Place. It's similar in many ways to Lajpat Nagar, although it is a bit bigger. Popular buys include saris and jewelry, ranging from costume items to exquisite diamond-studded wedding pieces.

Young women won't want to miss the fabulous deals on surplus clothing at **Sarojini Nagar Market** (Brig Hoshiar Singh Marg, near Africa Ave., most shops 10 A.M.-8 P.M. Tues.-Sun.). India is a major producer of clothing for more developed countries, and the pieces that don't quite make the cut, usually due to a missing button or an inconsistent dye job, are sold here at rock-bottom prices. It's like an open-air version of a factory outlet store, and there is always lot of stuff from H&M, Esprit, FCUK, and Ralph Lauren.

The best deals on hippie gear, Hindu deity statues, tapestries, and costume jewelry are at **Paharganj** (across from New Delhi Railway Station, Qutab Rd., most shops 11 A.M.-8 P.M. Tues.-Sun.) and the **Tibetan Market** (Janpath, near Connaught Place, 11 A.M.-8 P.M. Mon.-Sat.). These two markets cater primarily to visitors, although plenty of Indian college students frequent them too. The goods on offer are inexpensive by Western standards, but most shopkeepers will start with high prices and expect you to bargain them down.

If you'd rather not have to negotiate a price, you'll love **Dilli Haat** (Auobindo Marg and Ring Rd., 10:30 A.M.-9 P.M. daily, Rs. 20 adults, Rs. 10 children). This government-run market features artisans from across the country, and it's a great place to get the feel of a crafts market without the noise and pushy sales pleas that are common in most other markets. It's definitely on the artificial side, but the products here are of good quality. There's also an excellent food court featuring cuisine from across the country, and locals love to come here just to eat.

Sports and Recreation

Delhi is not a typical sports and recreation destination. Most of the sporting infrastructure, including the listings below, are aimed more at locals.

SPORTS FACILITIES

If your hotel doesn't have a gym and you are dying to work out, your best options are South Delhi's two major sports complexes, both of which offer temporary memberships. **Saket Sports Complex** (opposite Welcome Marriott Hotel, Saket, tel. 11/2956-1742, www.dda.org.in, 6:30 A.M.-11:30 P.M. Tues.-Sun., 4-8:30 P.M. Mon., gym Rs. 220 per hour), offers a large number of activities and classes, ranging from tae kwon do to ballroom dancing.

Another popular South Delhi option is the **Siri Fort Sports Complex** (August Kranti Marg, tel. 11/2649-7482, www.dda.org.in, 6 A.M.-9 P.M. daily, rates vary by activity), a sprawling sports facility offering everything from rifle shooting to Reiki. There are also 12 tennis courts on-site.

GOLF

The best place to go for golf in Delhi is the **Delhi Golf Club** (Dr. Zakir Hussain Marg, tel. 11/2430-7100, www.delhigolfclub.org, sunrise-sunset Tues.-Sun., 18 holes Rs. 3,000 Sat.-Sun., Rs. 2,000 Mon.-Fri., 9 holes Rs. 1,250 Sat.-Sun.). The club sits in the heart of central Delhi and comprises the 18-hole Lodhi Course and the 9-hole Peacock Course. A number of old Lodi-era tombs dot the grounds. There's also a pool and a bar on-site.

Delhi is also home to a much more affordable, and not nearly as nice, nine-hole course at **Siri Fort Complex** (August Kranti Marg, tel. 11/2649-7482, www.dda.org.in, 6 A.M.-9 P.M. daily, admission Rs. 40, Rs. 50 for 50 balls). This plain grass golfing facility has a driving range and a pitch-and-putt course.

HORSEBACK RIDING

There aren't many great places to go riding in Delhi, but you can always drop in to one of the lessons at the **Delhi Riding Club** (behind Safdarjung Tomb, Safdarjung Rd., Metro: Jor Bagh, tel. 11/2301-1891, 6:30-8:30 A.M. and 2:45-5:45 P.M. daily, Rs. 800 per adult's class, Rs. 600 per children's class). There are beginner and intermediate hunt-seat lessons (no jumping) for children and adults, and helmets are provided.

SWIMMING

For sport swimming rather than poolside lounging, there's a well-maintained Olympic-size swimming pool at **Siri Fort Sports Complex** (August Kranti Marg, tel. 11/2649-7482, www.dda.org.in, 6 A.M.-9 P.M. daily, Rs. 500). There's a similar pool at **Saket Sports Complex** (opposite Welcome Marriott Hotel, Saket, tel. 11/2956-1742, www.dda.org.in, 6:30 A.M.-11:30 P.M. Tues.-Sun., 4-8:30 P.M. Mon., Rs. 500). Both facilities are government-owned and are run by the Delhi Development Authority. The pool at the **Pacific Sports Complex** (Central School, near Moolchand Flyover, tel. 11/2645-2748, www.pacificsportscomplex.in, 6 A.M.-10 P.M. daily, Rs. 300 per hour) is popular, although it gets quite crowded in summer. Swimming sessions here start every hour on the hour, and at the end of your time slot, an attendant blows a whistle and forces everyone out. Note that a swim cap is required for people with long hair, and bikinis are frowned upon.

For something a bit more relaxed and considerably less sporty, check out the swimming pool at the **Park Hotel** (15 Parliament Rd., tel. 11/2374-3000, www.theparkhotels.com, 7 A.M.-7 P.M. daily, Rs. 700). This small pool is great for sunbathing and short swims, although it's a bit too shallow for diving. There's also a lovely poolside bar and restaurant.

YOGA

Delhi has plenty of places to practice yoga, and most of the five-star hotels and larger gyms offer guided sessions. For something a bit more traditional, drop in to one of the open classes at the **Sivananda Yoga Vedanta Centre** (A-41 Kailash Colony, Metro: Kailash Colony, tel. 11/3206-9070, www.sivananda.org/delhi, 6:30 A.M.-8 P.M. daily, Rs. 300 per class, packages available). The Delhi branch of the worldwide Sivananda Yoga organization offers 90-minute drop-in hatha yoga classes that concentrate on focusing the mind and opening the spine through breath, self-awareness, and an alternating mix of postures and relaxation. As it is a traditional center, dress modestly; tank tops are fine, but no sports bras or Speedos. If you are a complete beginner, you have to take an introductory course first to learn how to do the asanas (postures) correctly.

Delhi is also home to a number of centers of **Artistic Yoga** (F-7 Lower Ground Fl., Hauz Khas Enclave, opposite Laxman Public School, tel. 11/4176-7154, www.artisticyoga.com, 7 A.M.-8 P.M. daily, first class free), a unique take on yoga that moves away from the traditional yoga practiced in India as well as the forms of yoga common in the West. Instead, they focus on dynamic postures that help people get into shape. Check the website for a full list of centers and class times.

SPECTATOR SPORTS

Cricket fans can catch a match at **Feroz Shah Kotla** (Bhadur Shah Zafar Marg, near Delhi Gate, tel. 11/2331-4535, prices vary, call ahead for details). Built in 1883, it is the home stadium of Delhi's team, the Delhi Daredevils.

The enormous **Jawaharlal Nehru Stadium** (Bhisma Pitamah Rd., Lodhi Rd., Metro: Jawaharlal Nehru Stadium, tel. 11/2436-9400, prices vary, call ahead for details) also hosts international one-day test matches and a wide range of other sports. The 2010 Commonwealth Games and the 2012 Asian Games were held here.

Polo is quite popular in India; contact the **Army Polo and Riding Club** (B Squaron 61 Cavalry, Cariappa Marg, Cantonment, tel. 11/2569-9444, www.armypoloclub.com, prices vary) if you'd like to attend a match.

SPAS

One of the newest spas in Delhi, the ultra-modern **Aman Spa** (Aman Hotel, Lodhi Rd., tel. 11/4363-3333, 9 A.M.-10 P.M. daily) is also one of the city's best, featuring sleek treatment rooms and incredibly knowledgeable staff who have to go through intensive training before working here, even if they are experienced practitioners. A session at the spa's hammam (Turkish bath, Rs. 3,500-8,000) is a perfect way to end your India visit—after relaxing in a steamy chamber, you'll be brought into a treatment room, where a therapist will expertly scrub away an entire layer of dead skin from your body, making you feel soft, rejuvenated, and incredibly clean.

The beautiful **Amatrra Spa** (50-B Diplomatic Enclave, Chanakyapuri, tel. 11/2412-2921, www.amatrraspa.com, 7 A.M.-10 P.M. daily) offers a huge range of treatments that follow the principles of ayurveda (traditional Indian medicine). The signature treatment is the ayurvedic *abhiyanga* massage (Rs. 5,500), a relaxing massage using long sweeping motions to improve circulation and overall wellness. Use of a common jetted tub, steam, and sauna area is included in the price of all treatments.

The quiet **Oasis Spa** (Grand Hotel, Nelson Mandela Marg, Vasant Vihar, tel. 11/2677-1234, 7 A.M.-10 P.M. daily, pool 7 A.M.-9 P.M. daily) is an excellent place to escape the noise and grime of New Delhi. The spa features all-natural products and offers everything from Thai massage to hot-stone therapy. The proactive manager ensures that the therapists are continually trained in new techniques and treatments. The Moroccan Spice Body Scrub (Rs. 4,500) is highly recommended—it is deeply exfoliating and leaves a Christmassy aroma on your skin. The immense pool is surrounded by lush gardens and is set far back from the main road, virtually eliminating traffic noise. Oasis is particularly popular with expats, who flock here en masse on Sunday for brunch and a swim.

Accommodations

Delhi has a wide range of accommodations options, from luxurious five-star hotels to simple guesthouses. There are a few decent places in North and Old Delhi, although most people prefer to stay in Central or South Delhi, which are more convenient for visiting the major sights. In terms of accommodations, Delhi is one of the more expensive Indian cities, although you can get some incredibly good deals in the Central Delhi backpacker enclave of Paharganj. An increasing number of bed-and-breakfasts and homestays have opened in Central and South Delhi. Most are located in residential areas and provide a more intimate way to experience the city and live like a (wealthy) local.

OLD DELHI
Rs. 1,000-3,000

Most of the accommodations options in Old Delhi are pretty grim, with the exception of **Hotel Tara Palace** (419 Esplanade Rd., Old Cycle Market, opposite Red Fort, Chandni Chowk, Metro: Chawri Bazaar or Chandni Chowk, tel. 11/2327-6465, www. tarapalacedelhi.com, Rs. 2,200-2,400 d). The entrance to the hotel is at the end of a ramshackle alley, and the furniture in the air-conditioned guest rooms looks like it belongs in a college dorm; these minor drawbacks aside, it's a great location and pretty good value for money, especially if you take into account that the kind folks at Tara Palace provide free airport transfers 24-hours daily.

NORTH DELHI
Rs. 3,000-10,000

The three-star **Broadway Hotel** (4/15A Asaf Ali Rd., Daryaganj, tel. 11/4336-3600, www. hotelbroadwaydelhi.com, Rs. 3,000-4,000 d) has reasonably-priced guest rooms in a great location, not far from the 17th-century sights in Old Delhi and just a couple of minutes from New Delhi Railway Station. The classic wood-floor guest rooms are kept in great shape and get plenty of sunlight. It's also home to one of Delhi's most famous restaurants, Chor Bizarre.

Dating to 1903, the historic **Maidens Hotel** (7 Sham Nath Marg, Civil Lines, Metro: Civil Lines, tel. 11/2397-5464, www.maidenshotel. com, 8,500-9,500 d) exudes Old World charm and is much more reasonably priced than other hotels of its quality. The guest rooms are simple but elegant, and those on the third and fourth floors were renovated in the mid-2000s. The grounds are spacious, and the Civil Lines Metro station is only a couple of minutes away on foot.

At the back of an early-20th-century tenement, **Nina Kochhar's Homestay** (2 Sham Nath Marg, Civil Lines, Metro: Civil Lines, tel. 9811/022-326, www.delhibedbreakfast. com, Rs. 3,500 d, breakfast included) is a one-room homestay in a colorful apartment that looks a bit like a cross between an antiques store and an art gallery; the owner's son is a talented painter, and his works are displayed on the walls. Run by a former employee of the sleek Oberoi Group of Hotels, the homestay offers guests the opportunity to experience living in an Indian home of the upscale variety.

DELHI

CENTRAL DELHI
Under Rs. 1,000

◖ **Hotel Relax** (4970-71 Ram Dwara Rd., Nehru Bazar, Panchkuian Rd., Paharganj, tel. 11/2356-2811, vidur109@hotmail.com, Rs. 800-1,200 d) is one of the best deals in Paharganj. This small family-run guesthouse sits over a shop selling beautiful ethnic furniture and statuettes, and much of the merchandise is featured inside the guesthouse's common areas. All the guest rooms are clean, although some are windowless—make sure to specify if you want sunlight included in your stay. There's also a small private balcony on top where guests can take meals.

From the outside, and even from the lobby, the budget-friendly **Hotel Shelton** (5043, Main Bazaar, Paharganj, Metro: New Delhi or Ramakrishna Ashram Marg, tel. 11/2358-0673, sheltonh@rediffmail.com, Rs. 600-1,200 d) looks a bit grubby, but the guest rooms are surprisingly well-maintained, with comfy beds ornamented with pretty cushions. All guest rooms have TVs (some even have plasma flat-screens), and some of the pricier guest rooms have rain showerheads, a blessing in a place where many showers offer nothing more than a trickle. Note that a few of the guest rooms are windowless, but these are also much quieter. Specify at the time of reservation whether you want a window.

One of Paharganj's most popular options, the humorously named **Cottage Yes Please** (1843-44 Laxmi Narayan St., Raj Guru Rd., Chuna Mandi, Paharganj, Metro: New Delhi or Ramakrishna Ashram Marg, tel. 11/2356-2100, www.cottageyesplease.com, Rs. 900-2,500 d) guesthouse offers spotless guest rooms at reasonable prices. Marble floors dominate the interiors, and guest rooms feature 1970s-style wooden accents and chintzy wall plaques featuring Egyptian deities. The lobby is prettily adorned with colored glass lanterns, and there's a tiny elevator. The larger guest rooms

feature two double beds—perfect for groups and families.

Rs. 1,000-3,000

If price is your priority and you don't want to stay in Paharganj, **Hotel Alka Annexe** (M-20 Connaught Circus, Connaught Place, Metro: Rajiv Chowk, tel. 11/2341-4028, www.hotel-alka.com, Rs. 2,000-2,500 d) might be your best bet. Although it calls itself a hotel, it's really just a guesthouse, and the guest rooms are clean but really nothing special. If you can, try to get a top-floor room; these open onto a courtyard and are sunnier. Bargain hard and you can probably get a discount, or at least a free breakfast.

If Ikea did hotels, they would look something like the **Ginger Hotel Delhi** (IRCTC Rail Yatri Niwas, Bhav Bhutti Marg, New Delhi Railway Station, Metro: New Delhi, tel. 11/6663-3333, www.gingerhotels.com, Rs. 1,300-1,600 d), a comfortable and practical hotel that features self-check-in kiosks and a small gym. The McRooms here are clean, modern, and super-cheap, and it doesn't get more convenient for those with early morning trains from New Delhi Train Station, unless you don't mind squatting on the platforms.

Conveniently located right on the main bazaar, the 60-room **Hotel Hari Piorko** (4755 Main Bazaar, Paharganj, Metro: New Delhi or Ramakrishna Ashram Marg, tel. 11/2358-7999, www.hotelharipiorkodelhi.com, Rs. 1,200-1,500 d) is large enough to be called a hotel but has the homely feel of a guesthouse. The guest rooms here are clean, simple, and have a light aroma of rose water. Some of the larger guest rooms have aquariums built into their walls. The prices are a bit steeper than in some other Paharganj properties, but the service is decent and the place is well looked-after.

It's not exactly fun to stay at the **New Delhi YMCA Tourist Hostel** (Jai Singh Rd., Metro: Patel Chowk or Shivaji Stadium, tel. 11/4364-4047, www.newdelhiymca.org, Rs. 2,900-3,700 d), but it's certainly not bad either, and you'd be hard-pressed to find a central Delhi hotel with both a pool and fitness facilities at a better rate. Rates include breakfast and dinner. All guest rooms have air-conditioning, and triple-bed guest rooms are also available.

YWCA Blue Triangle Family Hostel (Ashoka Rd., Metro: Patel Chowk, tel. 11/2336-0133, www.btfhonline.com, Rs. 2,250-2,850 d) is one of the best deals in the otherwise exorbitantly priced Central Delhi hotel market. It's a bit institutional (this is the Y, after all), but the guest rooms are spacious, and the baths are modern. There is also an air-conditioned dormitory for groups of six or more. Wi-Fi is available at a modest cost (Rs. 50 per day), and breakfast is included in the room rate. Note that in order to stay here, you must purchase a one-month YWCA membership (Rs. 50) when you check in.

Rs. 3,000-10,000

There are only two guest rooms in the intimate **Amaaya BnB** (D-36 Nizamuddin East, tel. 9819/686-020, www.amaayadelhi.com, Rs. 4,300 d), which is really more of a homestay than a full-on B&B (although a hearty breakfast is included). Amaaya is in the elegant home, filled with art and books, of Ruma Devichand, a gracious and absolutely lovely textile designer. Both guest rooms are air-conditioned and have balconies.

A short walk from Humayun's Tomb, **Eleven Nizamuddin East** (11 Nizamuddin East, tel. 11/2435-1225, www.elevendelhi.com, Rs. 5,000 d) is essentially a converted bungalow, directly managed by a warm and hospitable owner. The guest rooms are tastefully decorated, well maintained, and have pretty modern baths. Allergy sufferers and parents of little ones may want to note that they have a big dog who's perfectly agreeable but doesn't like being touched.

If location and value are your primary concerns when choosing a hotel, you may want to consider **Hotel Alka** (P-16 Connaught Circus, Connaught Place, Metro: Rajiv Chowk, tel. 11/2334-4000, www.hotelalka.com, Rs. 5,500-6,000 d). Located on the outer ring of Connaught Place, this affordable hotel isn't much to look at (unless you are a huge fan of leopard murals, circa 1977) and is a bit overpriced, but its air-conditioned guest rooms are well-maintained by incredibly sweet housekeeping staff. Note that some guest rooms lack windows.

The lovely **◖ Hotel Bright** (M-85, opposite Super Bazar, Outer Circle, Connaught Place, Metro: Rajiv Chowk, tel. 11/4330-2222, www.hotelbrightdelhi.in, Rs. 5,500 d) is one of the nicest hotels of its price range in all of Delhi. From the outside, this 10-room property doesn't look like anything special, but the interiors are surprisingly modern and well kept. Guest rooms have wooden floors and beautiful linens and feature little extras not normally found in Indian hotels of this category, such as minibars, electronic keys, and ayurvedic toiletries.

There are only three guest rooms (all with two twin beds) in the recently opened **Jor Bagh BnB** (197 Jor Bagh, Metro: Jor Bagh, tel. 9811/079-029, http://jorbaghbnb.com, Rs. 5,400 d), an intimate guesthouse on the main road of Delhi's posh Jor Bagh neighborhood, just a couple of minutes' walk from the local Metro station. This family-run B&B opened in 2010, so all the fixtures and furnishings in the guest rooms are pretty new. Long-term visitors will appreciate the discount offered for stays of a week or longer: seven nights for the price of six. There's also a washing machine, which means you won't have to worry about your clothes being beaten beyond recognition by a local washer.

It's a real treat staying in the converted family home of Shukla Nath, owner of **◖ Luteyens Bungalow** (39 Prithviraj Rd.,

DELHI

tel. 11/2461-1341, www.lutyensbungalow.co.in, Rs. 6,500-7,000 d). This historic bungalow was built in 1935 and sits on spacious lawns that feature an old neem tree that's home to a flock of green parrots. The bungalow opened to the public in 1967 with a single guest room; now there are 16, and the ones in the main house are the most old-fashioned. Breakfast, tea, Wi-Fi, and use of the pool are included in the rates.

One of the best budget options in town, the conveniently located **Prem Sagar Guest House** (1st Fl., P Block, near Hotel Saravana Bhavan, Connaught Circle, Connaught Place, Metro: Rajiv Chowk, tel. 11/2334-5263, www.premsagarguesthouse.com, Rs. 3,500-4,500 d) offers clean air-conditioned guest rooms with granite floors in a semi-outdoor hotel filled with potted plants. Breakfast is included and served on a charming covered rooftop terrace.

Rs. 10,000 and Up

The newest top-end hotel to come up in the capital, the ◖ **Aman New Delhi** (Lodhi Rd., tel. 11/4363-3333, www.amanresorts.com, Rs. 38,500-42,500 d), has already made a name for itself as the most exclusive place to stay in town. Like other Aman properties, the resort does its best to remain low-key, making it a favorite with celebrities and pretty much anyone wanting a discreet place to get away. The interiors are minimalist and a bit dark, but this isn't necessarily a bad thing in a city where the sun blazes through most of the year. All guest rooms have heated plunge pools on their balconies, and many have exceptional views of Central Delhi. The suite on the top floor, Room 802, has a direct view of Humayun's Tomb. The Aman Spa is one of the best in town.

Arguably the chicest place in town, ◖ **The Imperial** (Janpath, tel. 11/2334-1234, www. theimperialindia.com, Rs. 17,500-30,000 d) was built in 1936 and exudes vintage charm. This classic property manages to radiate opulence without ostentation. The enormous pool is one of the largest—and most beautiful—in Delhi. Guest rooms feature spacious rosewood wardrobes, comfortable beds, and marble floors, and if you're the type to judge hotel rooms by their complimentary toiletries, you'll be pleased to know that the Imperial's choice is from French perfume house Fragonard.

If you're interested in learning more about contemporary Indian art and don't have time to venture out to the city's excellent galleries, you may want to stay at the **ITC Maurya** (Diplomatic Enclave, Sardar Patel Marg, Chanakyapuri, tel. 11/2611-2233, www.itchotels.in, 13,500-16,500 d). The common areas of this massive five-star hotel feature art from some of India's best-known artists, including a large mural in the lobby by Bengali artist Sanjay Bhattacharya and a series of stained-glass pieces from India's best-known artist of our time, the late M. F. Hussain. It's also home to the world-renowned Bukhara restaurant. The guest rooms are contemporary, and it's the first hotel in India to offer "pure rooms," special guest rooms designed for allergy sufferers that feature air filters and special allergen-focused cleaning methods.

Nobody does elegance quite like the Oberoi Group, and the **Oberoi Delhi** (Dr. Zakir Hussain Marg, tel. 11/2436-3030, www. oberoihotels.com, Rs. 19,500-28,500 d) is certainly no exception. This luxurious hotel is right in the center of town, and it's easy to reach most Central and South Delhi attractions in just a few minutes (depending on traffic, of course—this is Delhi, after all). It's a bit more suited for business travelers than some of Oberoi's properties, but it still has all the charm and sophistication one would expect from one of India's top hotel groups.

In the heart of Connaught Place, the modern **Park Hotel** (15 Parliament Rd., Connaught Place, Metro: Rajiv Chowk, tel. 11/2374-3000, www.theparkhotels.com, Rs. 11,750-13,250 d) lacks some of the charm of Delhi's more classically appointed five-stars, but nevertheless it is a lovely place to retreat after a long day in Delhi. It's also slightly cheaper than the average Delhi five-star. Note that the pool is quite small, and nonguests can use it for a fee.

Popular with CEOs and visiting dignitaries, the **Taj Mahal Hotel** (1 Mansingh Rd., tel. 11/2302-6162, www.tajhotels.com, Rs. 22,000-55,000 d) is one of Delhi's most popular five-stars; locals refer to it almost exclusively as the Taj Mansingh. This 294-room property in the heart of Lutyens' Delhi features ultra-clean guest rooms. Some of the guest rooms on the higher floors have incredible views of Central Delhi, including the Rashtrapathi Bhawan (Presidential Palace). Guests staying in the Club Rooms get access to an exclusive lounge where complimentary high tea and evening cocktails are provided.

Right next to Delhi's upscale Khan Market, **Vivanta by Taj Ambassador** (Sujjan Singh Park, Subramania Bharti Marg, Metro: Khan Market, tel. 11/6626-1000, www.vivantabytaj.com, Rs. 17,000 d) is a quiet choice for those looking for five-star quality without any unnecessary fanfare. Guest rooms incorporate a lovely blend of Indian textiles and modern furnishings into their design. There's also a 24-hour fitness center and an excellent spa. Unfortunately, there's no pool on-site, but guests can go for a swim at the Taj group's Taj Mahal Hotel nearby.

SOUTH DELHI
Rs. 1,000-3,000

The tiny **Urban Ashram** (D-12 Hauz Khas, tel. 11/4615-1818, www.myurbanashram.com, Rs. 2,960-3,250 d, breakfast included) has only three guest rooms, and while it's nothing special, it is excellent value for money. The guest rooms are kept clean, and there's a common dining area and small library for guests. Note that there is no signage leading to this place—the

entrance is down a narrow path on the right side of the hair salon on the ground floor.

One of the best deals in South Delhi, **White House Bed and Breakfast** (A-36 Kailash Colony, Metro: Kailash Colony, tel. 11/4652-3636, whitehousebedandbreakfast@gmail.com, Rs. 2,500-3,500 d) offers six clean air-conditioned guest rooms with LCD TVs and free Wi-Fi. Breakfast is included, and there's a small kitchen that guests can use on request. The B&B is right at the edge of Kailash Colony Market, which has plenty of small supermarkets and diners; it's just a few minutes from the Metro station. Note that the cheaper guest rooms here don't have proper windows.

Rs. 3,000-10,000

Occupying a nondescript house in a quiet South Delhi neighborhood, the cozy **Amarya Haveli** (P-5 Hauz Khas Enclave, tel. 11/4175-9268, www.amaryagroup.com, Rs. 6,900 d, breakfast included) has all the amenities and grace of a major hotel but with a much more intimate ambience. Run by two Frenchmen who are both married to Indians and have lived in India for a long time, this boutique hotel has beautiful, colorful guest rooms (all with air-conditioning, of course) and a well-stocked library full of travel guides.

Amarya Villa (A-2/20 Safdarjung Enclave, tel. 11/4103-6184, www.amaryagroup.com, Rs. 4,900-8,900 d, breakfast included) is the newer of the two French-owned Amarya properties in South Delhi. The guest rooms are beautifully decorated by the wife of one of the partners, who happens to be a talented textile designer, but it's the service that really makes this place so special. Every morning the staff list local cultural events on a chalkboard and are eager to help guests determine their day's itinerary. They also loan guests local cell phones during their stay, free of charge. Unlike most hotels, you can have breakfast whenever you wake up—even if it's a jet-lagged 4 P.M.

An excellent South Delhi business choice, the **Ashtan Sarovar Portico** (C-2 Green Park Extension, Metro: Green Park, tel. 11/4683-3333, www.sarovarhotels.com, Rs. 6,000 d) opened in 2011 and has contemporary decor, professional staff, and plenty of parking. The guest rooms are a bit small, and the glass wall that divides the sleeping area from the bath may not be to everyone's liking (there is a privacy screen), but you'll be hard-pressed to find such modern accommodations in South Delhi at such a low price.

The guest rooms at the **Cabana Hotel** (R-23 Greater Kailash I, Metro: Kailash Colony, tel. 11/4074-7474, www.hotelcabana.in, Rs. 5,200 d) are on the small side, but the building is sleek and the beds are big at this modestly priced business hotel. It is also close to good shopping at Greater Kailash's M- and N-Block market and not too far from the Metro. Unfortunately, the guest rooms aren't very well ventilated, and the smoking rooms have an unfortunate lingering stench; make sure to specify if you want a nonsmoking floor.

With its slightly crammed common area, the foreigner-owned **Colaba House** (B2-139 Safdarjung Enclave, tel. 11/4067-1773, www. colabahouse.com, Rs. 5,300-6,500 d) feels a bit like a youth hostel, but it is intimate, comfy, and well looked after. The guest rooms are a bit on the small side, and what they call suites are actually just large guest rooms, but it is in a quiet location and there's a rooftop terrace. Breakfast, tea, and coffee as well as Wi-Fi are included in the rates.

In the heart of South Delhi's upscale Defence Colony neighborhood, **Colonel's Retreat** (D-418 Defence Colony, Metro: Lajpat Nagar, tel. 9999/720-024, www.colonelsretreat.com, Rs. 4,100-4,800 d, breakfast included) offers spacious, sunny guest rooms decked out with colorful contemporary murals and beautiful furnishings. The common areas have computers, large tables, and plenty of books (and not just the discarded mass-market paperbacks that often constitute guesthouse "libraries"). Wi-Fi is complimentary.

Although **Hotel Gaiety Palace** (A-14 Kailash Colony, Metro: Kailash Colony, tel. 11/2923-2064, www.gaietypalace.com, Rs. 3,600-4,100 d) is located on a busy thoroughfare, the large air-conditioned guest rooms are clean, well-insulated, and quiet; all come with fake wood floors (with rugs), refrigerators, and coffeemakers. Some of the higher-end guest rooms are more like suites and have spacious sitting areas. Secure parking is also available.

Home@f37 (F-37, east of Kailash, Metro: Kailash Colony, tel. 11/4669-0200, www. f37.in, Rs. 3,650 d) has sunny, spacious guest rooms in a converted house just across from the Kailash Colony Metro Station. All 21 guest rooms are air-conditioned, and the furnishings are newish; some guest rooms also have desks. Breakfast, bottled water, Wi-Fi, and a daily newspaper are included in the rates.

Luxurious yet low-key, **The Manor Hotel** (77 Friends Colony West, tel. 11/4323-5151, www. themanordelhi.com, Rs. 9,000 d) is located at the very end of a long, quiet residential road flanked with beautiful mansions. There are only 15 guest rooms in this boutique garden hotel, making it easy for the friendly and attentive staff to give personal attention to guests. The guest rooms are sunny and feature sophisticated furnishings highlighted with beautiful Indian linens. The on-site restaurant, Indian Accent, serves delicious contemporary takes on classic Indian dishes.

One of the cleaner options in the string of garish low-cost hotels that flank the national highway across from the airport, the **Hotel Shanti Palace** (NH-8 Mahipalpur, near the airport, tel. 11/3061-7316, www.shantipalace. com, Rs. 5,450-6,600 d) is a good place to stay if you need to be at the airport early the next day and don't want to spend much on a hotel. The centrally air-conditioned guest rooms are kept in fairly good shape, and there's a bar and restaurant on-site. There's also a small business center, and the hotel has Wi-Fi.

Rs. 10,000 and Up

If you need a place to stay near the airport and want somewhere on the comfortable side, **Radisson Blu** (NH-8 Mahipalpur, near the airport, tel. 11/2677-9191, www.radissonblu.com, Rs. 12,500-18,000 d) is your best choice. This business hotel has modern guest rooms with rain showerheads, flat-screen TVs, and a safe you can actually fir your laptop in. Wi-Fi and airport transfers are included in the rates. The spa has a huge selection of services—perfect for relaxing between flights—and best of all, the Radisson Blu is home to the flagship branch of the delicious Great Kebab Factory.

Ever dreamed of what it would be like to live in a shopping mall? If so, you'll love the **Svelte Hotel Saket** (A-3 District Centre, Select Citywalk, Saket, tel. 11/4051-2000, www.svelte.in, Rs. 9,500-16,500 d). If an overnight stay in a mall sounds more like a nightmare, you'll be happy to know that this hotel has a private entrance, so you won't have to pass by hordes of shoppers on your way in. All of the guest rooms are actually suites designed to cater to long-term travelers; they have kitchenettes, and the staff can even fetch groceries for you. Suites range 42-102 square meters in size.

Food

Delhi has one of the best culinary scenes in the country, and you can get most types of cuisine, often at excellent prices by Western standards. Family restaurants and roadside cafés tend to be the cheapest places to eat, although they most often serve only Indian or occasionally Indo-Chinese fare. Slightly more upscale restaurants are more likely to focus on "continental" food. This often translates simply to pasta and pizza, but the term is sometimes used to mean anything that's not Indian or Chinese.

Coffee shops are increasingly popular in Delhi, and Indian chains such as Barista and Café Coffee Day, as well as foreign franchises such as Costa and Coffee Bean & Tea Leaf, serve decent espresso-based drinks. In budget restaurants, with the exception of South Indian joints, *coffee* means Nescafé, although some backpacker dives serve real coffee (advertised as "filter coffee").

OLD DELHI
Indian

One of Delhi's most famous restaurants,

Chor Bizarre (Hotel Broadway, 4/15-A Asaf Ali Gate, near Delhi Gate, Daryaganj, tel. 11/4366-3600, www.chorbizarre.com, 7:30-10 A.M., noon-3:30 P.M., and 7-11 P.M. daily, Rs. 500) serves delicious fresh food from across the country. The decor here is vintage and the walls are decked with old photos and memorabilia; there is a huge classic car in the middle of the restaurant. Lunch and dinner have all-you-can-eat buffets, but for something really special, opt for the Kashmiri Wazwan platter (vegetarian options available), a sampler featuring the distinctive cuisine of the mountainous Kashmir region. According to a Kashmiri friend, the Wazwan is missing a couple of essential components to make it authentic, but it's still an excellent choice in this pan-Indian eatery.

If you're in Old Delhi and want a quick snack, head to the local branch of the vegetarian snack-food chain **Haldiram's** (1454/2 Chandni Chowk, Metro: Chandni Chowk, tel. 11/2883-3007, www.haldiram.com, 9 A.M.-11 P.M. daily, Rs. 80). You'll find a huge selection of Indian snacks and light eats, ranging from a cold *raj*

BHAWAN DINING

A great way to sample regional cuisine from around the country is to visit a few of Delhi's many state *bhawans*, large complexes that house the offices (and oftentimes the residences) of state representatives in the capital. These institutions are dotted around central Delhi and often have guesthouses for visiting state dignitaries and inexpensive canteens serving the specialty food of their regions.

The mother of all *bhawans*, at least in terms of popularity, is **Andhra Bhawan** (1 Ashoka Rd., tel. 11/2338-2031, 7:30-10 A.M., noon-2:45 P.M., and 7:30-10 P.M. daily), which serves cuisine from the southern state of Andhra Pradesh. Here you can order a vegetarian *thali*, or platter meal, with unlimited free refills, for under Rs. 100. Add another Rs. 50 and you'll get a meat-based side dish too.

If you're interested in Rajasthani food and don't plan to go all the way to Jaipur, the Rajasthani government's **Café Bikaneer** (Pandara Rd., India Gate, tel. 11/2338-7731, noon-11 P.M. daily) serves up fiery meals consisting of both vegetarian and meaty Rajasthani dishes.

Carnivorous types will love the meat dishes at **Nagaland House** (29 Aurangzeb Rd., tel. 11/2379-4166, 11:30 A.M.-2 P.M. and 7:30-9:30 P.M. daily). The food from this northeastern state is often boiled rather than fried and is eaten with rice rather than bread.

Near the U.S. Embassy, the **New Sikkim House** (14 Panscheel Marg, tel. 11/2611-5171, call for hours) serves delicious food that is closer to Chinese than Indian, including huge plates of steaming hot *momos* (dumplings similar to dim sum) and excellent noodle dishes. It was temporarily closed at the time of writing, so call ahead to see if it has reopened.

kachori (huge crisp puffs filled with potatoes and bean sprouts, topped with sweetened yogurt, mint, and tamarind chutneys) to piping hot *chole bathura* (seasoned chickpeas served with deep-fried puff bread). There is also a huge selection of Indian sweets—try the *kaju barfi*, a super-sweet blend of cashews and sugar covered with a light dusting of edible silver foil.

Perhaps the most famous of Old Delhi's restaurants, **Karim's** (Gali Kababian, Jama Masjid, Chandni Chowk, Metro: Chandni Chowk, tel. 11/2326-9880, www.karimhoteldelhi.com, 9 A.M.-1 A.M. daily, Rs. 200) was founded in 1913 and has stayed in the same family ever since. Karim's specializes in Mughalai food (North Indian cuisine inspired by the Mughal invaders), and most of the dishes are either made from chicken or "mutton" (goat, not sheep). There's nothing much for vegetarians. The food is rich and spicy, and if you're not in the mood for something too heavy, you can always have one of the signature rolls: wraps made with chapatis and filled with meat and vegetables.

CENTRAL DELHI
Cafés and Patisseries

Chocoholics can get their fix at **Choko La** (38 Middle Lane, Khan Market, Metro: Khan Market, tel. 11/4175-7570, www.chokola.in, 8 A.M.-11 P.M. daily, Rs. 200). This incredible chocolatier makes every type of truffle you can imagine, plus a large array of hot chocolates, milk shakes, mochas, pastries, and desserts, most of which are made from chocolate, although there are a few fruity options too. There are also a few nonsweet meal items, but with this much chocolate around, do you really want to spoil your appetite with something mildly nutritious?

The absolutely charming **Latitude 28** (9 Khan Market, Metro: Khan Market, tel. 11/2462-1013, www.diva-italian.com, 11:30 A.M.-11 P.M.) is the best place for a coffee break in Khan Market. This beautifully appointed café features classic wallpaper, beautiful candelabras, fluffy cushions, and a luminous sunroom. You'll find high-quality coffees and teas; light, primarily continental dishes; and an excellent selection of desserts (the strawberry cheesecake is a must). To reach the third-floor café, you'll have to pass through luxury interior design store Good Earth, a treat in itself.

Arguably Delhi's best bakery, and certainly one of the oldest, **Wenger's** (A-16 Connaught Place, Metro: Rajiv Chowk, tel. 11/2332-4403, www.wengerspastry.com, 10:45 A.M.-7:45 P.M. daily, Rs. 70) does a better job at croissants then even the swankiest five-star joints in town. This Connaught Place institution was founded in the 1920s by an Austrian-Swiss couple and taken over by an Indian family in 1945, who manage it to this day. This historic bakery stocks nearly 200 different products, including 60-plus types of pastries. They also have some of the best chocolates in town, if not in India, and Chiranjeet Singh, the manager who stands at the back of the store near the chocolate counter most days, will happily entice you with a free sample.

Continental

Designed to look like a 1950s-era American diner, the **All-American Diner** (India Habitat Centre, Lodhi Rd., tel. 11/4366-3333, www.habitatworld.com, 7 A.M.-midnight daily, Rs. 350) is one of the top breakfast spots in Delhi and a good place to grab a burger or nachos any time of day. The restaurant features plenty of cozy booths and a long silver-colored bar with black-and-white checkerboard trim (think the side of a New York taxicab or the band of a London police officer's hat). There are also plenty of neon lights, and the finishing touch is the huge vintage-style jukebox. And if you're asking yourself why you'd come all the way to India to eat in an American diner, here's the answer: because the food, especially the heavy breakfasts, are some of the best you'll find in the States or otherwise.

Amici (47 Middle Lane, Khan Market, Metro: Khan Market, tel. 11/4358-7191, 11 A.M.-11 P.M. daily, Rs. 450) offers some of the best—and most affordable—Italian food in town. The interior of this two-story restaurant features big picture windows and a mix of artsy and cheeky black-and-white photographs, and there's a small outdoor seating area at the back of the top floor. Amici is best known for its thin-crust pizzas and huge selection of toppings, and they also do a mean tiramisu. The *spremuta,* a mix of lemon, mint, soda, and lots of crushed demerara sugar, is delicious and incredibly hydrating. The only drawback is that Amici doesn't serve beer or wine, a shortcoming to an otherwise excellent restaurant.

The poolside **Aqua** (15 Parliament Rd., Connaught Place, Metro: Rajiv Chowk, tel. 11/2374-3000, www.theparkhotels.com, 11 A.M.-1 A.M. daily, Rs. 700) is a good place to sip incredibly overpriced cocktails. They also serve a small selection of pizza, pastas, wraps, and lots of little appetizers. The food is really good, but it's the ambience that makes this place such a hit: You can eat inside in the slick restaurant or, if it's not too hot, take over a private mini cabana (complete with a fan and a small TV) and eat by the pool. There are often semiprivate parties on Sunday, usually sponsored by alcohol companies, and if you manage to talk your way in, you can use the pool for free.

Tucked away in the corner of Central Delhi's discreet Sunder Nagar Market, **Baci** (23 Sunder Nagar Market, tel. 11/4150-7446, noon-midnight daily, Rs. 600) serves up delicious traditional Italian cuisine and has an amazingly well-stocked bar. Along with pastas, pizzas, and antipasti, there is also an excellent selection of fresh seafood dishes. The place is romantic and understated but elegant, and it's popular with the younger generation of Delhi's most fabulous. DJs occasionally play on weekends.

The Big Chill Café (68-A Khan Market, Metro: Khan Market, tel. 11/4175-7588, 2-11 P.M. daily, Rs. 450) is a well-known Delhi institution popular with expats, splurging college students, and young families and is decked out from floor to ceiling with copies of vintage Hollywood posters. They serve up a delicious assortment of pizzas, pastas, and fresh salads—favorites include the vodka penne, penne drenched in a thick tomato cream sauce that supposedly includes an undetectable splash of vodka. However, the real draw here is the desserts-people come from all over town for a fix of Big Chill's famous chocolate squidgy cake or a thick Oreo milk shake.

Most people, including Australians themselves, have a hard time defining the culinary repertoire of the land down under, but the folks at **Café Oz & Bar** (52 Khan Market Khan Market, Metro: Khan Market, tel. 11/4359-7162, http://cafeozindia.com, 11 A.M.-12:30 A.M. daily, Rs. 350) seem to have an idea. Café Oz's offerings include delicious burgers, sandwiches, and a lot of pizza and risotto (not originally Australian, but whatever). There's also a good selection of beer, including an Indian version of Foster's, the quintessentially Australian beer that nobody in Australia claims to drink. The decor exudes casualness—think dark wood furnishings with exposed red-brick walls and large, colorful pop art posters of things people normally associate with Australia, such as Vegemite.

The food at **Lodi-The Garden Restaurant** (opposite Mausam Bhawan, near Gate 1, Lodhi Rd., Jor Bagh, tel. 11/2465-5054, www.sewara. com, noon-midnight daily, Rs. 500) is pretty good—try the gazpacho in the summer—but the charming atmosphere of this indoor-outdoor restaurant is what really makes it stand out. It's located on a wide plot right at the edge of the Lodi Gardens (unfortunately there's no gate connecting the two), and the spacious outdoor area is filled with large trees and lush plants, making it feel a bit like a secret garden. The interior part of the restaurant is in a two-story house-like structure, and there are great views of the garden from the upstairs veranda.

Fancy breakfast for dinner? Make a beeline to ◖ **Mrs. Kaur's Crepes and More** (66 Middle Lane, Khan Market, Metro: Khan Market, tel. 11/4352-8300, www.mrskaurs. com, 7:30 A.M.-11 P.M. daily, Rs. 275). This restaurant was opened a few years ago by Mrs. Kaur's, Central Delhi's beloved cookie maker, and serves a ton of good breakfast foods, including baked beans and Belgian waffles topped with strawberries and whipped cream. As the name implies, Mrs. Kaur's is also big on crepes—the Mediterranean savory crepe is a personal favorite.

Indian

Touted as one of Bill Clinton's favorite restaurants, ◖ **Bukhara** (ITC Maurya, Diplomatic Enclave, Sardar Patel Marg, Chanakyapuri, tel. 11/2611-2233, 12:30-2:30 P.M. and 7-11:45 P.M. daily, Rs. 1,200) specializes in North-West Frontier cuisine, from the rugged border region between Pakistan and Afghanistan: hearty, meat-dominant dishes marinated and then cooked in a tandoor (Indian clay oven). They also have plenty of vegetarian choices, and their buttery black dal (lentils) is cooked to the perfect consistency. The restaurant is designed with earthy tones and faux-rustic low tables, and guests are expected to eat in the "traditional" manner, meaning with their hands (but they will bring you silverware if you ask).

If you want the experience of eating in one of North India's beloved *dhabas* (roadside eateries) but are afraid your tummy won't stand up to it, you can always try **Dhaba at the Claridges** (Claridges Hotel, 12 Aurangzeb Rd., tel. 11/3955-5000, 12:30-2:30 P.M. and 7:30-11:30 P.M. daily, Rs. 1,200). This upscale restaurant does its best to reproduce the feel of a *dhaba,* with bench seating, metal dinnerware, and huge vats of food. The food is of the heavy North Indian variety, but they don't make it too spicy unless you ask for it that way.

A Khan Market institution, **Khan Chacha**

(50 Middle lane, Khan Market, Metro: Khan Market, tel. 11/2463-3242, noon-11 P.M. daily, Rs. 110) is the favorite choice of generations of Delhiites who come for the soft meat kebabs and wraps. It was originally nothing more than a hole-in-the-wall street vendor but recently moved into a slightly nicer but still charmingly bare-bones restaurant that has a few tables. The mutton Kakori rolls are especially popular. Make sure to ask them to go easy on the chutneys if you don't like your food too spicy.

The Connaught Place branch of **C Rajdhani** (9-A Atmaram Mansion, Scindia House, Connaught Circus, Connaught Place, Metro: Rajiv Chowk, tel. 11/4350-1200, www.rajdhani.co.in, noon-midnight daily, Rs. 300) is an excellent spot to go if you have a ravenous appetite or want to try the best of Rajasthani and Gujarati cuisine. The focus of this vegetarian restaurant is *thalis*, assorted platters featuring a wide array of breads, curries, vegetables, salads, and sweets. *Thalis* can either be "fixed" or "limited" (meaning that you don't get free refills) or "unlimited" (meaning that the servers will keep trying to force food on you until you feel ready to explode). Rajdhani *thalis* are of the unlimited variety, and the eager waiters will be happy to douse your food in delicious and incredibly fattening ghee (clarified butter).

Delhi has plenty of good South Indian joints, but **C Saravana Bhawan** (46 Janpath, Metro: Rajiv Chowk, tel. 11/2331-6060, www.saravanabhavan.com, 7:30 A.M.-11 P.M. daily, Rs. 90) is among the few that South Indians regularly patronize. This simple cafeteria-style family restaurant serves all the classics, such as *idlis* and *dosas* as well as some dishes that are more unusual in the north, such as *idiyappam,* also called string hoppers (rice noodles served with coconut milk or rich gravy). It's also a good place to try South Indian-style coffee: sweet and milky coffee blended with chicory that tastes a lot like coffee ice cream, only much hotter.

Multicuisine

One of the nicest of Paharganj's many rooftop restaurants, the Nepali-run **Everest Kitchen** (Lord Krishna Deluxe Inn, 1171-75 Main Bazaar, Paharganj, Metro: New Delhi or Ramakrishna Ashram Marg, tel. 11/2356-1456, 8:30 A.M.-11:30 P.M. daily, Rs. 100) tries to recreate the feeling of being in a garden, and there are lots of potted plants. Everest serves up a great selection of backpacker fare, from burgers to the Himalayan staple *dal baat* (dal and rice). Fresh salads washed in filtered water and real espresso are also offered.

A Paharganj classic, **Metropolis Restaurant** (1634 Main Bazaar, Paharganj, Metro: New Delhi or Ramakrishna Ashram Marg, tel. 11/2356-1782, www.metropolistravels.com, 11 A.M.-11 P.M. daily, Rs. 250) opened its doors in 1928 and has been serving an assortment of Indian and continental dishes ever since. It's nothing fancy, even by Paharganj standards, but the Western food is pretty good, and the drinks are plentiful—and served stiff. There's an indoor section that could use a remodel and a much more popular covered rooftop dining area.

Arguably the most popular spot for backpackers to congregate in Paharganj, the alfresco **Sam's Café** (Vivek Hotel, 1534-1550 Main Bazaar, Paharganj, Metro: New Delhi or Ramakrishna Ashram Marg, tel. 11/4647-0555, www.vivekhotel.com, 8 A.M.-10:30 P.M. daily, Rs. 120) is a great place to go for delicious falafels, pastas, Indian food with the spice levels tuned down, and palatable pizzas. The decor is nothing fancy, and the waiters here seem pretty indifferent for the most part, but the food is good and the beer is cheap. You can get some great views of Paharganj, and there's also a "German bakery" on the ground floor of the Vivek Hotel that's associated with the restaurant, but the pastries are on the dry side.

If you've ever fantasized about living in the good old days, you'll adore the molded ceilings and aging genteel waiters at the old-fashioned

United Coffee House (15-E Connaught Place, Metro: Rajiv Chowk, tel. 11/2341-1697, 10 A.M.-11:30 P.M. daily). This coffee shop is actually more of a restaurant that serves a huge selection of continental grills and Indian curries as well as sandwiches, pasta, and a few Indo-Chinese concoctions. The food is OK, but the atmosphere is the main selling point, and it is a good place to grab a coffee or a pot of tea and soak in the elegant ambience.

The funky **Urban Café** (70 Khan Market, 1st Fl., tel. 9999/918-034, www.urbancafe.in, 11 A.M.-1 A.M. daily) features soft sofas, colorful pop art murals, and an outdoor area for smoking hookahs. The ambience is jovial, and the clients tend to be of the well-heeled variety. Indian and continental food, including prawns and some decent pasta dishes, are served, and the wine list is pretty good for the area. If you have a sweet tooth, you'll definitely be into this place—although the dessert menu is fairly small, what they do serve is delicious and, unlike many places in India, not overly sweetened.

SOUTH DELHI
Cafés and Patisseries

A good spot for lunch or coffee, **Café Turtle** (N-16, 3rd Fl., N-Block Market, Greater Kailash I, Metro: Kailash Colony, tel. 11/2924-5641, www.cafeturtle.com, 9:30 A.M.-8:30 P.M. daily) has a decent selection of vegetarian sandwiches, pasta, quiches, and platters as well as delicious cakes and cookies. They also serve a huge selection of fresh juice concoctions and rich *lassis* and milk shakes. This café has a laid-back vibe, and the service is friendly and very attentive. There's also an outdoor seating area.

The low-key **Flipside Café** (7 Hauz Khas Village, Metro: Green Park, tel. 11/2651-6341, www.flipsidecafe.in, 10:30 A.M.-10 P.M. Wed.-Mon., Rs. 150) sits at the top of a narrow set of creaky stairs flanked by walls plastered with posters advertising upcoming concerts. With its red walls and chalkboard menus, this little *crêperie* has the look and feel of a college hangout, and it's a good place to loiter with a laptop and a cup of street-style Indian *chai*. There's also a small balcony (standing room only) for smokers. The specialty is crepes of both the sweet and the savory *galette* variety, but coffees, cakes, pizzas, and a rotating selection of daily specials are also served.

Part bookshop, part café, part photo gallery, and part hangout, the charming **⬛ Kunzum Travel Café** (T-49 Hauz Khas Village, Metro: Green Park, tel. 11/2651-3949, http://kunzum.com, Tues.-Sun. 11 A.M.-7:30 P.M., donation) is an ideal spot to socialize with other travel enthusiasts. There's also a wide variety of travel magazines and guidebooks on both India and other countries, and travel-themed events are held regularly. It's not a good place to get a proper meal, but they do offer coffee, tea, and biscuits. Best of all, there's no fixed price on the snacks, beverages, and Wi-Fi—instead, guests are asked to drop a donation in the donation box, depending on what they can afford.

Mocha (28-A Defence Colony, Metro: Lajpat Nagar, tel. 11/4658-8447, www.mocha.co.in, 10 A.M.-midnight daily, Rs. 250) is a leader in the Indian obsession with smoking *shisha* (flavored tobacco), and this darkly lit hookah bar-cum-coffee shop is a popular hangout for teetotal teenagers and anyone who appreciates a good cup of joe: The coffee beans are imported from all over the world. The food is so-so but the milk shakes, many of which are inspired by chocolate bars, are excellent. Now, if they could just turn the music down a bit.

Continental

One of the newest ventures by Ritu Dalmia, India's best-known chef of Italian cuisine, **Café Diva** (N-8 N-Block Market, Greater Kailash I, Metro: Kailash Colony, tel. 11/4101-1948, www.diva-italian.com, 11 A.M.-11:30 P.M. daily, Rs. 500) serves fine cuisine in a laid-back bistro-style environment. Dalmia is a hands-on restaurateur, and she may very well be at Café Diva, helping out in the kitchen, when you arrive (that's right: a celebrity chef cooking your lunch; how often does that happen?). There's a good mix of continental food, although naturally Italian dishes predominate. Don't miss the pumpkin-stuffed ravioli and the delicious Italian coffees.

If you're looking for a romantic alfresco dining experience, look no farther than **C Magique** (Gate 3, Garden of the Five Senses, Saket, tel. 9717/535-544, www.magique.in, 12:30-3:30 P.M. and 7 P.M.-1 A.M. daily, Rs. 750). This beautiful garden restaurant is great for lunch or dinner, but if you have to choose, go at night when the outdoor area is lit by strings of twinkling lights. The food is just as incredible as the ambience, and they serve a good blend of East Asian and continental dishes, including some excellent seafood. The wine list is extensive and well suited to the cuisine.

As implied by the name, **Moet's Sizzler** (26 Defence Colony Market, Metro: Lajpat Nagar, tel. 11/4655-5777, www.moets.com, noon-midnight daily, Rs. 400) specializes in "sizzlers": assortments of meats or vegetables served sizzling and smoking on a hot plate, similar to fajitas only generally served without bread (although the garlic bread makes a delicious side order). Sizzlers are noisy, smoky, and very popular in India, and if you've never had one, this is the place to try this popular cooking style.

Olive (One Style Mile, Mehrauli, tel. 11/2957-4444, www.olivebarandkitchen.com, noon-midnight daily, Rs. 800) is one of South Delhi's more sophisticated options. The food is primarily Italian, and everything is delicious and of impeccable quality, especially the pizzas. The decor is rustic chic, and there's both indoor and outdoor seating; the rooftop area is good for big groups. The courtyard, with its enormous banyan tree, is especially enchanting at night when illuminated by candlelight. Note

that it's not well signposted, and vehicle entry is through a nondescript gate, so you might have to ask directions once you get to Mehrauli.

Shalom (N-18 N-Block Market, Greater Kailash I, tel. 11/4163-2280, www.shalomexperience.com, noon-1 A.M. daily, Rs. 600) is one of Delhi's most established lounges, and it's a popular nightspot thanks to its well-stocked bar and regular guest appearances by top DJs and musicians. The atmosphere is chic without being overly formal, and the tables are few enough that patrons can expect a lot of personalized attention from servers. The focus is on Middle Eastern food and Mediterranean grills, and the mezze platters are the best in town. They also have an excellent wine list, and the mojitos are to die for.

One of the most popular eateries in South Delhi, the trendy **TLR** (31 Hauz Khas Village, Metro: Green Park, tel. 11/4608-0533, www.tlrcafe.com, 11 A.M.-midnight daily, Rs. 450) was instrumental in transforming Hauz Khas Village from an arts and couture district into one of the best-known dining spots in town. TLR is especially popular among Delhi's growing number of expatriates, who come for the continental menu of pastas, sandwiches, lamb chops, fish-and-chips (a rarity in Delhi), fresh juices, and coffee. There is also a good selection of beer, wine, and spirits. If you're here in the holiday season, drop by for a traditional English Christmas dinner. TLR also hosts DJs, bands, open mike nights, and the occasional pub quiz.

East Asian

If you're tired of heavy North Indian food and want something on the lighter side, you'll appreciate the food at **Ai-The Love Hotel** (MGF Mall, 2nd Fl., District Centre, Saket, tel. 11/4065-4567, noon-midnight daily, Rs. 700). A Japanese restaurant that was originally more of a nightspot, now that its reputation as an electronic music venue has been reined in, diners are starting to realize that Ai has some of the best Japanese food in town, serving up authentic main dishes along with popular sushi and sashimi. There are often brunch specials on weekends, and the food is quite popular with Japanese expats.

Korean food in India? It might sound like a weird idea, but if you've never had Korean cuisine before, it's worth trying at **Gung, The Palace** (D-1 B Green Park, near Ashirwad Complex, Metro: Green Park, tel. 11/4608-2663, noon-3 P.M. and 6-10:15 P.M. daily, Rs. 1,000). Because Gung is in a neighborhood with a lot of vegetarians (there's a large Jain community in Green Park), it even makes meat-free dishes, and not just kimchi. Most of their food, however, is based on imported meat. Gung is very popular with Delhi's constantly growing number of Korean expats and focuses on the traditional, both in cuisine and in decor. The tables are inside screened chambers, and guests are expected to take off their shoes and sit on the floor. There is a table for those who have trouble with low seating, though. Also, as the restaurant is both very small and very popular, reservations are a must.

Among the newest restaurants to open in Hauz Khas Village, **Yeti Tibetan Kitchen** (50A, 2nd Fl., Hauz Khas Village, Metro: Green Park, tel. 11/4067-8649, 12:30-11 P.M. daily, Rs. 250) is done up in a contemporary-rustic fashion, with exposed brick walls and lots of dark wood, adorned with strings of colorful Tibetan prayer flags. Try to get a window seat, from where you can take in spectacular views of Deer Park's crumbling monuments. Yeti specializes in cuisine from Tibet, Nepal, and Bhutan, including Tibetan classics such as *momos* (similar to dim sum) and *tingmo* (steamed Tibetan bread). Mutton, pork, and "buff" (buffalo beef) feature heavily on the menu, but there are also plenty of vegetarian options. Some of the dishes are very spicy.

Riding on the popularity of pan-Asian restaurants, **The Yum Yum Tree** (opposite Nathu Sweets, 1st Fl., New Friends Colony, tel. 11/4260-2020, www.theyumyumtree.in, 12:30-4 P.M. and 7-10:45 P.M. daily, Rs. 500) focuses primarily on dim sum and sushi, and the Chinese food is much less Indianized than in most places in Delhi. The restaurant is divided into a formal dining area and a relaxed lounge that features a sushi train and large panels on the walls covered with hundreds of tiny stickers. On Tuesday nights a special package (Rs. 777) is offered that includes all-you-can-eat sushi, all-you-can-drink cocktails, a main course, and a dessert.

Indian

Even the most voracious appetites will be stretched to their limits at the ◖ **Great Kebab Factory** (Radisson Blu Hotel, NH-8 Mahipalpur, near the airport, tel. 11/2677-9191, www.thegreatkababfactory.com, noon-midnight daily, Rs. 700). You start off with flatbreads and a selection of kebabs, either vegetarian or meaty, that literally melt in your mouth (pardon the cliché, but it's true). Then they bring you more, and more. When you finally protest that you simply can't take another bite, they bring you the main course of the day, served with rice or *biryani*. That is followed with four different types of delicious desserts. You probably won't want to eat again for the next 24 hours, but when you do, you'll realize that most food pales in comparison to the incredible kebabs served at this amazing restaurant.

Specializing in home-style South Indian food, **Gunpowder** (22 Hauz Khas Village, Metro: Green Park, tel. 11/2653-5700, noon-3 P.M. and 7:30-11 P.M. daily, Rs. 200) has remained immensely popular since it opened in 2009. The restaurant is half indoors and half outdoors and overlooks the massive lake in Deer Park. The food is not too spicy, and those who want a bit more bite need only order the restaurant's namesake "gunpowder":

a mix of ground spices that can be mixed in a bit of oil and added to your food to spice it up. The tamarind rice and the hot flaky Malabar *paranthas* are the most delicious ways to add a little starch to the restaurant's excellent curries.

If you've developed a hankering for some good old Mughalai food, you'll adore **Moti Mahal Deluxe** (11 Defence Colony Market, Metro: Lajpat Nagar, tel. 11/2433-0263, www.motimahalindia.com, noon-midnight daily, Rs. 350). This typically North Indian restaurant is popular with locals and focuses on rich, creamy Indian dishes, best eaten with thick tandoori naan bread smothered with butter. The decor is plain, but you'll be focusing on the rich food, which includes everything from the unusual dal (lentils) with meat to *chana chili* (spicy-hot chickpeas). They also have Indo-Chinese food, but it is best avoided. The quintessential Delhi dish—butter chicken—was invented at this restaurant (though not at this branch).

At the edge of Deer Park, **Naivedyam** (1 Hauz Khas Village, Metro: Green Park, tel. 11/2696-0426, 10 A.M.-11 P.M. daily, Rs. 140) features some of the tastiest South Indian food in town. They offer all the classics—*idlis,* masala *dosas,* curd rice—as well as a few more unusual specialties, such as *idiyappam* (rice noodles served with sweetened coconut milk). The juices are exceptionally tasty, and the coconut water is served in the coconut, roadside-style. The interior is more elegant than one would expect from such an affordable restaurant and features frescoes of scenes from India's vast repertoire of mythological tales.

Bengali food doesn't usually end up on the menus of Indian restaurants in the West, even those run by Bengalis, so if you'd like to try the regional cuisine of West Bengal, head to **Oh! Calcutta** (E-Block, International Trade Towers, Nehru Place, Metro: Nehru Place, tel. 11/3040-2415, www.speciality.com, 12:30-3:30 P.M. and 7:30-11:30 P.M. daily). This restaurant serves a huge selection of vegetarian and meat-based dishes, including plenty of high-quality seafood options; seafood plays a big role in Bengali food, not surprising given that Bengal is a coastal region.

One of South Delhi's most celebrated restaurants, **Park Balluchi** (inside Deer Park, Metro: Green Park, tel. 11/2685-9369, www.parkballuchi.com, noon-midnight daily, Rs. 350) is popular with Indian families and offers heavy Indian dishes, including kebabs, *biryanis,* and creamy curries. While the food is delicious, it's the ambience that makes this place so special. The interiors are reminiscent of a cabin in the forest, with cobbled stone walls and dark wood beams. Best of all, Park Balluchi is located in the middle of Deer Park, near the deer cages, and is surrounded by greenery.

Many people are surprised to learn that Indian cuisine goes far beyond curries, flatbreads, and rice dishes. South Indian vegetarian food, such as that served at **Sagar Ratna** (Shop 18, Defence Colony Market, Metro: Lajpat Nagar, tel. 11/2433-3658, www.sagarratna.in, 8 A.M.-11 P.M. daily, Rs. 90), is worlds away from what is typically served in most Indian restaurants overseas. South Indian food uses elements such as lentil-rice flour and fresh coconut to make a variety of delicious treats, including the masala *dosa,* an eggless crepe stuffed with mildly spiced potatoes, and the *idlis,* round spongy cakes most often served with lentil stew. Avoid coming on Tuesday—many Hindus abstain from eating meat on this day, and Sagar Ratna seems to be many a Delhiite's vegetarian restaurant of choice.

Information and Services

TOURIST INFORMATION

Delhi Tourism (8-A DDA SCO Complex, Defence Colony, tel. 11/2461-8026, www.delhitourism.nic.in, 10 A.M.-5 P.M. Mon.-Fri.) is the city's government-run tourist board. The main office is in South Delhi and is visible from the Ring Road. This is primarily an administrative office and not worth visiting unless you're already in the area; you're better off paying a visit to the Central Reservation Office (Coffee Home I, Baba Kharak Singh Rd., tel. 11/2336-3607, 7 A.M.-9 P.M. daily), where you can also obtain information on hotels and tours.

MONEY

There's no shortage of ATMs in Delhi, and all of them accept international debit cards. Using ATMs is the easiest and cheapest way to get rupees, but if you have traveler's checks or, better, hard cash, you won't have a problem exchanging those either. Traveler's checks are accepted at some large shops, but this is becoming increasingly less common as plastic gains popularity.

Both traveler's checks and cash can be traded for Indian currency at foreign exchange bureaus, and some hotels run exchange bureaus for their guests (at five-star hotels, these are usually commission-free). Most foreign exchange bureaus are in Connaught Place, and they're usually legitimate. The internationally trusted **Thomas Cook** has bureaus around town, including one at Connaught Place (Janpath, tel. 11/2341-5848, www.thomascook.in). **RRSB Forex** (50-68, Ground Fl., World Trade Centre, Babar Rd., Connaught Place, tel. 11/2341-2180, www.rrsbforex.com) is another reputable Connaught Place money changer. South Delhi options include **LKG Forex** (E-35, Ground Fl., Lajpat Nagar I, near Central Market Rampul, tel. 11/2981-7772,

www.lkgforex.co.in), near the rowdy Lajpat Nagar Central Market, and **Princess Forex** (M-29 Greater Kailash I, tel. 9811/093-767). Always make sure to ask for a receipt.

HOSPITALS AND PHARMACIES

Delhi is filled with pharmacies, and if you need something, it's best to ask at the front desk of your hotel where the closest one is. Many pharmacies also offer delivery services.

If you need urgent medical care, there are quite a few excellent options in Delhi, including **Apollo Hospital** (Sarita Vihar, Delhi-Mathura Rd., tel. 11/2692-5858, www.apollohospdelhi.com) and **Max Hospital** (2 Press Enclave Rd., Saket, tel. 11/2651-5050, www.maxhealthcare.in). **East West Medical Centre** (28 Greater Kailash I, tel. 11/2464-1494) does not provide urgent care but has a more personalized and homely feel and very sweet staff. For heart conditions, contact **Fortis Escorts Heart Institute** (Okhla Rd., tel. 11/4713-5000, www.fortisescorts.in).

INTERNET ACCESS

All major hotels in Delhi offer Internet access via Wi-Fi for guests; in five-star hotels it can cost upward of Rs. 250 per hour. Many of the restaurants and cafés in Khan Market have free Wi-Fi for patrons, including *Amici* (47 Middle Lane, Khan Market, Metro: Khan Market, tel. 11/4358-7191, 11 A.M.-11 P.M. daily, Rs. 450) and *Mrs. Kaur's Crepes and More* (66 Middle Lane, Khan Market, Metro: Khan Market, tel. 11/4352-8300, www.mrskaurs.com, 7:30 A.M.-11 P.M. daily, Rs. 275). There are Internet cafés on every corner in Central Delhi's Paharganj—Internet access will set you back around Rs. 30 per hour. Make sure to bring your ID with you, as Internet cafés are legally required to log your personal details before you start surfing.

POSTAL SERVICES

There are post offices all around Delhi; a full list is available at www.indiapost.gov.in. The biggest post office in Central Delhi is the **New Delhi GPO** (Gole Dak Khana, Baba Kharak Singh Rd., tel. 11/2336-4111), near Connaught Place. This is the place to go with packages, which need to be wrapped in white cloth and sewn up before you ship them. There's a tailor on-site, just inside the main doors, who has plenty of white cloth for this purpose.

If you're staying in South Delhi, there's a tailor who will sew up your parcels just outside the **Hauz Khas Post Office** (Aurobindo Marg, near IIT Gate, Hauz Khas, tel. 11/2652-3059). His makeshift tailor shop is located against the outside northern wall of the post office complex.

If you don't want to deal with queues at the post office, some high-end hotels will ship parcels for their guests for a price. Most bookshops and boutiques can pack and send your purchases home for you, and they're usually pretty reliable. There are also plenty of shops in the backpacker haven of Paharganj that ship parcels on their customers' behalf for a small fee, but they aren't always reliable, and packages shipped through these services don't always reach their destinations. As the old adage goes, if you want it done right, do it yourself.

LAUNDRY

No matter where you are in Delhi, the easiest way to get laundry done is through your hotel. If you're staying in a five-star place, they'll arrange for machine-wash service or dry-cleaning and can often get your clothes back to you the same day. Guesthouses and budget hotels often outsource the work to a *dhobi* (washer man or woman), who will take your clothes down to a nearby body of water or clothes-washing area known as a *dhobi ghat* and wash your clothes there, often flogging them with sticks or rocks to get all the dirt out. This can be disastrous for finer fabrics, and the laundry detergent they use can sometimes turn whites a cornflower blue, so it's best not to hand your Sunday finest to them. There are dry cleaners of varying quality in every market in Delhi. The most reputable, **Four Seasons** (tel. 11/2681-0056, www.fourseasons.in), specializes in fine garments and delicate fabrics. They have locations around the city and have a pickup and drop-off service.

LUGGAGE STORAGE

There are 24-hour left-luggage facilities, known as "cloakrooms," in all of Delhi's train stations. Luggage storage costs start around Rs. 20 per 24-hour period. Baggage must be locked and can be stored for up to a month.

In Paharganj, **Ajay Guest House** (5084-A Main Bazar, Paharganj, tel. 11/2358-3125, www.ajayguesthouse.com) offers luggage storage at a shockingly low Rs. 5 per day per item, and they'll allow you to leave your stuff here for a year or two if you feel like it. The luggage room is open 8 A.M.-8 P.M. daily.

Getting There and Around

GETTING THERE
Air
Delhi is India's number-one point of entry, and most major carriers fly to the **Indira Gandhi International Airport** (DEL), about 16 kilometers southwest of town. The domestic terminal and the international terminal (the brand-new ultramodern Terminal 3) are far from each other, although a shuttle service operates between the two for passengers with onward journeys.

The easiest way to get to Delhi from the airport is by booking a prepaid taxi at one of the Delhi Police-operated prepaid taxi booths, inside the arrivals terminal. You'll be asked to pay in advance and will be given a slip with a number written on it, indicating which of the 20-odd clearly-numbered taxi posts to go to. A taxi shouldn't cost you more than about Rs. 400 no matter where you want to go in Delhi, and it will likely cost a bit less. A number of private radio cab operators also have booking offices at the airport, a good option if you want something with air-conditioning.

Buses also run from the airport to the Interstate Bust Terminal (ISBT) at Kashmiri Gate, although the service is crowded, slow, and generally not a good idea, especially for first-time visitors to India. You are better off with a taxi, or if you're really trying to save money, you can take the **Airport Express** (www.delhiairportexpress.com) branch of the Metro. It runs from 5:30 A.M. to just after 11 P.M. daily and costs Rs. 60-80 to reach Central Delhi.

Train
The main train stations in Delhi are the **New Delhi Railway Station** in Central Delhi near Connaught Place and Paharganj, the **Delhi Railway Station** in Old Delhi near the Red Fort, and the **Hazrat Nizamuddin Railway Station** in Central Delhi near Humayun's Tomb. Tickets sell out fast, but select trains have special "tourist quota" tickets, reserved for foreign visitors. These tickets can be purchased at the **International Tourist Bureau** (1st Fl., New Delhi Railway Station, Paharganj side, tel. 11/4262-5156, 8 A.M.-8 P.M. Mon.-Sat., 8 A.M.-2 P.M. Sun.). Make sure to bring your passport, and to prove that you obtained your rupees legally, an ATM receipt or receipt from a foreign exchange bureau is also required, although they don't usually ask for it.

Bus
You can get pretty much anywhere in India from Delhi by bus. The **Interstate Bus Terminal** (ISBT) at Kashmiri Gate in Old Delhi is where most public buses leave from. Buses to Agra (4-5 hours, Rs. 221-371) depart 6 A.M. to 7 P.M. from Sarai Kale Khan Bus Stand; the cost varies depending on the type of bus. The Rajasthan State Road Transport Corporation (RSRTC) operates a variety of bus types. Some leave from the ISBT, but most depart from Bikaner House (tel. 11/2338-3469) near India Gate in Central Delhi. Buses to Jaipur (about 5 hours, Rs. 400-730) arrive at Jaipur's Central Bus Stand (tel. 141/237-3044). Buses that arrive in Jaipur in the middle of the night drop passengers at Badi Chaupur in the old Pink City.

Taxi
Delhi is connected to Jaipur by National Highway 8 and to Agra by National Highway 2. Many people opt to take a taxi around India's Golden Triangle, and this will cost at least Rs. 11,000-12,000 for a three-night, four-day trip in a Tata Indigo or Toyota Etios sedan. This fare includes taxes, tolls, and up to around 900 kilometers of travel; additional days and kilometers will cost extra. A day trip to Agra

SHATABDI TRAINS TO AND FROM DELHI

You can get direct trains from Delhi to all of the destinations mentioned in this book. The fastest and most comfortable trains to Agra and Jaipur are the *Shatabdi Express* category. These are seated trains and include meal services. All cars are air-conditioned. *Janshatabdi* trains are similar in speed and layout, but meals are not served, and only certain cars have air-conditioning.

The three major Shatabdi trains that collectively cover most of the destinations in this book are the *Agra*, the *Ajmer Shatabdi Express,* and the *Kota Janshatabdi.* Their schedules:

Departure station	Arrival station	Name	Number	Departs	Arrives
New Delhi	Agra Cantt.	*Bhopal Shatabdi*	12002	6:15 A.M.	8:12 A.M.
Agra Cantt.	New Delhi	*NDLS Shatabdi*	12001	8:25 P.M.	10:30 P.M.
New Delhi	Jaipur	*Ajmer Shatabdi Express*	12015	6:05 A.M.	10:30 A.M.
Jaipur	New Delhi	*Ajmer Shatabdi Express*	12016	5:50 P.M.	10:40 P.M.
New Delhi	Alwar (for Sariska)	*Ajmer Shatabdi*	12015	6:05 A.M.	8:39 A.M.
Alwar (for Sariska)	New Delhi	*Ajmer Shatabdi*	12016	7:30 P.M.	10:40 P.M.
New Delhi	Ajmer (for Pushkar)	*Ajmer Shatabdi*	12015	6:05 A.M.	12:40 A.M.
Ajmer (for Pushkar)	New Delhi	*Ajmer Shatabdi*	12016	3:50 P.M.	10:40 P.M.
New Delhi	Haridwar (for Rishikesh)	*Dehradun Shatabdi*	12017	6:50 A.M.	11:25 P.M.
Haridwar (for Rishikesh)	New Delhi	*Dehradun Shatabdi*	12018	6:13 P.M.	10:45 P.M.
New Delhi	Dehradun (for Mussoorie)	*Dehradun Shatabdi*	12017	6:50 A.M.	12:40 P.M.
Dehradun (for Mussoorie)	New Delhi	*Dehradun Shatabdi*	12018	5 P.M.	10:45 P.M.
Hazrat Nizamuddin	Bharatpur (for Keoladeo Ghana)	*Kota Janshatabdi*	12060	1:20 P.M.	3:48 P.M.
Bharatpur (for Keoladeo Ghana)	Hazrat Nizamuddin	*Kota Janshatabdi*	12059	9:25 A.M.	12:30 P.M.
Hazrat Nizamuddin	Sawai Madhopur (for Ranthambore)	*Kota Janshatabdi*	12060	1:20 P.M.	6:02 P.M.
Sawai Madhopur (for Ranthambore)	Hazrat Nizamuddin	*Kota Janshatabdi*	12059	7:05 A.M.	12:30 P.M.

takes four hours each way by taxi and will set you back around Rs. 6,000-7,000, including all taxes and tolls, in a Tata Indigo sedan.

Jaipur, 5-6 hours from Delhi, is a bit far to do in one day. A two-night, three-day trip in a Tata Indigo or Toyota Etios sedan costs around Rs. 6,500-7,500, including taxes and tolls, for 600 kilometers of travel; additional kilometers cost extra. While taxis can be booked through your hotel, they will charge a high commission. It's a lot cheaper to go through a private agent. Your best bet is to contact the government-approved, family-run **Destination India Travel Centre** (78 Janpath, 1st Fl., tel. 11/2371-2345, www.indiatripmakers.com). It has its own small fleet of pristine vehicles with English-speaking drivers and is very tuned in to the needs of overseas visitors.

GETTING AROUND

There's no shortage of transportation options in Delhi, and depending on where you need to go, you have your choice of cycle rickshaws (for short distances), autorickshaws, taxis, and the Delhi Metro. There are public buses as well, but they are crowded, confusing to use, and best avoided. Delhi Tourism has launched a sightseeing bus, known as HOHO, which is quite good.

Cycle Rickshaw

In certain parts of Delhi, especially the older parts of town, cycle rickshaws (half bicycle, half cart, used to pedal passengers around) are a popular way of making short jaunts between two points when it is slightly too far to walk. They are commonly used to get to nearby Metro stations. There's no fixed rate—just ask how much ahead of time, and be generous. Pulling a cycle rickshaw is a lot harder than it looks, and the people who do this job are usually really struggling even to feed themselves.

Autorickshaw

One of the cheapest and quickest ways to get around Delhi is by autorickshaw, usually shortened simply to "auto." These green-and-yellow vehicles are easy to flag down on the street in most parts of Delhi, although they'll often refuse to go to a destination that they find too out-of-the-way, usually giving the excuse that they're out of gas. It's sometimes easier to book an auto through one of Delhi Police's prepaid booths, which charge fixed rates (pay in advance at the counter). There are booths at all the major train stations and bus terminals as well as at some touristed sites, including Dilli Haat, Janpath, and the Inner Circle at Connaught Place. If you end up hailing an auto instead, note that they are expected to go by the meter, although most drivers don't like to do this, preferring to negotiate a fixed rate in advance. If you're not familiar with Delhi, they can easily take you for a ride—the city is not well signposted, and following a map while zooming around in one of these little scooters is tricky. If they do end up going by the meter, expect to pay Rs. 19 for the first two kilometers (or parts thereof) and Rs. 6.50 per additional kilometer. They also charge Rs. 7.50 per item of luggage (drivers usually try to round this up to Rs. 10, which is really too trivial to debate). It is common practice to round up the fare when you arrive at the destination, especially if you don't have change (a Rs. 46 fare will become Rs. 50). Rates are displayed in rupees and the obsolete paise (Rs. 1 = 100 paise). From 11 P.M. to 5 A.M., fares increase by 25 percent; this is called a "night charge."

Taxi

Taxis are a slightly less convenient but certainly more comfortable way to get around. You can occasionally hail a black-and-yellow public taxi from the street, but it's more common to book one at a taxi stand. There's at least one in every neighborhood—in central Delhi, these stands are often right next to

© RAJAT DEEP RANA

Autorickshaws are a popular way to get around Delhi.

major hotels. They usually try to negotiate fixed rates, but they do have meters. The official government-approved meter fare is Rs. 20 for the first kilometer and Rs. 11 for each additional kilometer (Rs. 13 per additional kilometer in the odd instance when they have air-conditioning). You can usually hire one of these taxis for a whole day, although you're more likely to end up with a plain white "private cab," like the type used for longer trips. Rates start at around Rs. 850 for eight hours and a maximum of 80 kilometers (you can pay extra for additional hours or kilometers) in a small unair-conditioned vehicle and can increase significantly if you want a large car or air-conditioning. For point-to-point travel, you can also call a radio cab. Delhi has plenty of operators; the most popular are **Meru Cabs** (tel. 11/4422-4422, www.merucabs.com), **Mega Cabs** (tel. 11/4141-4141, www.megacabs.com), and **Easy Cabs** (tel. 11/4343-4343, www.easycabs.com).

Metro

One of the fastest and easiest ways to get around town is by **Delhi Metro** (www.delhimetrorail.com), an enormous rapid-transit system with 142 aboveground and underground stations spread around the city and surrounding suburbs. The Metro runs every day from around 6 A.M. until 11 P.M. There's a special women-only compartment at the end of each train, usually much less crowded and much more hospitable to solo female travelers.

If you don't plan to use the Metro much during your stay, you can buy single-use tokens (fares range Rs. 8-30, depending on the distance traveled). However, the lines at ticket counters can get quite long, so it's easier to purchase a Tourist Card or Travel Card. Tourist cards are valid for unlimited travel for a duration of either one (Rs. 100) or three (Rs. 250) calendar days. Travel Cards, sometimes referred to as Smart Cards, work on a per-journey basis (fare is deducted for each journey). You need to put at

The Delhi Metro is a convenient and inexpensive way to get around town.

© RAJAT DEEP RANA

least Rs. 50 (and up to Rs. 800) credit on your card when you get it. There's a Rs. 50 refundable deposit on both Tourist and Travel Cards.

HOHO

Delhi Tourism's **Hop On–Hop Off (HOHO)** (tel. 1800/102-9500, www.hohodelhi.com) bus is a great way to see the sights at your leisure. This air-conditioned sightseeing bus covers most of the major attractions in Delhi and runs every 30 minutes 8:45 A.M.-7:15 P.M.; tickets (Rs. 300 adults, Rs. 150 children under 90 centimeters) can be bought online or at any one of the 19 bus pick-up points around town. An English-speaking "Guest Relations Executive" sits on board all the buses and can give advice and itinerary suggestions to passengers.

Tours

Delhi Transport Corporation's **Delhi Darshan** (Delhi Darshan Counter, Scindia House, Connaught Place, tel. 11/2884-4192, ext. 244, www.dtc.nic.in, Rs. 200 adults, Rs. 100 ages 5-12, free under age 5) tour bus leaves from Scindia House in Connaught Place every morning at 9:15 A.M. and picks up passengers at Delhi Tourism on Baba Kharak Singh Road and India Tourism on Janpath before starting the day's tour. They stop at Raj Ghat, Red Fort, the Birla Mandir, Qutb Minar, Lotus Temple, and Humayun's Tomb before dropping all passengers at the Akshardam Temple; you must then find your way home independently.

Delhi Tourism operates half-day (Rs. 200) and full-day (Rs. 300) tours of Delhi's top sights Tuesday-Sunday. Morning tours run 9 A.M.-1:30 P.M. and cover the Gandhi Smriti, Birla Mandir, Qutb Minar, and Lotus Temple. Afternoon tours run 2:15-5:45 P.M. and go to the Red Fort, Rajghat, and Humayun's Tomb. Tours can be booked from Delhi Tourism's office (Baba Kharak Singh Rd., tel. 11/2336-3607, www.delhitourism.gov.in, 7 A.M.-9 P.M. daily).

A number of private operators also provide

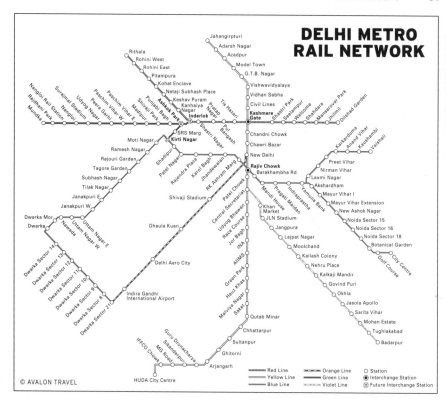

DELHI METRO RAIL NETWORK

Jahangirpturi
Adarsh Nagar
Rithala
Azadpur
Rohini West
Model Town
Rohini East
Pitampura
G.T.B. Nagar
Kohat Enclave
Vishwavidyalaya
Netaji Subhash Place
Vidhan Sabha
Keshav Puram
Civil Lines
Ashok Park
Kanhaiya Nagar
Kashmere Gate
Inderlok
SRS Marg
Chandni Chowk
Kirti Nagar
Chawri Bazar
Moti Nagar
New Delhi
Ramesh Nagar
Rajiv Chowk
Rajouri Garden
Preet Vihar
Tagore Garden
Barakhambha Rd
Nirman Vihar
Subhash Nagar
Laxmi Nagar
Tilak Nagar
Akshardham
Janakpuri E
Mayur Vihar I
Janakpuri W
Shivaji Stadium
Patel Chowk
Mayur Vihar Extension
Dwarka Mor
Central Secretariat
Khan Market
New Ashok Nagar
Dwarka
Udyog Bhawan
JLN Stadium
Noida Sector 15
Uttam Nagar E
Race Course
Jangpura
Noida Sector 16
Nawada
Uttam Nagar W
Jor Bagh
Lajpat Nagar
Noida Sector 18
Dhaula Kuan
INA
Moolchand
Botanical Garden
Delhi Aero City
Kailash Colony
City Centre
AIIMS
Nehru Place
Golf Course
Green Park
Kalkaji Mandir
Indira Gandhi International Airport
Hauz Khas
Govind Puri
Malviya Nagar
Okhla
Saket
Jasola Apollo
Qutab Minar
Sarita Vihar
Guru Dronacharya
Chhattarpur
Mohan Estate
Sikanderpur
Sultanpur
Tughlakabad
IFFCO Chowk
Ghitorni
Badarpur
MG Road
Arjangarh
HUDA City Centre

Tis Hazari
Pul Bangash
Shastri Nagar
Shadipur
Patel Nagar
Rajendra Place
Karol Bagh
Jhandewalan
RK Ashram Marg

Shastri Park
Seelampur
Welcome
Shahdara
Mansarovar Park
Jhilmil
Dilshad Garden

Karkarduma
Anand Vihar
Kaushambi
Vaishali

Yamuna Bank
Indraprastha
Pragati Maidan
Mandi House

Nangloi Rail Station
Nangloi
Rajdheni Park
Mundka
Surajmal Stadium
Udyog Nagar
Peera Garhi
Paschim Vihar W
Paschim Vihar E
Madipur
Shivaji Park
Punjabi Bagh

Dwarka Sector 14
Dwarka Sector 13
Dwarka Sector 12
Dwarka Sector 11
Dwarka Sector 10
Dwarka Sector 9
Dwarka Sector 8
Dwarka Sector 21

Legend:
Red Line — Orange Line — Station
Yellow Line — Green Line — Interchange Station
Blue Line — Violet Line — Future Interchange Station

© AVALON TRAVEL

---

tours in Delhi, with Old Delhi being the most popular; it's also the most walkable and one of the more historic parts of town. **When in India Tours** (R-6 South Extension II, tel. 9958/077-066, www.wheninindia.com) operates three-hour tours of Old Delhi using cycle rickshaws. These tours cost a whopping Rs. 2,560 but include informative guides, tea and water, and transportation on cycle rickshaws. Admission to monuments is extra.

The more adventurous can go on a much more reasonably priced early-morning bike tour with **Delhi by Cycle** (Siddarth Niwas 144/3, Hari Nagar Ashram, tel. 11/6464-5906, www.

delhibycycle.com, Rs. 1,450). The cost of the three-hour tour includes a bicycle and optional helmet rental, guide fees, tea, water, breakfast, and snacks. Four tours that cover different parts of the city are offered.

Escape Delhi (C-192 Sarvodaya Enclave, tel. 9999/438-784, www.escapedelhi.com) offers weekend outings from Delhi, usually involving outdoor activities such as river rafting, trekking, parasailing, and even skiing. They also organize weekends of camping and music at a lakeside luxury campsite about 1.5 hours' drive from Delhi.

AGRA AND THE TAJ MAHAL

Most Indian people will tell you that if it weren't for the Taj Mahal, the sweltering Uttar Pradesh city of Agra would be a destitute and rather uninviting place. There is some truth to this statement; Agra lacks both the charm of many of India's old towns and the modernity of the country's thriving cities. It's also true that the Taj Mahal is the main reason to visit Agra, and were the city not home to this world-famous monument, the government and hospitality industry would not have pumped the kind of funds into the city that they have. However, many people erroneously assume that the Taj Mahal is the only sight worth visiting in Agra and end up missing out on some of the city's most fascinating attractions.

For many years, Agra was viewed as a stopover city, and many visitors would come to see the Taj Mahal and then leave the following morning. Admittedly, it was also a less inviting place in those days, and the touts, heat, and dust could be overwhelming. However, the city, at least the area around the Taj, has really improved over the past few years, and the increased presence of police combined with better road maintenance has reduced obnoxious touting and dust, respectively. In fact, hoteliers have reported a sharp spike in the average length of stay of their guests over the past three years. This is likely attributable to the increased exposure the Taj Mahal has garnered since gaining a place on the list of the New Seven Wonders

HIGHLIGHTS

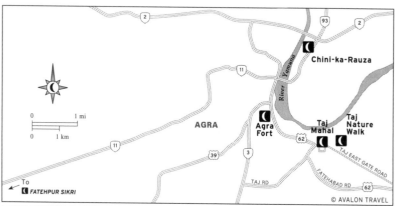

© AVALON TRAVEL

LOOK FOR 🌙 TO FIND RECOMMENDED SIGHTS, ACTIVITIES, DINING, AND LODGING.

🌙 **Taj Mahal:** India's most famous monument, this incredible marble structure symbolizes the ultimate in love and husbandly devotion (page 87).

🌙 **Agra Fort:** This massive 16th-century fort is worth exploring for anyone curious about how the royal Mughals lived (page 92).

🌙 **Chini-ka-Rauza:** Few visitors make it out to this old mosaic-covered tomb built in the

Persian style (page 95).

🌙 **Taj Nature Walk:** Catch beautiful tree-framed glimpses of the Taj Mahal from this lush eco-park (page 97).

🌙 **Fatehpur Sikri:** This sprawling ghost town was once the capital of Mughal emperor Akbar and was built almost entirely in red sandstone (page 99).

of the World, combined with Agra's increasing popularity as a conference destination for Indian businesspeople.

However, while Agra is a much easier place to deal with than it used to be, the city is still very, very hot most of the year, so remember to drink plenty of water and wear cool loose-fitting clothes. Note that covering your legs and shoulders will not only protect your skin from the sun, it will also be appreciated by the local population, who favor conservative dress for both men and women.

HISTORY

Most of the stories you will hear and the sights you visit during your trip will be related to the Mughal Empire, but historians believe that Agra was inhabited long before the Mughals made it their base. Some believe that the city was settled by Aryan tribes and that it was once called Arya-Griha, or "dwelling place of the Aryans." Others believe that Agra was founded by the maternal grandfather of the Hindu god Krishna (many Hindus believe that their deities once walked the earth). Although there are conflicting theories about Agra's early roots, most believe that the city in its present form was founded in 1504 by the Afghan ruler Sultan Sikandar Lodi of the pre-Mughal Delhi Sultanate, who made it his capital. He was succeeded by his son, who was killed by Babur's troops in 1526 at the third Battle of Panipat. Babur, the founder of the Mughal Empire, made Agra his home until his death in 1530.

The city would go on to be ruled by a succession of Mughal emperors: Babur's son Humayun, then Akbar, who called the city Akbarabad and then briefly shifted base to Fatehpur Sikri. Akbar's grandson Shahjahan would later build the Taj Mahal in memory of his beloved deceased wife, Mumtaz Mahal. Mumtaz and Shahjahan's notoriously fun-hating and ultraorthodox son Aurangzeb would later usurp the romantic Shahjahan, locking him up in Agra Fort, where he would remain until his death.

Under Aurangzeb's rule, all the beauty, art, and culture that had defined the courts of the Mughals disappeared from Agra. He destroyed temples, forced Hindus to convert to Islam, and rid his empire of any art depicting human and animal forms, considering them idolatrous. His life marked the end of the artistic splendor of the Mughal Empire. The entire empire gradually declined, and Agra was briefly taken over by the Jaat people (from what is now Haryana and parts of Uttar Pradesh) before coming under the control of the British in 1803, under which it remained until India's independence in 1947.

PLANNING YOUR TIME

If you are really only in Agra to see the Taj Mahal and perhaps the Agra Fort, a day trip or overnight trip from Delhi or Jaipur is feasible. However, if you have the time, a stay of

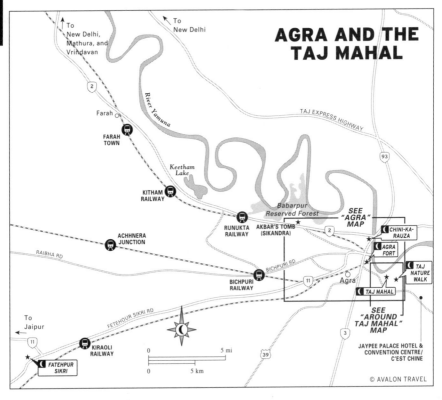

AGRA AND THE TAJ MAHAL

© AVALON TRAVEL

2-3 days is a better idea, as this will allow you to visit the area's many sights at a leisurely pace and give you time for excursions to nearby attractions such as Fatehpur Sikri.

It's also worth noting that temperatures in Agra are notoriously high during most of the year, so if you're visiting at any time except the winter months, it's best to take things slowly and give yourself some buffer time in case you want to retire to your hotel room during the early afternoon, the hottest part of the day.

Admission Prices in Agra

The pricing system for the monuments in Agra and vicinity is a bit complex. There are different prices for Indians and foreigners (including resident foreigners), and citizens of South Asian Association for Regional Cooperation (SAARC) member states get discounts at some attractions. Moreover, some of the sights are doubly ticketed by both the Archaeological Survey of India and the Agra Development Authority (ADA). The charges levied by the ADA are referred to as "toll tax" and apply only to the Taj Mahal, Fatehpur Sikri, Agra Fort, Itmad-ud-Daulah's Tomb (Baby Taj), and Akbar's Tomb at Sikandra. Foreigners paying the Rs. 500 toll tax required to enter the Taj Mahal can present their Taj ticket at the other monuments for a full waiver of additional toll tax, but only if they visit on the same day. This works out to a discount of Rs. 50 on the total ticket cost at Agra Fort, but only Rs. 10 off at the other attractions.

The prices listed below are the full ticket cost, including toll taxes. Children under age 15 are admitted to most of Agra's sites at a reduced rate or for free, regardless of their country of origin.

SAFETY AND SCAMS

Touting is a huge problem in Agra, so be wary of rickshaw, bus, and taxi drivers who try to convince you to visit shops—chances are you will be vastly overcharged to compensate for the Rs. 50-plus commission these touts get just for bringing you into the shop (they also get a hefty cut of whatever you decide to purchase). In many shops that work regularly with touts, you'll notice a room off to the side of the main entrance—this is a waiting lounge for touts, where they also go to collect their finder's fees.

ORIENTATION

Agra is a relatively small city and fairly easy to navigate, although you'll need a taxi or autorickshaw to get to most of the sights. The Yamuna River runs north-south through the northern part of the city; its trajectory turns east just before the Taj Mahal.

Most of Agra's food and accommodations options are found either in Taj Ganj—a congested neighborhood just south of the Taj Mahal—or along the busy Fatehabad Road. Taj Ganj and Fatehabad Road are linked by Taj East Gate Road, sometimes called VIP Road. The majority of the sights in Agra are north of the Taj Mahal, including Agra Fort, which is on the same side of the river as the Taj. Many of the city's best-known tombs and Mughal gardens are situated on the east bank of the Yamuna River, just off National Highway 93. If you travel north toward Delhi on National Highway 2, you'll pass Sikandra (site of Akbar's Tomb and Mariam's Tomb), and then the twin cities of Mathura and Vrindavan. If you're headed toward Agra via National Highway 11, you'll pass the fantastic ghost town of Fatehpur Sikri, which sits at the border of the states of Uttar Pradesh and Rajasthan.

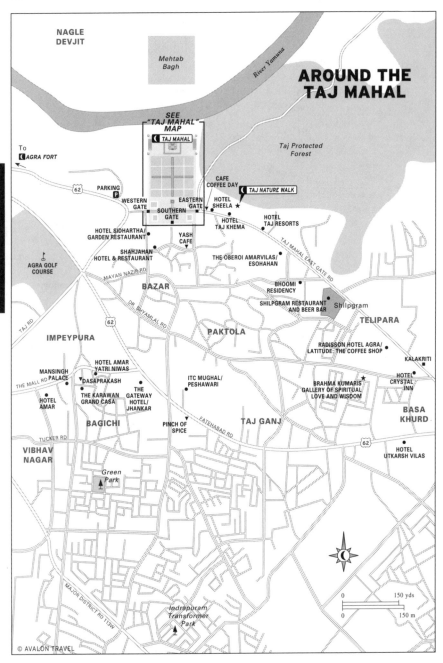

NAGLE
DEVJIT

*Mehtab
Bagh*

River Yamuna

AROUND THE
TAJ MAHAL

SEE
"TAJ MAHAL"
MAP

☾ TAJ MAHAL

*Taj Protected
Forest*

To
☾ AGRA FORT

62

PARKING
P

WESTERN
GATE

EASTERN
GATE

SOUTHERN
GATE

CAFE
COFFEE DAY

☾ TAJ NATURE WALK

HOTEL
SHEELA ★

HOTEL
TAJ RESORTS

HOTEL SIDHARTHA/
GARDEN RESTAURANT

YASH
CAFE

HOTEL
TAJ KHEMA

AGRA GOLF
COURSE

SHAHJAHAN
HOTEL & RESTAURANT

THE OBEROI AMARVILAS/
ESOHAHAN

TAJ MAHAL EAST GATE RD

MAYAN NAZIR RD

BAZAR

BHOOMI
RESIDENCY

DR. SHYAMLAL RD

62

PAKTOLA

SHILPGRAM RESTAURANT
AND BEER BAR

Shilpgram

TELIPARA

TAJ RD

IMPEYPURA

RADISSON HOTEL AGRA/
LATITUDE: THE COFFEE SHOP

KALAKRITI

THE MALL RD

MANSINGH
PALACE

HOTEL AMAR
YATRI NIWAS

▼ DASAPRAKASH

ITC MUGHAL/
PESHAWARI

BRAHMA KUMARIS ★
GALLERY OF SPIRITUAL
LOVE AND WISDOM

HOTEL
CRYSTAL
INN

HOTEL
AMAR

THE KARAWAN
GRAND CASA

THE
GATEWAY
HOTEL/
JHANKAR

BASA
KHURD

BAGICHI

PINCH OF
SPICE

FATEHABAD RD

TAJ GANJ

TUCKER RD

62

VIBHAV
NAGAR

*Green
Park*

HOTEL
UTKARSH VILAS

MAJOR DISTRICT RD 113W

*Indrapuram
Transformer
Park*

0   150 yds

0   150 m

© AVALON TRAVEL

The Taj Mahal

India's most famous monument, the Taj Mahal (tel. 562/233-0498, sunrise-sunset Sat.-Thurs., Rs. 750 foreigners, Rs. 20 Indians) is considered the finest example of Mughal architecture as well as the ultimate expression of love. This extraordinary monument is India's most famous sight, and its spectacular beauty is the main reason most people come to Agra.

HISTORY

The Taj Mahal was built by a mourning Shahjahan in memory of his beloved wife Mumtaz Mahal. Mumtaz was the emperor's constant companion and would accompany Shahjahan on his military campaigns across the empire. It was during one such campaign, when the royal couple had traveled to Burhanpur on the Deccan Plateau, that Mumtaz gave birth to her 14th child, only to die soon after from complications. While on her deathbed, she asked Shahjahan to build a monument over her grave as a symbol of their undying love, and thus the idea of the Taj Mahal was born. Mumtaz Mahal was buried temporarily in Burhanpur immediately after her death, and her remains were transferred to Agra six months later.

Construction of the Taj Mahal began at the end of 1631, but there are conflicting views about when it was completed. It is claimed to have taken 22 years to erect, although there is evidence that the main building was already finished by February 1643. An estimated 20,000 builders worked on the mausoleum. Materials were brought from across northern India, and many of the gems used for the inlay work were given to the empire by royals from abroad. The marble used to construct the mausoleum was sourced from Makrana in Rajasthan, where some of the hardest marble in India is mined to this day. Nobody is really sure how much the entire project cost, although historians estimate that the total was somewhere in the region of 30 million rupees.

Although the Taj Mahal is a quintessentially Indian symbol, it's actually a fine example of international architectural collaboration. It was designed by the Persian architect Ustad Isa, although much of the detailing and artisanal work on the building is of Indian origin. The gardens were rebuilt by the British during the rule of then-viceroy Lord Curzon, who had them redesigned in a more English style while maintaining the traditional Mughal layout.

◖ VISITING THE TAJ MAHAL

The best time to visit is at sunrise, before the heat gets too intense or the crowds too large. It's also an enchanting sight to watch the sparkling glint of the sun on the white marble monument as it rises over the Yamuna River above the Taj. Tickets are available at the southern and western gate entrances. If you're approaching from the eastern gate, you have to purchase your tickets from the Shilpgram complex on Taj East Gate Road. Audio guide company Audio Compass has a stall at the complex where you can book a headset-style audio guide (Rs. 105); you pick up the device inside the complex and leave a piece of ID as a deposit. From Shilpgram you can take an electric-cart shuttle to the monument (free for foreigners, Rs. 10 for Indians). Foreigner tickets include a small bottle of water and special disposable shoe covers that you will be required to wear inside the main monument if you don't want to go barefoot.

If you are in Agra during the five days around the full moon (two days before and two days after), you can also participate in one of the small night viewings of the Taj (8:30 P.M.-12:30 A.M., Rs. 750 foreigners, Rs. 510 Indians, Rs. 500 children). Tickets must be purchased

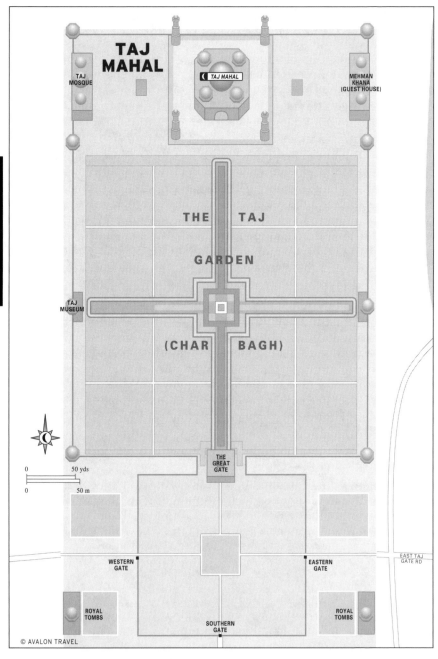

© AVALON TRAVEL

The layout of the Taj Mahal is perfectly symmetrical.

24 hours in advance from the Archaeological Survey of India (22 Mall Rd., tel. 562/222-7261, asiagra@vsnl.net). Groups of up to 50 people at a time can attend the night-viewing sessions, which last 30 minutes each; a visiting time is assigned when you buy your ticket. Note that night visitors can view the Taj from the interior courtyard but are not allowed to enter the mausoleum.

All three gates have heavy security, and while camcorders, cameras, and mobile phones are allowed, candies, cigarettes, and oversize handbags are not. Secure locker facilities are available at the western and southern gates and at Shilpgram. After security, you'll enter an exterior courtyard; this is also where the audio guides can be picked up.

THE GREAT GATE

In the center of the first courtyard stands the octagonal **Darwaza-i-Rauza**, the "Great Gate" of the Taj Mahal. This spectacular structure, made of red sandstone and inlayed with Makrana marble, is beautiful enough to be touted as a monument on its own, with its beautiful floral gem inlay work and its border of Koranic verses, inlayed in black marble on a white background. As you pass into the interior of the gate, admire the beautiful Egyptian blue glass lamp above, which was installed by Lord Curzon during renovations in 1906. Make sure you have your camera ready: As you approach the opposite end of the gatehouse, the Taj Mahal will come into view.

The viewpoint just beyond the gate is the most popular spot for photographs, and if for some reason you didn't bring a camera, you can have yourself photographed by a licensed photographer for a fixed price ranging Rs. 20-80, depending on the size of the print. If you're eager to take one of those snapshots where you hold out your hand to create the illusion that you are pinching a tiny Taj between your fingers, this is the place to do it. However, if you don't want throngs of unknown tourists to make an appearance in your photos, it's best to take a right and descend down to the benches just below the platform, where remarkably few people go to take pictures. On your way down, you'll pass the southern galleries, where Agra's poor used to go three times a week during the monsoon season to receive alms from Shahjahan.

THE TAJ GARDEN

One of the most charming features of the Taj Mahal complex is the beautiful *char bagh* (four-quarter) garden in which the great monument sits. The garden, believed to have been designed by noble Mughal Ali Mardan Khan, features a symmetrical layout of fountains and green areas, including a long reflecting pool that extends from the Great Gate to the Taj Mahal itself. In Mughal times, the garden's fountains were regularly replenished with water from the nearby Yamuna River, which

Carved floral reliefs decorate a wall at the Taj.

© MARGOT BIGG

was drawn by the bucketful and transported to on-site reservoirs on the garden walls. The water was then pumped into the fountain via iron pipes.

MEHMAN KHANA AND TAJ MOSQUE

Continue along the path flanking the reflecting pool and you will soon reach the raised platform on which the Taj Mahal was built. To the right of this platform is the **Mehman Khana** (guesthouse), which was built to host visitors during the *urs* (annual festival marking the death of a revered figure) of Mumtaz Mahal, which took place annually until 1653. Resist heading straight to the mausoleum and have a look around this structure; it's not as deep as it appears. The spiral design on the interior of the dome in the main part of the building is remarkable, albeit a bit dizzying to stare at. Just next to the structure is a digital

signboard that displays information on the actual pollution levels of the Yamuna River. On the opposite side of the Taj Mahal is the Taj Mosque, almost identical to the Mehman Khana it faces, which was likely done to preserve the symmetry of the complex.

INSIDE THE TAJ

Walk across the platform to the slippery stairway leading up to the Taj Mahal. Note that photography is not allowed inside the mausoleum, although a lot of people do manage to sneak in a cell-phone shot of the interior. Once inside, you'll notice an intricately carved eight-sided marble screen, behind which are the two symbolic sarcophagi of Mumtaz and Shahjahan (the actual tombs are purportedly in the basement, which is closed to visitors). This surrounding screen is inlaid with precious stones; it took about 10 years to create. Originally it had a door made of jasper, which

WHO WAS MUMTAZ MAHAL?

The Taj Mahal is often touted as the most elaborate expression of worldly love on the planet today, but little is known about the woman for whom this grand mausoleum was built.

Arjumand Banu Begum was born in Agra to an aristocratic family of Persian origin who are believed to have hailed from present-day Afghanistan. Her father was the governor of Lahore, and her aunt was Nur Jehan, the favorite wife of Emperor Jahangir. She was betrothed to Shahjahan when she was only a teenager, and although the emperor had more than one wife, she was clearly the main object of his affections. It was he who gave her the name Mumtaz Mahal, meaning "Distinguished Palace" and often interpreted as "Jewel of the Palace."

The bond between Mumtaz and Shahjahan was very strong, and she was considered an ideal wife as she lacked any desire for political power. Mumtaz and Shahjahan were rarely apart, and the empress would travel with her husband on his numerous campaigns around the empire. It was during one such trip that she met her demise, in the throes of labor with her 14th child. Her first son, Aurangzeb, would later rule the Mughal Empire.

has since disappeared. Unlike the other screens at the complex, this one uses floral, not geometric, patterns. The floor is covered with geometric inlay patterns, said to be symbolic of harmony. At the apex of the interior dome is a medallion of the sun, symbolic of Allah's presence. The interiors are decorated with inscriptions in Arabic, which, interestingly, are not Koranic verses but poetry exalting the pleasures of paradise.

TAJ MUSEUM

After your visit to the monument's interiors, you may want to stop briefly at the Taj Museum, inside what was once a *jal mahal* (water palace). An identical building stands on the east side of the garden, directly across from the east-west canal from the museum. The museum houses some of Shahjahan's old documents, sketches of the Taj Mahal, and plenty of old sabers, scimitars, and examples of calligraphy dating from the 17th century. Photography is prohibited inside.

GETTING THERE

The Taj Mahal sits along the banks of the Yamuna River in the southern part of Agra. If you're staying in the Taj Ganj area, you can get here by foot or cycle rickshaw, although if you plan to enter via the East Gate, you have to pick up tickets at the government-run Shilpgram complex first. If you're staying in the Fatehabad Road area, you're better off taking an autorickshaw or taxi. Note that the last 500-meter stretch before the Taj is closed to motorized traffic, so if you are coming by car or auto, you have to get out and either walk or take an cycle rickshaw the remainder of the way. Alternatively, you can ask to be dropped at Shilpgram, from where you can take an electric-cart shuttle (free for foreigners, Rs. 10 for Indians) to the Taj East Gate.

Other Sights

◖ AGRA FORT

The second-most visited attraction in town, the gargantuan Agra Fort (Yamuna Kinara Rd. and NH 3, tel. 562/296-0457, sunrise-sunset daily, Rs. 300 foreigners, Rs. 20 Indians), a UNESCO World Heritage Site, is spread out over about four square kilometers and merits a visit of at least 2-3 hours. Independent guides are available for hire at the main entry at Amar Singh Gate, and they will likely find you before you find them. Alternatively, you can rent an audio guide (Rs. 105) from the Audio Compass booth at the same gate. Audio guides are available in a wide variety of Indo-European and East Asian languages, but note that you will need to leave your passport or another form of ID as a deposit. Agra Fort closes at sunset, although visitors are welcome to return for the evening Agra Fort Sound and Light Show (in English 8:15 P.M. daily, Rs. 150 foreigners, Rs. 40 Indians, Rs. 25 students).

The fort was built of red sandstone by Akbar the Great over a period of eight years at a cost of 3.5 million rupees. It was completed in 1573, although additions were made by Akbar's grandson, Shahjahan, who used the fort as a palace (he was later imprisoned here by his son Aurangzeb). Some believe that the fort was constructed over the old Badalgarh Fort that was used by Rajput rulers before the Mughals took control of the area.

Agra Fort originally had four gates, two of which are now sealed. Today, visitors must access the fort through the southern **Amar Singh Gate,** built by Shahjahan. According to local legend, Amar Singh killed imperial treasurer

Agra Fort is a UNESCO World Heritage Site.

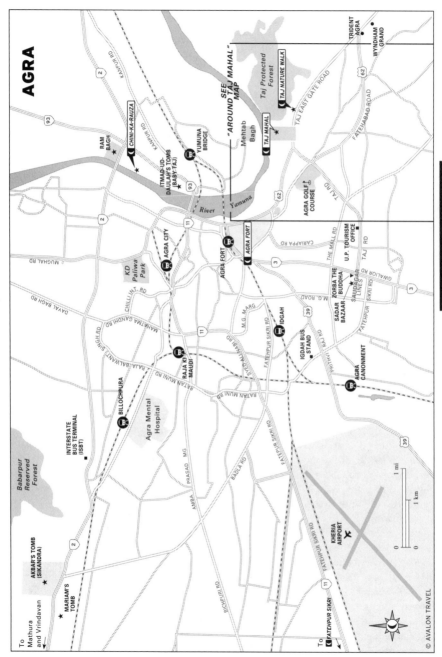

AGRA

AGRA AND THE TAJ MAHAL

© AVALON TRAVEL

Salabat Khan here. Straight ahead is **Akbari Gate,** which leads to the interior of the fort complex. If you take the first right, you'll end up in the **Akbari Mahal,** now in ruins. Akbar's harem lived here during his reign. Just north of the Akbari Mahal is the better-preserved and undeniably captivating **Jehangir Mahal,** arguably the highlight of the fort complex. This two-story building served as the *zenana,* or women's palace, meant for women of the court. The palace includes a temple and a breezy courtyard, featuring a mixture of decorative styles. In fact, the most notable feature of the palace is its blend of Central Asian and indigenous Indian architectural elements.

To the north of Jehangir Mahal, the white marble **Khas Mahal** was used as a harem room as well as a bedroom by Shahjahan. The structure's interiors feature intricately carved pillars and large domed pavilions, which were later used as residences for Shahjahan's daughters. The centerpiece of the palace was a large fountain that continuously spouted rose water through its 32 jets; this was probably an old-fashioned approach to air freshener. Just outside the Khas Mahal is the **Angoori Bagh** (Grape Garden), where grapes, flowers, and pomegranates once grew in soil that was allegedly brought to Agra all the way from Kashmir.

Continuing north, the octagonal **Musamman Burj,** or Jasmine Tower, is where Shahjahan was held captive and later died, supposedly while gazing at the Taj Mahal through a window. The tower features a lot of floral stone inlay work, including a considerable number of images of jasmine. Just across from the tower is the white marble **Meena Masjid,** built by Aurangzeb for the use of Shahjahan during his captivity in the fort.

The two large halls that comprise the **Diwan-i-Khas,** built in 1637 by Shahjahan, is the next major structure in the complex. This building was believed to have been designed and

THE ART OF *PIETRA DURA*

One of the most prominent features on many of the Mughal-era monuments in Agra is the extensive use of *pietra dura* or stone inlay. This craft has its roots in the ancient Roman craft of *opus sectile* and is distinguishable from mosaic and other types of inlay in that it incorporates single stones cut into their final shape before being pasted into place. Using large stones, especially those with a lot of grain and variation, such as marble and lapis lazuli, adds texture and depth to the images. The Mughals called this art *parchin kari* and used it extensively in their architecture to create geometric and floral adornment as well as religious motifs for the walls of their palaces and tombs. As they were wealthy rulers, a great deal of attention went into selecting the finest stones for their works of art, and while some pieces have been chipped away and stolen over the centuries, the majority remain on the walls of Agra's many fabulous monuments to this day for the enjoyment of all.

constructed by the same artisans who built the Taj Mahal. It was here that Shahjahan would hold audiences with ministers and high-ranking officials. Akbar's nearby hall of public audiences, the **Diwan-i-Aam,** was built by Akbar and later remodeled by Shahjahan using the emperor's characteristic white marble and semi-precious stone inlay.

ITMAD-UD-DAULAH'S TOMB (BABY TAJ)

Partially due to its slight resemblance to the Taj Mahal and mostly because of its not-so-catchy name, Itmad-ud-Daulah's Tomb (NH 93, near Kanpur Rd., sunrise-sunset daily, Rs. 110 foreigners, Rs. 20 Indians) is referred to more often than not as the Baby

© RAJAT DEEP RANA

The tomb of Itmad-Ud-Daulah is often referred to as Baby Taj.

Taj (ironically, this structure was completed in 1629, two years before work on the Taj Mahal even began). The Baby Taj sits on the eastern banks of the Yamuna River and is the final resting place of Mirza Ghiyas Beg, who hailed from what is now Iran and served as prime minister at the Mughal court. It was built for Beg by his daughter, Empress Begum Noor Jahan. The exterior is covered with *pietra dura* inlays in which geometrical arabesque designs feature heavily. The interiors are decorated with intricate carvings of flora and inscriptions from the Koran as well as delicate mosaic work featuring a rainbow of semiprecious stones. Like the Taj Mahal, this monument sits on a raised platform and is made entirely of marble. Historians consider this building to mark the transition between red sandstone and white marble architecture that took place in the 17th century.

CHINI-KA-RAUZA

The dilapidated old Chini-ka-Rauza (NH 93, south of NH 2, sunrise-sunset daily, free) lacks the glitz of many of the better-maintained attractions of Agra, but it's actually one of the most enchanting and undervisited sights in town. It is surrounded on three sides by gardens, remarkably well-kept compared to the building itself, and it overlooks the Yamuna River. This is the mausoleum of Afzal Khan Alami, better known as "Shukrullah," who served under Shahjahan. It was constructed during Shukrullah's lifetime and completed around 1635, some four years before his death in Lahore. The tomb's most prominent characteristic is the extensive glazed tile mosaic work that flanks its exterior. The tile work consists primarily of tiny pieces of glazed tiles, about 16 millimeters in size, painstakingly embedded into a plaster base. A banner runs along the exterior, featuring Koranic inscriptions

AGRA AND THE TAJ MAHAL

© RAJAT DEEP RANA

Take a break from the crowds at the lesser-known Chini-ka-Rauza.

interspersed with floral motifs. The cool interior of the tomb also features a considerable amount of colorful tile work, although much of it has deteriorated over time. The tomb is notably more Persian than Indian, and there's a marked absence of pillars, *jalis* (marble screens), and other indigenous features typical of Mughal architecture in India.

MEHTAB BAGH

Translated as the "Moonlight Gardens," Mehtab Bagh (across the river from the Taj Mahal, sunrise-sunset daily, Rs. 100 foreigners, Rs. 5 Indians) is directly opposite the Taj Mahal and was once a popular place to view the famous structure. Unfortunately, extensive flooding over the years has turned this garden into a bit of a dump, and there's not much in terms of astonishing plant life. It is admittedly a great place for photographers, but if you're only here for the much-talked-about views of the Taj Mahal, you can save your money by turning

right when facing the entrance and heading down the road about 100 meters. You'll pass a small Buddhist shrine on your right before reaching the muddy banks of the Yamuna River, where you can take postcard-worthy snapshots of India's most famous monument to your heart's content. Just beware of the mud!

RAM BAGH

Believed to be one of the earliest Mughal gardens in the country, this red sandstone park (NH 93, north of NH 2, sunrise-sunset daily, Rs. 100 foreigners, Rs. 5 Indians) was built on the four-quarter *char bagh* plan and incorporates design elements brought from Persia, including terraced fountains that allow water to cascade down. As there is no spring at the site, the water had to be drawn from the nearby Yamuna River and sent through a series of canals with the help of waterwheels. Ram Bagh also served as a royal orchard and housed numerous ornamental plants and fruit trees. Ram

© MARGOT BIGG

Enjoy incredible Taj views just down the road at Mehtab Bagh.

Bagh was laid out in 1526 by Barbur, founder of the Mughal Empire, whose body was temporarily stored here after his death. At the time it was known as Aram Bagh (Relaxation Garden) and was used as a place of respite in the hot summers. Visitors today will find it difficult to believe that Ram Bagh was considered a spot to cool down; although the garden is filled with greenery, there's limited shade, and the old fountains, which likely once helped reduce temperatures, are now dry.

◖ TAJ NATURE WALK

If you need a quiet place to escape from the constant cries of touts and tour guides, head straight to the rambling Taj Nature Walk (Taj East Gate Rd., tel. 562/233-1297, www.tajnaturewalk.in, sunrise-sunset daily, Rs. 100 foreigners, Rs. 10 Indians). This beautifully lush expanse was turned into a park in 1998 and is managed by Agra's Social Forestry Division. The Taj Nature Walk features well-paved trails,

including four vantage points, named after historical figures, where visitors can view and photograph the Taj Mahal. It's also a lovely place for bird-watching, and colorful murals depicting the various types of birdlife that visit the park cover the wall at the park's entrance. Rumor has it that hyenas and jackals also live in the park, although they only come out early in the morning and late at night, when the Taj Nature Walk is closed to the public.

BRAHMA KUMARIS GALLERY OF SPIRITUAL LOVE AND WISDOM

Housed in a building shaped a bit like a spaceship at the end of Taj East Gate Road, the Brahma Kumaris Gallery of Spiritual Love and Wisdom (Taj East Gate Rd., tel. 562/223-2221, 8 A.M.-8 P.M. daily, free), refreshingly has absolutely nothing to do with the Mughals. This small museum, run by the Brahma Kumaris, a Hindu sect with a large international following,

MUGHAL GARDENS

The Taj Mahal's verdant garden was constructed in the *char bagh* style.

One of the most noticeable architectural relics of the Mughal Empire are the many well-planned gardens they laid out during their rule. The tradition started in India with Babur, who built Agra's Ram Bagh in the 16th century, and was carried on by his descendants. Most were built in the quadrilateral *char bagh* style, the roots of which can be traced to ancient Persia. *Char bagh* gardens feature a geometrically exact series of pathways, rectangular green spaces, and terraced cascading fountains, and are designed with four quadrants to represent Eden and the concept of paradise on earth. The garden of the Taj Mahal was also built in this style.

is filled with plaster statues and information panels describing the beliefs of the organization with regard to self-mastery, reincarnation, and karma. Ask to see the peaceful meditation room in the basement.

AGRA'S OUTSKIRTS
Akbar's Tomb (Sikandra)

About six kilometers north of Agra on the road to Delhi, Akbar's Tomb (NH 2, Sikandra, sunrise-sunset daily, Rs. 110 foreigners, Rs. 10 Indians) is often referred to simply as Sikandra, the name of the township in which it stands. Akbar the Great selected this location as his final resting place, although he died before the tomb could be completed; his son Jehangir finished the job in 1613. Akbar's daughters, Aram Bano and Shakrul Nisha Begum, are also interred here. This five-story tomb is made of red sandstone and combines elements of both Hindu and Muslim architecture, a reflection of the interfaith tolerance that marked the latter part of Akbar's reign. Unlike many structures of

© MARGOT BIGG

Akbar's Tomb in Sikandra

the era, it does not have a domed roof. The stunning entryway at the southern gate features intricate floral and geometrical designs that appear to be *pietra dura* but are actually mosaics. The 16-hectare garden surrounding the tomb is a beautiful place to lounge and is home to herds of deer and plenty of primates, most of which are relatively nonaggressive Hanuman langurs.

Mariam's Tomb

If you're already in Sikandra and have some spare time, Mariam's Tomb (sunrise-sunset daily, Rs. 100 foreigners, Rs. 5 Indians), west of Akbar's Tomb, is worth a visit. Here lies the remains of Akbar's wife, Mariam Zamani, who was the Princess of Amber (near Jaipur). Originally built as a pavilion by Sikandar Lodi in 1495, this elongated red sandstone building still contains the faint remains of murals painted during the Lodi era. Mariam's cenotaph sits on the open-air upper floor of the structure.

◀ Fatehpur Sikri

No visitor to Agra should miss a visit to the UNESCO World Heritage Site city of Fatehpur Sikri (sunrise-sunset daily, Rs. 260 foreigners, Rs. 20 Indians), 37 kilometers west of Agra on the Jaipur-Agra Highway (NH 11). The city was established as a new capital by Akbar in 1570, after local Sufi saint Salim Chishti blessed Akbar with a son, Jehangir. According to local legend, the saint actually sacrificed his own six-month-old son, thereby sending the soul of the infant into the womb of Akbar's wife. The delighted Akbar built extensive palaces and courtyards out of red sandstone. The city was later abandoned, likely due to a lack of potable water in the area.

The primary entry is next to **Jodh Bai's Palace.** This structure was built between 1570 and 1574, and despite its name the Archeological Survey of India believes it has nothing to do with Jodh Bai. The western part of the palace hosts a small Hindu shrine, and

© MARGOT BIGG

Sheikh Salim Chishti's shrine in Fatehpur Sikri

the roof is covered with azure-hued glazed tiles. Next to this structure is **Mariam's Palace,** a two-story structure built for Akbar's wife. Continue toward the five-story **Panch Mahal,** a beautiful pavilion that slightly resembles a pagoda, with progressively smaller floors from bottom to top. The building was used for recreation by the women of the court. The **Diwan-i-Khas** (Hall of Private Audiences) used to be elaborately embellished with painted Persian verses and murals, but only traces remain today. The structure has built-in shelves that were likely used to store books. The southern window was known as the Darshan Jharoka (Viewing Window), and Akbar appeared here daily to greet his subjects. Just next to the Diwan-i-Khas is the Hall of Public Audiences, the **Diwan-i-Aam,** where Akbar made rulings. The building is surrounded by large cloisters on three sides in which litigants would sit. The fourth side was reserved for the royal women.

Near the main complex and up some dizzyingly steep stairs sits the **Buland Darwaza** (Victory Gate), built by Akbar in the late 16th century in commemoration of his victory over Gujarat. The sandstone gate is inlayed with geometric designs in black and white marble. The main archway is flanked with verses from the Koran on three sides as well as a quote from Jesus, reflective of Akbar's staunch pluralistic ideals. Some claim the 54-meter-high structure to be the largest gateway in the world.

Behind the gate is the **Jama Masjid,** an immense mosque dating from 1571, as well as the white marble *dargah* (shrine) of Salim Chishti, where Salim Chishti's *urs* festival is held every year during Ramadan. The shrine is supported by pillars that contain a built-in drainage system that drains water into a tank below. Devotees come to the *dargah* to honor the saint and make wishes by tying red string to the interior latticed screens. Qawwali (Sufi devotional music) performances are held regularly. Note that men and women alike should cover their heads when entering the shrine;

© RAJAT DEEP RANA

Fatehpur Sikri's Buland Darwaza is believed to be the world's largest gate.

if you don't have a hat or a scarf, you can borrow a plastic skullcap at the entrance in exchange for a small donation of your choosing. Entry to the mosque complex and the shrine are free, regardless of whether you have a ticket to the main Fatehpur Sikri monument.

GETTING THERE

Fatehpur Sikri is best accessed by road, and run-down local buses (Rs. 40) run regularly from Agra's Igdah Bus Stand. A few buses stop at the bus stand in Fatehpur Sikri, a short walk from the monument; alternatively, any bus to Jaipur or Bharatpur will drop you at the Bypass Road, from where you can take a shared autorickshaw (Rs. 5 pp, but foreigners are often asked to pay more) to central Fatehpur Sikri. Uttar Pradesh Tourism also offers half-day tours to Fatehpur Sikri (Rs. 550 foreigners, Rs. 300 Indians, Rs. 300 children, includes entrance to the monument); these leave at 10:30 A.M. from Agra's Cantt. Railway station and get you back to Agra at 3 P.M. Bookings can be made at tourism offices or through UP Tours (Rahi Tourist Bungalow, near Raja ki Mandi Railway Station, tel. 562/285-0120, rahitbagra@up-tourism.com).

Mathura and Vrindavan

About 50 kilometers from Agra on National Highway 2 on the way to Delhi, the twin holy towns of Mathura and Vrindavan are perfect for a pit stop. Mathura is believed to be the birthplace of Lord Krishna, an avatar of the Hindu god Vishnu, and every year thousands of Vaishnavites (devotees of Vishnu) come to pay their obeisance. The town is also famous for its elaborate celebrations of the Holi festival, where people throw powdered colors (and sometimes mild dyes) on each other to welcome the onset of spring. The area is particularly known for the Lath mar Holi celebration, where women arm themselves with long sticks to chase color-throwing men away. There's not a lot to do in this town except visit a few unspectacular

LORD KRISHNA

One of the best-known and most beloved Indian deities, Lord Krishna is believed to be the eighth avatar of Vishnu, the preserver in the Hindu trinity. He is believed to have once walked the earth and spent much of his time in Vrindavan and Mathura, where he was born. The great Indian epic the *Mahabharata* contains many tales of the god's life, and the best-known section, the Bhagavad Gita, recounts a conversation between Krishna and the prince Arjuna.

Many of the stories of Krishna recount his childhood in a cow-herding community. He was often mischievous and was known for stealing butter and playing pranks with his friends. He was also a great protector of his people, and even as a child he was known to kill adversaries. Krishna's uncle Kansa, the ruler of the Vrishni kingdom where Krishna grew up, had

been trying to assassinate Krishna since the child was born. Krishna eventually destroyed Kansa and made Ugrasena king. Krishna later went to battle as a charioteer (so that he would not have to wield weapons) in the Kurukshetra War. He is believed to have died when a hunter shot him in the foot, mistaking it for a deer, and Krishna's mortal death is believed by many to mark the beginning of the Kali Yuga, the final of four cycles that the world goes through before starting over again.

Krishna is worshiped across India by Vaishnavites, devotees of Vishnu and his incarnations. He also figures prominently in the bhakti (devotional) form of worship. Krishna is often paired with his consort Radha, his most beloved milkmaid, in the form of Radha Krishna.

temples, but many visitors like to make a quick stop at the government-run **Mathura Museum** (Dampier Park, 10:30 A.M.-4:30 P.M. Tues.-Sun., tel. 565/250-0847, Rs. 25 foreigners, Rs. 5 Indians), a beautiful red sandstone archaeological museum housing centuries' worth of religious statuary, pottery, and coins.

About 10 kilometers from Mathura, Vrindavan is the prettier and more interesting of the two towns, filled with enough temples and little lanes to keep visitors of any faith occupied for an hour or two. The most famous temple is the 19th-century **Banke Bihari Mandir** (town center, 7 A.M.-9 P.M. daily), home to a mysterious idol of Lord Krishna that, according to local belief, can cause devotees to

faint if they look into its eyes. The idol is therefore kept behind a curtain that is only opened for a few seconds at a time before being quickly shut again. The **Krishna Balaram Mandir** (Bhaktivedanta Swami Marg, Raman Reti, tel. 936/447-8207, www.24hourkirtan.com, 24 hours daily), run by the International Society for Krishna Consciousness (ISKCON), a.k.a. the Hare Krishnas, hosts a never-ending session of *kirtan* (devotional singing) that has been going nonstop for the past 25-plus years. There's also a branch of ISKCON's vegetarian restaurant **Govinda's** (tel. 565/254-0021, 8 A.M.-3 P.M. and 5-9:30 P.M. daily, Rs. 80) in the temple guesthouse. This is arguably the cleanest place to eat in town.

Entertainment and Events

NIGHTLIFE

When it comes to nightlife, Agra is as dead as it gets. It's a fairly conservative city with strict liquor laws, and as there are no major universities, the club scene is pretty much nonexistent, save for one hotel club that closes at 11 P.M. Most locals party at friends' houses or brave the four-hour drive up to Delhi if they want to go out. If you feel like drinking, your best bet is to head to the bar in one of the many five-star hotels in town.

Inside the Jaypee Hotel complex, **2010** (Jaypee Palace Hotel, Fatehabad Rd., tel. 562/233-0800, www.jaypeehotels.com, 7-11 P.M. Sat.-Sun., Rs. 500) is the only nightclub in town. This small, shady "discotheque," if you can call it that, only admits couples and is only open on Saturday and, oddly, Sunday. The DJ plays a collection of Bollywood hits, American pop, and hip-hop. You can rent out the whole club for private events, although you're better off waiting until you get to Delhi to do any clubbing.

The Radisson's chichi **Lizard Lounge** (Radisson Hotel Agra, Taj East Gate Rd., tel. 562/405-5555, www.radisson.com, noon-midnight daily) provides a nice modern break from all the pomp and marble of Agra. Like the rest of the hotel, the interiors here border on futuristic and feature glass-beaded curtains and velveteen chaise longues. Check out the trippy false ceiling, which resembles a motherboard. There's a wide selection of imported liquor, including lots of single-malt scotch. The bar attracts a mix of mature Indian guests and foreigners of all ages, and it is quiet enough that you can enjoy a good chat without having to yell into your interlocutor's ear.

Although far from happening, the bar at **The Oberoi Amarvilas** (Taj East Gate Rd., tel. 562/223-1515, www.oberoihotels.com, noon-midnight daily) is open to nonguests and provides a great opportunity to catch a glimpse of the interiors of Agra's most spectacular hotel. The furnishings are elegant and old-fashioned, giving the impression of a gentlemen's club (in the traditional sense of the word) from days of yore. The views of the Taj Mahal are among the best in town, especially from the small adjoining terrace.

THE ARTS

Sadly, and surprisingly, Agra has very little going on when it comes to the arts, perhaps because it's hard to compete with a masterpiece such as the Taj Mahal. There are no proper art museums to speak of, and most of the self-proclaimed art galleries are nothing more than glorified souvenir shops. However, fans of the performing arts will appreciate Agra's two major spectacles.

Part play, part sound-and-light show, the dramatic **Mohabbat the Taj: The Saga of Love** (41/142 A-1 VIP Rd., tel. 562/223-1011, www.kalakritionline.com, 6:30 P.M. daily, Rs. 400-3,000) narrates the tale of how the Taj Mahal came to be through the love story of Mumtaz and Shahjahan. The spectacle features a meticulously crafted Makarana marble replica of the Taj Mahal as its centerpiece, which, at the crescendo of the performance, rises up onto the stage.

Agra's other major performance, the hour-long **Agra Fort Sound and Light Show** (in English 8:15 P.M. daily, Rs. 150 foreigners, Rs. 40 Indians, Rs. 25 students), provides insight into the history of the fort and to Agra, accompanied by brilliant lighting. Showtimes are known to change frequently, so check ahead at the fort if possible.

Cinemas

Agra has a couple of comfortable air-conditioned

cinemas. The four-screen **Fun Cinemas** (Pacific Taj Mall, Fatehabad Rd., tel. 562/200-8045, www.funcinemas.com) shows both English and Hindi films throughout the day and well into the night. **BIG Cinemas** (TGI Mall, Fatehabad Rd., tel. 936/810-3619, www.bigcinemas.com/in) also shows a mix of Bollywood and Hollywood films.

FESTIVALS AND EVENTS
Taj Mahotsav

Every year, the Uttar Pradesh Tourism Department invites artisans from across India to hawk their regional wares at the government-run Shilpgram complex for Taj Mahotsav (Feb. 18-27). Although Shilpgram is a great place to shop year-round, the selection during the festival is considerably better, when the number of booths swells to around 400. Taj Mahotsav is essentially one big shopping fest, although performances, mostly of traditional dances from various regions of India, and an assortment of regional food stalls make the festival a bit more palatable for people who are all shopped out.

Sheetala Fair

The annual religious Sheetala Fair (July-Aug.) is held in honor of Sheetala Ashtami, a goddess revered by people of the local village of Chakshu for her ability to prevent and cure smallpox. Numerous ceremonies are held to appease her and to guarantee the good health of devotees for the year to come.

Kailash Fair

Held near Sikandra, the Kailash Fair (Aug.-Sept.) honors Lord Shiva, the destroyer in the Hindu pantheon, whom devotees believe manifested himself here at the Kailash Temple in the form of a stone lingam. People come to make offerings, chant, and pray to the deity.

Bateshwar Fair

The monthlong Bateshwar Fair (Oct.-Nov.), held in honor of Lord Shiva, takes place in Bateshwar, about 65 kilometers from Agra. Pilgrims from across India descend on Bateshwar to bathe in its holy waters during this auspicious month. It's also one of the best-known cattle fairs in North India, and herders from across the region come to show off and sell their livestock.

Ram Barat

One of Agra's most famous events, the Ram Barat (Oct.-Nov.) is a symbolic reenactment of the marriage procession of the Hindu god Rama, the protagonist of one of India's best-known religious texts, the *Ramayana*. The location of this three-day festival shifts to a different part of Agra every year, and the area is decorated with flowers and lights to prepare for the procession.

Salim Chishti's *Urs*

It's common in India for Muslims make pilgrimages to shrines of saints on the anniversary of their deaths, where huge ceremonies known as *urs* are held. Fatehpur Sikri hosts one such *urs* every year during the Islamic calendar's month of Ramadan at the mausoleum of Sufi saint Salim Chishti, where Muslims and non-Muslims alike gather to pay homage to Chishti and partake in festivities that range from Qawwali performances to camel rides.

Shopping

When it comes to shopping, Agra pales in comparison to Delhi and Jaipur, but there are still a few places to pick up interesting souvenirs. The most popular Agra craft is marble inlayed with semiprecious stones; marble boxes, coasters, fridge magnets, and tabletops dominate most of the city's handicraft emporiums. *Zari*, gold string embroidery originating from Persia (in Iran today it's known as *zardozi*), is also big in Agra. Brassware, woven rugs, jewelry, and carved elephants made of light-brown Indian jade are also popular souvenirs. Agra has a large leather industry, and many European shoe manufacturers get production work done here.

HANDICRAFT EMPORIUMS

Most of the handicraft emporiums are located along Fatehabad Road, and the majority of them sell more or less the same type of merchandise, namely marble inlay tchotchkes, *zari* embroidery work, saris, costume jewelry, woven rugs, and books on India.

Next to Hotel Sheela, just a few steps away from the Taj Mahal's East Gate, **Agra Cottage Industry** (Eastern Gate Rd., tel. 562/329-4231, 7 A.M.-7 P.M. daily) is an excellent place to pick up marble inlay pieces. The staff here are polite and less pushy than most Agra shopkeepers, and there's often a marble worker crafting away just in front of the shop.

The cozy **Anokhi Handicraft** (opposite Hotel Atithi, Fatehabad Rd., tel. 562/401-2898, mehraj1970@yahoo.com, 8 A.M.-8 P.M. daily) stocks a small assortment of typical Agra souvenirs as well as vases, sandalwood carvings, and beautiful (but quite overpriced) sitars. There is also an excellent selection of coffee-table books.

The enormous **Kalakriti** (41/142 A-1 VIP Rd., tel. 562/223-1011, www.kalakritionline.com, 9 A.M.-8 P.M. daily) is one of the few handicraft emporiums in Agra that's actually fun to shop at. Beautiful statues are strewn throughout the garden surrounding this massive red building. There's a huge showroom inside featuring high-quality and tasteful handicrafts from across India, all carefully selected with a more art-oriented customer base in mind. The play *Mohabbat the Taj*, which tells the story of the Taj Mahal, is also staged here.

The Agra branch of Rajasthan's state government–run handicraft emporium **Rajasthali** (Taj Complex, tel. 562/233-0417, www.rajasthali.gov.in, 10:30 A.M.-7 P.M. Mon.-Sat.) is the perfect place to pick up any items that you wished you'd bought in Jaipur. The emporium sells everything from the mirrored cushion covers ubiquitous in Rajasthan to beautiful silver and enamel jewelry. It may come as a relief to know that there's no need to bargain in this fixed-price shop.

You could easily get lost in the sprawling **U. P. Handicrafts Development Centre** (Handicraft Nagar, Fatehabad Rd., tel. 562/233-3167, 10 A.M.-8 P.M. daily). The lobby houses a 60-centimeter-tall marble replica of the Taj Mahal, and various doors lead to different sections of the complex, each of which focuses on a particular handicraft. They often showcase live displays of marble working, and the staff are happy to explain the process to visitors. The center is popular with large tour groups, so visit on your own for better prices.

MARKETS

In the backyard of the Shilpgram tourist complex, the open-air government-managed **Shilp Haat** (Shilpgram, Taj East Gate Rd., 8:30 A.M.-6:30 P.M. Sat.-Thurs.) is clean, tourist-friendly, and a little bit Disneyesque. Traders from across India come to hawk everything from plastic Taj Mahal key rings to pashmina shawls. It's a comfortable place to browse, and although the

© MARGOT BIGG

Agra is known for its *zari* embroidery.

prices are a bit inflated, you'll be helping someone make an honest living rather than lining the pockets of conniving touts.

In the leafy Agra Cantonment area, **Sadar Bazaar** (Saudagar Lines, between MG Rd. and Gwalior Rd., most shops 10 A.M.-8 P.M. Wed.-Mon.) is popular with both visitors and locals alike. You'll find plenty of restaurants and a smattering of standard handicraft dealers. If you're looking for leather, don't miss the great selection of "export-quality" goods on sale at **Taj Leather World** (B-28 Shopping Arcade, Sadar Bazar, tel. 562/222-5076, noon-10 P.M. daily), which stocks an extensive selection of products ranging from jackets to luggage in pretty much every color you could imagine. Another Sadar Bazar must is **Pancchi Petha** (Sadar Bazar, tel. 562/325-3478, www.pancchipetha.com, 9 A.M.-9 P.M. daily), the most famous and hygiene-conscious manufacturer of *petha*, Agra's signature sweet, made from white pumpkin and sugar. The company has been in operation for over 70 years and produces all types of *petha,* ranging from the traditional plain variety to *petha* flavored with cherry and coconut.

Hing ki Mandi is the traditional stronghold of Agra's shoe industry, and it's a great place to pick up footwear and other leather goods at rock-bottom prices. Be prepared to bargain, and beware of shoddy quality; a lot of substandard pieces end up here. A number of shoe manufacturers and importers are headquartered on the Bypass Road toward Delhi, before you reach Sikandra—you can find amazing deals on shoes that would likely cost a fortune back home.

If you'd like to see where locals go to buy everything from plastic buckets to bangles, head to **Kinari Bazaar** (near Agra Fort). This loud and chaotic market isn't great for souvenirs, but it's a wonderful place to take photos and people-watch. If you're in the market for saris or other traditional clothing, you'll get a much better deal here than in any of the handicraft emporiums.

SHOPPING MALLS

Agra has two major shopping malls, **TDI Mall** and **Taj Pacific Mall** (both on Fatehabad Rd.), and as is most Indian cities, they are right next door to each other. The shops in both malls focus on shoes, Indian women's wear, and sportswear, although they are best known by locals for their cinemas. TDI is also home to one of Agra's rare branches of McDonald's, not the most appealing choice for foodies, but a potential boon for people with small children who can't stomach Indian food. Neither mall is particularly worth a visit unless nature happens to call while you're nearby or you need a place to take an air-conditioned break.

Sports and Recreation

Agra has very little going on in terms of sports, and most people rely on their hotel gyms, pools, and yoga classes to stay fit during their trips to the city. Spas, on the other hand, are much more abundant, and although the best ones are generally located in hotels, most, including those listed below, are open to nonguests.

GOLF

If you'd like to putt with the Taj Mahal in the background, your best option is the 18-hole **Agra Golf Course** (191 The Mall, MG Rd., tel. 562/222-6579, www.agraclub.com, 6 A.M.-4:30 P.M. daily, Rs. 1,000 pp). The course is run by the Agra Club, one of the many old-school membership clubs that still abound in India, so you'll likely get the chance to meet a few local golfers during your round.

SPAS

The flagship location of the ITC Hotel Group's **Kaya Kalp** (ITC Mughal, Fatehabad Rd., tel. 562/402-1700, www.itchotels.in, 8 A.M.-10 P.M. daily), a growing chain of spas, has been awarded numerous accolades, and it's no wonder why: This enormous spa is among India's most impressive, and many clients come to Agra not for the Taj Mahal but simply to experience the treatments here. The signature Kaya Kalp massage (60 minutes Rs. 3,750, 90 minutes Rs. 4,800) focuses on tension relief, and therapists are good at finding the exact amount of pressure appropriate for each individual client. There are eight treatment rooms, including a large hammam (Turkish bath) and an ayurvedic treatment room. Like the rest of the ITC Mughal, Kaya Kalp's interiors are inspired by Mughal art with a modern twist. The main theme is the pomegranate, believed to have been brought to India by the royal Mughal rulers, and ruby red curlicue motifs with integrated pomegranates run along the walls and floors of the spa. There's also a large outdoor area that hosts a variety of tropical plants as well as a plant-filled conservatory. Spa guests can use the 25-meter lap pool after their treatments.

The quiet **Radisson Agra Spa** (Taj East Gate Rd., tel. 562/405-5555, www.radisson.com, 9 A.M.-9 P.M. daily) specializes in massage and offers a number of relaxing and stress-relieving treatments that range from Swedish massage (Rs. 2,600) to the signature Thai massage (Rs. 2,500), an oil-free, fully-clothed style of bodywork in which the therapist stretches and flexes tired muscles. In line with the treatment focus, the decor is more Thai than Indian, and the darkened lighting and soft music are likely to send you off to sleep during your treatment.

For good old-fashioned ayurvedic treatments at reasonable prices, head to a branch of

Verma's Kairali Ayurvedic Health Spa (tel. 983/728-4249, hours vary), a chain of hotel-based ayurvedic spas run by Dr. K. S. Verma. Dr. Verma is trained in yoga, ayurveda, and Reiki, and he integrates these different teachings into his therapies. Specialties include *shirodhara* (Rs. 2,000), a traditional ayurvedic massage in which medicated oil is slowly dripped onto the client's forehead, creating a sense of well-being while simultaneously moisturizing the hair. The spa has plenty of outlets around town, including at the **Hotel Crystal Inn** (Behind TDI Mall, Fatehabad Rd., tel. 562/405-3400), **Bhoomi Residency** (1 Amar Lok, Taj Link Rd., near Shilpgram, tel. 562/223-2101), and the **Raj Mahal Hotel** (AC 1-2 Taj Nagri Phase II, tel. 562/402-3625), to name a few.

SWIMMING

If you're staying somewhere without a pool and feel like taking a dip, you have quite a few options in Agra. Water parks and municipal pools tend to be loud, crowded, and primarily patronized by young men who consider boxer shorts proper swimming attire; they are best avoided, especially by women. Instead, try one of the hotel swimming pools that are open to nonguests. The **Mansingh Palace** (Fatehabad Rd., tel. 562/233-1771, 6 A.M.-7 P.M. daily, Rs. 300 pp, Rs. 500 per couple) offers one of the best deals in town. Alternatively, try the pool at **Hotel Amar** (Tourist Complex Area, Fatehabad Rd., tel. 562/233-1884, 6 A.M.-7:30 P.M. daily, Rs. 400 pp). The staff at both places are pretty laid-back, and once you've paid, they're not too strict about how long you stay.

Accommodations

Agra has accommodations to suit all budgets, from tiny backpacker holes-in-the-wall to opulent award-winning properties. Although there are hotels scattered around the city, the majority are on Fatehabad Road and Taj East Gate Road, never more than a few kilometers from the Taj Mahal. Most of the very low-cost guesthouses are in the area around the Taj Mahal known as Taj Ganj; surprisingly, this prime location is one of the shabbiest parts of town and thus has only a handful of midrange and upscale options.

The high season in Agra is October-March, although some hoteliers start their high-season rates in September. Outside this period, it's advisable to bargain hard—it's not unheard of for hotel rooms to go for less than half their published rate. Peak occupancy at most hotels is over the Christmas-New Year's holidays, so if you plan to travel during this time, it's a good idea to book well in advance.

UNDER RS. 1,000

If you're after a bargain, it doesn't get much cheaper than the **Shahjahan Hotel & Restaurant** (South Gate, Taj Ganj, tel. 562/320-0240, shahjahan_hotel@hotmail.com, Rs. 450-850 d). This small, ultrabudget guesthouse operates with the backpacker set in mind, and the guest rooms are bare-bones but relatively clean. The more expensive rooms have air-conditioning, a bonus in the summer months but a waste of money November-February. They also offer free pickup from Agra's train and bus stations.

Hotel Sheela (Taj East Gate Rd., Taj Ganj, tel. 562/233-3074, www.hotelsheelaagra.com, Rs. 600-800 d) offers clean, backpacker-focused accommodations at excellent prices. The grounds are set back a bit from the road, and there's a guard at the gate at night, making it a good choice for solo female backpackers. A pair of fluffy Pomeranians live on-site, and light sleepers should be prepared for early-morning yapping sessions. The guest rooms are clean, and many of the air-conditioned guest rooms have recently been refurbished, but some lack hot water. If you book ahead, make sure to confirm the rate quoted to you, as this guesthouse has been known to attempt to overcharge weary travelers. The on-site restaurant is clean, but the food is nothing special.

A stone's throw from the western gate of the Taj Mahal, **Hotel Sidhartha** (Western Gate, Taj Ganj, tel. 562/223-0901, www.hotelsidhartha.com, Rs. 600-800 d) has long been a popular spot for backpackers and other travelers trying to keep their lodging expenses to a minimum. The air-conditioned and unair-conditioned guest rooms are simple and don't feature extras such as TVs or telephones. However, the location is hard to beat, and the quiet garden courtyard is a good place to unwind after a long day of sightseeing.

RS. 1,000-3,000

The major selling point of the state-run **⟨ Hotel Taj Khema** (Taj East Gate Rd., Taj Ganj, tel. 562/233-0140, www.up-tourism.com, Rs. 1,600-2,600 d) is its grassy hillock with spectacular views of the eastern side of the Taj Mahal, some 200 meters away. Nonguests have to pay Rs. 200 for a cup of tea and a few biscuits on the mound (Rs. 300 on Fri., when the Taj is closed to the public), but hotel guests can while away as much time as they want with the great monument as the backdrop. There's a small playground and a larger bird feeding area, popular with resident peacocks. Book early if you are coming in high season, as there are only 14 guest rooms. Eight of these are charming "Swiss Cottages," all of which feature balconies with swing seats.

Set back from the main drag of Fatehabad Road, **The Karawan Grand Casa** (8 Bansal Nagar, Tourist Complex Area, Fatehabad Rd., tel. 562/405-3000, www.karawanhotels.com, Rs. 2,000 d) offers relatively quiet, spotless

guest rooms that are good value despite being slightly on the small side. Because the hotel is off the main road, the guest rooms are a bit quieter than those in neighboring properties. Sadly, unlike most hotels in the area, there's no pool. There is, however, free Wi-Fi throughout the property. The rates are flexible, so bargain hard, especially during the off-season.

Hotel Amar Yatri Niwas (Tourist Complex Area, Fatehabad Rd., tel. 562/233-3030, www.amaryatriniwas.com, Rs. 1,800-2,100 d) boasts a welcoming and professional staff, clean guest rooms (all with bathtubs, a rarity in India), and room service from its hygienic on-site restaurant. The hotel also offers group discounts and a variety of meal plans, but with only 41 guest rooms, it's a cozier and more personable place to stay than your average Fatehabad Road tourgroup haven. There's also a branch of British coffee chain Costa Coffee and a Thomas Cook office on the ground floor. Unfortunately, there's no pool, but guests can swim for Rs. 200 per hour (half the normal fee) at the nearby Hotel Amar.

RS. 3,000-10,000

A favorite with both Indian and overseas package tourists, the three-star **Hotel Amar** (Tourist Complex Area, Fatehabad Rd., tel. 562/233-1884, www.hotelamar.com, Rs. 3,800-5,000) is clean, well-maintained, and a decent value. Some of the guest rooms are a bit gaudy, with an overuse of mismatched fabrics and cheaply designed columns, but this adds an Indian-kitsch flavor and keeps the Amar from being drab. The staff are knowledgeable and helpful, although not exactly friendly, in stark contrast to the lovely staff at Amar Yatri Niwas, the sister property up the road. The pool has a small waterslide and is open to nonguests willing to pay Rs. 400 per hour for the privilege.

The **⟨ Radisson Hotel Agra** (Taj East Gate Rd., tel. 562/405-5555, www.radisson.com, Rs. 8,500-9,500), one of Agra's youngest luxury hotels, opened for business in mid-2011 and quickly became one of the most popular hotels in town, perhaps because the rates are shockingly good. The contemporary decor is a relieving contrast to the marble- and sandstone-gone-wild themes that the majority of Agra's high-end hotels are fond of. The lobby is music-themed; notice the abstract statues of musical notes and bongos. Although this property is more leisure-oriented than the average business-focused Radisson in the United States, it is still quite a good place to hold conferences, and there's even an entire floor designed with the requirements of executive clientele in mind.

The 67-room **◖ Hotel Utkarsh Vilas** (Fatehabad Rd., tel. 562/223-0056, www.utkarshvilas.com, Rs. 8,000 d) is among the most sophisticated midrange options in Agra, with friendly but nonintrusive staff and spick-and-span facilities. This centrally air-conditioned property features a beautiful marble lobby adorned with hand-painted pillars and arches, a relieving contrast to the dusty and traffic-laden Fatehabad Road. The guest rooms are elegantly appointed, with floor-to-ceiling windows and light wood floors. Like many of Agra's properties, a little bargaining will get you a large discount, so try to book over the phone and ask for a better price.

A short jaunt from the Taj Mahal's East Gate, **Hotel Taj Resorts** (near Shilpgram, Taj East Gate Rd., tel. 562/223-0160, www.hoteltajresorts.com, Rs. 4,000-6,000 d) offers spotless guest rooms that are surprisingly quiet considering the hotel's main road location. The staff are charming and go out of their way to make guests feel well looked-after. The small rooftop pool doesn't have Taj Mahal views, but it's still great for cooling down at the end of the day.

Bhoomi Residency (1 Amar Lok, Taj Link Rd., near Shilpgram, tel. 562/223-2101, www.bhoomiresidency.com, Rs. 3,500-4,500 d) offers some of the best accommodations deals in the Taj Ganj area, although it's the incredibly charming and helpful staff that make this property stand out from the other less-inspiring hotels around it. The guest rooms are simply decorated but very clean, and all feature LCD TVs. There's a small ayurvedic spa on-site as well as a rooftop pool with views of the Taj Mahal.

Hotel Crystal Inn (behind TDI Mall, Fatehabad Rd., tel. 562/405-3400, www.hotelcrystalinn.com, Rs. 4,000-5,500 d) features clean guest rooms, all of which are equipped with a medium-size fridge. Executive rooms include a small futon lounge area that can double as an extra bed. There's also a tiny ayurvedic spa (really just a massage room) on-site. The air-conditioned rooftop restaurant is entirely encased in glass and serves Indian, Chinese, and continental cuisine. Room service is available 24 hours daily.

Tucked away from the main drag of touts and tourist traps, the **Trident Agra** (Fatehabad Rd., tel. 562/223-5000, www.tridenthotels.com, Rs. 8,000 d) is popular with families and independent travelers. Dishes from the wood-fired oven in the restaurant (aptly named The Restaurant) are some of the best in town. The lobby is decorated in welcoming yellows and whites, with plenty of vases of freshly cut yellow roses. The colorful patterned carpeting in the halls looks better suited to an airport than a hotel, but the guest rooms, with their deep pastel hues and Santa Fe–inspired upholstery, give the place a less institutional feel. The Trident is run by the Oberoi Group, and the staff here meet and exceed the parent company's high standards.

Considering its prime location just over one kilometer from the Taj Mahal, the **Hotel Pushp Villa** (Taj East Gate Rd., near Fatehabad Rd., tel. 562/329-0267, www.hotelpushpvilla.com, Rs. 3,600-4,600 d) is an excellent value. The guest rooms are kept in tip-top shape, and some even have views of the Taj Mahal. There's a branch of the omnipotent Kairali Ayurvedic Spa as well as a beauty salon and a banquet hall—expect to come across an Indian wedding or two if you come during the winter wedding season. Although the hotel is certainly a decent place to rest your head, it's best known for its revolving rooftop restaurant, Merry Go Round, which is popular with locals and travelers alike.

Popular with tour groups and middle-class Indian travelers, the **Mansingh Palace** (Fatehabad Rd., tel. 562/233-1771, www.mansinghhotels.com, Rs. 8,000 d) has all the Indo-bling of a five-star hotel at reasonable prices. The musty lobby, which looks like it was plucked from the set of a 1960s James Bond film, and aloof reception staff are a bit off-putting, but the hotel redeems itself with clean, well-maintained guest rooms and facilities. The halls feature green marble offset with dark wood, adding to the old-school understated elegance that the property seems to be going for.

RS. 10,000 AND UP

◖ **The Oberoi Amarvilas** (Taj East Gate Rd., tel. 562/223-1515, www.obberoihotels.com, Rs. 30,000-40,000 d) is without a doubt the most luxurious property in Agra, although it comes at a high price. The marble-dominated interiors are Mughal inspired without being over-the-top, and they incorporate elements such as *pietra dura* floral inlays, geometric patterns, and gold-leaf embellishment. The spa features ayurvedic and Western massage treatments as well as excellent revitalizing facials. The outdoor pool is enchanting, with built-in archways and a covered section. The property is especially impressive at night, when the terraced fountains that lead down to the pool are lit up. All of the guest rooms here have teak floors, large baths with tubs, and stunning views of the Taj Mahal.

Proudly touting itself as the largest hotel in Agra, **Jaypee Palace Hotel & Convention Centre** (Fatehabad Rd., tel. 562/233-0800, www.jaypeehotels.com, Rs. 10,000-11,000 d) is a popular conference and convention spot. It seems to have been designed with the domestic guest in mind, with features like a private cinema and a gaming arcade among its top selling points. The 341 guest rooms are furnished with light wood floors and come with bathtubs. Some also have balconies overlooking the expansive property. Because of its size, the hotel can feel a bit institutional, but at least the separate check-in and checkout sections of the lobby help reduce the potential for chaos.

Formerly known as the Mughal Sheraton and still referred to as such by locals, the massive **ITC Mughal** (Fatehabad Rd., tel. 562/402-1700, www.itchotels.in, Rs. 11,800 d) is a destination in itself, with recreational activities ranging from an all-terrain vehicle track to a butterfly garden. The spa, Kaya Kalp, has been voted one of the best in Asia. The design of the hotel acts as a history lesson, and each area is named after a Mughal emperor. The recently refurbished lobby houses modern interpretations of Mughal designs, including a mesmerizing chandelier made of smaller Mughal-era lanterns. About one-quarter of the guest rooms fall into the suite category; the most impressive are in the newest wing, the Khwab Mahal (Palace of Dreams). Honeymooners should ask for one of the romantic presidential suites, all of which feature private outdoor pools and en-suite therapy rooms.

Formerly known as the Taj View Hotel, **The Gateway Hotel** (Fatehabad Rd., tel. 562/660-2000, www.thegatewayhotels.com, Rs. 11,000-14,500) is among the best-known hotels in town. The standard guest rooms here are furnished with modern fixtures, whereas the Executive Taj Facing guest rooms incorporate marble and red sandstone in their interiors, a nod to the Taj Mahal. There's a whole slew of activities on this 2.4-hectare property, including puppet shows, tennis, cooking demonstrations, temporary-tattoo artists, and even an Indian astrologer. Another bonus is that the entire property is Wi-Fi enabled, even at the pool. There's an ayurvedic spa specializing in detox therapies, open only to hotel guests.

If you've ever dreamed of spending the night in the Taj Mahal (a bit of an alarming concept, considering it's a tomb), you'll adore the lavish **C Wyndham Grand Collection, Agra** (7th Milestone, Fatehabad Rd., tel. 562/223-7000, www.wyndham.com, Rs. 18,000-25,000 d), with its white marble centerpiece of a lobby surrounded by red sandstone wings. The hotel, formerly known as the Orient Taj, sits on 10 hectares and boasts the biggest pool in Agra; the complex took a decade to build. The deluxe guest rooms have fireplaces, and some even have steam showers. The standard guest rooms are organized in house-like clusters that wrap around sprawling Mughal-style gardens.

Food

Agra is not exactly known as a dining destination, and most of the good places to eat are in hotels and guesthouses. The main cuisine available is what's known as Mughalai food: rich, spicy, usually meat-based dishes favored by rulers during the Mughal Empire. Agra is best known for its local sweet specialty, *petha,* a glutinous dessert made from boiled white pumpkin.

Because Agra has a very strong culture of touting, even by Indian standards, you may find yourself dragged to one of the many overpriced stand-alone restaurants that flank Fatehabad Road and some parts of Agra Cantonment. These are generally safe places to eat, but the prices are inflated in order to subsidize the heavy commissions paid to tour guides and drivers, and the quality is generally not very high.

CAFÉS AND PATISSERIES

Lovingly abbreviated as CCD by most Indian coffee drinkers, **Café Coffee Day** (21/101 East Gate, Taj Ganj, tel. 9319/922-112, 6 A.M.-8 P.M. daily, entrées Rs. 60) is one of the few places in town (outside of the major hotels) where you can get a cup of fresh-brewed coffee. The pastries could use some work, but the coffee is wonderful, especially if you are planning a sunrise visit to the Taj Mahal. There are also outlets on Taj East Gate Road and Fatehabad Road.

EAST ASIAN

If you're in the mood for authentic Chinese food that hasn't been Indianized beyond recognition, **C'est Chine** (Jaypee Palace Hotel, Fatehabad Rd., tel. 562/233-0800, 12:30-3 P.M. and 7:30-11:30 P.M. daily, entrées Rs. 650) is your answer. The sous chef is originally from Hong Kong, and you can see him and his staff in action in the semi-open kitchen. The ground-floor restaurant incorporates a lot of gold into its interiors, and the floor-to-ceiling windows look out onto a reflecting pool. The specialty is chicken, although there are plenty of other options, ranging from soups and dim sum to the ever-popular prawns in oyster sauce.

INDIAN

In a city where heavy Mughalai food is the standard fare of most eating joints, the relatively light food at South Indian specialist **Dasaprakash** (9 Bansal Nagar, Fatehabad Rd., tel. 562/223-0089, 8 A.M.-10 P.M. daily, entrées Rs. 120) is a nice change. This small, simple, and very clean restaurant serves up the South Indian favorites *dosas* and *idlis.* For a more unusual concoction, try the cheese *uttapam,* a lentil-flour pancake with onion, coriander, and cheese mixed into the batter. The ice cream sundaes are equally noteworthy and feature local ice cream flavors such as mango, lychee, and pistachio.

Inside the Oberoi Amarvilas, **C Esphahan**

(Taj East Gate Rd., tel. 562/223-1515, seatings 7:30 and 9:30 P.M. daily, entrées Rs. 1,200) is among the most elegant and romantic choices in town. The restaurant is only open for dinner, and as there are only two seatings, reservations are strongly advised. Esphahan is intimate and well-staffed, and all the food is prepared in an open-view "live kitchen." The dishes are predominantly Mughalai, with a few items from other parts of India, such as the extra-spicy Kerala shrimp curry. Favorites include the quail curry (quail stuffed with chicken mince and served with saffron sauce) and the vegetarian *palak ke kofta,* spinach and cottage cheese dumplings in spinach gravy. If you can't make up your mind, vegetarian and nonvegetarian sampler platters known as *thalis* are available. Gluten-free and sugar-free options are also available.

For five-star dining at much lower prices, look no farther than ◖Jhankar (The Gateway Hotel, Fatehabad Rd., tel. 562/660-2000, 7:30 A.M.-11:30 P.M. daily, entrées Rs. 400), the smaller of the two restaurants in the Gateway Hotel. Like many of the hotel dining options in Agra, Jhankar features a live kitchen, and the crystal beaded curtains adorning its entryway add an elegant flair. The dishes here are inspired by local flavors but with much less spice. The delicious *shahi kaju aloo,* potato dumplings cooked in cashew gravy, is sweet and not too hot. The *dhania murg,* spiced chicken flavored with coriander, is equally appetizing. Don't miss the chef's own version of the local sweet, *petha.*

The gimmicky **Merry-Go-Round** (Top Fl., Hotel Pushp Villa, Taj East Gate Rd., near Fatehabad Rd., tel. 562/329-0267, 6:30-10:30 A.M., noon-3 P.M., and 7-11 P.M. daily, entrées Rs. 300) prides itself on being the only revolving restaurant in the state of Uttar Pradesh. The floor of this glass-walled restaurant completes one full rotation every 45 minutes, slow enough that you hardly notice it (a boon for those prone to motion sickness). The special of the house is the Merry-Go-Round

chicken, served in sweetish cashew gravy. They also have a well-stocked bar and serve classic cocktails such as gimlets and planter's punch.

Specializing in food from the Northwest Frontier, now the border between Pakistan and Afghanistan, the acclaimed **Peshawari** (ITC Mughal, Fatehabad Rd., tel. 562/402-1700, www.itchotels.in, 12:30-2:45 P.M. and 7:30-11:45 P.M. daily, entrées Rs. 2,000) is done up in a faux-rustic style in an attempt to give it the look of a rural roadside café. The result is slightly kitschier than perhaps was intended, but it's still a fun place to eat. The restaurant focuses on mutton-based kebabs, although there's still plenty of choice for vegetarians. Guests are encouraged to eat with their hands in the traditional way and are provided with checkered aprons for damage control. Cutlery, however, is available on request.

Pinch of Spice (1076/2 Fatehabad Rd., opposite ITC Mughal Hotel, tel. 562/404-5252, www.pinchofspice.in, noon-11:30 P.M. daily, entrées Rs. 200) is among the few stand-alone restaurants in Agra. The decor here is modern, with cubic lamps made of frosted glass and black, gray, and white furnishings. Somewhat oddly, the place smells of rose oil. They specialize in Punjabi food but also have a few pasta dishes and a smattering of Indo-Chinese favorites. Try the vegetarian *paneer* butter masala or the butter chicken, both of which are cooked in a rich and creamy tomato gravy and are best eaten with fluffy oven-baked naan bread.

Just behind the Shilpgram handicraft village, **Shilpgram Restaurant and Beer Bar** (Shilpgram, Taj East Gate Rd., tel. 562/223-3056, 7:30 A.M.-10:30 P.M. daily, entrées Rs. 100), looks like it was modeled after a high school cafeteria, but the food is good and the beer cold and cheap. Owned and operated by the Uttar Pradesh state tourism board, the restaurant serves up a variety of vegetarian and meat-based North Indian dishes made with fresh ingredients and spiced to order. If you come in the evening after the handicrafts village is closed for the night, you may even get the place to yourself.

MULTICUISINE

In the small garden courtyard of the Hotel Sidhartha, the **Garden Restaurant** (Hotel Sidhartha, Western Gate, Taj Ganj, tel. 562/223-09018, 6:30 A.M.-10 P.M. daily, entrées Rs. 60) dishes up Western breakfast omelets and toast as well as a large selection of North and South Indian specialties. They also have a few interpretations of Korean dishes, such as *dak juk,* a chicken porridge. Just don't expect to be transported to Seoul through your taste buds—the food is decisively Indianized. Don't miss the *puri sabzi,* deep-fried puffed breads similar to savory elephant ears served with vegetable curry; it's traditionally a breakfast food but great any time of day.

Although it only opened in mid-2011, **◖ Latitude: The Coffee Shop** (Radisson Agra, Taj East Gate Rd., tel. 562/405-5555, www.radisson.com, 24 hours daily) has already become a popular spot for well-heeled locals to meet and eat. The open-plan restaurant features slick contemporary furnishings and attentive service, although the main draw is the wide array of innovative dishes, including plenty of choices that you won't find anywhere else in town. Not only is there a huge selection of Indian kebabs inspired by regional cuisines from across the subcontinent, there's also a substantial selection of European food, ranging from lemon-crusted prawns to pork chops. If you're after something sweet, the quintessentially Rajasthani *malpuas* (white flour pancakes

soaked in sugar and rosewater syrup) are the best in Agra.

Yash Café (3/317 Chowk Kagziyan, Taj Ganj, tel. 9760/418-604, 7 A.M.-10:30 P.M. daily, entrées Rs. 80) has been a favorite with backpackers for many years, and for good reason: This cozy restaurant serves better food at better prices than most of the other backpacker joints around. Unlike most eateries in the area, Yash is not on a rooftop but in a heavily windowed room one floor above ground level. The brick pillars adorned with strings of lights give the place a college clubhouse feel, and there always seems to be a classic Bollywood film playing on the small TV set. Most of the food is Indian, although they also serve pizzas and a few interesting breakfast concoctions, such as the Indian French Toast, served with ground coconut.

If your trip to Agra is starting to take a toll on your waistline, you had best head to **Zorba the Buddha** (E-19 Shopping Arcade, Sadar Bazar, Agra Cantt., tel. 562/222-6091, www. zorbarestaurantagra.com, 10 A.M.-10 P.M. daily, Rs. 200), a quaint and very hygienic vegetarian café where the cook makes a point of going easy on the oil. It's hard not to raise an eyebrow at the restaurant's tagline, "Explore new heights of vegetarian delights," but that's exactly what you will do. Most of the food is Indian, although there are a few East-meets-West fusion dishes; try the Fiesta, a mix of local vegetables cooked in a tomato cashew gravy and topped with cheese and honey. It sounds odd, but it's delicious, especially with a bit of the house specialty: cheese and spinach naan. The only complaint is that the portions are a bit small and the prices a bit too high.

Information and Services

VISITOR INFORMATION

There are two visitor information centers in Agra operated by Uttar Pradesh Tourism (www. up-tourism.com), the state tourism board. The **Uttar Pradesh Government Tourist Office** (64 Taj Rd., tel. 562/222-6431, 10 A.M.-5 P.M. Mon.-Sat., closed public holidays) is the closest to Taj Ganj and Fatehabad Road. There's also a visitor information counter at the **Agra Cantt. Railway Station** (tel. 562/242-1204, 8 A.M.- 10 P.M. daily, closed public holidays). Uttar Pradesh Tourism also has interactive kiosks at both their offices as well as at Shilpgram, the Tourist Bungalow at Delhi Gate, and at Fatehpur Sikri. The **Government of India Tourism Office** (191 The Mall, tel. 562/222-6378, 10 A.M.-5 P.M. Mon.-Sat., closed public holidays) is useful for information about travel in other parts of the country.

MONEY

There are literally hundreds of ATMs spread across Agra, and you may find that this is the cheapest way to obtain rupees. Most have a withdrawal limit of Rs. 10,000 per transaction. Money changers also abound, and you can't walk far in Taj Ganj without having someone offer to buy your dollars or pounds at a commission-free rate. Most of these are government authorized; if in doubt, ask to see their certificate, and always make sure you get a receipt. A few banks can change money, although their hours (10 A.M.-2 P.M. Mon.-Sat.) make them fairly inconvenient choices. The rates are just as good, and sometimes better, at foreign-exchange bureaus. Money changers include **Sehra Creative Forex** (11 ABC, T. S. Sehra Bldg., Fatehabad Rd., tel. 562/400-9765), **Raj Travel and Internet** (East Gate, Taj Mahal, tel. 562/223-4232), and **Thomas Cook** (181/1 Tourist Complex Area, Fatehabad Rd., tel.

562/233-0480; New Taj Entry, Shilpgram, tel. 562/645-8192).

HOSPITALS AND PHARMACIES

Like most Indian cities, there's a pharmacy on every corner, all of which sell genuine high-quality medicines at much lower rates than you'd expect back home. Many pharmacies will also deliver medicine right to your hotel. Note that pharmacists in India may try to dispense antibiotics even for a small cough; never take antibiotics without consulting a doctor first. Most hotels have a doctor on call 24-7, so you'll never need to go searching for medical care.

If you fall seriously ill and need to be admitted to the hospital, avoid one of the many government hospitals if possible, as private hospitals generally have better service and equipment. **Asopa Hospital** (Gaicana Rd., Bypass, tel. 562/260-4606) is reputed to offer the best care in town.

INTERNET ACCESS

Broadband Internet access is widely available at Internet cafés throughout Taj Ganj and on Fatehabad Road, with rates as low as Rs. 10 per hour and as high as Rs. 30 per hour. An increasing number of midrange hotels and all upmarket properties also offer Wi-Fi access.

POSTAL SERVICES

Agra's **General Post Office** (Mall Rd., tel. 562/246-3886, 10 A.M.-6 P.M. Mon.-Sat.) is the largest and most conveniently located post office in town. Most crafts emporiums can also arrange to have your purchases shipped home for a fee.

LAUNDRY

Every hotel in Agra will have laundry service, which can cost as little as a few rupees per item at guesthouses and considerably more at midrange and upmarket hotels. Clothes are often hand washed by *dhobis* or local washer men and women, who are known for beating clothes clean with sticks and leaving them outside to dry. While this method is highly effective against the dust that is prevalent in North Indian cities, it can wreak havoc on delicate items.

LUGGAGE STORAGE

Most hotels will store their guests' luggage free of charge after checkout. There's also a 24-hour left-luggage facility (known as a "cloakroom") at the Agra Cantt. Railway Station. Locks are required on all luggage left here, and charges start at Rs. 10 per 24 hours. Note that the facility occasionally closes for meals, so double-check the hours with the attendant, especially if you are on a tight schedule. Small lockers are also available at Shilpgram and at the Taj Mahal ticket offices, although these are intended for storage of prohibited items, not for suitcases.

Getting There and Around

GETTING THERE

Agra is well connected to other points in the Golden Triangle by road and rail. National Highway 2 connects Delhi to Agra; Jaipur and Agra are linked by National Highway 11.

Air

Agra's **Kheria Airport** (AGR) is located at the Agra Air Force base, six kilometers from the city center. **Kingfisher Airlines** (Hotel Clarks Shiraz, 54 Taj Rd., 1800/209-3030, www.flykingfisher.com) operates daily flights between Agra and Delhi. Flights depart from Terminal 3 of Delhi's Indira Gandhi International airport at 10:45 A.M., reaching Agra at 11:45 A.M. The flight from Agra to Delhi leaves at 12:10 P.M., arriving in Delhi at 1:10 P.M. This was the only commercial flight operating at the airport at press time.

Train

A number of trains run between Delhi and Agra, the fastest of which, the *Shatabdi Express,* takes around two hours to reach Central Delhi's New Delhi Railway Station. The *Shatabdi* is scheduled so that a day trip from the capital to Agra is possible, with trains departing Delhi at 6:15 A.M. and arriving at Agra Cantt. Railway Station at 8:12 A.M. The evening *Shatabdi*

departs Agra Cantt. at 8:30 P.M. and reaches Delhi at 10:30 P.M. Hygienic (although not very palatable) meals are served on board and are included in the cost of tickets.

Many regular trains also make the 240-kilometer journey between Jaipur and Agra; most of these take 4-5 hours, and almost all of them depart and arrive at Agra Fort Railway Station (the exception is the *Gwalior Udaipur Super Express* train, which arrives at Agra Cantt.).

Bus

Agra has two major bus stands, with the Igdah Bus Stand serving most coaches to and from Rajasthan and Delhi. Most other buses use the **Interstate Bus Terminal** (tel. 562/260-3536), referred to by the acronym ISBT. Uttar Pradesh Tourism publishes a useful timetable of major trains and buses from Agra, available at both their offices (64 Taj Rd., tel. 562/222-6431, 10 A.M.-5 P.M. Mon.-Sat., closed public holidays; Agra Cantt. Railway Station, tel. 562/242-1204, 8 A.M.-10 P.M. daily, closed public holidays).

Government-run air-conditioned buses to Delhi leave from Igdah Bus Stand every hour 6 A.M.-6 P.M. daily. Buses to Agra leave from Delhi's Sarai Kale Khan Bus Stand 6 A.M.-7 P.M. daily. The journey between the two cities takes 4-5 hours and costs Rs. 221-371, depending on the type of bus.

Buses to Jaipur take 4-5 hours and depart every 1-1.5 hours 6:30 A.M.-midnight daily. The most comfortable of these is the air-conditioned Volvo bus (Rs. 367), which leaves at 2:30 P.M. daily. A seat in a regular deluxe bus will set you back Rs. 178. For information call the **Rajasthan State Road Transport Corporation** (tel. 562/242-0228), located across from the Igdah Bus Stand.

Taxi

As renting a car and driving yourself is neither widely available nor advisable (driving in India is notoriously maddening), renting a car with a driver is a popular way of getting around the Golden Triangle, and many people hire a taxi in Delhi to take them to Agra, Jaipur, and back to Delhi. Fuel costs are always included, but be sure to check whether quoted charges also include tolls and the obligatory road tax that all vehicles are required to pay when entering the state of Uttar Pradesh. Also note that some taxi providers charge a flat fee while others charge a per-kilometer rate on top of "out-of-station charges" (additional charges for out-of-town travel). Rates are higher if you decide to use the air-conditioning. If you just want to be dropped in Agra from Delhi or Jaipur, you will usually be charged for a round-trip journey, as the driver has to return the vehicle to its point of origin.

The journey between Delhi and Agra takes about four hours by taxi, and a return day trip in a Tata Indigo sedan will cost you around Rs. 6,000-7,000, including all taxes and tolls. This is not the fastest way to get between the two cities, but it does allow you to stop at some interesting sites on Agra's outskirts, namely Sikandra, Mathura, and Vrindavan. It's also convenient if you want to arrive at the Taj Mahal in time for sunrise—you have to leave Delhi around 2 A.M. to make it in time. Driving from Jaipur also takes around four hours, a bit

less than the amount of time it takes to travel by train. Fatehpur Sikri is on the way, as is Bharatpur, home to Keoladeo Ghana National Park. Rental charges from Jaipur to Agra are equivalent to charges from Delhi to Agra.

GETTING AROUND

Agra is fairly compact, although traffic can snarl at times, and getting from one point in the city to another can take ages. Fortunately, most of the attractions and hotels are close to each other.

The three main modes of transportation used by visitors are autorickshaws, cycle rickshaws, and taxis. Motorized vehicles (with the exception of motorcycles) are banned in the area immediately around the Taj Mahal's three gates, so most people trying to get from point to point in this area either walk or take cycle rickshaws. Electric-cart shuttles also make regular runs from Shilpgram to the Taj Mahal's East Gate, about 800 meters away. Rides are free for foreign visitors.

For farther distances, both taxis and autorickshaws make more sense, although many cycle rickshaw wallahs are willing to go long distances. Both forms of rickshaws can be hailed on the street, and make sure to negotiate a price ahead of time. An autorickshaw will usually charge at least Rs. 400-500 for a half-day trip from Taj Ganj with stops at Agra Fort, Baby Taj, and Ram Bagh—tack on another Rs. 300 or so if you want to drive out to see Akbar's tomb in Sikandra. Taxis can be booked through travel agents or pretty much any hotel and will generally charge at least Rs. 1,200 per day for a basic car. Cycle rickshaws may charge a bit less than taxis or autorickshaws, and a trip on this ecofriendly form of transportation takes longer than it would in a motorized vehicle. Again, rates are negotiable, but be generous—pulling a rickshaw is an extreme workout, and cycle rickshaw wallahs are among India's poorest.

JAIPUR

Perhaps the most visitor-friendly city in North India, Jaipur attracts visitors for its bounty of well-maintained historic sites, beautiful heritage hotels, and top-notch shopping. Often referred to as the Pink City for the salmon-hued walls of its old town, Jaipur is the capital of Rajasthan and the state's best-known destination. Rajasthan is known for its hospitality, and you'll notice the grace and warmth of Jaipur's citizenry from the moment you arrive.

At the edge of the massive Thar Desert, Jaipur is an enchanting city with plenty to offer visitors. You will find ornately decorated Old World palaces, stunning hilltop forts, beautifully decorated camels and elephants, and historic old *havelis* elegantly converted into charming heritage hotels, all set against the rugged background of the arid Aravalli Range, one of the oldest mountain ranges in the world. Of course, Jaipur also has its fair share of modernity, including hordes of ugly new shopping malls and a lot of noisy traffic, but the pure magic of this romantic desert city tends to overshadow its few annoyances.

The gateway to Rajasthan also has an amazing concentration of architectural masterpieces and visitor attractions. It is the arts and culture epicenter of Rajasthan and an excellent place to catch a showcase of traditional Rajasthani performing arts. The shopping is some of the best in the country, and even the shopping-phobic won't want to miss the colorful street markets that

HIGHLIGHTS

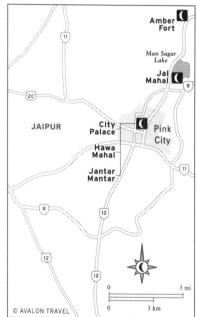

© AVALON TRAVEL

LOOK FOR [TO FIND RECOMMENDED SIGHTS, ACTIVITIES, DINING, AND LODGING.

[**City Palace:** The current home of Jaipur's royal family, this beautiful palace complex seamlessly blends elements of Mughal, European, and Rajasthani architecture (page 122).

[**Hawa Mahal:** This airy palace covered with tiny windows was once used by the women of Jaipur's royal court to watch passersby below (page 122).

[**Jantar Mantar:** This remarkable observatory has an impressive collection of gigantic, centuries-old astronomical tools (page 124).

[**Amber Fort:** Take an elephant ride to the top of this stunning hilltop fort, which took two centuries to complete (page 128).

[**Jal Mahal:** This recently restored water palace is filled with fascinating exhibits on miniature art and crowned with a gorgeous rooftop garden (page 130).

occupy much of the old part of the city. Jaipur is a popular destination year-round, although it can get quite hot during the April-June summer season, so it's important to come prepared to take it easy if you are visiting at this time.

HISTORY

Jaipur was founded in 1727 by Maharaja Sawai Jai Singh I, who needed to shift his capital from nearby Amber (which had been around since the 12th century) due to a growing population and a shortage of water. Jaipur was among the first planned cities in India, and its grid-like system of streets was designed by Bengali architect Vidyadhar Bhattacharya, who developed the city's layout in accordance with the principles outlined in the Shilpa Shastra, an ancient treatise on Indian architecture. It took four years to build, and although Jaipur has since expanded significantly, the old part of town remains the heart of the city.

Jaipur continued to flourish after Sawai Jai Singh's death despite numerous invasions by Maratha and Jaat people. The British later took over the kingdom, indirectly administering Jaipur and surrounding states under the collective state of Rajputana. Relations with the British remained relatively stable, and in 1883 the entire city was painted pink to honor a state visit by the Prince of Wales. The old

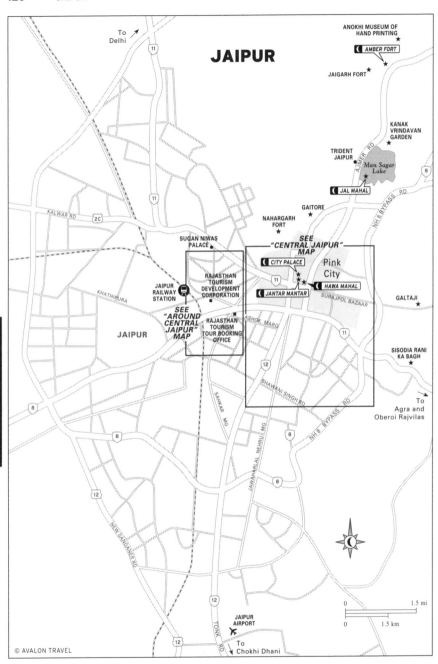

JAIPUR

town retains its rosy hue to this day, and all building owners in this part of Jaipur are prohibited from painting their properties any other color. However, you'll notice that most of the buildings in the old town are more salmon than pink—rumor has it that this slightly orangey paint is cheaper than the purely pink stuff.

After India's independence from the British, Jaipur and other neighboring states were merged. Jaipur's maharaja at the time, Man Singh II, was given the title of Rajapramukh and gained power over the region. His rule was short-lived, however, and in November 1956 Rajasthan was formed and incorporated into the Republic of India, with Jaipur as its capital.

PLANNING YOUR TIME

Many people breeze through Jaipur, spending two full days before heading to the next destination on their itinerary. While it is possible to cover the highlights of the city in just a couple of days, three days will allow you to soak in some of the sights at a leisurely pace, do some shopping, and perhaps take in a cultural performance. Tack on a fourth day in the hot summer months (Apr.-June), when temperatures hover well over 38°C day and night; this will allow you to retire to your hotel room during the most unbearably hot part of the day.

SAFETY AND SCAMS

There are plenty of shops in Jaipur hawking handicrafts as well as quite a few large tourist-trap emporiums that work in conjunction with touts to take as much money as possible from visitor. Autorickshaw drivers in Jaipur are notorious for trying to lure tourists into these shops, and many stores pay touts a set fee for every tourist they bring in, regardless of whether that person buys anything. Taxi and autorickshaw

drivers might also try to lure you to the nearby "crafts villages" of Sanganer and Bagru; note that these are commission-driven tourist traps, and you can get most of the handicrafts available there much cheaper in Jaipur city.

It's also a good idea to be vigilant of anyone who tries to get you to carry gems back to your home country in return for a bit of cash. In this classic scam, a traveler is approached and befriended by a local, whose main goal is to convince the traveler to carry "gems" back to his or her home country. The unsuspecting foreigner is asked to leave a small deposit or a signed carbon-copy credit card imprint as a guarantee. Upon returning home, the victim will find that the gems are fake and that his or her credit card has been maxed out in a single charge by the so-called gem dealer.

ORIENTATION

Jaipur is a well-planned city, although its numerous traffic circles and one-way streets (some of which become two-way at certain times of day) make it a bit confusing for newcomers to get around. Most of Jaipur's sights are concentrated in central Jaipur, the old Pink City, and in the outlying village of Amber. The old Pink City in the northeastern part of town is a bit more straightforward, simply because it's designed on a grid and all the major streets have names. The newer parts of town are to the south and west of the Pink City in central Jaipur. Major neighborhoods include Bani Park, west of the Pink City, where most of the heritage hotels are; C-Scheme, south of the Pink City; and Civil Lines, west of C-Scheme. The older city of Amber, where you'll find a number of attractions, including the area's three major forts, is about 10 kilometers from central Jaipur on National Highway 8 toward Delhi.

Sights

Like most monuments in India, there are separate rates for foreigners and Indians at most of Jaipur's sights. A good way to save money is by purchasing a "composite ticket" (Rs. 300 foreigners, Rs. 150 foreign students), which is valid for five days and will give you access to Amber Fort, the Albert Hall, the Hawa Mahal, the Jantar Mantar, and Nahargarh Fort.

PINK CITY

◖ City Palace

A must-visit for history buffs, the City Palace (Tripolia Bazaar, Pink City, tel. 141/408-8888, 9 A.M.-5 P.M. daily, Rs. 300 foreigners, Rs. 75 Indians) blends Rajasthani, Mughal, and European architectural styles into a splendid complex of courtyards, gardens, pavilions, and royal halls. Construction on this royal residency began in 1729 under Sawai Jai Singh II, although additions and alterations took place well into the early 1900s. The palace has remained the home of Jaipur's royal family since it was first built, and the titular maharaja and his family live in the striking **Chandra Mahal** to this day.

The City Palace is fairly large and packed with things to see, so it's a good idea to plan at least two hours here. The colorful peacock gate at the entrance of the Chandra Mahal stops many visitors in their tracks, and there's usually a group of awestruck people gaping at the amazingly intricate representations of India's national bird that adorn the gate's arches. As the Chandra Mahal is a home, only the ground floor is open to the public. You'll find paintings of past rulers along with plenty of informative plaques detailing the history of the royal family.

Another important part of the palace is the **Diwan-i-Khas** (Hall of Private Audiences), a multiple-domed chamber with a marble floor that resembles a life-size chessboard. The biggest attraction is a pair of enormous silver vessels, alleged to be the world's largest silver creations, commissioned by Madho Singh II to carry water from the holy Ganges River to England for King Edward VII's 1901 coronation. Don't miss the palace's **museum,** a series of rooms showcasing musical instruments, equestrian tack, armory, bejeweled weaponry, and beautifully preserved royal costumes, including some of the gargantuan robes of the obviously very heavyset Sawai Madho Singh I. There's also an art gallery in the **Diwan-i-Aam** (Hall of Public Audiences) featuring everything from miniature paintings and calligraphic work to woven carpets. A small crafts market operates here as well, and it's a nice place to pick up souvenirs without much risk of being harangued. Just outside the door sits a palmist, who will happily tell your fortune for a small fee.

◖ Hawa Mahal

Jaipur's most iconic landmark, the five-story Hawa Mahal (Palace of Winds, Tripolia Bazaar, Pink City, tel. 141/261-8862, 9 A.M.-4:30 P.M. daily, Rs. 50 foreigners, Rs. 10 Indians) was built in 1799 by Maharaja Sawai Pratap Singh as a safe place for royal women to watch royal processions and other happenings in the market below through tiny windows without having to reveal themselves to the general public.

The eastern facade of the sandstone structure contains 953 latticed windows, known locally as *jharokas,* although the other sides of the Hawa Mahal are quite plain in comparison. The building was designed to allow cool breezes to circulate throughout its interiors. Royal servants were also employed to pour water on the lattices, which helped keep the place even cooler. Although air-conditioning has since made this type of architecture obsolete, the Hawa Mahal remains an excellent

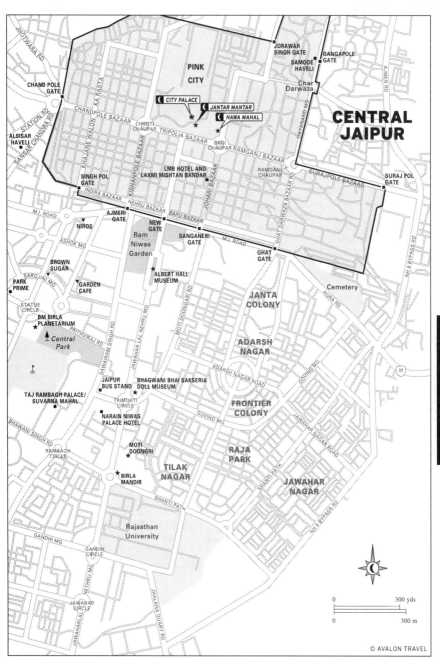

JAIPUR

© MARGOT BIGG

the naturally air-conditioned Hawa Mahal

place to cool down (plus you never have to worry about the electricity going out).

The sight is a fun spot to wander around, although be prepared to climb a few sets of narrow stairs to get from floor to floor. The inside of the building features a number of small enclaves surrounding a courtyard, set off by long rows of pillars and arches, some of which are painted with fading floral motifs. There are numerous little nooks, each with its own canopy and lattice, that make excellent vantage points for taking aerial snapshots of street scenes.

Jantar Mantar

The largest of the five observatories built across North India by Sawai Jai Singh II, the Jantar Mantar (Tripolia Bazaar, Pink City, tel. 141/261-0494, 9 A.M.-4:30 P.M. daily, Rs. 100 foreigners, Rs. 20 Indians, audio guides Rs. 150) is an impressive collection of enormous stone and marble instruments used for measuring astronomical phenomena. It was built between 1727 and 1734, and although it was modeled after Delhi's astronomical tool collection of the same name, the Jaipur version is larger and considerably more remarkable. The observatory was originally built of marble and stone, although a considerable amount of additional marble was added during a 1901 renovation.

The giant immovable tools here can be used for everything from predicting eclipses and monsoon rains to tracking stellar movements. There's even a set of devices known as the Ram Yantras that are used for gauging altitude. The largest tool here is the Samrat Yantra, a sundial measuring 27 meters high. Another point of interest is the Rasavilaya, a collection instruments for measuring the celestial latitude and longitude of each of the twelve constellations in the zodiac. This function is unique to the Jaipur Jantar Mantar. Each instrument has a small plaque with an image of the astrological sign to which it corresponds. Both Western and

The Jantar Mantar is filled with unique astronomy instruments.

Vedic astrology are very popular in India, and many visitors to the site make a point of seeking out their sign.

The Jantar Mantar is set up in a large outdoor courtyard across from the City Palace. This open-air plan is essential to the observatory's function, but the lack of shade can be troublesome on hot days, so you may want to bring an umbrella or parasol. The sight is pretty well signposted, and most of the instruments have corresponding plaques explaining how they work. Some visitors prefer to hire a guide at the entrance to the monument, and this is useful if you want an in-depth explanation of how the instruments function. Guides charge Rs. 200-400 depending on the number of people in your group; there's an additional Rs. 150 surcharge for languages other than English or Hindi.

CENTRAL JAIPUR
Albert Hall Museum

Perhaps one of the world's finest examples of Indo-Saracenic architecture, along with the Brighton Pavilion in England, the Albert Hall Museum (Ram Niwas Bagh, tel. 141/257-0099, 9 A.M.-5 P.M. daily, Rs. 50 foreigners, Rs. 10 Indians) is definitely worth a visit, even if just to gawk at the stunning sandstone and white marble facade. Its first stone was laid by the Prince of Wales (later King Edward VII) during his state visit in 1876, and it opened to the public 11 years later. The Albert Hall is the work of Sir Samuel Swinton, who also designed the Rambagh Palace, and is modeled after the Victoria and Albert Museum in London. It's especially beautiful here at night, when the hall's domes and arches are lit up. Today it operates as the Government Central Museum and houses an odd assortment of art and artifacts, including an Egyptian mummy. The museum is on the grounds of Ram Niwas Bagh, a large garden that was built to create employment after a famine devastated Jaipur in 1868.

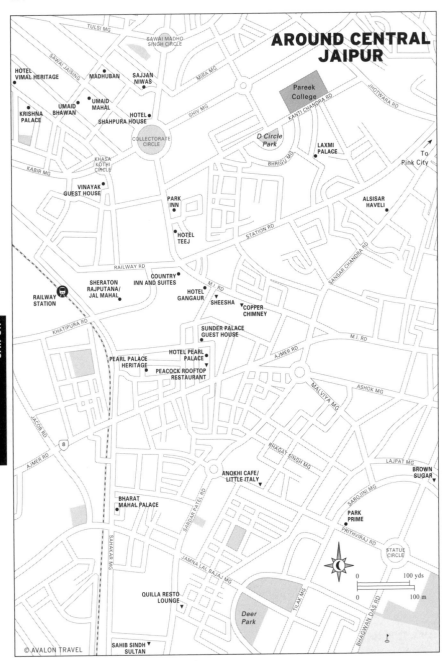

JAIPUR

© RAJAT DEEP RANA

Jaipur's Albert Hall Museum is one of the world's most stunning examples of Indo-Saracenic architecture.

Birla Mandir

The youngest of Jaipur's visitor attractions, the Birla Mandir (Indira Circle, Jawaharlal Nehru Marg, Bapu Nagar, 6:30 A.M.-noon and 3-8:30 P.M. daily Oct.-Mar., 6 A.M.-noon and 3-9 P.M. daily Apr.-Sept., free) was built in 1988 under the benefaction of the Birlas, a prominent family of industrialists who have built a number of temples around the country and continue to do so to this day. The temple is often referred to as the Lakshmi Narayan Temple after its two principle deities: Lakshmi, goddess of fortune, and her consort Narayan (a form of Vishnu, the preserver). The interiors of this triple-domed white-marble temple are adorned with stained glass scenes from the *Ramayana* and enormous idols. The intricately carved ceilings are worth craning your neck for. Note that photography is prohibited inside the structure.

Birla Planetarium

The major reason to visit the Birla Institute of Scientific Research is to catch a show at the Birla Planetarium (Birla Institute of Scientific Research, Statue Circle, tel. 141/238-5367, www.bisr.res.in, 11 A.M.-6 P.M. daily, Rs. 40). This planetarium's aim is to help the Indian public understand and appreciate the science of astronomy, and while it's not exactly one of Jaipur's must-see sights, it's a great place to go if you're traveling with kids or anyone fond of attempting to understand the cosmos. As showtimes often change, call ahead to find out about screenings in English.

Bhagwani Bhai Sakseria Doll Museum

The adorable little Bhagwani Bhai Sakseria Doll Museum (Jawaharlal Nehru Marg, Narayan Singh Circle, tel. 141/261-9359, 8 A.M.-6 P.M. daily, donation) was inaugurated in 1979. It is run by the government, and the proceeds from the museum help support

© RAJAT DEEP RANA

The Birla Mandir is one of Jaipur's newest tourist attractions.

programs for deaf and mute people. The museum is a simple room filled with glass cases displaying dolls from around the world wearing the traditional clothing of their respective countries, including a few rather humorous specimens. There's also a small collection of Indian dolls wearing regional apparel. It's a fun and educational stop and definitely worth a 20-minute visit if you are traveling with children or are interested in dolls or costumes.

Moti Doongri and Ganesh Temple

Overlooking the Birla Mandir, Moti Doongri (Hindi for Pearl Hill) is one of Jaipur's best-known landmarks, although it's not easily visited and is used more as a backdrop for photos. The hill is crowned by a palace, also known as Moti Doongri, designed to resemble a Scottish castle. Sawai Man Singh once lived here, and it remains the property of Jaipur's royal family. The main draw for most visitors is the hilltop Ganesh Temple, only open once a year on

Shivaratri, the holy night of Lord Shiva, celebrated in February or March. The closest you can get to Moti Doongri the rest of the year is the **Ganesh Temple** (8 A.M.-5:30 P.M. Thurs.-Tues., 8 A.M.-11 P.M. Wed.) at the base of the hill, just a few paces from the Birla Mandir. This simple temple, dedicated to the elephant-headed son of Shiva, is not as ornate as the Birla Mandir, but most pious Hindu visitors to the area make a point of stopping to pay their respects to the god.

AMBER AND VICINITY
◖ Amber Fort

Amber Fort (Ameer Rd., tel. 141/253-0293, 8 A.M.-5:30 P.M. daily, Rs. 200 foreigners, Rs. 25 Indians) looks over the township of Amber (pronounced "uh-meer," rhymes with *here*), once the regional capital. The area was first settled by the Meena people, Jaipur's original rulers, who claimed to come from a common ancestor, the Matsya avatar of Lord Vishnu. In

© RAJAT DEEP RANA

Moti Doongri was designed to look like a Scottish castle.

the 11th century, Amber was conquered by the Kachwahas, who later went on to create Jaipur, and it is believed that the fort sits on the ruins of a Meena site. Construction likely began in the late 16th century under the rule of Raja Man Singh I, although it's alleged to have taken about two centuries to complete the structure.

The fort is made of red sandstone and white marble and contains a fine collection of palaces, halls, and *char bagh* (four-quarter) Mughal gardens. The entire complex combines Rajput and Mughal architectural influences, including stone lattice screens, intricate mirror work, and paintings. There's also a famous **temple** here dedicated to Sheetala Mata (the goddess Kali). The idol in this temple is believed to have been recovered from what is now Bangladesh by Raja Man Singh, who located the statue in a prophetic dream. Beyond the temple is the **Ganesh Pol** gate, which leads to the palace's many rooms.

Highlights of the Amber Palace include the magnificent **Sheesh Mahal** (Mirror Palace), a small room covered with mosaics made of thousands of little shards of mirrors. Sheesh mahals exist in many Rajasthani forts and palaces and were lit by candlelight at night to create a dazzling play of light and color. It's fun to get lost in the **Zenana,** a series of frescoed rooms that all open onto a common courtyard. This is where the wives and mistresses of the king once lived. There's also a subterranean passageway connecting the Amber Palace and Jaigarh, although unfortunately it's not open to the public.

It's a steep climb up many stairs to the top of the fort, but you can opt to ride up on the back of an elephant from the base of the complex to the Singh Pol entry gate (Rs. 900 one-way for two people). There's also a sound-and-light show at the fort's Kesar Kyari (Amber Palace, tel. 141/253-0844) most evenings, but call ahead for showtimes as they change frequently.

© MARGOT BIGG

Construction of Amber Fort took centuries to complete.

Anokhi Museum of Hand Printing

If you're interested in the local craft of block printing, you won't want to miss the Anokhi Museum (Chanwar Palkiwalon ki Haveli/ Anokhi Haveli, Kheri Gate, Amber, tel. 141/253-0226, www.anokhi.com, 10:30 A.M.-5 P.M. Tues.-Sat., 11 A.M.-4:30 P.M. Sun., Rs. 30, camera Rs. 50, video Rs. 150). This museum is run by the owners of one of Jaipur's best-known clothing boutiques and features examples of textiles from Ajrakh, Bagru, Balotra, Sanganer, and, of course, Jaipur. The museum also houses examples of the tools used for hand printing as well as live demonstrations and the odd special exhibition. The crafty can even attend workshops and learn how to make pieces themselves (contact the museum well in advance for details). There's also a small museum shop selling cards, clothes, and interior furnishings as well as a café on-site.

◖ Jal Mahal

Jaipur's beloved water palace, the Jal Mahal

(Amber Rd., tel. 141/263-0714, 9:30 A.M.-5:30 P.M. daily, www.jaltarang.in, call for admission) sits in the middle of the Man Sagar Lake on the Amber Road. It was built by Sawai Jai Singh II as a pleasure palace for royal Jaipurites and their friends. For many years, however, this palace was in a state of ruin, and visitors were limited to photographing it from the road. Management of the palace has recently been taken over by Jal Mahal Resorts, which spent six years restoring the property to its former glory. Until recently, there was a well-accepted rumor going around Jaipur that the palace had four floors below the water level, including one that housed a temple. During renovations, however, it was discovered that there's actually only one basement level, devoid of any temple.

The main floor of the Jal Mahal has been beautifully restored and features galleries with blown-up copies of some of Rajasthan's finest miniature paintings as well as the aromatic

ELEPHANT RIDING

Elephants are believed to have been used as beasts of burden in India for 4,000 years, and they have been used in battle since Vedic times. Domestic elephants are looked after by keepers known as mahouts, who spend their entire lives in close contact with the animals. Elephants are used for tasks ranging from transporting goods to giving rides to tourists, and some temples dedicated to the Hindu god Ganesh, who has an elephant's head, keep one or two of the auspicious animals on the grounds for good fortune.

Elephant riding is especially popular in the rainforests of South India, but if you can't make it down there during your trip, you can still take a ride on one of these animals at Jaipur's Amber Fort. Females are usually used for riding, as the bulls are more temperamental. Basket-style saddles can accommodate 2-3 people at a time. While most mahouts take pretty good care of their animals (remember, elephants are their livelihood), do keep an eye out for signs of neglect, such as animals whose ankles are chaffed from the overuse of chains. If you are interested in learning more about elephant handling, you can ask any autorickshaw or taxi driver to take you to the nearby "Elephant Village" in the town of Kunda, about two kilometers from Jaipur, where most of the Amber Fort elephants and their handlers live.

© MARGOT BIGG

an elephant and his mahout

JAIPUR

Ittar Mahal, a hall filled with bottles of different essential oils that people used to sniff to get a bit of relief back in the days when the lake smelled of waste. The rooftop garden, the **Chameli Bagh,** is the best part of this amazing site and features a magnificent array of white marble fountains, canopies painted with delicate frescoes, and plenty of trees and flowers. The garden also includes translucent marble designs with LED lights underneath that light up at night, creating a dazzling image of an illuminated lotus.

As the Jal Mahal is in the middle of a lake, the only way to get to it is by driving to the dock (inside the Jal Tarang grounds) and taking one of the property's beautiful wooden paddleboats, each of which features a different animal at its bow. Unfortunately, at the time of writing, a number of disagreements with the government, coupled with unbalanced coverage by a local newspaper, have prevented the Jal Mahal from opening to the general public. Groups and dignitaries can apply for special permission to visit, and if the palace hasn't yet opened to everyone at the time of your trip, it's well worth contacting them ahead of time to request a visit.

Kanak Vrindavan Garden

The beautiful Kanak Vrindavan Garden

© RAJAT DEEP RANA

the Jal Mahal's beautiful rooftop gardens

(Amber Rd., north of Mansagar Lake, 8 A.M.-5 P.M. daily, Rs. 4) is tucked in a valley just before Amber Fort and has some excellent views of the surrounding forts. It's a good place for picnicking in cooler winter months. The garden was named by Maharaja Sawai Jai Singh, who thought it resembled Vrindavan, the North Indian city near Agra where Lord Krishna once frolicked. The well-manicured garden is divided into eight rectangular sections and features grass patches interspersed with fountains, terraces, stone walkways, and a set of intricately designed temples commissioned in the Rajasthani style by Sawai Jai Singh II.

Gaitore

The royal cremation ground of Gaitore (Gaitore Bazaar Rd., off Amber Rd., 9 A.M.-4:30 P.M. daily, Rs. 50 foreigners, Rs. 10 Indians) has been around since Jaipur was founded and remains in excellent condition today. This is the final resting place of Jaipur's

rulers, each of whom has his own cenotaph, or *chhatri* (literally "canopy," which refers to the onion dome covering the shrine). Many believe that Gaitore gets its name from a mispronunciation of the phrase *gaye ka thor*, which means "resting place of those who have gone." Like much of Jaipur's architecture, the cenotaphs blend Islamic tomb–style construction with traditional Rajput design elements. Each *chhatri* is designed to reflect the personality of the ruler to whom it is dedicated and features elaborate stone carvings of flowers, curlicues, and animals. These highly detailed cenotaphs, set against the arid, sparse backdrop of the Aravallis, gives Gaitore a spooky, enchanted air, appropriate given that it is, after all, a place for the dead.

Jaigarh Fort

The massive red sandstone military structure that is Jaigarh (Victory Fort) (behind Amber Fort, off Amber Rd., tel. 141/267-1848,

© RAJAT DEEP RANA

stunning royal centopaths at Gaitore

9 A.M.-4:30 P.M. daily, Rs. 75 foreigners, Rs. 25 Indians) houses a number of palaces, gardens, and temples within its walls. Built between the 15th and 18th centuries, Jaigarh is a good place to explore Jaipur's military history, and there's an armory housing a large variety of weapons and armor that were used in various battles through the centuries. There's also a museum, filled with photos and knickknacks from Jaipur's royal family, that provides interesting insight into how royal life has changed over the years. Jaigarh also once housed a great cannon foundry during the Mughal Empire, and to this day Jaigarh is also home to a number of cannons. The most famous is the Jai Baan, built in 1720, with a 55-ton barrel, claimed to be the world's largest wheeled cannon.

Nahargarh

Up an alarmingly steep road not far from Amber Fort, Nahargarh (Ameer Rd., tel. 141/518-2957, 10 A.M.-5:30 P.M. daily, Rs. 30

foreigners, Rs. 10 Indians), often called the "Tiger Fort," was the first of three forts built by Sawai Jai Singh in 1734, with later additions made by Sawai Ram Singh II and Sawai Madho Singh II. According to legend, the site on which the fort now stands was once haunted by the ghost of a prince, who agreed to leave only if the fort was named after him; the place still feels a bit eerie at night. Much of the fort is now in ruins, but it has one of the best vantage points in town. There's also a series of rooms that were once used for women of the court, and some of the original frescoes still remain. The fort also has an impressive system of underground rainwater-harvesting tanks that could allegedly sustain the fort for two years. The best time to visit is after sunset, when the fort is lit up. There's also a cozy café with good Indian meals, snacks, and drinks—you'll get dinner included here if you take the Rajasthan Tourism Development Corporation's Pink City by Night tour (tel. 141/247-5466, tours@rtdc.in).

OUTSKIRTS OF JAIPUR
Chokhi Dhani

If you want to experience Rajasthani rural life without compromising your comfort levels, take a taxi to the ultrakitschy Chokhi Dhani (Tonk Rd., tel. 141/277-0555, www.chokhidhani.com, Rs. 500). Spread over four hectares, this award-winning "village complex" has all the makings of a village, only it's cleaner and people speak English. It is admittedly a bit artificial and slightly reminiscent of a miniature golf course, but once you get over the initial cheesiness of it, you'll soon be having a blast. Highlights include live dance performances, camel rides, traditional huts, and even a full-fledged village fair that features crafts from around the state. There are also regular demonstrations of various traditional crafts. Admission includes an all-you-can-eat spread of rich Rajasthani specialties, including local desserts; this is one of the main reasons to visit. Note that Rajasthani food is known for its spiciness, so ask which dishes are spicy before you indulge. There's also a luxury village hotel on-site.

Galtaji

The beautiful pilgrimage site of Galtaji (Galta Gate, off NH 8 Bypass Rd., tel. 141/268-0951, 6 A.M.-7 P.M. daily, camera Rs. 50, video Rs. 150) is a bit far from town but well worth the trip for its beautiful *kunds* (water tanks) and enchanting temples. Referred to in the tourist trade as the "Monkey Temple," the complex was built in the 18th century by Diwan Rao Kriparam, and the main pink stone temple at the summit of the hill is dedicated to Surya, the sun god. Galtaji attracts both foreign visitors and pious Hindus, who come en masse during the annual Makar Sankranti holiday in mid-January. It's also very popular with monkeys of the pesky rhesus macaque variety, so keep a tight hold on your belongings and be prepared for a possible simian mugging if you're

carrying snacks with you. The water tanks hold spring water, although some dry up in years with weak monsoons, and you will likely see pilgrims bathing, especially in the most auspicious of the tanks, Galta Kund, with its cow-head spout.

Sisodia Rani ka Bagh

Five kilometers east of the Pink City, the terraced garden and palace complex of Sisodia Rani ka Bagh (NH 11 toward Agra, tel. 141/268-0494, 8 A.M.-8 P.M. daily, Rs. 10, camera Rs. 20) is one of the more scenic gardens in Jaipur. This multitiered Mughal garden was built in 1728 by Sawai Jai Singh for his queen and features intricate waterways, pavilions, statues, and a lot of colorful flowers. Sawai Jai Singh also built his queen a beautiful palace that features murals of Lord Krishna. The garden very much has a fairytale feel to it, and visitors today will appreciate its beautiful architecture, well-maintained grounds, and numerous varieties of flowers and shrubbery.

Entertainment and Events

There are plenty of entertainment options in Jaipur, although most take the form of traditional dances and performances. While a few of these are staged at cultural centers, the majority take place on hotel lawns, and many of the city's heritage and luxury hotels have nightly music and dance performances. There are also a number of festivals and religious events held throughout the year, including the annual Elephant Festival, one of Jaipur's best-known events. The city's nightlife scene, however, could use some work.

NIGHTLIFE

Nightlife options in Jaipur are limited; most of the decent bars are in five-star hotels.

Formerly known as Back to Basics, **B2B** (Country Inn and Suites, Khasa Kothi, MI Rd., tel. 141/403-3300, 9:30 P.M.-1:30 A.M. Wed. and Fri.-Sat., 4-8:30 P.M. Sun., Rs. 1,200 per couple) is the most convenient place to go clubbing if you're staying on MI Road or in the Bani Park area. The interiors of this small basement nightclub are minimalistic, and the music varies between house and Bollywood dance hits. B2B operates a strictly couples-only door policy, and the crowd is dominated by wealthy Jaipur professionals.

Raja Park's **Club Oxygen** (Hotel Dodas Palace, Lane 2, Raja Park, tel. 9983/000-031, 8:30 P.M.-3 A.M. Fri.-Sat.) is an underground (both literally and figuratively) nightclub that attracts a good mix of expats, travelers, and chilled-out locals. The clientele are generally friendly and unpretentious and come to dance the night away to everything from electronic dance music to hip-hop. The trippy interiors blend intricate black-light murals with complex lighting systems (including a color-changing LED-lit DJ console) to create a visually stimulating environment unparalleled in Jaipur. It's a good idea to call ahead to check the cover charge and guest-list requirements.

On the ground floor of Park Prime Hotel, **Henry's** (C-59 Prithviraj Rd., C-Scheme, tel. 141/236-0202, noon-11:45 P.M. Sun.-Thurs., noon-1:45 A.M. Fri.-Sat.) is decorated to look like a British pub but unfortunately lacks any British ale. The beer is of the Indian-made foreign variety (think Foster's, Carlsberg, and Heineken); there's also a local beer called Golden Peacock on tap. They also have a cocktail menu that features pretty much every mixed drink imaginable as well as a small wine list. Henry's food menu includes Indian and Chinese takes on pub fare along with, as in any authentic British pub, very ordinary vegetarian lasagna.

Inside the Ramada Jaipur, **The Fire Ball** (Govind Marg, Raja Park, tel. 141/406-6666, www.ramadajaipur.com, noon-midnight Mon.-Sat., nightclub Sat. evening only) is an amusing place to spend a few Saturday-night hours sipping cocktails and dancing to blaring Bollywood music. The lighting is minimal verging on pitch black, and you'll probably need to use the backlight of your cell phone to read the menu. The selection of drinks is far better than in most Indian nightclubs and includes rarities such as tequila and Jägermeister. The bouncers try to ensure a balanced male-to-female ratio, not an easy feat in India, so single men are sometimes turned away, although foreigners of any gender usually don't face problems getting in.

THE ARTS
Art Galleries

Next to the Amber Fort exit gates, **Gallery Art Chill** (Amber Palace, West Wing, tel. 141/253-0025, www.artchill.com, 8 A.M.-6 P.M. daily) specializes in contemporary art from some of India's most prolific painters as well as some up-and-coming visual artists. They also have a small collection of landscapes. Purchases can be shipped overseas on request.

Kanchan Art Gallery (D-255 Shubham Apt., Devi Marg, Bani Park, tel. 141/220-8379, www.kanchanartgallery.com, 10 A.M.-8 P.M. daily) has a large selection of contemporary and traditional paintings from across the country, including many spiritually themed pieces. Regular group and single-artist exhibitions are held regularly.

Mukesh Art N Frame (41 Girdhar Marg, adjoining Fortis Hospital, JLN Marg, tel. 141/401-1829, www.mukeshartandframe.com, 11 A.M.-9 P.M. Mon.-Sat., 3-8 P.M. Sun.) sells contemporary and traditional art—primarily paintings—and has a section devoted to miniatures. Mukesh stocks up to 5,000 paintings at any given time; all of the art is sold framed, and custom framing is available.

Cinemas

The modern and very comfortable **Inox** (4th Fl., Crystal Palm Mall, Bais Godam Circle, C-Scheme, tel. 141/511-7298, www.inoxmovies.com) screens both Hollywood and Bollywood films. They have a number of locations around town, most of which are in shopping malls.

The landmark **Raj Mandir** (Ashok Nagar, tel. 141/237-4694) cinema is one of Jaipur's funkiest buildings and is often likened to a wedding cake because of its unusual curlicue-shaped roof. It was constructed in the 1970s in the streamline modern style and first opened its doors in 1976 with a screening of the now cult classic *Charas;* the Raj Mandir continues to screen Hindi films today.

Cultural Centers

The government-run **Jawahar Kala Kendra** (Jawahar Lal Nehru Marg, tel. 141/270-6560, www.jawaharkalakendra.rajasthan.gov.in, 9:30 A.M.-7 P.M. daily, Rs. 100) is a multipurpose arts and culture center featuring a library, museum, theater, and art gallery. Music and dance performances showcasing talent and traditions from across the country are frequently held.

Performances are also regularly staged at the **Birla Auditorium** (Statue Circle, tel. 142/238-5224) and **Ravindra Manch** (Ram Niwas Bagh, tel. 141/261-9061).

FESTIVALS AND EVENTS
Makar Sankranti Kite Festival

In January, the Makar Sankriti Kite Festival marks the transition of the sun into the northern houses in Indian astrology. It's known as an auspicious day to harvest crops, but in Jaipur and other parts of Rajasthan, Makar Sankranti is celebrated with kite flying. Residents congregate on rooftops to fly kites, and many also engage in friendly (albeit very dangerous) kite battles, in which kite strings coated with glass shards are used to cut other kites loose from their strings.

Jaipur Literature Festival

Among Jaipur's newest festivals, the Jaipur Literature Festival (www.jaipurliteraturefestival.org), an annual late-January gathering of Indian and international literati, has already become one of the city's most popular events. Hosted primarily on the grounds of the Hotel Diggi Palace, the festival features free lectures and panel discussions and has showcased some of the world's most prolific writers, from Salman Rushdie to Pico Iyer.

Elephant Festival

Held every year in March on Holi, India's

JAIPUR LITERATURE FESTIVAL

Every January, writers from around the world descend on Jaipur for the annual Jaipur Literature Festival (www.jaipurliteraturefestival.com), a celebration of literary arts both in India and abroad. Since its inception in 2006, it has grown to be the biggest literary festival in Asia. The five-day festival features panel discussions, book readings, and Q&A sessions from a wide selection of authors as well as evening performances by well-known Indian and international acts. The festival has featured a number of world-renowned authors among its delegates, including Vikram Seth, Pico Iyer, Alexander McCall Smith, and Ian McEwan. The festival gained international attention in 2012 when Salman Rushdie canceled his visit after receiving information about alleged death threats. The author of the controversial 1988 novel *The Satanic Verses* previously spoke at the festival in 2007.

famous festival of color, Jaipur's Elephant Festival is a spectacular showcase of one of India's most beloved animals. This festival is held at the Chagan grounds and includes a number of elephant-related activities, including elephant polo, an elephant-versus-humans tug-of-war, competitions for the best-decorated elephants, and, of course, elephant rides. There are also folk-dance performances and food stalls.

Gangaur

The 16-day Gangaur festival (Mar.-Apr.) honors the goddess Gauri, a form of Parvati, Shiva's consort, and is particularly auspicious for women. If you visit during this time, you are likely to see women carrying earthenware pots on their heads in procession, and you'll probably overhear a lot of chanting in local Shiva temples. The last days of this festival culminate with large, elaborate processions featuring effigies of the goddess.

Sheetala Ashtami

Celebrated with fervor in March-April in Chaksu, 40 kilometers south of Jaipur, Sheetala Ashtami, sometimes referred to as Basoda, is a festival held six days after Holi and devoted to the goddess of smallpox, Sheetala Mata. On this day, people give food offerings to the deity in the hope that she will protect them from any epidemics in the following year, and women do not enter the kitchen. A small fair is also set up in Chaksu for the festival.

Teej

Although the Teej festival (July-Aug.) is feted throughout northern India, it is celebrated with the most gusto in Jaipur. During Teej, women pray to the goddess Parvati and ask for her blessings in their marriage. The festival also honors the monsoon, and women wear green to commemorate the benefits of the rains. Swings are also hung in trees at this time. A large and colorful procession is held in Jaipur on Teej, and the tradition is to eat the local sweet treat *ghewar* (spongy funnel cake) on this day.

Shopping

Jaipur is a fabulous place to shop, and one can easily spend days sorting through the many wares on offer. Popular souvenirs include glass bangles, fine jewelry, leather shoes and bags, silk and cotton textiles and bedspreads, parasols, puppets, and blue pottery made from quartz mixed with fuller's earth. It's important to bargain hard—Jaipur is one of the main stops on most Northern Indian package tours, and many shopkeepers will quote you exorbitant prices in U.S. dollars, hoping that you fail to realize that handicrafts cost considerably less in India than in the United States.

HANDICRAFT EMPORIUMS

For guaranteed quality, the government-run **Rajasthali** (opposite Ajmer Gate, MI Rd., tel. 141/510-3329, www.rajasthali.gov. in, 11 A.M.-7:30 P.M. Mon.-Fri.) is the best place to go. They stock everything from locally woven silk saris to stunning pieces of furniture as well as a selection of ethnic artifacts from across the country. The reasonable fixed prices mean you won't have to haggle here.

MARKETS

The best markets are in the old Pink City part of town, and each specializes in a different type of handicraft. The shops on all three market streets listed here are usually open by 10 A.M. and close by 8:30 or 9 P.M. All but a handful of shops are closed on Sunday.

Bapu Bazaar Road runs parallel to MI Road, between Ajmer and Sanganeri Gates. You'll find a wide range of colorful textiles and handicrafts of varying quality, ranging from mirrored bedspreads to cloth parasols. Many of the merchants here specialize in traditional leather shoes or *jootis*. It's one of the city's more colorful streets, and there are some great photo ops.

Johari Bazaar Road runs north from Sanganeri Gate to the Badi Chaupur traffic circle. This market street is the hub of Jaipur's gem and jewelry trade and is a good place to pick up silver and enamel bracelets and bibelots. You'll find everything from gold bangles to cheap costume jewelry in the shops that line this road.

Kishanpole Bazaar runs north from Ajmer Gate all the way to the Choti Chaupur traffic circle. This street is more popular with locals than with travelers, although many of the shops

BLUE POTTERY

One of Jaipur's best-known crafts, blue pottery is believed to have come to Jaipur from Persia during the days of the Islamic Sultanate. However, it wasn't until the 19th century under the patronage of Sawai Ram Singh II, a great lover of the arts, that the craft began to flourish.

Although blue pottery traditionally consisted of blue-and-white glazed tiles and vessels, today you can get everything from picture frames to ashtrays in a variety of colors. Although artisans have begun creating a wider range of products, they continue to make the pottery by hand using a mixture of substances that include quartz, fuller's earth, glass, and sodium borate. Blue pottery is widely available around town, but the best place to pick it up is at **Neerja International** (Anand Bhawan, Jacob Rd., Civil Lines, tel. 9829/010-239, www.neerjainternational. com, 10 A.M.-9 P.M. daily), which sources all of its wares directly from village craftspeople.

do stock handicrafts. It's the best place to pick up handcrafted wooden furniture, rugs, and textiles. They also sell a range of metal trunks and utensils, including some funky handmade scissors.

BOUTIQUES

Run by an Indian designer and her Portuguese husband, **Ambika** (2 Jacob Rd. Civil Lines, tel. 141/410-8276, www.ambikaconcept.com, 9:30 A.M.-8 P.M. daily) stocks whimsical cotton dresses, tunics, and accessories. Most of the clothes are for women, although they plan to launch a line of children's wear soon.

For all things block printed, stop by the popular **Anokhi** (2nd Fl., KK Square, C-11 Prithviraj Rd., C-Scheme, tel. 141/400-7244, www.anokhi.com, 9:30 A.M.-8 P.M. daily). This boutique sells women's tunics, dresses, and pajamas as well as lovely cotton bedspreads. The mostly organic café is excellent.

Jaipur's most famous jeweler, **Gem Palace** (MI Rd., tel. 141/237-4175, www.gempalacejaipur. com, 11 A.M.-8 P.M. daily) has been selling beautifully crafted jewelry since 1852. The glittering showroom is full of everything from antique costume jewelry to exquisite (and very expensive) fine gems. They also have an excellent selection of local *meenakari* (inlaid enamel) pieces.

The Franco-Indian **Hot Pink** (Narain Niwas Palace, Kanota Bagh, Narain Singh Rd., tel. 141/510-8932, www.hotpinkindia.com, 10 A.M.-8 P.M. daily) stocks vibrant clothing, accessories, and cushion covers from a host of up-and-coming designers based in India. They also have a line of cute, colorful children's wear embellished with elephantine designs.

If you're looking for a piece of the famous Jaipur blue pottery, head to **Neerja International** (Anand Bhawan, Jacob Rd., Civil Lines, tel. 9829/010-239, www.neerjainternational.com, 10 A.M.-9 P.M. daily), where you'll find everything from traditional blue bowls to modern multicolored candelabras. All items are handmade and bought directly from the craftspeople who make them.

BOOKSTORES

Books Corner (MI Rd., near Niros, tel. 141/236-6323, 10 A.M.-9:30 P.M. daily) stocks a variety of books, from novels to coffee-table picture books about Jaipur and India. They also have a decent selection of nonfiction titles on Indian culture and spirituality.

Crosswords (1st Fl., KK Square, C-11 Prithviraj Rd., C-Scheme, tel. 141/237-9400, 10:30 A.M.-9 P.M. daily) is among India's most popular bookstore chains. This branch stocks books aimed at Indian readers, so there are a lot of novels from both Indian and international authors as well as business books. There are also titles on subjects of local significance.

SHOPPING MALLS

Jaipur is increasingly a mall city, and as in many Indian cities, Jaipur's traditional markets and plazas are facing fierce competition from the air-conditioned megamalls that are popping up around the city. Most malls have one large department store, a food court, and a collection of shops specializing in toys, high-end Indian women's wear, shoes, and sportswear. Some of the most popular include the massive **Crystal Palm Mall** (opposite MGF Metropolitan, Bais Godam Circle, C-Scheme), **Gaurav Towers** (off Pradhan Marg, Malviya Nagar), and **MGF Metropolitan** (opposite Crystal Palm Mall, Bais Godam Circle, C-Scheme). The shops in Jaipur's malls are nothing spectacular, but they're a great place to dip into when you're in need of a little air-conditioning.

Sports and Recreation

Jaipur is not a major sports and recreation destination, and if you want to keep up your workout while in the city, your hotel gym is the best bet. The most popular sports are cricket, like everywhere in India, and polo. Most hotels have pools, and many allow nonguests to use them for a small fee.

CRICKET

If you want to learn how to play cricket or brush up on old skills, you can get personal training at the **Jaipur Cricket Academy** (Jori Farms, near 200 Feet Express Hwy., Khirni Phatak, Jhotwara, tel. 9828/019-300, www.jaipurcricketacademy.com). The academy also runs short holiday clinics for children and teens.

HORSEBACK RIDING

Horseback riding sessions and lessons can be arranged through the **Silver Spurs Farm** (Dhaka Marg, Sirsi Rd., tel. 141/224-0344, www.silverspursjaipur.com), which also has a small B&B, and the **Jaipur Polo Club** (B-21 Tulsi Marg, Hanuman Nagar, Khatipura, tel. 141/224-0196, www.jaipurpolo.com).

GOLF

Among India's most famous golf courses, the 18-hole **Rambagh Golf Club** (Bhawani Singh Rd., tel. 562/238-5482, www.rambaghgolfclub.com, 6 A.M.-5 P.M. daily, Rs. 1,150 pp) is set on the grounds of the former royal residence, next to the Taj Rambagh Hotel. You can see the Moti Doongri Fort from parts of the course.

SPECTATOR SPORTS

Jaipur doesn't have a lot of spectator sports, although there are cricket matches at the massive **Sawai Mansingh Stadium** (Rambagh Circle, tel. 141/274-2511), locally abbreviated as SMS Stadium. Indian cricket matches tend to be more energetic affairs than you might find elsewhere in the cricketing world, and matches in Jaipur are no exception. Information and schedules are available on the Rajasthan Cricket Association website (www.cricketrajasthan.in).

Polo is another popular sport in Jaipur, and tournaments are often held by the **Jaipur Polo Club** (B-21 Tulsi Marg, Hanuman Nagar, Khatipura, tel. 141/224-0196, www.jaipurpolo.com) and the **Rambagh Polo Club** (Bhawani Singh Rd., tel. 141/283-5380). These matches are excellent for people-watching and often attract an interesting mix of Rajasthani aristocrats and business types. Check ahead with the clubs for details, as schedules and ticket prices vary. The Royal Jaipur Polo Foundation sometimes organizes elephant-back polo games; for more information contact Maharaj Narendra Singh (tel. 9828/199-991, maharajnsingh@gmail.com).

SAFARIS

If you'd like to explore the desert and villages around Jaipur, **Dera Amer** (2 Yudhishtra Marg, C-Scheme, tel. 141/222-8468, www.deraamer. com) can arrange for one-hour safaris in jeeps (Rs. 3,000 pp) or on elephant-back (Rs. 4,500 pp). A meal back at the camp is included in the price, and children under age eight can come along for free. Jeep safaris travel along a forest track between Amber and the camp in Kukas, north of the city. The trip passes by a medieval stepwell (a well with a set of steps descending to the water), a tiger rescue center, and a village. Elephant safaris take place around the camp's arid golden landscape. The area is home to hyenas and leopards that thankfully only come out at night. Jackals and antelopes are spotted occasionally, however, and you'll probably see plenty of native birds, including flycatchers and peacocks. The company also organizes elephant polo matches, visits to elephant camps, and bird-watching outings.

SPAS

For a city of its size and popularity, Jaipur has remarkably few noteworthy spas. The fantastic **Kaya Kalp Spa** (Sheraton Rajputana, Palace Rd., tel. 141/510-0100, 8 A.M.-10 P.M. daily) is a beautiful, dimly lighted spa painted in hues of marble white and pomegranate red. The signature Kaya Kalp massage treatment (Rs. 3,750 for 60 minutes, Rs. 4,800 for 90 minutes) combines a variety of massage styles and will likely relax you to sleep. All treatments include a complimentary steam, sauna, and jetted tub as well as a fresh glass of cleansing pomegranate juice.

For something more traditional, namely ayurvedic treatments, visit one of the two branches of **Kerala Ayurveda Kendra** (F-34 Azad Marg, Jamnalal Bajaj Marg, C-Scheme, tel. 141/510-6743; D-259 Devi Marg, Bani Park, tel. 141/400-6000, www.keralaayurvedakendra.com), where you can get everything from a classic oil massage to a 90-minute *shirodhara* (Rs. 2,000) treatment in which heated medicated oil is poured onto the forehead. This place is not as luxurious as what you would find in a five-star hotel, but the prices are low, the facilities clean, and the treatments fantastic. They also offer training programs for aspiring ayurvedic therapists.

SWIMMING POOLS

If your hotel doesn't have its own swimming pool, you can always go for a dip at one of the many hotel pools in Jaipur that allow nonguests to swim. Some of the nicest, although not necessarily the largest, include the one on the verdant grounds of **Madhuban** (D-237 Bihari Marg, Bani Park, tel. 141/220-0033, 7 A.M.-10 P.M. daily, Rs. 100) and the pool at **Umaid Bhawan** (D1-2A, behind Collectorate, Bani Park, tel. 141/231-6184, 8 A.M.-8 P.M. daily, Rs. 200).

Accommodations

Sleeping options in Jaipur abound, and the city is home to some spectacular heritage properties that won't cost you a fortune to stay in. Most of these are located in the posh Bani Park neighborhood, a stone's throw from the bus stand and railway station. Bani Park also has a few budget options, as does the Hathroi Fort area just south of MI Road. There are business hotels and luxury five-star accommodations throughout the city; many of the larger ones are located near Amber Fort on the road to Delhi. The old Pink City has very few hotels. Like most of North India, Jaipur's high season runs October-March, although most hotels keep their rates consistent throughout the year.

UNDER RS. 1,000

If you're looking for a good place to meet backpackers, you'll love **Akriti Guest House** (D-169-C Bhragu Marg, Bani Park, tel. 141/220-2800, akritiguesthouse@hotmail.com, Rs. 400-1,500 d). This ultra-low-budget guesthouse has basic rooms surrounding a small garden, which is where most of its guests seem to hang out. The staff are really friendly and speak excellent English. As the guesthouse is tucked inside the Bani Park neighborhood, traffic noise is rarely an issue at night.

Travelers with an appreciation for art will likely fall in love with **⬛ Hotel Pearl Palace** (Hari Kishan Somani Marg, Hathroi Fort, Ajmer Rd., tel. 141/237-3700, www.hotelpearlpalace.com, Rs. 900-1,150 d). This beautiful guesthouse is owned and operated by S. P. Singh, a charming hotelier with the soul and eye of an artist. All of the guest rooms are decorated with a mixture of local and imported furnishings, and some are covered floor-to-ceiling with beautiful blue tiles. There's also a small dorm room on-site for those on a very tight budget (Rs. 175 pp) as well as a reading room and the funky Peacock Rooftop Restaurant. Guests are also treated to a free tourism brochure written and published by Mr. Singh himself, titled "Jaipur for Aliens," which provides information and anecdotes about Jaipur's main attractions as well as a few pages explaining topics ranging from Sikhism (Mr. Singh's religion) to India's cricket obsession.

If Hotel Pearl Palace is fully booked, as it often is, your next best budget option in the area is the **Sunder Palace Guest House** (Sanjay Marg, Hathroi Fort, Ajmer Rd., tel. 141/236-0178, www.sunderpalace.com, Rs. 600-1,200 d). The rooms in this family guesthouse are exceptionally clean and well maintained, and most have intricate floral designs hand-painted on the ceiling. The cheapest guest rooms on the ground floor are noisy and best avoided. The rooftop restaurant serves delicious vegetarian food; note that the management do not permit nonvegetarian food to be carried onto the premises.

One of the best deals in town, **⬛ Krishna Palace** (E-26 Durga Marg, Bani Park, tel. 141/220-1395, www.krishnapalace.com, Rs. 650-1,350 d) is a family-run budget hotel that could easily be converted into a midrange hotel with just a few tweaks. As it stands, this budget property is a steal, with beautiful high-ceilinged guest rooms featuring Edwardian-style furniture with Rajasthani touches. Tall travelers will love that the beds are well over two meters long, 30 centimeters longer than most beds in India. The owner is enthusiastic and friendly and goes out of his way to make guests happy.

The very affordable and super-cozy **Vinayak Guesthouse** (Plot 4, Kabir Marg, Bani Park, tel. 141/324-9963, vinayaguesthouse@yahoo.co.in, Rs. 300-650 d) is operated by a friendly family that lives on-site and often invites hotel guests into their home. The guest rooms are basic but clean, and the cheaper ones have shared baths. There's also a cute rooftop restaurant and a Wi-Fi lounge featuring a small book exchange. Note that Vinayak is located in the middle of a strip of low-quality, overpriced guesthouses that are notorious for reeling in guests via touts and unscrupulous rickshaw drivers, so be firm if anyone tries to lure you to one of the neighboring hotels.

RS. 1,000-3,000

If you're on a tight budget but still want little luxuries (like air conditioning, TV, and a Western-style toilet), you may strike a good balance at the Rajasthan Tourism Department's **Hotel Gangaur** (Near Khasa Kothi, MI Rd., tel. 141/237-1641, www.rtdc.in, Rs. 1,500-2,300). This midsize hotel is clean, very well maintained, and has room service. There's also a gift shop selling all the Rajashtani kitsch you could ever dream of, along with a small travel office with details about the tourism department's daily tours and activities. It's a short walk or rickshaw ride away from the old town and the train station. There's plenty of parking and a dormitory for drivers.

Rajasthan Tourism's **Hotel Teej** (Collectorate Rd., Bani Park, tel. 141/220-5482, www.rtdc. in, Rs. 1,400-2,000 d) is a clean and reliable (albeit a bit ramshackle) option, right between the bus stand and the train station. The guest rooms are basic, and the friendly staff are knowledgeable about local history and attractions. There's an inexpensive but good Indian restaurant on-site as well as a small playground.

A 70-year-old *haveli* turned hotel, **Madhuban** (D-237 Bihari Marg, Bani Park, tel. 141/220-0033, www.madhuban.net, Rs. 1,900-3,600 d) is in a big garden filled with bougainvillea in a quieter part of Jaipur's residential Bani Park neighborhood. The guest rooms are situated around spacious courtyards, and all have safes.

There's also a small pool in a side courtyard and a quaint restaurant filled with antique decorations and elegant chandeliers.

If you want to stay right in the middle of the hectic Pink City, **LMB Hotel** (Johari Bazar, tel. 141/257-8276, www.hotellmb.com, Rs. 2,525-2,925) is not a bad choice. This simple hotel above Jaipur's most famous sweets shop, with the same name, offers clean guest rooms that smell like rose petals and come equipped with fridges and TVs. Although it's not the most charming hotel in Jaipur, it's certainly among the most convenient, and a stay is warranted only if you prefer accessibility over ambience.

The lovely **Laxmi Palace** (Vijay Path, Bani Park, tel. 141/220-0922, www.suganniwaspalace.com, Rs. 2,600-2,900 d) is a comfortable and affordable heritage property in an old house with a small garden. The guest rooms feature four-poster beds, and some have enormous balconies. There are beautiful hand painted ceilings throughout the property and a small restaurant serving family-style Indian cuisine. Free parking and same-day laundry service are also offered.

Jaipur is filled with jaw-droppingly impressive accommodations, but perhaps the most stunning, and certainly the best value for money, is the enchanting **◖ Pearl Palace Heritage** (54 Gopal Bari, Lane 2, tel. 141/237-5242, www.pearlpalaceheritage.com, Rs. 1,500-2,100 d). Built and designed by the ultracreative S. P. Singh, also the proprietor of Hotel Pearl Palace, this faux-heritage hotel offers most of the amenities of a five-star heritage hotel at shockingly budget prices. Each guest room is themed after a different aspect of Indian culture, and all guest rooms come equipped with computers, built-in music systems, fridges, and extralong beds. The hallways are adorned with sandstone bas reliefs inspired by artifacts from museums around the world, all of which were hand-sculpted by a team of artists brought specially to Jaipur from Gujarat from the project. The hotel is still being completed, and future additions include a semi-subterranean swimming pool and a restaurant.

The neo-heritage **Sajjan Niwas** (behind Collectorate, Bani Park, tel. 141/231-1544, www.sajjanniwas.com, Rs. 2,600-3,000 d) seems to be riding on the coattails of the far more popular Umaid Bhawan next door, although it's still a decent place to stay. The guest rooms here are clean and spacious, and many feature beautiful windows of multicolored glass, adding an enchanting touch to the interiors. There's also an elevator and a small swimming pool.

Rajasthani meets rococo at ◖ **Umaid Bhawan** (D1-2A, behind Collectorate, Bani Park, tel. 141/231-6184, www.umaidbhawan. com, Rs. 2,400 d), a maze of a hotel covered with ornate decorations and plenty of nooks and balconies to relax in. The property was built by the Maharaja of Jaipur's former army chief in the 1920s and was turned into a family hotel in 1993. The guest rooms are not as over-the-top as the exteriors, and some have views of Amber Fort. There's a rooftop restaurant serving Rajasthani food, a small shop, and a compact outdoor swimming pool.

The younger sister of the popular Umaid Bhawan, **Umaid Mahal** (C-20 B/2 Bihari Marg, Bani Park, tel. 141/220-1952, www.umaidma-hal.com, Rs. 2,000-3,500 d) is lovely in its own right. This hotel cutely touts itself as a "heritage castle," and while such a description might be a bit gratuitous, it's still a fun place to play prince and princess for a few nights. The whole place is covered with gorgeous green marble floors, and the walls are adorned with intricate and colorful hand-painted floral borders. The lower basement level has a large and ornately decorated restaurant and a small outdoor lap pool with a fountain.

For a glimpse into the lives of Jaipur's

aristocracy, book a room at ◖ **Sugan Niwas Palace** (Vijay Path, Bani Park, tel. 141/220-0922, www.suganniwaspalace.com, Rs. 2,800-4,800 d). This hotel was built as a family house in 1946 and later transformed into a hotel by the original owner's grandson. Sugan Niwas exudes Old World charm and is furnished with antiques and family memorabilia; the common sitting room is filled with fascinating curios. The whole building is surrounded by a flower-filled garden, and there's a large pool out back. The on-site restaurant, Saffron, also serves a nice selection of Indian and Rajasthani specialties.

RS. 3,000-10,000

If you are traveling with energetic young children, you might want to consider a stay at the 90-year-old **Bharat Mahal Palace** (16 Parivahan Marg, C-Scheme, tel. 141/236-5498, www.bharatmahalpalace.com, Rs. 3,000 d), close to the railway station. This is one of the more simply decorated heritage properties and offers some of the largest guest rooms you'll find in this category. There's also a large walled-in garden with plenty of room to run around, a restaurant serving Indian and Western meals, and a small swimming pool.

Alsisar Haveli (Sansar Chandra Rd., tel. 141/236-8290, www.alsisarhaveli.com, Rs. 4,800-5,600 d) is full of pleasant surprises. You'll be surprised that such a work of art can exist on such a dusty, noisy street, surprised at how quiet it is, and surprised at how you can get a chance to stay in such a lovely place at relatively low rates. This heritage hotel was built in 1892 and retains much of its original charm and decorations, and many of the guest rooms have four-poster beds and quaint reading nooks. The beautiful pool is shaped like a traditional Rajasthani archway and is set in a leafy courtyard.

Characterless but convenient, **Country Inn**

JAIPUR

HERITAGE STAYS

If you've ever dreamed of living like royalty, even if just for one night, Jaipur can help you make that dream come true. The city is home to a huge number of "heritage" properties, historic mansions and palaces that have been converted into hotels. After India's independence, many of Rajasthan's aristocrats and royals lost much of their wealth, and by the end of Indira Gandhi's time as prime minister, most were trying to maintain palatial properties without any help from the state. Many noble families ended up converting their *havelis* (city manors) and palaces into family-run hotels; others leased or sold their properties to enterprising hoteliers and

chains. These days, heritage hotels abound in Jaipur, especially in the upscale Bani Park area.

Many of the city's newer purpose-built hotels also try to emulate the heritage look and feel, and they often have all the beauty and splendor characteristic of heritage hotels without the crumbly walls. These properties use elements of Indo-Saracenic and Rajasthani architecture to give the impression that they were built long, long ago. On the other hand, these newer hotels have excellent infrastructure and are often as beautiful as their historic counterparts; if the look and feel of a place is more important to you than its age, you may actually prefer to go faux.

and Suites by Carlson (Khasa Kothi, MI Rd., tel. 141/403-3300, www.cisindia.com, Rs. 9,500 d) is a clean and reliable option just a few minutes from the train and bus terminals. The guest rooms here are meticulously maintained and come equipped with large flat-screen TVs. The only complaint: The baths are a bit on the small side. There's a pool, a nightclub called B2B, and even a shopping mall on-site.

Built in 1956 by the former rulers of the Rajasthani principality of Shahpura, the family-run **Hotel Shahpura House** (Devi Marg, Bani Park, tel. 141/220-2293, shahpurahouse.com, Rs. 3,500-4,500 d) is one of the more elegant heritage options in Jaipur. The guest rooms feature intricate mirror work on the ceilings and are furnished with beautiful silk bedspreads. The rooftop restaurant hosts regular cultural performances and live cooking demonstrations. The pool in the courtyard looks fantastic when lit up in the evenings. Wi-Fi is included.

Situated around a peaceful courtyard featuring a wide pool, **Hotel Vimal Heritage** (D-148 A/2 Durga Marg, Bani Park, tel. 141/220-1333, www.hotelvimalheritage.com, Rs. 4,000 d) blends colonial architecture with Rajasthani

elements. The guest rooms in this suburban heritage property feature large beds and small sitting nooks, some of which feature decorative colored-glass windows. There's also a jetted tub (a rarity in Jaipur), a poolside bar, and an air-conditioned restaurant featuring rich local cuisine.

If you grew up reading Hansel and Gretel, it's likely that at some point you have dreamed of visiting a house made of candy. The closest you will get in Jaipur is the stately **Narain Niwas Palace Hotel** (Kanota Bagh, Narain Singh Rd., tel. 141/256-1045, www.hotel-narainniwas.com, Rs. 5,800-7,400 d). With its exteriors painted in subdued pastel yellows and pinks, this place looks like a giant piece of confectionary, and with its sprawling lawns, errant peacocks, large pool, and plentiful nooks to explore, it's an easy place to revert to childhood if you're so inclined. The guest rooms are clean and elegant and feature antique furniture. There's also a small collection of designer boutiques on the property.

India is a noisy place, and decibel levels generally peak on the country's busy main roads. It's therefore usually a better idea to choose accommodations situated slightly away from busy thoroughfares if you want to get a good night's sleep. Occasionally, however, you'll find a main-road place that manages to maintain pin-drop silence, such as the quiet **Park Inn** (A-28/C/3, Sawai Jaisingh Hwy., Bani Park, tel. 141/415-1000, www.sarovarhotels.com, Rs. 6,500-10,000 d). The guest rooms are of the standard business variety but are kept in great condition and are peacefully quiet. South-facing guest rooms have excellent views of the city and the Aravalli mountain range.

Park Prime (C-59 Prithviraj Rd., C-Scheme, tel. 141/236-0202, www.parkprime.net, Rs. 9,000 d) is a reliable choice for business travelers and anyone who prefers something a bit more contemporary. The guest rooms focus on function rather than form and lack the often-times frilly "ethnic" decor common to most Rajasthani properties. There's also a pub, Henry's, and a few very good restaurants as well as a rooftop swimming pool.

One of the first five-star properties to open in Jaipur, the 218-room **Sheraton Rajputana** (Palace Rd., tel. 141/510-0100, www.starwood-hotels.com, Rs. 7,000-12,500 d) is particularly popular with business travelers, families, and tour groups, and it has plenty to offer in terms of meeting and banquet facilities. This purpose-built hotel has all the standard amenities one would expect from an international brand as well locally inspired art and decor to add a bit of Jaipuri flavor. It's also home to the luxurious Kaya Kalp Spa, arguably the best spa in the city.

RS. 10,000 AND UP

Oberoi Rajvilas (Goner Rd., Babaji-ka-Mod, tel. 141/268-0101, www.oberoihotels.com, Rs. 35,000-230,000) is the perfect place to make believe that you are a Rajasthani prince or princess from days past. This massive property on the outskirts of Jaipur is big enough that many guests prefer to be escorted from their guest rooms to the reception area in a golf cart. This is not a bad idea if you have luggage, but if it's not too hot and you like to walk, you may find a wander in the property's whimsical gardens more enjoyable. The guest rooms are all luxurious, ranging from simple garden cottages to private villas with their own pools, and the friendly yet discreet staff go out of their way to make you feel welcome and well looked after.

At the edge of the old Pink City sits the delightful **Samode Haveli** (Samode House, Gangapole, tel. 141/263-2407, www.samode. com, Rs. 13,000 d), a luxurious royal residence turned hotel built in the Indo-Saracenic style in the 19th century. The place is strewn with memorabilia left by the former occupants, and the staff are warm and knowledgeable about the property's history. The guest rooms have been restored with period furniture to reflect the *haveli*'s history, but they include all the modern amenities you'd get in a five-star hotel. The restaurant is situated in what was once a royal dining hall and contains an amazing collection of well-restored frescoes.

Run by the Taj Group, one of India's top luxury chains, the 19-hectare **Taj Rambagh Palace** (Bhawani Singh Rd., tel. 141/221-1919, www.tajhotels.com, Rs. 31,500-45,100 d) is one of the snazziest places to stay in town. This revamped palace was built over 200 years ago and converted into a hotel in 1957 by Maharaja Sawai Man Singh II. Many of the guest rooms have recently been refurbished and incorporate fine silk drapes and bedding, hand-painted walls, and all the amenities you'd expect from a hotel of this level. Rambagh also offers some of the best fine-dining experiences in town, especially at the elegant Survana Mahal.

Couples and families looking for a bit of privacy and serenity will adore **❰ Tree of Life Resort and Spa** (Kacherawal-Kukas, www.treeofliferesorts.com, tel. 9602/091-000, Rs. 15,500-19,000 d). This sprawling

JAIPUR

a pool of one's own at Tree of Life Resort and Spa

COURTESY OF TREE OF LIFE RESORT & SPA

resort, situated 30 minutes' drive from central Jaipur, consists of 14 luxury villas, each with either a small garden or a private outdoor swimming pool (those without private pools can always swim at the large shared infinity pool). The small spa is designed especially for couples and only takes one individual or couple at a time. There's also a big focus on cuisine, and the chef creates custom menus for all guests. Culture buffs will appreciate the owner's large collection of Ganesh statues from around the world.

Simple, clean, and conveniently located near Amber Fort and the Jal Mahal, **Trident Jaipur** (Amber Fort Rd., tel. 141/267-0101, www.tridenthotels.com, Rs. 13,500-14,500 d) is a spacious, modern property with a design based on local aesthetics. With plenty of conference and business facilities, the Trident seems to be aimed more at those on work trips, but the guest rooms and facilities are not nearly as sterile as an average business hotel. The lakeview guest rooms have romantic views of the Jal Mahal.

Food

Jaipur is hardly a foodie's paradise, although there are a few good places to eat. A good percentage of Jaipur's restaurants serve only vegetarian food, and most of the nonvegetarian restaurants focus on rich Mughalai and tandoori dishes. Most restaurants aimed at visitors

focus on North Indian and Rajasthani dishes, such as *lal maas* (spicy mutton curry) and *dal baati churma* (lentils served with flour dumplings and unleavened bread). Street snacks such as *kachoris* (deep-fried round pastries stuffed with lentils or onions) and sweets such as *ghewar* (syrupy sweet funnel cakes) are considered local specialties and can be found at most sweets shops.

CAFÉS AND PATISSERIES

Inside one of Jaipur's best-known garment boutiques, the adorable ◖ **Anokhi Café** (2nd Fl., KK Square, C-11 Prithviraj Rd., C-Scheme, tel. 141/400-7245, www.anokhicafe.com, 10 A.M.-8 P.M. daily, Rs. 120) is an excellent place for good coffee and cakes as well as healthy vegetarian food. This self-service café is popular with expats and anyone dying for a decent salad. The desserts are not overly sweet, and many a Western visitor appreciates that the savories are not loaded with chili powder. Most of the food is organic or partially organic, with ingredients sourced from Anokhi's farm.

A short walk from C-Scheme's Statue Circle, **Brown Sugar** (Axis Mall, Bhagwan Das Rd., tel. 141/401-6611, 11 A.M.-11 P.M. daily, Rs. 50) is a popular hangout for young Jaipurites. This little café is on the ground floor of a small shopping mall, and while the interiors are nothing special, it's a great place to satisfy late-night sweet cravings. Most of the items on the menu are rich cakes and pastries, including quite a few eggless options. They also serve palatable sandwiches, noodles, and forgettable pizzas as well as a selection of espresso-based coffee drinks.

INDIAN

For a taste of Rajasthani cuisine toned down to suit the Western palate, book a table at ◖ **Jal Mahal** (Sheraton Rajputana, Palace Rd., tel. 141/510-0100, 12:30-3 P.M. and 7:30-11:30 P.M. daily, Rs. 600), the Sheraton Rajputana's spacious buffet restaurant. Chef Akshraj Jodha has designed a menu dubbed "Royal Repast," which includes specialty dishes from across the desert state, including rotis made of millet, *papadum* curry, and the quintessential *lal maas* (spicy lamb curry). There's a marked lack of fresh vegetable dishes on the menu; this is because

the staple foods of the state are legumes, grains, and meats due to its desert climate. Dishes are served with buttermilk, which aids in the digestion of heavy spices. *Thalis* (platters) are also available for those who want to try a bit of everything, and there's a buffet serving a variety of Indian and continental dishes for the most indecisive.

Gimmicky nostalgia abounds at **Sahib Sindh Sultan** (3rd Fl., Crystal Palm Mall, Bais Godam Circle, C-Scheme, tel. 141/406-4444, www.bjngroup.in, noon-3:30 P.M. and 7-11:30 P.M. daily, Rs. 375), a restaurant designed to recreate the train dining-car experience of days of yore. The centerpiece of the restaurant is a large Raj era–style railcar, a bit of an oddity for a restaurant in a modern shopping mall. Only four people can fit into one of the train booths, but there are tables outside the train for larger groups. And while the train theme likely draws in families and lovers of all things kitschy, the real reason to come is the delectable Mughalai and Punjabi food, featuring rich poultry and mutton dishes and plenty of vegetarian fare. There is even mildly spiced lobster stewed in pomegranate juice.

Popular with well-off Jaipurites is the trendy hookah bar **Sheesha** (Top Fl., City Pearl, MI Rd., near Khasa Kothi, tel. 141/403-3669, 11 A.M.-midnight daily, Rs. 250). This spacious restaurant resembles a redbrick loft and is illuminated with strings of multicolored lights. The background music is of the annoying techno-pop variety, but it's not loud enough to encumber conversation. Hookah serves up a vast selection of tandoori kebabs and breads as well as rich curries and rice dishes, and the cuisine is inspired by the royal cuisine of Mughal-era *nawabs* (rulers) and created by a chef from Lucknow, India's capital of nonvegetarian delights. Order cautiously—the portions are too large for all but the most voracious of eaters. Beer and wine are served, but not liquor.

It doesn't get any more elegant than the

beautiful **Suvarna Mahal** (Taj Rambagh Palace, Bhawani Singh Rd., tel. 141/221-1919, noon-3 P.M. and 7 P.M.-midnight daily, Rs. 800). Dining in this formal restaurant is like going back in time 100 years, thanks to its rose-hued interiors covered with large area rugs, period furniture embellished with petit point designs, massive crystal chandeliers hung from a frescoed ceiling, and gold-plated cutlery. The food is almost as exquisite as the ambience, and the menu is based on royal cuisines from across India.

MULTICUISINE

Known for its rich North Indian food and variety of meat-based dishes, MI Road's **Copper Chimney** (MI Rd., near GPO, tel. 141/237-2275, 11 A.M.-11:30 P.M. daily, Rs. 300) is the place to go if you are ravenously hungry: The portions are enormous, and most of the dishes are on the heavy side. There are also a few interesting continental dishes (gratins and the like), and alcohol is served. While it's definitely a safe and hygienic place to eat, the food is not the tastiest in town, and it seems that they rely more on the patronage of foreign and domestic travelers than on repeat local customers. The service is friendly but notoriously slow.

The vegetarian **Garden Café** (A-6 Mahaveer Marg, C-Scheme, tel. 141/237-9397, www.gardencafe.in, 11 A.M.-11 P.M. daily, Rs. 130) is neither a café in the strict sense nor in an actual garden (it's more of a patio), but it's still one of the best places to take a break from the heavy Rajasthani and Mughalai food that most of Jaipur's hotels are simply mad about. They do serve plenty of North and South Indian food as well as Indianized Chinese dishes, although the continental dishes, especially the nachos, moussaka, and wood-fired pizzas, are the main reason to come. There's also an air-conditioned indoor seating area for hot days.

Popularly abbreviated LMB, **Laxmi Mishtan Bandar** (Johari Bazar, tel. 141/257-8276, www.hotellmb.com, 8 A.M.-11:30 P.M. daily, Rs. 200) is Jaipur's best-known sweets shop, selling a huge choice of local and pan-Indian sweets and savory snacks. They also have a large vegetarian restaurant serving everything from North and South Indian specialties to macaroni and cheese. They also have a decent selection of Rajasthani dishes and *thalis.* The decor is nothing special (the place resembles a 1980s American chain hotel) but the waiters are prompt, although some are not particularly fluent in English. LMB is popular with Indian families and can get a bit noisy during peak meal times, but if you come in the late afternoon, you may get the place to yourself.

If you have reached the point where you can no longer stand the sight of curry, you'll find salvation at **Little Italy** (KK Square, C-11 Prithviraj Rd., C-Scheme, tel. 141/402-3444, www.littleitaly.in, noon-11 P.M. daily, Rs. 375), arguably the most authentic Italian joint in town. The interiors are classically simple without being institutional, but the main reason to visit is the food. The extensive menu includes everything from asparagus salad to cheese fondue as well as pizzas and every possible pasta concoction imaginable. They also have a few Indo-Chinese and North Indian dishes along with passable enchiladas. With such a wide selection, you won't even notice that this restaurant is strictly vegetarian.

A Jaipur institution, **Niros** (MI Rd., tel. 141/237-4493, www.nirosindia.com, 10 A.M.-4 P.M. and 6-11 P.M. daily, Rs. 250) has been serving a wide selection of dishes to Jaipurites and visitors since the 1960s. The interiors don't appear to have changed a lot since Niros first opened its doors half a century back, which gives it a bit of vintage charm. This multicuisine restaurant dishes up everything from tandoori chicken to baked fish florentine and prides itself as being the first place in Jaipur to serve Chinese food, which they do quite well. The servers are reasonably friendly and speak English well enough to explain some of the menu's less obvious dishes. Beer and wine are served.

On the roof of Hotel Pearl Palace, overlooking the ruins of the Hathroi Fort, the charming **Peacock Rooftop Restaurant** (Hari Kishan Somani Marg, Hathroi Fort, Ajmer Rd., tel. 141/237-3700, 7 A.M.-11 P.M. daily, Rs. 120) is a charming place to dine on cheap, unexceptional backpacker fare, including plenty of meat dishes. This outdoor restaurant is filled with plants and decorated with a combination of frescoes and replicas of ancient *warli* art, which match the funky rust-colored handmade wrought-iron chairs. It's especially pleasant at night when the sun goes down and strings of lights go on. Croissants and other pastries are on sale every morning 7-9 A.M. These are not as good as what you'd find in France or in most Indian five-star hotels—they taste like salty Indian butter—but nevertheless they're far superior to what you get in most of India's ubiquitous backpacker-focused "German bakeries."

Hookah smoking, or *shisha,* is a popular pastime in Jaipur, and one of the best places to puff is **Qilla Resto-Lounge** (E-145 Ramesh Marg, C-Scheme, tel. 141/401-7615, 10:30 A.M.-11 P.M. daily, Rs. 180). If you don't mind the smoky atmosphere, it's also a good place to grab a light meal. Like many of Jaipur's eateries, this place is "pure" (no eggs) vegetarian, but it makes up for its lack of meat-based ingredients with a wide selection of dishes, including a few attempts at Mexican cuisine and plenty of soups. Indian food, unsurprisingly, is also available. If you're feeling hungry, don't miss the *chaats,* light Indian snack foods that are normally served as street food.

Information and Services

VISITOR INFORMATION
The **Rajasthan Tourism Development Corporation** (RTDC, www.rajasthantourism. gov.in) is the governmental body in charge of administering state-run tourism services throughout Rajasthan. The RTDC-run tours can be booked at the RTDC's office (Government Hostel, MI Rd., tel. 141/511-0598, 7 A.M.-10 P.M. daily) or at Hotel Gangaur (near Khasa Kothi, MI Rd., tel. 141/237-1641) and Hotel Teej (Collectorate Rd., Bani Park, tel. 141/220-5482). Additional visitor information, maps, and planning assistance are provided at the RTDC's new office (Paryatan Bhawan, Khasa Kothi Hotel Campus, MI Rd., tel. 141/511-0598, 9 A.M.-7:30 P.M. Mon.-Fri.). There are also visitor information counters at Platform 1 of Jaipur's Railway Station (Railway Rd. and Khatipura Rd., tel. 141/231-5714, 7:30 A.M.-9:30 P.M. daily), at Deluxe Platform 3 of the Central Bus Stand (Narayan Singh Circle, Sawai Ram Singh Rd., tel. 141/220-6720, 7 A.M.-9 P.M. daily), and at Jaipur's Sanganer Airport.

MONEY
ATMs are ubiquitous in Jaipur, although many will only allow you to withdraw Rs. 10,000 at a time. The city also abounds with money changers, including quite a few unauthorized ones. Remember that changing money on the black market is a crime, and if you doubt the legitimacy of a money changer, ask him or her to furnish a certificate of authorization. Always ask for a receipt.

The largest number of foreign-exchange bureaus are on MI Road. Legitimate money changers here include **Thomas Cook** (Jaipur Tower, MI Rd., tel. 141/236-0940) and

Frequent Forex (Ganpati Plaza, MI Rd., tel. 141/239-7504, and 2916 Tiwari Bldg., opposite Niros, MI Rd., tel. 141/237-9422).

HOSPITALS AND PHARMACIES

Jaipur has plenty of pharmacies, and your hotel can advise you on where to find the closest one. Many close by 8-8:30 P.M., but **Maliram Sitaram Ayurvedic & Medical Store** (37 Kishan Pole Bazar, tel. 141/232-2568) in the Pink City is open until 10:30 P.M. Be wary of overzealous pharmacists; many will happily dole out huge doses of antibiotics for even the smallest of complaints. Most hotels have a doctor on-call 24-7, but if you feel in need of urgent care, your best option is **Fortis Hospital** (Jawahar Lal Nehru Marg, Malviya Nagar, tel. 141/254-7999).

INTERNET ACCESS

There's no shortage of Internet cafés in Jaipur, and most charge around Rs. 30 per hour for broadband access. Many hotels and guesthouses have Internet access in their lobbies or business centers. Wi-Fi is becoming increasingly popular, and these days even budget guesthouses offer free Wi-Fi to their guests; conversely, five-star and business hotels often charge a small fortune for access.

POSTAL SERVICES

Jaipur's **General Post Office** (GPO, MI Rd., tel. 141/236-8740, 10 A.M.-6 P.M. Mon.-Sat.) is the most convenient place in town to send packages home. There's also a smaller branch just up the road at **Sanganeri Gate** (tel. 141/257-1087). International parcels need to be stitched up in white fabric and sealed with a bit of red wax; this can be done at the GPO for a small fee, depending on the size of the package. Most reputable shops and emporiums can also arrange to ship purchases home on your behalf; some even offer this service free of charge.

LAUNDRY

The easiest way to get your clothes cleaned in Jaipur is by asking the front desk of your hotel or guesthouse to arrange for laundry services. High-end hotels will have machine laundry and dry-cleaning available; everyone else will rely on the hand washing services of the local *dhobi* (washer person), who will scrub, beat, and wring your garments until they are good as new. If you have delicate garments, it's better to wash them yourself or wait until you get home to have them laundered. Dry cleaners of varying repute are scattered throughout the city; **Ambassador Dry Cleaners** (MI Rd., near Niros Restaurant, tel. 141/237-2549) is popular with travelers.

LUGGAGE STORAGE

Most hotels and guesthouses are willing to store guests' luggage free of charge, and some will even hold onto it for a few days. There's also a left-luggage facility (known as a "cloakroom") at Jaipur's Railway Station, but you may be required to lock your luggage to use the facility. Charges start at Rs. 10 per day. The cloakroom is open 24 hours daily, although it can close for up to half an hour at a time for staff breaks. Check the closing times when you deposit your luggage to avoid showing up during a break time.

Getting There and Around

GETTING THERE

Jaipur is well connected to Delhi and Agra by road and rail. Delhi and Jaipur are linked by National Highway 8; National Highway 11 connects Jaipur and Agra.

Air

Jaipur's Sanganer Airport (JAI) is in the suburban district of Sanganer about 13 kilometers south of central Jaipur. There are direct flights between Delhi and Jaipur from early in the morning until about 9 P.M. Operators on the Delhi-Jaipur route include Air India, Jet Airways, Kingfisher Airlines, and SpiceJet. There are also direct flights to other major cities around India. Currently, the only direct international flights operating from Jaipur are to the United Arab Emirates and Oman in the Middle East. There are no flights between Jaipur and Agra.

Train
DELHI TO JAIPUR

There are plenty of trains linking Delhi and Jaipur, and all take 4.5-6 hours. The *Shatabdi Express* leaves New Delhi Railway station every morning at 6:05 A.M., reaching Jaipur at 10:30 A.M. The *Shatabdi* leaves Jaipur for Delhi every evening at 5:50 P.M. and arrives in Delhi at around 10:40 P.M. All of the compartments are air-conditioned, and meals, included in the ticket price, are served on board.

AGRA TO JAIPUR

On most days there are five trains between Jaipur and Agra, and the journey takes 4-5 hours. Most trains use the Agra Fort Railway Station; the *Gwalior Udaipur Super Express* train arrives at Agra Cantt.

OTHER TRAINS

There are also a number of regular trains to Ajmer (for Pushkar, 2-3 hours), Sawai Madhopur (for Ranthambore National Park), Alwar (for Sariska National Park), and Bharatpur (for Keoladeo Ghana National Park). The *Haridwar Adi Mail* is the only train that connects Jaipur to Haridwar (for Rishikesh); it leaves Jaipur at 11:15 P.M. daily.

Bus

There are a number of buses of varying quality between Delhi and Jaipur, from basic, usually crowded "local" buses that stop for passengers along the way to more comfortable air-conditioned Volvo buses that have assigned seats and only stop once along the way for tea and a restroom break. The most reliable are those operated by the **Rajasthan State Road Transport Corporation** (RSRTC, www.rsrtc.gov.in). These range from basic unair-conditioned buses to more deluxe buses with LCD TVs (best avoided unless your idea of a peaceful bus journey includes five hours of blaring Bollywood movies) and cost Rs. 400-730. Most buses use **Jaipur's Central Bus Stand** (Narayan Singh Circle, Sawai Ram Singh Rd., tel. 141/237-3044), although buses that arrive in Jaipur in the middle of the night drop passengers at Badi Chaupur in the old Pink City (it's best to avoid arriving in the middle of the night).

In Delhi, most buses use **Bikaner House** (tel. 11/2338-3469) near Central Delhi's India Gate, although some go to the Interstate Bus Terminal (ISBT) in Old Delhi instead or in addition.

Taxi

It's a common practice for visitors to hire a taxi in Delhi and cover the entire Golden Triangle by car. Fuel costs are always included, but be sure to check whether quoted charges also include tolls and pocket money for drivers. You can usually negotiate a flat rate or a per-kilometer rate plus "out-of-station" (out-of-town) charges. Rates are higher if you decide to use the air-conditioning. Even if you only want to be dropped in Jaipur from Delhi or Agra, you will still have to pay for a round-trip journey. The drive between Delhi and Jaipur is smooth, thanks to recent repaving of National Highway 8, which connects the two cities. The drive takes 5-6 hours by taxi, and a two-night, three-day trip in a Tata Indigo or Toyota Etios sedan costs Rs. 6,500-7,500, including taxes and tolls, for 600 kilometers of travel (additional fees apply if you exceed your kilometer limit). For the best deals, avoid booking through hotels, which take hefty commissions, and go straight to travel agents. Your best bet is to book a car in Delhi through the very reliable **Destination India Travel Centre** (78 Janpath, 1st Fl., tel. 11/2371-2345, www.indiatripmakers.com), who have their own fleet of cars complete with English-speaking drivers. They can also arrange tours and cars for people already in Jaipur. Another reputable, though more expensive, option is **Rajasthan Tours** (Rambagh Palace, Bhawani Singh Rd., tel. 141/238-5141, www.rajasthantouronline.com), which has branch offices all over Rajasthan.

GETTING AROUND
Autorickshaw

Jaipur is fairly easy to get around, and the most common way to get from point A to point B is by autorickshaw (sometimes referred to as *tuk-tuks* in Jaipur). Most autorickshaws charge Rs. 400-450 per day, although they subsidize these low rates by getting visitors to stop at commission-paying handicraft shops. If you don't want to shop, you can either explain that you don't want to shop and negotiate a higher rate at the beginning of your trip, or just not say anything and refuse when your driver tries to take you

anywhere you don't want to go. Note that there have been cases where drivers ditch passengers who refuse to go shopping, so make sure not to leave anything in the autorickshaw while visiting sites. It's also a good idea to write down the driver's name, phone number, and license plate details. Never take an autorickshaw without negotiating the price first.

Taxi

Taxis are another way to get around town, and the drivers are somewhat less likely to be touts than rickshaw drivers are. Unfortunately, they also aren't as easy to park, so using this form of transportation can sometimes take longer than the slower but more compact autorickshaw. Taxis charge Rs. 700-1,200 per day. Metered radio cabs are also available and charge Rs. 12-15 per kilometer, plus a 25 percent surcharge at night. Established operators include **Metro Cabs** (tel. 141/424-4444, www.metrocabs.in) and **My Cab** (tel. 141/500-0000, www.mycabs.in).

Cycle Rickshaw

For short distances, you can also take an eco-friendly cycle rickshaw, which is essentially a three-wheeled hybrid between a bicycle and a cart. The rates are negotiable and usually start at about Rs. 20, depending on the distance covered. Be generous: Pulling a cycle rickshaw is even harder than it looks, especially in sweltering desert heat, and India's rickshaw wallahs are among the poorest people in the country.

Metro

A mixed aboveground and underground Metro is currently being constructed in Jaipur and is expected to start running in early 2013. The Metro will connect Badi Chaupur in the Pink City with Man Sarovar in the suburbs, stopping at the railway station and Civil Lines en route. A second north-south line has also been proposed.

Tours

The **Rajasthan Tourism Development Corporation** (RTDC, tel. 141/247-5466, tours@rtdc.in) also offers bus tours. The **half-day tour** (8 A.M.-1 P.M., 11:30 A.M.-4:30 P.M., and 1:30-6:30 P.M., Rs. 250) includes visits to the Birla Mandir, the Albert Hall, the Jantar Mantar, the City Palace, and Amber Fort. They also drive by the Hawa Mahal, Gaitore, and the Jal Mahal. The **full-day tour** (9 A.M.-6 P.M., Rs. 300) includes all of these sites plus a visit to the forts of Jaigarh and Nahargarh, where they stop for lunch. They also go by the Birla Planetarium and will drop you here if you want. The **Pink City by Night tour** (6:30-10:30 P.M., Rs. 375) is mostly bus-based, and although they stop quickly for photo ops in front of most of the monuments visited, the only long stops are at an over-priced handicraft emporium and the enchanting Nahargarh (Tiger Fort), where an included vegetarian buffet supper is served (this is the highlight of the tour). Tours can be booked at the following pickup points: Transport Unit (Government Hostel Campus, MI Rd., tel. 141/237-5466), RTDC Hotel Gangaur (near Khasa Kothi, MI Rd., tel. 141/237-1641), RTDC Hotel Teej (Collectorate Rd., Bani Park, tel. 141/220-5482), and at the visitor information counters at the bus stand (tel. 141/231-5714) and railway station (tel. 141/220-6720). Note that admission fees to the monuments are not included in the ticket price of these tours.

JAIPUR

EXCURSIONS AROUND THE TAJ MAHAL, DELHI, AND JAIPUR

If you have the time, a side trip from Delhi, Jaipur, or Agra will give you an excellent feel for life in India beyond the big cities. Fortunately, there are plenty of great spots to visit around the Golden Triangle, all of which have excellent infrastructure for visitors and plenty of fascinating things to see and do.

If you're interested in Hinduism and other Indian spiritual traditions, you'll adore Rishikesh, a charming holy town on the banks of the sacred Ganges River in the Himalayan foothills. It seems like you can't take more than two steps in Rishikesh without bumping into an ashram or temple, and its dozens of yoga schools have earned the settlement the nickname "yoga capital of the world." The spiritually minded will also enjoy Pushkar, an oasis town east of Jaipur, built around a holy lake that attracts Hindu pilgrims from across the country. This little town is popular with backpackers and budget travelers and is a perfect base for short camel safaris into the desert.

History buffs will take interest in Mussoorie, a colonial town with a distinctly British feel to it. This wooded hill station is also one of the closest places to Delhi to get away from the summer heat, and it is a great place to hike year-round. Art lovers will appreciate the famous frescoes of the Shekhawati region, often touted as India's "open-air art gallery."

Nature enthusiasts won't want to miss one of

HIGHLIGHTS

◖ Parmarth Niketan Ashram: Don't miss the chanting and ritual offerings that take place every evening at this Rishikesh ashram's *aarti* (prayer ceremony) on the banks of the Ganges River (page 159).

◖ The Mall: Take a walk in the clouds and enjoy the views from Mussoorie's main strip (page 167).

◖ Jagatpita Shri Brahma Temple: One of the only temples dedicated to creator god Brahma in the world, this Pushkar temple is one of the holiest spots in an already very holy town (page 175).

◖ Dr. Ramnath A. Podar Haveli Museum: This old *haveli* in Shekhawati is literally covered with beautiful frescoes and has been turned into an interesting museum highlighting local culture (page 184).

◖ Ranthambore National Park: If you're going to spot a tiger during your India trip, this is the most likely place. While you're at it, don't miss the fascinating old ruins at Ranthambore Fort, near the entrance to the park (page 185).

LOOK FOR ◖ TO FIND RECOMMENDED SIGHTS, ACTIVITIES, DINING, AND LODGING.

the region's national parks. Bird-watchers will love the variety of avian species that flock to the Keoladeo National Park every year. Those traveling by road from Delhi to Jaipur can easily make a stopover at Sariska Tiger Reserve, a national park that is home to a huge variety of wild cats, including a few tigers. If tigers are really what you're after, your best bet is Ranthambore National Park, one of the world's most famous tiger reserves.

PLANNING YOUR TIME

All of the destinations in this chapter are within easy reach of the Golden Triangle. Rishikesh and Mussoorie, in the Himalayan foothills,

both make great side trips from Delhi, and each merits two nights' stay. Pushkar can be done as a day trip from Jaipur, although you'll get more out of the experience if you allow yourself to fall into the town's intrinsic slow pace and give yourself a few days here. The Shekhawati region and Sariska Tiger Reserve are both located between Delhi and Jaipur and make excellent stopovers en route between the two cities, but only if you are traveling by car. Keoladeo National Park near Bharatpur is located on the road between Agra and Jaipur and can be visited on a day trip from Agra (if you start early, you can combine it with a visit to the ruins at Fatehpur Sikri). Ranthambore is nearest to

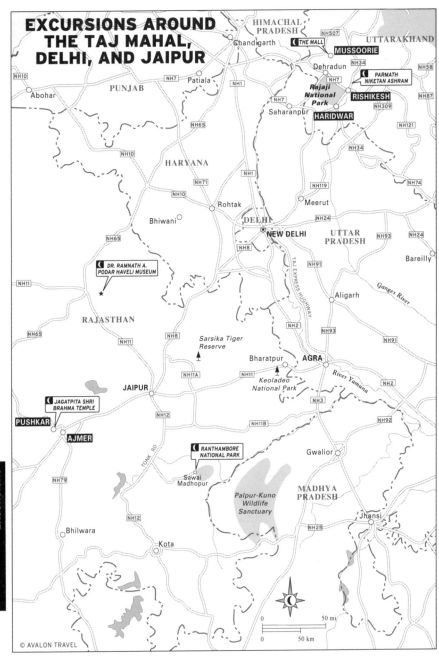

EXCURSIONS

© AVALON TRAVEL

Jaipur and can be done as a day trip (if you leave very early), although most people prefer to stay one night and go on an early morning tiger safari the next day.

The Himalayan Foothills

There are a few real gems of towns just north of Delhi in the Himalayan foothill region known as Garhwal in Uttarakhand state. On the banks of the Ganges River, the holy towns of Rishikesh and Haridwar are recommended for those interested in visiting temples, and Rishikesh in particular is known internationally as a center for yoga and meditation studies. A bit higher up is the old Raj-era hill station of Mussoorie, notable for its cool climate and many walking circuits. Hill stations were used by the British during colonial times as summer retreats when the heat of Delhi was too much to handle. This tradition of heading to the hills in the summer has continued to this day, although these days, most people come only for weekend breaks.

RISHIKESH

On the banks of the River Ganges, the most sacred body of water to Hindu people, Rishikesh is a charming little town filled with ashrams, temples, and shops selling New Age gear. There are also a lot of stalls scattered throughout the city, most of which sell more or less the same thing: inexpensive religious iconography, gemstones for astrological use, and yoga paraphernalia. Some of the local yoga centers and ashrams organize musical performances from time to time, but there are few regular events and virtually nothing in terms of nightlife.

Rishikesh is touted widely as the "yoga capital of the world," and for good reason: There's seemingly a yoga school on every corner, and it is especially popular with foreign yoga aficionados. It's also an important pilgrimage spot—stories of Rishikesh appear in ancient Vedic texts—and the little city attracts Hindus from across the country, who come to seek blessings by bathing in the holy river.

The town is divided into a lot of small areas and is most congested around the city center, on the southwest banks of the Ganges. This is the least pleasant part of town, and most foreign visitors prefer to stay near one of the two suspension bridges: Ram Jhula and Laxman Jhula. Ram Jhula attracts a more sedate crowd, and travelers here tend to be a bit older and more yoga-focused than the people who stay in Laxman Jhula. The majority of the hotels and guesthouses near Ram Jhula are on the eastern banks of the river, in and around a tiny ashram-filled area known as Swargashram. About two kilometers upstream, the Laxman Jhula area has tons of guesthouses on both sides of the bridge; it is a bit more of a backpacker scene. There's also a small beach that's popular with swimmers, but be aware that the current in the Ganges is much more powerful than meets the eye, and swimmers unfamiliar with the river have been swept away to their deaths.

Sights and Activities
BHARAT MATA MANDIR AND TRIVENI GHAT

Just west of Swargashram, near Rishikesh city center, is the most important bathing ghat (set of stairs) in town. This is where the Ganges, the Yamuna, and the mythical Saraswati Rivers merge, and evening prayer ceremonies known as *aartis* are held. Near the ghat stands the famous Bharat Mata Mandir, a white-domed temple dedicated to Lord Vishnu, the preserver in the Hindu trinity. The original temple structure was built by renowned saint Adi Shankaracharya in the 12th century, only to be destroyed by Timur in 1398.

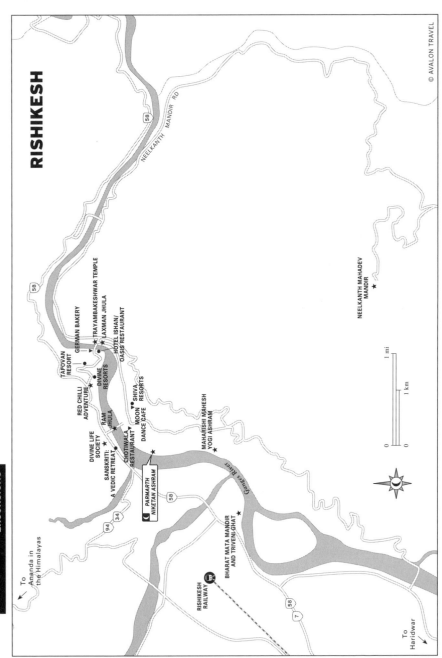

RISHIKESH

© AVALON TRAVEL

©RAJAT DEEP RANA

pilgrims bathing in the Ganges River in Rishikesh

DIVINE LIFE SOCIETY

One of the most significant ashrams in Rishikesh, the Divine Life Society (Shivanandanagar, Muni ki Reti, tel. 135/243-0040, www.sivanandaonline.org) was established in 1936 by Swami Sivananda Saraswati, a doctor turned guru whose influence on the international popularity of yoga is notable to this day. There's a long list of daily activities (a schedule can be obtained from the main office), including yoga classes (separate for men and women), chanting, and an evening ritual *aarti* on the banks of the Ganges. There's also a small bookshop (9-11:30 A.M. and 2-5 P.M. daily) affiliated with the ashram that stocks most of Sivananda's many books. Serious yogis can also apply for a residency at the ashram.

◖ PARMARTH NIKETAN ASHRAM

This famous ashram (Swargashram, tel. 135/243-4301, www.parmarth.com) has pretty gardens filled with colorful plaster statues of various deities, but the main draw is the evening *aarti* ceremony that the ashram stages at its ghat, in front of a giant statue of Lord Shiva. Every evening at sunset, devotees, swamis, and students from the ashram's yoga *gurukul* (essentially a spiritual boarding school for children) come to the ghat to chant, perform rituals, and send their prayers off into the Ganges by launching offerings in the form of little banana-leaf boats containing flowers and small lit candles. It's a beautiful, and, for many, mystical experience, and visitors are welcome to join in. You can purchase offerings from one of the many vendors in the area and say a prayer yourself. The ashram also offers a residential yoga program.

LAXMAN JHULA AND RAM JHULA SUSPENSION BRIDGES

While many visitors enjoy the romance of taking a riverboat across the Ganges, it's much easier just to cross one of the two suspension

EXCURSIONS

bridges. The oldest of these, the 165-meter-long **Laxman Jhula** (near Tapovan, upstream from Ram Jhula) was built in 1927-1929 to replace a shorter bridge downriver that had been washed out during a flood in 1924. The bridge is built on the same spot where Laxman, brother of Ram (the protagonist of the great Hindu epic the *Ramayana*), is believed to have crossed the Ganges on a jute rope. A little under two kilometers west of Laxman Jhula, **Ram Jhula** (downstream from Laxman Jhula toward Rishikesh city center) connects Shivanandanagar with Swargashram. This bridge was built in the 1980s. Both bridges attract lots of monkeys, and children often gather on both bridges to sell fish food; on clear-water days, those with good vision can see the fish below. Laxman Jhula in particular has a lot of touts, including postcard hawkers and priests who will perform a small ceremony on you and then demand a donation.

© RAJAT DEEP RANA

the serene grounds of Parmarth Niketan Ashram

NEELKANTH MAHADEV MANDIR

One of the area's most significant pilgrimage sites, this forest temple (sunrise-8 P.M. daily) is dedicated to Lord Shiva, in his blue-faced form of Neelkanth (*neelkanth* means "blue throat" in Sanskrit). According to legend, gods and demons churned the sea in order to create divine nectar (*amrit*). A deadly poison known as *halahala* was created as a by-product of the process, and to save the world from ingesting this toxic substance, Shiva drank it all himself. When his consort, Parvati, saw what he'd done, she quickly strangled him to stop the poison from passing into his belly. Doing this caused his neck and face to turn blue, earning him the name Neelkanth. The temple is about 13 kilometers on foot (the fairly easy trek from Swargashram takes 3-4 hours) or 38 kilometers by road (via Neelkanth Mandir Rd., east of Rishikesh). Avoid coming in the holy month

of Shravan (usually July-Aug.), when the place is overrun with devotees.

TRAYAMBAKESHWAR TEMPLE

The 13-story Trayambakeshwar Temple (Ganges River south bank, near Laxman Jhula suspension bridge, 5:30 A.M.-8 P.M. daily) contains multiple floors of deities and picture-window displays of scenes from Vedic texts. The floors get progressively smaller as you climb to the top (you have to walk around each floor), and there are some exceptional vantage points from the narrow higher levels.

JUMPIN' HEIGHTS

Thrill seekers won't want to miss a visit to Jumpin' Heights (Badrinath Rd., Laxman Jhula, tel. 135/2443-1000, www.jumpin-heights.com, Wed.-Mon.). This self-proclaimed "extreme adventure zone" offers three main

YOGA IN RISHIKESH

There are dozens of yoga courses to choose from in Rishikesh. These are a few of the most popular.

PARMARTH NIKETAN ASHRAM

The Parmarth Niketan Ashram (Swargashram, tel. 135/243-4301, www.parmarth.com, www.internationalyogafestival.com) offers yoga, meditation, and philosophy courses for people of all experience levels. Most range two weeks to one month in length. They also host the International Yoga Festival every winter.

PATANJALI INTERNATIONAL YOGA FOUNDATION

The non-residential Patanjali yoga center (opposite Tapovan Resort, tel. 941/136-1825, www.patanjali-yogafoundation.com) offers certificate programs in ayurveda therapy and yoga teacher training.

RISHIKESH YOG PEETH

Two-week yoga courses for beginners and yoga teacher training as well as short yoga, ayurveda, and meditation retreats are the main offerings of the residential Rishikesh Yog Peeth yoga center (Krishna Cottage, Swargashram, tel. 135/244-0193, www.rishikeshyogpeeth.com), in a converted guesthouse.

TRIKA YOGA AND MEDITATION

Affiliated with the Agama Yoga movement, daily courses in yoga and philosophy are taught at Trika (Gaddi Hall, Swargashram, tel. 989/737-1217, www.trika.agamayoga.com), often by non-Indian instructors.

YOGA NIKETAN ASHRAM

A residential program in yoga and philosophy is offered at Yoga Niketan Ashram (Muni-ki-Reti, tel. 135/243-0227, www.yoganiketanashram.org). A minimum stay of 15 days is required in most cases.

---

activities: bungee jumping, flying-fox ziplining, and a giant swing (similar to bungee jumping, except that after you jump, you swing upright, as if on a pendulum). Adventure specialists from New Zealand designed all of the infrastructure. Shuttles from Laxman Jhula to the sight run hourly 8:30 A.M.-2:30 P.M.

RAFTING

Rishikesh is a well-known rafting destination, and almost all travel agents can organize rafting trips. The most established rafting company is **Red Chilli Adventure** (Tapovan, Laxman Jhula, tel. 135/243-4021, www.redchilliadventure.com). Most customers opt for a 26-kilometer half-day circuit (Rs. 800) or a 35-kilometer full-day trip (Rs. 1,500, lunch included), although you can also opt for longer rafting expeditions lasting 12 days or longer. Note that trips occasionally get canceled on rainy days due to unsafe weather conditions.

MAHARISHI MAHESH YOGI ASHRAM

Often referred to as the Beatles Ashram in honor of its most famous guests, the rundown Maharishi Mahesh Yogi Ashram complex (Swargashram, 10 minutes on foot west of Ram Jhula) was once the headquarters of the Maharishi Mahesh Yogi, the pint-size founder of Transcendental Yoga. Through the 1960s and 1970s the Maharishi taught this form of nondenominational mantra meditation to an entire generation of Westerners, including a few celebrities. The Beatles lived here for a few weeks, and the song "Fool on the Hill" is said to be about the guru. Today, the ashram is in ruins and has been overtaken by rainforest plants, langurs, and more than a few huge spiders. Nevertheless, it's an interesting place for a stroll, and it's especially fun to climb inside the egg-shaped meditation domes where devotees used to stay. The bottom floor of these rooms served as sleeping quarters, while the upper dome-like part was reserved strictly

SEA OF ORANGE: THE KANVAR YATRA

Every summer during the Hindu month of Shrawan, Rishikesh fills up with thousands of saffron-clad Shiva devotees, known as *kanvariyas*, who travel from villages across Northern India to collect Ganges River water from sacred spots to bring back to their hometowns. Many of the participants are men in their late teens or early 20s, for whom participation in this annual pilgrimage informally marks their coming-of-age within the community. They are supposed to travel on foot (although they often rent large trucks and semis) and take turns carrying water while their companions drive alongside. At night, the groups of young men often park their trucks on the side of the road and dance wildly to blaring remixes of devotional music; it looks a bit like a religious rave. Rishikesh and the other holy sites get very crowded and rowdy during this time, and some people prefer to schedule their visits so that they don't coincide with the Kanvar Yatra.

for meditation. Note that the ashram property is owned by the government and not officially open to the public, but a Rs. 50 "donation" to the guard at the gate will get you access.

Accommodations
UNDER RS. 1,000

Next to Laxman Jhula, the backpacker favorite **Hotel Ishan** (near the bridge, Laxman Jhula, tel. 135/244-2192, Rs. 300-800 d) is one of the best deals in town. The pricier guest rooms are on the upper floors, and some have spectacular views of the Ganges. The cheaper guest rooms (101-104) on the lower floors can be a bit on the loud side during the day, mostly due to the record shop below, which has blasted the same CD of Hindu chanting on repeat mode for years now, much to the chagrin of long-term guests of the hotel.

A 10-minute walk uphill from Swargashram, the peaceful **Shiva Resorts** (tel. 135/244-0094, Rs. 250 d) has been a favorite with yogis on a budget for many years. Guest rooms wrap around a grassy garden with a small fountain. The accommodations are basic, and most rooms are without air-conditioning, but the prices are reasonable and the property is well maintained. Although it's more of a guesthouse than a resort, the numerous amenities, including an ayurvedic spa, a yoga hall, and a clean

restaurant, make it possible for guests to stay occupied without stepping off the property.

RS. 1,000-3,000

Tapovan Resort (Tapovan, Laxman Jhula, tel. 135/249-192, tapovanresort@yahoo.com, Rs. 1,480-2,250) is one of the quieter spots in town, owing primarily to its location off the main road, away from the majority of foot traffic. The guest rooms on the upper floors have excellent views of the hotel's garden, with the Ganges in the background. There's a decent Indian restaurant on-site, and daily yoga classes are offered in the ground-floor yoga studio. Guest rooms are air-conditioned and equipped with TVs; the deluxe guest rooms also have balconies, although some are on the garden levels and are better described as patios.

RS. 3,000-10,000

For some of the best Ganges River views in town, check in to the popular **Divine Resorts** (Tapovan, Laxman Jhula, tel. 135/244-2128, www.divineresort.com, Rs. 3,500-5,500 d), a short stroll from Laxman Jhula. All the guest rooms are spacious, with marble floors, sofas, and small fridges. The executive guest rooms, which are reached by a vertigo-inducing glass elevator, have uninterrupted views of

EXCURSIONS

the Ganges and are close enough to the sacred river that guests can actually hear the water as it rushes by.

On the banks of the Ganges, just next to the Sivananda Ashram, the peaceful **Sanskriti: A Vedic Retreat** (Swargashram, Yatri Niwas, Ram Jhula, tel. 135/244-2444, www.sanskritivedicretreat.com, Rs. 3,000 d) offers all of the personalized service of a boutique hotel at great rates. The six guest rooms are decorated in a rustic-chic fashion, with faux rosewood floors and furnishings complimented by traditional Indian upholstery in earthy hues. All of the guest rooms are river-facing—unfortunately, they're also on the second floor, so the views aren't great. There's also an ayurvedic restaurant, which serves food tailored to guests' ayurvedic constitutions, along with massage facilities and yoga classes.

RS. 10,000 AND UP

Considering Rishikesh's reputation as the yoga capital of the world, it's no surprise that one of the world's top destination spas, **◖ Ananda in the Himalayas** (The Palace Estate, Narendra Nagar, tel. 1378/227-500, www.anandaspa.com, Rs. 30,500-47,500 d), is based here. On a hilltop 16 kilometers from Laxman Jhula, a stay at this haven of peace will quickly make you forget about all of the more stressful aspects of traveling in India. This spa resort uses ayurveda, India's ancient system of healing, to help guests with everything from weight loss to stress management, and ayurvedic systems prevail everywhere from the spa to the restaurant. The daily wellness menu has meals tailored to guests' dominant *doshas,* or body constitutions, as determined by the on-site ayurvedic doctor. Daily group activities include yoga classes, lessons in classical Indian music, and lectures on Vedanta, the philosophy behind much of the Hindu belief structures. There's also a heated swimming pool, a six-hole golf course, and a number of beautiful yoga and meditation pavilions, all with stunning views of the Ganges River some 900 meters below.

Food

Established in 1958, Rishikesh's most famous place to eat is **Chotiwala Restaurant** (Atma Prakash Marg, Swargashram, tel. 135/243-0070, www.chotiwalarestaurant.com, 7 A.M.-10 P.M. daily, Rs. 100), a must-visit for domestic travelers and a good place to rub shoulders with religious pilgrims while feasting on vegetarian Indian fare. There are actually two Chotiwalas next to each other, each of which has a man dressed as their mascot (a priest-like character with a shaved head and a rat tail, commonly worn by Hindu Brahman men). The owners of each diner are brothers, in friendly competition to get the most customers.

The tastiest cakes and pastries in town are served at the open-air **German Bakery** (tel. 135/212-2055, 8 A.M.-9 P.M. daily, Rs. 120), at the west end of the Laxman Jhula suspension bridge. Although this place is best known for its baked goods (the cinnamon rolls are to die for), an excellent array of Indian, Chinese, and continental meals, including delicious homemade spinach pasta dishes, are also served. The bakery is almost as popular with local rhesus macaques as it is with foreign travelers—tempting as it may be, feeding leftover scraps to monkeys will only encourage them to come foraging in the restaurant.

Popular with Western yoga students, the semi-enclosed rooftop **Moon Dance Café** (near the taxi stand, Ram Jhula, tel. 8126/527-922, 8 A.M.-10 P.M. daily, Rs. 110) serves up a variety of affordable snacks and meals, including veggie burgers, lasagnas, and vegetarian takes on full English breakfasts. The daily menu often features some interesting tofu concoctions. Avoid the far-too-oily pad thai, but don't miss the French onion soup. While the food here is delicious, it's not a great place to go when you are famished—the kitchen is tiny and thus meals can take ages to prepare.

The menu of **Oasis Restaurant** (Hotel Ishan, near the bridge, Laxman Jhula, tel. 135/244-2192, 8 A.M.-10 P.M. daily, Rs. 90), lists every possible backpacker concoction imaginable, from avocado *lassis* to Russian beet soup. The Indianized Tex-Mex food is nothing like what you might find in El Paso, but it's still some of the best in India. The staff is friendly, and the service is much prompter than in most backpacker cafés. You can opt to sit in the airy main restaurant, with large glass windows overlooking the Ganges, or in the smaller windowless bakery section below, with floor seating and cable TV.

Information and Services

Most travel agencies in Rishikesh double as Internet cafés and charge Rs. 30 per hour for high-speed Internet access. Unfortunately, most of them don't have power backup for their computers, so remember to save your work, as power cuts are frequent. The majority of guesthouses and hotels in Rishikesh are yet to offer Wi-Fi.

Travel agents can book private vehicles and train tickets as well as give advice on day trips and local attractions. In Rishikesh town there's also a state-run **Tourist Bureau** (Haridwar Bye Pass Rd., tel. 135/243-0209, 9 A.M.-5 P.M. Mon.-Sat.), where you can pick up maps. Its primary specialty seems to be assisting religious pilgrims in the area, however, so unless you plan to book a pilgrimage somewhere, you may find a visit to be a waste of time.

Both the Ram Jhula and Laxman Jhula areas have **post offices**. The Swargashram branch (tel. 135/243-0019, 10 A.M.-4 P.M. Mon.-Fri., 10 A.M.-1 P.M. Sat.) is located near the Sivananda Ashram on the Muni-ki-Reti side of the bridge. The Laxman Jhula branch (tel. 135/243-0292, 10 A.M.-4 P.M. Mon.-Fri., 10 A.M.-1 P.M. Sat.) is on the road that connects Swargashram with Laxman Jhula. You can get parcels packed here for a small fee.

Most of the travel agencies in town can exchange currency for a nominal fee. The only **ATMs** in the touristed part of Rishikesh are in Swargashram, near the Ram Jhula suspension bridge. If you're coming from the bridge, the Axis Bank ATM is on the right, just before Chotiwala Restaurant. If you continue uphill past Chotiwala, the State Bank of India ATM is on the left.

There are not many pharmacies in the touristed part of town, although you can easily get ayurvedic medicine all over town. One of the best selections can be found at **Divya Ganga Herbals** (Swargashram, near Divine Life Society, tel. 135/244-2115, 10 A.M.-8 P.M. daily). For allopathic medicines, head into Rishikesh city center, where there are dozens of pharmacies on the main street (Haridwar Rd.). The closest hospital to Ram Jhula is the **Nimral Ashram Hospital** (off Haridwar Rd., Mayakund, tel. 135/243-0942, www.nirmalhospitals.com).

Getting There and Around

Although Rishikesh does have its own railway station, only a handful of local trains come here. If you're coming from Delhi, Jaipur, or Agra, take a train to Haridwar; from Haridwar, the easiest way to get to Rishikesh is by taxi (25-30 minutes, about Rs. 500) or by taking a shared autorickshaw (also called a Vikram, 45-60 minutes, Rs. 35-40 pp). Make sure to specify whether you want to be dropped at Rishikesh city center, Ram Jhula (for Swargashram and Muni-ki-Reti), or Laxman Jhula (for Tapovan). Note that about halfway along your journey, once you cross the border between greater Haridwar and greater Rishikesh, you may be asked to switch to a different shared autorickshaw. This is pretty standard and helps keep both Rishikesh and Haridwar rickshaw operators in business. Just remember not to pay anyone until the end of your journey.

FROM DELHI

Trains from Delhi to Haridwar take 4-5 hours. Most people prefer to book a seat on the comfortable *Dehradun Shatabdi Express,* which leaves Delhi at 6:50 A.M. and gets to Haridwar about 4.5 hours later. The return journey from Haridwar on this train leaves at 6:13 P.M. and reaches Delhi just before 11 P.M.

Once in Haridwar, you can take a taxi, bus, or shared Vikram (basically a large autorickshaw) to Rishikesh. Buses stop at Rishikesh's main bus stand, so from here you have to arrange an autorickshaw to Ram Jhula or Laxman Jhula, depending on where you are staying. Some Vikrams will take you all the way to Ram Jhula or even Laxman Jhula and will charge around Rs. 35 per person for the trip.

Rishikesh is fairly walkable, and most people get around on foot or motorcycle. Shared jeeps (Rs. 10) run between the south side of Laxman Jhula and Swargashram, southeast of Ram Jhula. Vikrams run between Laxman Jhula and Ram Jhula (Rs. 5 pp). You can also take a shared Vikram from either of the suspension bridges to Rishikesh town (Rs. 5 from Ram Jhula, Rs. 10 from Laxman Jhula).

There are also plenty of local buses that link Delhi to Haridwar and Rishikesh. For many years, two private nonstop buses left the Muni-ki-Reti petrol pump every day, although at the time of writing this service was suspended. Local buses (that make many stops) leave from Rishikesh's bus stand every 30-60 minutes and usually take about 7-8 hours to reach Delhi's main bus terminal (ISBT). A taxi from Delhi to Rishikesh and back costs Rs. 5,000 and up, depending on how long you stay; the drive takes around six hours.

FROM AGRA AND JAIPUR

Two trains run between Haridwar and Agra Cantonment. Both leave Agra in the morning and take 9.5 hours. The *Haridwar Mail* connects Haridwar to Jaipur and Ajmer (for Pushkar). The journey between Jaipur and Haridwar takes 13 hours; Haridwar to Ajmer takes 15.5 hours.

FROM MUSSOORIE

Trains also run between Dehradun (for Mussoorie) and Haridwar and take about 1.5 hours, but if you're coming from Dehradun or Mussoorie, it's easier—and slightly faster—just to take a local bus, shared jeep, or private taxi directly to Rishikesh.

You can also fly from Delhi to Dehradun's Jolly Grant Airport (DED) and then travel to Rishikesh from there. If you take into account airport check-in times and the hour or so it will take you to reach Rishikesh from Jolly Grant, however, it's probably not worth it. Moreover, the road between Rishikesh and Jolly Grant is often closed in the evening due to the risk of elephant attacks.

HARIDWAR

Anyone with an interest in Hinduism will adore Haridwar. This busy city attracts pilgrims from all over India who come to pray to the Ganges River. It's also the sight of the site of the Ardh and Purna Kumbh Melas, huge pilgrimages that rotate among four major Ganges River locations every 6-12 years. The Kumbh Mela is considered the largest religious gathering in the world.

Haridwar is the gateway to Rishikesh, and while it has a lot of hotels, most are aimed at Indian visitors and lack some of the charm (and standards of cleanliness) of the hotels in Rishikesh. If possible, try to stay in Rishikesh and either visit Haridwar as a day trip or stop off for a couple of hours en route to Delhi.

Sights and Activities
HAR KI PAURI

The main bathing ghat (set of stairs) in Haridwar, Har ki Pauri is awash with the devout year-round and is always filled with activity. Daytime is marked by crowds of religious visitors praying and bathing, and it's a vibrant place to people-watch or browse the dozens of little stalls nearby selling religious paraphernalia. Just make sure to avoid taking photos of people while they are taking a dip. Har ki Pauri is also quite enchanting at night, when priests and pilgrims descend on the ghat to perform the evening *aarti* ritual. If you have a good camera, you can get some great shots of little flower-filled offering boats containing lighted candles as they drift downstream. Just make sure you don't take any photos of bathers—this is strictly prohibited at all holy sites in India, not to mention a bit invasive for the person taking a dip.

MANSA DEVI MANDIR

Just west of Har ki Pauri, the busy hilltop Mansa Devi Mandir temple (8 A.M.-noon and 2-5 P.M. daily), dedicated to the goddess Mansa, is among Haridwar's most popular sights, and pilgrims come to ask the goddess to grant their wishes. The temple itself is a bit crowded most of the time, but the area around it is good for a breather. On clear days the view of Haridwar and the Ganges River from the temple is excellent. You can either walk a strenuous 1.6 kilometers uphill or take a clunky cable car (Rs. 48 round-trip) to the summit.

Food

If you have some time to kill before your train, or if you are hungry when you arrive in Haridwar, the air-conditioned **Big Ben** (Hotel Ganga Azure, near Shivmurti, tel. 1334/220-938, 8:30 A.M.-11 P.M. daily, Rs. 120), opposite the railway station, is clean and quiet and serves delicious continental, Chinese, and North Indian vegetarian food. The tea is also excellent and can be ordered by the pot. The food is on the spicy side, but they're accustomed to foreigners and can make milder versions on request.

Just east of Har ki Pauri ghat, **Mohan ji Puri Wale** (Shalesh Modi, near Police Chowk, Har ki Pauri, tel. 9411/100-388, 8 A.M.-10:30 P.M. daily) is a popular spot for street food and sweets. It specializes in *aloo puri,* spicy potatoes served with deep-fried puff bread. There is also a good selection of *lassis,* juices, Indian sweets, and savory snacks, and takeout is available. The only issue is that there's not much room to sit near the eatery.

Information and Services

The most convenient place to pick up maps and tourism brochures in Haridwar is at the railway station's **Tourist Information Centre** (tel. 1334/265-305, Mon.-Sat. 9 A.M.-5 P.M.).

Haridwar's **post office** (Station Rd., tel. 1334/227-025, 10 A.M.-5 P.M. Mon.-Sat.) is conveniently located between the railway station and Har ki Pauri. You'll find a number of small Internet cafés and pharmacies along this street, Station Road, which is also lined with ATMs; The State Bank of India and the Union Bank both have ATMs directly across from the station.

The private **City Hospital** (NH 58, Ranipur More, tel. 1334/220-180) is a 10-minute walk west of the train station.

Getting There and Around

Haridwar Junction is the city's only train station, where you can get onward train transportation to Delhi, Jaipur, and Agra or hop on a bus to Mussoorie. From Rishikesh, you can catch a shared rickshaw (also known as a Vikram) from Tapovan (near Laxman Jhula), Ram Jhula (Muni-ki-Reti side), or Haridwar Road in Rishikesh city center, all of which take about an hour and will drop you near Har ki Pauri or directly across the street from Haridwar's railway station. Just let the driver know where you want to get off at the time you board. There are plenty of cycle rickshaws in Haridwar; a trip between Har ki Pauri and the railway station takes about five minutes, depending on how congested the streets are.

MUSSOORIE

Nicknamed the "Queen of the Hills," Mussoorie is a popular spot for visitors from India's Indo-Gangetic Plain, who come to escape the oppressive heat that descends on Northern India during the summer. It was established as a hill station in 1825, when a British military officer and a government official constructed a shooting lodge here. Within a few years, the Raj government created a convalescent depot in the suburb of Landour, just above present-day Mussoorie. The Dalai Lama established the Tibetan Government in Exile here in 1959, and although he later moved to Dharamsala, there's still a large Tibetan population in the area. Because of the cool climate, there's also a large number of retirees, and during the Indian wedding season (Nov.-Dec.), swarms of honeymooning couples visit the town.

Although there are plenty of hill stations in the Himalayan foothills, Mussoorie is by far the easiest to access from Delhi, and it can get quite crowded on weekends. The tourism industry is largely geared for domestic travelers, which means that many of the activities are family-focused (think video arcades and ice cream shops) and most of the restaurants serve primarily Indian food. It's also very hilly, and it's not an easy place to navigate if you have compromised mobility. Cycle rickshaws are available in certain areas, but most people get around town on foot. With its fresh air, quaint English churches, towering deodar trees, and beautiful views of the Doon Valley below, Mussoorie is worth the climb.

Sights and Activities
CAMEL'S BACK ROAD
Mussoorie's most popular walking circuit, this 3.2-kilometer-long loop of hilly road gets its name from a rock formation shaped like a camel that can be seen from the summit of the hill. The road is paved and thickly lined with deodar trees, and there are pleasant valley views along the way. If you don't want to walk it, you can rent a horse (Rs. 300) at the base of the hill at the Library Bazaar end of Mall Road. You can also access the road at the east end of Mall Road, near the Picture Palace Bus Stand.

◖ THE MALL
Mussoorie's main street, known as "The Mall," is a hilly collection of shops and restaurants between the old Picture Palace cinema to the east and the Library Bazaar to the west. This is the hub of Mussoorie's commercial activity, and it is possible to spend your entire stay walking between the two ends of the strip. It's not a good place for handicrafts and authentic Indian souvenirs; rather, you'll get your pick of shawls and other winter wear, scary masks, wooden tchotchkes, cheap lingerie (for the honeymoon set), and imported candies. Every Saturday 4-6 P.M., celebrated Anglo-Indian author Ruskin Bond signs copies of his books at

©MARGOT BIGG

Take a stroll through the forest in Mussoorie.

EXCURSIONS

EXCURSIONS

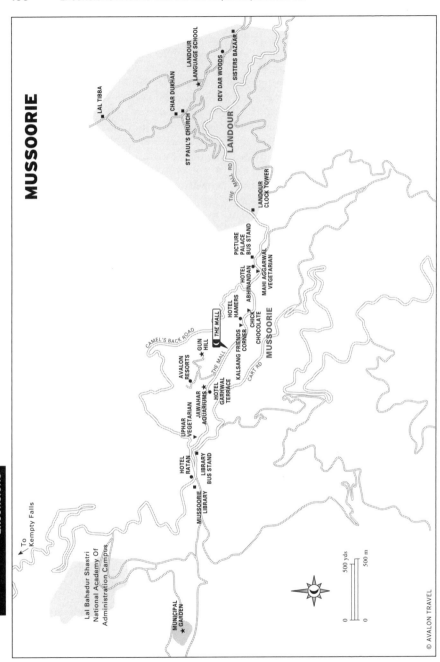

MUSSOORIE

LANDOUR LANGUAGE SCHOOL

SISTERS BAZAAR

DEV DAR WOODS

LANDOUR

CHAR DUKHAN

ST PAUL'S CHURCH

LAL TIBBA

THE MALL RD

LANDOUR CLOCK TOWER

PICTURE PALACE BUS STAND

HOTEL ABHINANDAN

MAHI AGGARWAL VEGETARIAN

HOTEL HAMERS

CHICK CHOCOLATE

CAMEL'S BACK ROAD

GUN HILL

THE MALL

KALSANG FRIENDS CORNER

MUSSOORIE

AVALON RESORTS

THE MALL

CART RD

HOTEL GARHWAL TERRACE

JAWAHAR AQUARIUMS

UPHAR VEGETARIAN

HOTEL RATAN

LIBRARY BUS STAND

MUSSOORIE LIBRARY

To Kempty Falls

Lal Bahadur Shastri National Academy Of Administration Campus

MUNICIPAL GARDEN

500 yds

500 m

0

0

© AVALON TRAVEL

weekend crowds at The Mall, Mussoorie

the well-stocked **Cambridge Book Depot** (The Mall, tel. 135/263-2224, 10 A.M.-9 P.M. daily). There's also a small branch of the Uttarakhand Tourism Office (tel. 135/263-2863, 10 A.M.-5 P.M. Mon.-Sat.), about 800 meters east of Library Bazaar.

GUN HILL

The second-highest peak of Mussoorie, Gun Hill has spectacular views and a few shops where you can get your photo taken in traditional Garhwali costumes, along with stalls hawking overpriced tea and Maggi instant noodles. The views are fantastic, as is the steep hike up. However, most people opt to take the **Cable Car** (The Mall, 10 A.M.-7 P.M. daily, Rs. 75 round-trip) from the Mall up to the summit.

JAWAHAR AQUARIUMS

It's really more of a collection of tropical fish tanks than a bona fide aquarium, but the Jawahar Aquariums (The Mall, 10:30 A.M.-9 P.M. daily, Rs. 20) are worth a quick visit, especially if you have children with you. Note that the admission fee is redeemable against your food bill at the adjoining Sagar Ratna South Indian restaurant.

KEMPTY FALLS

Kempty Falls (north on Cart Rd. from the Library Bazaar end of Mall Rd.) is the largest waterfall in the area and is very popular with Indian families. You have to take a taxi (Rs. 720) to get here as it's about 16 kilometers outside Mussoorie. Alternatively, the Garhwal Mandal Vikas Nigam (GVMN, the government tourism board) operates tours (Rs. 50) to the falls; these can be booked at the tourism office on Mall Road.

The water at Kempty Falls descends into a small basin that unfortunately is a bit too shallow to swim in. It's a beautiful spot but has lost a lot of its charm due to a proliferation of tea stalls and commercial activities in the area coupled with piles of litter left by blasé visitors. Note that most people take a dip in their clothes, and wearing a bikini would likely attract more than a few stares. Kempty Falls is also home to the Himalayan Adventure Institute (tel. 1376/213-806, www.himadven.com), which organizes rope courses and other outdoor adventure activities.

LANDOUR

A steep hike uphill from the Mall, the suburb of Landour is a quiet spot to escape the crowds of Mussoorie. Landour proper starts at a large clock tower just north of the old Picture Palace building. Just past the clock tower is an array of **shops** selling old paintings, books, and antique odds and ends. Keep walking uphill for about 20 minutes and you'll reach **Char Dukhan** (literally "four shops"), a small commercial center with a few teashops and an Internet café as well as **St. Paul's Church,** built in 1840.

EXCURSIONS

From here, turn right and continue up toward **Sisters Bazaar,** which is really just a handful of shops, including one selling homemade cheddar cheese and jam, passing the **Kellogg Church,** home to the Landour Language School, on the way. From here, take a ramp up to **Lal Tibba** (also known as TV Tower Hill, as it's used as a broadcasting station), an ideal sunset viewpoint that stands over 2,700 meters in elevation.

MUNICIPAL GARDEN

Also known by its former name, Company Bagh, this garden was created by geologists during the Raj. It's popular for picnicking, and there's a small artificial lake with pedal boats available to rent. It's four kilometers by road past Mall Road, at the western Library Bazaar end, but pedestrians can walk via Waverley Convent Road, which shortens the journey to less than two kilometers. It's nothing spectacular, but the walk is pleasant, and the greenery is refreshing.

Accommodations
UNDER RS. 1,000

If you want to be smack in the middle of all of Mussoorie's "action," you won't get any closer to the center of town than the budget **Hotel Hamers** (Kulri, The Mall, tel. 135/263-2818, Rs. 800-2,250 d). Some of the guest rooms are absolutely charming, with unusual interiors and nice balconies. Others could use a bit of work or, as is the case with many of the hotels in Mussoorie, some new carpets. The room rates are highly flexible; if you're able to bargain hard, you'll likely get something much lower than advertised. The hotel also offers free parking.

RS. 1,000-3,000

A few kilometers uphill from the Mall, in the suburb of Landour, **◖Dev Dar Woods** (Sisters Bazaar, Landour, tel. 135/263-2544, www.

devdar.blogspot.com, Rs. 1,200) feels more like a home than a hotel. Housed in an old bungalow surrounded by pine-filled lawns, Dev Dar is popular with students from the local Hindi language school. The highlight is the huge living room with a fireplace, perfect for reading, socializing, or just warming up in the chilly winter months. People come from all over Mussoorie to sample the wood-fired pizzas, which admittedly are not life-changing but are pretty good by Indian standards.

At the library end of town, the quaint **Hotel Ratan** (Gandhi Chowk, tel. 135/263-2719, captkj@hotmail.com, Rs. 1,750-3,550 d) has very clean, basically furnished guest rooms, all with cable TV and small fridges. Despite its location on a busy thoroughfare, the guest rooms are fairly quiet. There's also a large outdoor terrace with valley views and a small restaurant serving clean, simple Indian meals and snacks.

The government-owned and operated **Hotel Garhwal Terrace** (The Mall, tel. 135/263-2683, www.gmvnl.com, Rs. 1,840-2,190 d) has clean, pretty guest rooms with views of the cloudy valley below. All guest rooms have light wood floors as well as lovely beds and tables to match, and the staff is friendly and accommodating. There's a bar and restaurant on-site, and parking is available. Rooms can be booked online or by visiting one of the offices of the government-run tourism initiative Garhwal Mandal Vikas Nigam (GVMN) located across India.

Conveniently located right next to the Picture Palace bus stop, **Hotel Abhinandan** (Picture Palace, tel. 135/263-1888, Rs. 2,800-3,800 d) is clean, cozy, and a decent value. Unlike many hotels in Mussoorie, you won't find any moldy carpets: All guest rooms have tiled or wood flooring or a combination of the two. The super-deluxe guest rooms have huge rain showerheads. There's also a rooftop restaurant, and families will appreciate the small children's library on-site.

RS. 3,000-10,000

A steep hike (or quick car ride) up from the Mall, **Avalon Resorts** (near Cart Rd., tel. 11/422-2411, www.avalonresorts.com, Rs. 6,000 d) offers a number of immaculate studio rooms and suites, all with basic kitchen facilities. The decor is modern yet cozy, and many of the guest rooms have huge balconies with panoramic views of the Himalayan foothills. There's also a bar and restaurant on-site, and even if you aren't staying here, you are welcome to come up for a beer and take in the stunning view. The property is popular with up-scale Indian honeymooners and families and is perfect for long-term visitors.

Food

Popular with local youth and urban Indian visitors, the quaint **Chick Chocolate** (Kulri, The Mall, tel. 135/263-2131, 10:30 A.M.-9 P.M. daily, Rs. 150) is as known for its funky interiors, featuring old film posters and 1960s diner-style seating, as it is for its pizzas, pastas, and pancakes. There's also a huge selection of candy on hand, ranging from homemade chocolates to imported gummy bears. The only drawback is that this eatery is self-service, so guests have to pay at one counter and then deliver their order slip to the kitchen themselves. This wouldn't be a problem except that the kitchen staff here is notorious for messing up orders.

No visit to Mussoorie is complete without trying the delicious Tibetan food at **◖ Kalsang Friends Corner** (near the post office, Kulri, The Mall, tel. 135/263-3710, 10:30 A.M.-11 P.M. daily, Rs. 160). This family-run restaurant has two floors of seating with great views of the Mall, making it an ideal spot for people-watching. The walls are red and gold and feature photos of the smiling Dali Lama. The uniforms of the waitstaff, in red Chinese silk, compliment the interiors. Kalsang is best known for its Tibetan food, ranging from *momos* (stuffed dumplings) to *thukpa* (noodle soup), although a decent selection of Thai and Chinese dishes is also served—spicy-food lovers should not miss the fiery Thai papaya salad.

Just across from the crumbling Picture Palace, **Mahi Aggarwal Vegetarian** (Kulri, The Mall, tel. 135/263-0995, 8 A.M.-11 P.M. daily, Rs. 100) captures the spirit of Mussoorie, with its beech wood walls and views of the noisy street below. This small vegetarian restaurant serves up pretty much every possible *paneer* concoction imaginable. They also have a huge selection of savory Indian breakfast foods as well as milk shakes and a few Chinese dishes thrown in for good measure.

At the library end of the Mall, the delicious **Uphar Vegetarian** (The Mall, tel. 135/263-0342, 8:30 A.M.-4:30 P.M. and 6:30-8:30 P.M. daily, Rs. 90) is a great place to get your South Indian food fix. The interiors are canteen-like, but the food is delicious. The friendly staff at this "pure" (no eggs) vegetarian restaurant serve a large selection of *dosas* and *idlis* as well as a number of North Indian curries and rotis made from every type of flour you could think of.

Information and Services

Mussoorie's **Tourist Office** (Mall Rd., near the Gun Hill Ropeway, tel. 135/263-2863, 10 A.M.-5 P.M. Mon.-Sat.) has friendly staff and a lot of brochures on different destinations in Uttarakhand state. You can also book local tours to destinations such as Kempty Falls. Note that the signposted tourism office on the road between Dehradun and Mussoorie is not operating.

There are couple of Internet cafés along Mall Road and one at Char Dukhan in Landour. They charge around Rs. 40 per hour for access. The post office (Kulri, The Mall, tel. 135/263-2206, 9 A.M.-5 P.M. Mon.-Sat.) is on Mall Road.

There are quite a few banks with ATMs in Mussoorie, including an Axis Bank (Library Bazaar, The Mall) and a State Bank of India (Kulri, The Mall). The only place in town that exchanges currency is **Trek Himalaya** (The Mall, next to the Gun Hill Ropeway, tel. 135/263-0491, 10 A.M.-5 P.M. daily).

There are plenty of pharmacies along Mall Road, and if you don't feel fit to walk, your hotel can usually send someone to pick up medication for you. The **Landour Community Hospital** (uphill from the Landour Clock Tower, tel. 135/263-2053) is a missionary hospital with friendly staff and an on-site dispensary.

LANDOUR LANGUAGE SCHOOL

Landour Language School (41/2 Landour Cantt., tel. 135/263-1487, www.landourlan-guageschool.com) was established at the turn of the 20th century with the aim of imparting Hindi language skills on foreign missionaries. Today the school teaches Hindi and other North Indian languages to hundreds of students every year. Most students take private lessons, although two people at the same level can opt for a semiprivate course. A minimum enrolment of two weeks is required. Each session is 50 minutes long, and classes run 8:20 A.M.-4:50 P.M. Students are advised to take a maximum of four sessions per day. Classes cost Rs. 210-350 each, depending on the number of students.

Getting There

Like most of India's hill stations, Mussoorie does not have a train station. The nearest railway station is in Dehradun, 39 kilometers away.

There are six trains connecting Delhi to Dehradun on any given day, including the comfortable *Dehradun Shatabdi,* which takes 5.5-6 hours. Hygienic, although not exactly delicious, meals are included in the fares on this seated, air-conditioned train.

The *Uttaranchal Express* runs daily and links Dehradun to Jaipur in about 13 hours. There are no direct trains between Dehradun and Agra, so all passengers must connect in Delhi. The *Dehradun Express,* however, links

Dehradun to Bharatpur (for Keoladeo) and Sawai Madhopur (for Ranthambore).

Buses of varying quality run between Dehradun and Delhi's ISBT, taking 8-9 hours. A taxi from Delhi to Mussoorie and back costs Rs. 5,000 and up, depending on how long you stay. The drive takes around seven hours. You can also fly from Delhi to Dehradun's Jolly Grant Airport (DED) and catch a taxi from there to Mussoorie. Kingfisher, Jet Airways, and Air India operate flights on this route, and the flight time is one hour.

FROM DEHRADUN

When you arrive at Dehradun's railway station, try to ignore the inevitable swarms of touting rickshaw and taxi drivers. Instead, walk out of the main doors and take a left. Walk for about 100 meters and you will reach the booking office of the local taxi drivers union (tel. 135/262-7877), where you can arrange for a prepaid Ambassador taxi (big enough to seat four if you have only a little bit of luggage). A one-way journey to Mussoorie's Picture Palace Bus Stand costs a fixed Rs. 610. Right next to the booking office is the local bus stand, where you can catch a local bus. Those susceptible to motion sickness might want to avoid this option, as the road to Mussoorie is of the hairpin-bend variety, and it's not uncommon for passengers on this service to lose their lunch.

Getting Around

Mussoorie is a small, walkable city, and most people come for strolls and hikes. If you are tired or have difficulty walking a lot, however, there's no shortage of cycle rickshaws. You can also rent taxis from the unionized taxi stands at both ends of the mall; the posted rates are a bit high by Indian standards, and bargaining doesn't generally work due to union rules. Alternatively, book through your hotel or call the Mussoorie Taxi Stand (tel. 135/261-0002).

Rural Rajasthan

Rajasthan is one of India's most vibrant states and one of the most popular with visitors. Its vast expanses of desert, variety of cultural traditions, and ornate architecture coupled with a well-developed tourism infrastructure make it one of the easier parts of the country to travel in. The region is also home to a number of fascinating small towns and villages, all of which are relatively easy to access from Jaipur or Delhi. One of the most popular is Pushkar, an entrancing town built around a small holy lake. Pushkar is significant for the Hindu god Brahma and is filled with temples and old pastel-hued *havelis,* making it a popular spot for photography enthusiasts. Near Pushkar, the railway town of Ajmer has a couple of places worth visiting, including one of the most important Sufi shrines in the world and a stunning Jain temple. If you really want to get out into the countryside, head to the Shekhawati region between Jaipur and Delhi. This part of Rajasthan is noted for its incredible old *havelis* covered with intricate hand-painted frescoes.

PUSHKAR

This captivating little temple town a couple of hours southwest of Jaipur is worth a visit for its scenic lake and mystical atmosphere. Pushkar is believed to be thousands of years old and is mentioned in many ancient sacred texts. While most of the original temples and havelis were destroyed during the Mughal invasion of India, it still has an ancient feel to it.

According to legend, Pushkar came into existence when the Hindu creator god Brahma was searching for a place to perform a *yajna* (fire ritual). He came across Pushkar, where a demon called Vajranabh was wreaking havoc. Brahma manifested a lotus flower with which to kill the demon, and in the process, petals from the flower landed in three spots, each of which transformed into a body of water. One of these was Pushkar, and today the town is associated with Brahma more than any other deity.

Although Pushkar is a holy site par excellence, it's also very touristy and attracts everyone from overseas package tourists to Indian religious pilgrims. It's also a must-see for the backpacker set, which means that there are excellent cheap restaurants, plenty of shops selling mass-produced hippie clothes, and tons of zealous touts. For some backpackers, one of the main draws is the ubiquitous "special *lassi,*" a yogurt drink made with a concoction of marijuana flowers known as bhang. Note that while bhang is more or less accepted in Pushkar, other intoxicants, including alcohol, as well as nonvegetarian food, are prohibited.

Safety and Scams

It's a good idea never to take flowers from strangers in Pushkar, unless you are looking for a quick way to be separated from your rupees. Many of Pushkar's priests earn a living by practicing *pujas* (religious ceremonies) at the banks of the town's holy lake. They try to lure you in by offering you a flower and trying to convince you to offer it to the lake. If you acquiesce, you'll soon find yourself being asked to repeat mantras and prayers for your family members. Once the ceremony is over, you'll likely be emotionally bullied into "donating" an exorbitant amount. Of course, you may want to oblige the priests for the sake of a cultural experience, but you have every right to name your price or simply say no. Refusing is not, as some will have you believe, disrespectful of the traditions of Pushkar, and most street-smart Indians would know to be wary of such behavior from self-labeled "holy men."

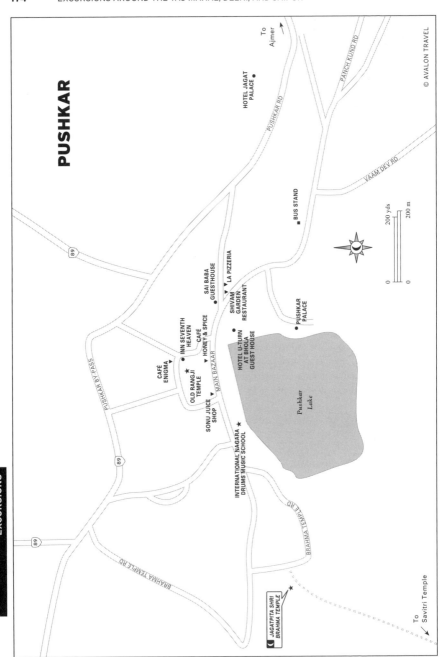

PUSHKAR

To Ajmer

PANCH KUND RD

PUSHKAR RD

HOTEL JAGAT PALACE

VAAM DEV RD

89

BUS STAND

200 yds

200 m

SAI BABA GUESTHOUSE

LA PIZZERIA

SHIVAM GARDEN RESTAURANT

PUSHKAR PALACE

INN SEVENTH HEAVEN

PUSHKAR BY-PASS

CAFÉ HONEY & SPICE

CAFÉ ENIGMA

OLD RANGJI TEMPLE

MAIN BAZAAR

HOTEL U-TURN AT BHOLA GUEST HOUSE

Pushkar Lake

SONU JUICE SHOP

89

INTERNATIONAL NAGARA DRUMS MUSIC SCHOOL

89

BRAHMA TEMPLE RD

BRAHMA TEMPLE RD

JAGATPITA SHRI BRAHMA TEMPLE

To Savitri Temple

© AVALON TRAVEL

EXCURSIONS

BAREFOOT COLLEGE

A couple of hours' drive southwest of Jaipur on the way to Pushkar is one of the most innovative social organizations on the planet. In the tiny village of Tilonia, Barefoot College (tel. 1463/288-205, www.barefootcollege.org) trains unskilled village people, many of whom can't read or write, to work in a variety of fields, ranging from health care to solar-energy engineering. The idea is to keep the project grassroots and sustainable. Rather than bringing in outside consultants who may not necessarily be able to relate to the students, the college is largely managed by rural men and women who graduated from Barefoot and decided to stick around to share what they learned.

Barefoot College also runs a handicraft collective that sells bedding, interior decor, and other textiles. Their products are available in shops across North America and online (www.tilonia.com). Alternatively, you can drop by the college yourself to pick up a few gift items and learn more about their many initiatives and programs.

Sights and Activities

☾ JAGATPITA SHRI BRAHMA TEMPLE

Pushkar's most famous attraction, the Brahma Temple (Pushkar Lake, western end of the main bazaar, 5:30 A.M.-12:30 P.M. and 3-9 P.M. daily) is believed to be India's only temple dedicated to Brahma, the creator in the Hindu trinity. The temple was built in the 14th century, but historians believe that a temple to Brahma has existed on this site for two millennia. This colorful temple, with its saffron-colored spire and blue pillars, is a must-visit site for Hindus who come to Pushkar for pilgrimages, and it is one of the few temples in the holy hamlet that allow visitors of all religious and cultural backgrounds. The idol of Brahma in the sanctum sanctorum is believed to have been blessed by Adi Shankara, one of India's most famous sages and the founder of Advaita Vedanta (nondualism). Note that cameras and phones are not allowed inside, but there is a small shop just to the left of the main entrance with locker facilities.

PUSHKAR LAKE

Pushkar's holy lake is the town's centerpiece and one of the most sacred bodies of water in India. It's surrounded by 52 marble ghats (sets of stairs) and some of Mahatma Gandhi's ashes are rumored to have been immersed in Gau Ghat, near the main market. Pushkar Lake is a beautiful place to relax, and there's something very magical about watching the sun cast shades of pink across the sky as it sets over the lake. Although most of the ghats and religious activity takes place on the northern and eastern banks, it's possible to circumambulate the entire lake in under an hour (just remember to take your shoes off).

OLD RANGJI TEMPLE

Built in 1823 by Seth Puran Mal Ganeriwal of Hyderabad (a South Indian tech city that was, at the time, a highly regarded princely state), the Old Rangji Temple (north of the main bazaar, near Varah Ghat) incorporates a fine balance of South Indian Dravidian-style architecture with design elements more common to the Rajput and Mughal traditions. Music performances are occasionally staged on the temple's large grounds.

SAVITRI TEMPLE

Dedicated to Brahma's first wife, the Savitri Temple (southwest of Pushkar lake, via Brahma Temple) sits atop a hill overlooking Pushkar. According to legend, Savitri refused to come down to Pushkar when she learned that her husband had married Gayatri, and her essence remains on the hill to this day. The temple is

EXCURSIONS

EXCURSIONS

© MARGOT BIGG

Pushkar's peaceful lake

small and houses a pretty statue of the goddess, but the main reason most people come up is for the excellent views of Pushkar below. Most people set out about an hour before sunrise to climb the hill—note that there are well-lit steps leading from the base to the summit. There are also a lot of monkeys and langurs en route, and women should avoid wearing long flowing skirts—the local primates are known to grab onto skirts and refuse to let go. Make sure to carry lots of water—there's a small stand selling tea and cold drinks next to the temple, but the journey up can be dehydrating.

INTERNATIONAL NAGARA DRUMS MUSIC SCHOOL

Percussionists of all skill levels are welcome at the International Nagara Drums Music School (Gangaur Ghat, tel. 9829/205-069 or 9283/97-045, nathunagara@yahoo.com). This is one of the best places in India to learn the *nagara,* a pair of kettle drums that can be found in different incarnations across South and Central Asia. The school is run by a world-renowned *nagara* maestro, the convivial Nathu Lal Solanki, who has performed with artists ranging from Susheela Raman to Mickey Hart. Solanki teaches here when he's not on tour abroad (which he often is).

CAMEL RIDES AND SAFARIS

If you've never ridden a camel before, Pushkar is a great place to try. There are plenty of open areas to tread, and the arid desert that surrounds Pushkar provides a beautiful backdrop for a camelback journey. Safaris can be organized by travel agents around Pushkar as well as through most hotels. Camel rides cost about Rs. 150 per hour, and safaris start from Rs. 700 for an overnight trip.

HORSEBACK RIDING

Run by a Franco-Canadian horse lover who has lived in Pushkar for over 25 years, **Shannus**

PUSHKAR CAMEL FAIR

The most popular time of year for a visit to Pushkar is during the annual Camel Fair, a five-day event in which camel traders from across the region descend on Pushkar to showcase their beasts. The Rajasthan Tourism Development Commission (RTDC) is also heavily involved in the proceedings, hosting a range of activities that include mustache-length competitions and camel races. The fair is held around the full moon of the month of Kartik in the Hindu calendar, usually in October or November. This is also considered the most auspicious time of year to take a dip in Pushkar's holy lake, which drives up the number of visitors even more. While it's definitely an exciting time to visit, it's also very crowded, and hotel rates increase dramatically.

Hotel and Horse Riding School (Punchkund Rd., tel. 145/277-2043, http://shannus.weebly.com) is the place to go if you feel like a hack through the desert. The school offers riding lessons for beginners, and experienced equestrians can ride independently (after passing an ability screening). There's also a hotel on-site, with lovely redbrick garden rooms. Riding costs Rs. 350 per hour.

Shopping

Pushkar is a great place to go shopping, especially if you're interested in picking up hippie clothing. The main market street that cuts across the northern end of the lake is filled with shops selling religious paraphernalia, such as statuary; CDs of mantras and Indo-electronic fusion music; leather bags, sandals, and journals, ironic in a vegetarian holy town inhabited primarily by Brahmans; psychedelic glow-in-the-black-light paintings of elves perched on mushrooms; and, of course, clothes. It's a one-stop shop for inexpensive T-shirts, peasant blouses, and cotton trousers (a.k.a. Ali Baba pants; if you're old enough, you'll know them as Hammer pants), and there's little variety among the shops. You'll also find a few decent jewelry shops, although the selection is much better in Jaipur. If you're looking for a unique Pushkar souvenir, you can either get a small image of Brahma on the lake (sold at almost every shop within a 100-meter radius of the Brahma Temple) or *gulkand,* a sweet, locally made rose jam that's often mixed with milk and made into a cooling tonic.

Accommodations

Pushkar is particularly popular with backpackers, and there's a good selection of ultracheap rooms in town. It's also one of the most tout-ridden places in India, so book ahead if you can and try not to let anyone drag you off to see another hotel, no matter how tired you are when you arrive. The rates listed below are for high season (Oct.-Mar.), but note that most properties raise their tariffs considerably during the annual camel fair in November.

UNDER RS. 1,000

Backpackers swear by the **Sai Baba Guesthouse** (Varah Temple St., Chhoti Basti, tel. 9636/459-481, Rs. 250-400 d), a clean and consistently reliable option run by a French-Indian couple. The guest rooms in this *haveli* property are situated around a massive courtyard with a small fire pit. As the property is a few paces off the main road, the guest rooms here are much quieter than many other options in town, and you won't be wakened by early morning lakeside prayers.

On the banks of Pushkar's holy lake, the quaint **Hotel U-turn at Bhola Guest House** (Varah Ghat, Chhoti Basti, tel. 9928/737-798, www.hoteluturn.com, Rs. 250-600 d) is arguably the most charming budget option in town. This intimate family *haveli* has six simple guest rooms with shared baths; some also have

learning to play *nagara* drums in Pushkar

lakeside views. The young owner, nicknamed Mogli, is an entertaining and helpful source of local information. There's also an equestrian-themed rooftop restaurant with spectacular views of the lake and excellent "pure" (no eggs) vegetarian food.

The midrange (by Indian standards) **Inn Seventh Heaven** (next to Mali Ka Mandir, Chhoti Basti, tel. 145/510-5455, www.inn-seventh-heaven.com, Rs. 900-2,600 d) is a tranquil option for travelers looking for a bit of respite from the constant touting of Pushkar. The guest rooms feature Rajasthani touches, including arched built-in bookshelves and *jharoka*-style windows, and some are air-conditioned. There's also a beautiful open courtyard and a rooftop restaurant serving hygienic Indian and continental food, including decent coffee.

RS. 3,000-10,000

A short stroll or taxi ride out of Pushkar, the beautiful ◖ **Hotel Jagat Palace** (behind Ramdwara, tel. 145/277-2001, www.hotelpushkarpalace.com, Rs. 6,000 d) is a good option for families and couples who don't want to stay in the heart of town. The 85-room property is surrounded by verdant gardens, and there's a large well-maintained pool. Guest rooms are appointed with art deco-style furniture and paintings of scenes from Indian mythology. Note that this hotel is also a popular spot for weddings and large groups, so there's a chance of feeling crowded out, especially if you come during the wedding season (Nov.-Jan.).

The lakeside **Pushkar Palace** (behind Ramdwara, tel. 145/277-2001, www.hotelpushkarpalace.com, Rs. 6,500 d) is the most popular of the higher-end hotels, so be sure to book well in advance during the high season. The guest rooms are spotless and have spacious marble baths and old-fashioned furniture. There's also a decent restaurant overlooking the lake, and meal packages are available. Unfortunately, there's no swimming pool, although guests are

EXCURSIONS

allowed to swim at Jagat Palace, the nearby sister property. The hotel is particularly popular with Western tour groups.

Food

Because of its status as a backpacker mecca, Pushkar has a fine selection of affordable, delicious, and hygienic places with cuisine from around the world. As in many of India's holy towns, all the food served in Pushkar is vegetarian, and many restaurants don't serve eggs. Alcohol is also prohibited, although some restaurants do serve beer disguised in tea cups.

It's easy to while away the hours at the laid-back **Café Enigma** (Near Old Rangji Temple, tel. 145/510-5029, www.cafe-enigma.com, 8 A.M.-midnight daily, Rs. 80). This rooftop restaurant offers a combination of chair and floor seating and offers spectacular views of the surrounding Aravalli mountains. Also served is a delicious selection of salads (washed in purified water), falafel, and pizza as well as the Indian backpacker-circuit classic "Hello to the Queen," a mash-up of bananas, crumbled biscuits, ice cream, and chocolate sauce.

Health nuts and vegans will appreciate the wholesome meals prepared at **Café Honey & Spice** (Laxmi Market, Old Rangji Temple, tel. 145/510-5505, 7:30 A.M.-6:30 P.M. daily, Rs. 120). Although the ambience is nothing special (the restaurant is inside an indoor market in a converted shop), the food is delicious and nutritious. Honey & Spice focuses on breakfast and lunch dishes—the tofu sandwiches are especially good. They also have soy milk shakes, ayurvedic herbal teas, and very strong coffee.

La Pizzeria (Varah Temple St., Chhoti Basti, tel. 9982/475-601, 8:30 A.M.-11 P.M. daily, Rs. 150), serves up some of the best Italian food in Pushkar, if not in India. Delicious pizzas come from the wood-fired stove; the risottos and pastas are equally amazing. The cheeses used are mostly imported from Europe, as is the Lavazza espresso. The people at La Pizzeria

even make their own pesto from basil grown on their rooftop garden. And if that weren't enough, this is one of the few restaurants in Pushkar with an air-conditioned section.

Although the ambience could use a bit of work, the food at **Shivam Garden Restaurant** (Varah Temple St., Chhoti Basti, tel. 145/510-5761, 8 A.M.-10 P.M. daily, Rs. 125) is exceptionally good. The small garden at this backpacker favorite is more of a patio, and it's cute but not exactly enchanting. The food, however, is delicious and always prepared fresh. Indian, Chinese, and continental favorites are served along with a wide variety of salads cleaned with filtered water. The minty falafel here is particularly worth a try. They also have a couple of guest rooms upstairs, perfect for long-term visitors or anyone having trouble finding a hotel.

Sonu Juice Shop (Main Bazaar, near Payal Guest House, tel. 9414/666-829, 8:30 A.M.-9 P.M. daily, Rs. 50) is Pushkar's most popular juice stand and a great place to meet up with foreign backpackers. This stand is known for its delicious fruit juice combinations, and if you're nice, you may even get a few free samples. The muesli is served with layers of curd, honey, and lots of fresh fruit and will turn even the most skeptical breakfaster into a hard-core granola muncher. The juices are all made with filtered ice.

Information and Services

The Rajasthan Tourism Development Corporation (RTDC) has a small **Tourist Information Bureau** (Hotel Sarovar, off the main bazaar, near Jaipur Ghat, tel. 145/277-2040, 9:30 A.M.-6 P.M. daily) where you can pick up old brochures and have a chat about local sites with the friendly staff.

There's a **post office** (tel. 145/277-3085, 9:30 A.M.-5 P.M. Mon.-Sat.) just behind the vegetable market across from Varah Ghat on the main road. There are a few tailors nearby who can pack your parcels in the standard white cloth for a small fee. There's a laundry service next to the post office that can get your clothes back to you the next day. They'll come back lightly scented with rose water.

It's difficult to take more than a few steps in Pushkar without bumping into a combination Internet café, travel agent, and money changer. They all charge around Rs. 30 per hour for Internet access and can change money legally. Make sure to check that all of your rupees are in good order—you're unlikely to get an incorrect amount, but agents sometimes try to pawn off torn bills, which are difficult to use, on travelers. There's also a branch of **Thomas Cook** (tel. 145/277-3193, 10 A.M.-6 P.M. daily) near New Rangji Temple on the main road. Punjab National Bank and the State Bank of India have ATMs on the road leading north from the Brahman Temple.

There are a few pharmacies on the main road. If you need to go to a hospital, your best bet is **Mittal Hospital and Research Centre** (Pushkar Road, Ajmer, tel. 145/260-3600, www.mittalhospital.com) in Ajmer.

Getting There
TRAIN
There is no railway station in Pushkar, so if you're coming by train, you have to go to Ajmer and then take a bus or taxi to Pushkar. Trains from Jaipur to Ajmer run every couple of hours and take about 2-3 hours. Four trains per day run from Agra to Ajmer via Bharatpur; these take 6-7 hours. There are plenty of train options if you're coming from Delhi; most take 6-8 hours. Many are overnight services, but if you want to watch the Rajasthani desert roll by, the most convenient is the *Ajmer Shatabdi,* which leaves Delhi at 6:05 A.M. and reaches Ajmer at 12:40 P.M. The same train then returns to Delhi, leaving Ajmer at 3:50 P.M. and reaching Delhi at 10:40 P.M.

Once in Ajmer, you can negotiate a taxi from the train station to Pushkar, although if you

organize it through your hotel ahead of time, you might get a better rate. If you are on a very tight budget, you can also exit the train station, cross the main road, and take a shared autorickshaw to the bus stand (Rs. 5). From the bus stand you can take a bus to Pushkar for under Rs. 20.

BUS
Regular buses of varying quality run the 145 kilometers between Jaipur and Pushkar and leave from Jaipur's main bus stand. Overnight buses also run from Pushkar to Delhi and take 10 hours. They can be booked at virtually all travel agents in town, or directly from **Naveen Travels** (12 Prem Prakash Marg, near Ajmer Bus Stand, tel. 145/277-3070). Both uncomfortable seats (Rs. 250) and beds (Rs. 450 pp s or d) are available on these buses, which depart Delhi at 11 P.M. and arrive in Pushkar at 9 A.M. They usually leave Pushkar around 7:30 P.M. and stop in Ajmer for about 30 minutes before continuing on to Delhi via Jaipur. Passengers are then dropped at Karol Bagh (although the bus drivers will cheekily tell passengers it's the main bazaar of Delhi's backpacker haven, Paharganj, some three kilometers away). If you are going to Paharganj, take an autorickshaw and insist on using the meter, or walk to the Karol Bagh Metro, from where you can take the Metro (toward Noida) to Ramakrishna Ashram Marg, two stops away.

Getting Around
Pushkar is a walkable city, and cars are not allowed on the main road (most residents use motorcycles to get around). Cycle rickshaws have recently been introduced to the city, which makes it easier to get to the bus stand if you have a lot of luggage with you. If you're staying in the outskirts of the city, you can arrange taxi transfers into Pushkar through your hotel or at any local travel agency, which seemingly occupy every other shop in town. You can also

rent a motor scooter (around Rs. 200 per day) or a bicycle (Rs. 100 per day).

AJMER

About 11 kilometers from Pushkar, the hectic city of Ajmer is worth a visit if you're already in the area but not an overnight stay. Most visitors to Pushkar end up here in transit (the closest railway station to Pushkar is in Ajmer), and if you happen to be passing through, you may want to leave your luggage in the left-luggage office (called a "cloakroom") at the railway station and spend a couple of hours visiting local sights. The main attractions are the famous Dargah Sharif, the shrine of one of South Asia's most loved Sufi saints. Another interesting site is the Nasiyan Jain Temple, home to a beautiful gilded statue depicting Jain religious scenes. Both attractions can easily be visited in two hours.

Sights and Activities
DARGAH SHARIF
About 10 minutes by cycle rickshaw from the train station, Ajmer's most famous attraction is the Dargah Sharif (tel. 9829/070-786, www. dargahajmer.com, 6 A.M.-3 P.M. and 4-9 P.M. daily, free), the *dargah*, or shrine, of Sufi saint Moinuddin Chishti. Chishti lived from 1141 to 1230 and was responsible for establishing the Chishti order of Sufism in the subcontinent. According to legend, during the annual hajj, when pilgrims flock to Mecca, Chishti would be spotted by devotees both in Mecca and in Ajmer, a miracle that would later contribute to the mystic's status as a significant saint.

The shrine is arguably the most important pilgrimage site for South Asian Muslims, and Emperor Akbar used to travel from Agra every year to pay his obeisance to Chishti. The city of Ajmer fills up during the annual *urs* (anniversary of Chishti's death), which takes place in the first week of Rajab, the seventh month of the Islamic calendar. During this time, pilgrims come from around the world to pay their respects, so if you happen to be in town during Rajab, which falls in a different month of the Western calendar each year, expect throngs of people.

To reach the *dargah,* follow the inevitable crowds through a labyrinth of little alleys lined with shops selling incense and other offerings. Eventually you'll reach the enormous main gate. Remove your shoes and put your camera away before entering. Inside, you'll see pilgrims bowing in prayer and offering flowers to the saint's shrine, surrounded by an intricately carved marble lattice. There are also two large cauldrons in the courtyard—you can't miss them—that are used for preparing meals for devotees. Every evening, Qawwali (Sufi devotional music) is staged; the energetic and moving performances attract people of all faiths.

NASIYAN JAIN TEMPLE (RED TEMPLE)
The area around Ajmer and Pushkar was once a stronghold of the Jain community, and Ajmer in particular still has a significant Jain population. The Nasiyan Temple (Vaishali Nagar, 8:30 A.M.-4:30 P.M. daily) is the most important Jain temple in the area. It's not particularly old (it was constructed in 1865), but nevertheless it is quite impressive. The most interesting part of the temple complex is the Svarna Nagri Hall, which contains an enormous gilded wooden sculpture depicting scenes from Jain religious stories. It is highly detailed, and you can easily spend hours looking at the model from different angles.

SHEKHAWATI REGION
Long before memories were kept alive through photos, family records and stories of times past were depicted through visual arts. In the Shekhawati Region of northeast Rajasthan, these memories exist to this day in the form of the beautiful vegetable-dyed frescoes that adorn the walls of the region's many *havelis*

EXCURSIONS

Finely painted *havelis* abound in the Shekhawati Region.

(city mansions). The region is often referred to as Rajasthan's "open-air art gallery." While this is a bit of an exaggeration, it's still a nice place to learn a bit about the region's history through beautiful depictions of times past.

Shekhawati is named after Rao Shekha, a chieftain who lived in the 15th century. Although the area has been inhabited since the Middle Ages, it wasn't until the middle of the 18th century that it really began to blossom, and most of the *havelis* and other interesting buildings date from 1750 to 1930. Most of the wall paintings are from the 19th and early 20th century. The 19th-century paintings tend to focus primarily on religious scenes, although by the turn of the 20th century, paintings began incorporating motifs of the industrial age (such as trains and cars) and merging Western and traditional schools of painting.

Getting There and Around

You really need a car in Shekhawati, and train service from Jhunjhunu to other cities is limited. Local buses are available, and it's possible to visit the entire region only by bus (starting in Jhunjhunu if you are approaching from Delhi, or Nawalgarh if you are coming from Jaipur), although this will add a lot of time to your trip. In fact, most people only visit as a detour between Delhi and Jaipur, and this is the best way to do it. If you plan to visit the area, negotiate this at the time you book a vehicle between Jaipur and Delhi. Also bear in mind that in some parts of the region, the roads are in very bad shape and have lots of potholes, especially in stretches between Delhi and Jhunjhunu and Mandawa, so make sure you allow plenty of time in your itinerary, especially if you visit during the sloshy monsoon season (late June–Sept.), when roads are at their muddy worst.

Jhunjhunu

If you're traveling from Delhi to Shekhawati, the first city you will hit is Jhunjhunu, the capital of the region. Jhunjhunu was established in the 15th century by the Kayamkhani Nawabs but was taken over by the Rajput Sardul Singh about 300 years later. Most of the architecture can be attributed to the Rajput period.

This dusty city is a bit noisy and lacks some of the quaint charm of the region's smaller destinations, but there are quite a few interesting spots to check out. The **Khetri Mahal** (Wind Palace) is the town's most famous attraction. Believed to have been built in 1760 or 1770, depending on who you ask, this deserted mini palace is an agglomeration of beautiful carved archways, high pillars, and lots of little balconies, all designed to allow air to pass through and cool the palace's interior. It's believed to have been the inspiration for Jaipur's famous Hawa Mahal. The 17th-century **Badalgarh** (Cloud Fort), a stark, high-walled structure atop a craggy hill, is worth a visit for its exceptional views. Devout Hindu travelers also make a point of visiting the **Rani Sati Temple,** dedicated to a minor goddess who committed the act of *sati* (ceremonial self-immolation) on the funeral pyre of her husband. Interestingly, there are no idols in this temple.

ACCOMMODATIONS AND FOOD

The lodging choices in Jhunjhunu are slim, but if you find yourself in need of a clean and comfortable place to rest your head for a night or somewhere to grab a meal, **Hotel Shiv Shekhawati** (near Muni Ashram, tel. 1592/232-651, www.shivshekhawati.com, Rs. 1,000-1,200 d) is your best bet. The restaurant (6 A.M.-10 P.M. daily) serves up a standard variety of vegetarian North Indian fare, plus a few Rajasthani specialties. They are accustomed to foreign guests and generally go easy on the chili powder. Meals can also be served on the large grassy lawns that surround the property. Their sister guesthouse, **Hotel Jamuna Resort** (tel. 1592/232-871, www.hoteljamuna.com, Rs. 1,100-1,850 d), is just down the road and offers

similar cuisine and slightly more elaborately decorated guest rooms, but parking is limited.

Mandawa

About 24 kilometers from Jhunjhunu is the 18th-century fort town of Mandawa. The fort, covered with intricate religious frescoes, has been converted into a heritage hotel known as **Castle Mandawa.** Another interesting place to stop, even if you aren't planning to stay, is **Hotel Mandawa Haveli;** the hotel is small, but the intricate fresco work, most of which is focused on stories from the life of Lord Krishna, is fabulous. If you're not staying at the hotel or eating at the restaurant, admission is Rs. 70. Tours are usually conducted 9 A.M.-10 P.M. daily. Nearby, the imposing **Sonthaliya Gate** is a good place to stop for a few snapshots. There's also a **Shiva Temple** in Mandawa that houses a large quartz-crystal lingam (symbolic representation of Shiva).

ACCOMMODATIONS AND FOOD

If you're after a fairy-tale experience in Shekhawati, a stay in ◖ **Hotel Mandawa Haveli** (near Sonthaliya Gate, tel. 1592/223-088, www.hotelmandawa.com, Rs. 2,250-2,950 d) is definitely in order. This small hotel is housed in an ornately painted 18th-century *haveli,* and each of the 21 guest rooms and suites is given one of the many names of Lord Krishna, the most popular Hindu deity in the region. All of the guest rooms are air-conditioned, and some have separate sitting areas with small windows overlooking the town. The receptionist, Bhawani, is amazingly hospitable and is an excellent source of historical information. The on-site restaurant, **Rasoi** (7:30-10 A.M., noon-3:30 P.M., 7:30-10:30 P.M. daily), is open to nonguests and serves up some interesting Indian dishes (Rs. 250) such as the unusual but delicious onion curry. They also have French-press coffee and soy milk, two rarities in the land of Nescafé and farm-fresh cow's milk.

EXCURSIONS

The **haveli** doubles as a visitor attraction, and the entrance fee (Rs. 70) is waived for hotel guests and those dining at Rasoi.

Nawalgarh

The mazelike 18th-century township of Nawalgarh has some of the region's finest *havelis.*

◖ DR. RAMNATH A. PODAR
HAVELI MUSEUM

Don't miss the spectacular Dr. Ramnath A. Podar Haveli Museum (Rambilas Podar Rd., tel. 1594/225-446, www.podarhavelimuseum. org, 8 A.M.-7 P.M. daily, Rs. 100 foreigners, Rs. 70 Indians, Rs. 40 children, camera Rs. 30, video Rs. 50). This *haveli* dates from 1902 and houses an array of three types of frescoes: decorative, portrait, and descriptive, the latter normally used to tell religious stories. There's a painting of a train above one of the main gates, apparently painted to show visitors what trains looked like, as there was no rail service in the area at the time. Be sure to check out the optical-illusion fresco above the gate on the inside of the back room. The painting depicts an elephant and a cow facing each other. A single head is used for both beasts, so it looks like an elephant or a cow, depending on your perspective. The cloistered courtyards of the *haveli* are surrounded with display rooms, each with a different theme. The most interesting is the turban room, which shows how turbans are worn in different parts of Rajasthan, and there is a gallery with dolls dressed in a variety of bridal costumes used by different castes found in the state.

MORARKA HAVELI MUSEUM

Next to the Podar Haveli, the **Morarka Haveli Museum** (Naya Bazar, tel. 9351/767-266, 8 A.M.-7 P.M. daily, Rs. 50) is also worth a visit. Built in 1900, this well-preserved *haveli*

features a lot of religious art, including, quite unusually, scenes from the life of Christ as well as beautiful mirror inlay work.

ACCOMMODATIONS AND FOOD

The charming **Koolwal Kothi** (House No. 40, Government Hospital Rd., tel. 1594/232-651, www.welcomeheritagehotels.com, Rs. 5,000) is housed in one of Nawalgarh's more impressive buildings, and while the property stretches over several lots, there are only 10 guest rooms, allowing for personalized service. The property was built in 1934 by a local philanthropist, and many of the fixtures and fittings are original, giving it a vintage feel. **Fresco** (7 A.M.-10:30 P.M.), the on-site restaurant, has an OK selection of affordable Indian vegetarian dishes (Rs. 150) and serves alcohol. All of the guest rooms have air-conditioning and cable TV.

A backpacker favorite, the family-run **Shekhawati Guesthouse** (near Roop Niwas Kothi, tel. 1594/224-658, www.shekhawatiguesthouse.com, Rs. 500-800 d) is among the best budget choices in the region. There are 10 guest rooms: five grass-roofed cottages, and five cheaper rooms in the main building that, while clean, were in need of a paint job at the time of writing. There is no air-conditioning, but the jungle coolers in some of the guest rooms are sufficient for keeping temperatures bearable.

Dundlodh

About eight kilometers from Nawalgarh, the **Dundlodh Fort** (Dundlodh, tel. 1594/252-519, 7 A.M.-7 P.M. daily, Rs. 20) is worth a visit if you are already in the area. The fort blends Rajput and Mughal architectural styles and has a lot of military memorabilia, an excellent reading room, and slightly garish interiors. It also functions as a hotel, and although it's not as luxurious as some of the other heritage hotels in Rajasthan, it certainly is authentic.

National Parks

India is home to numerous national parks and wildlife sanctuaries, three of which are easy to get to from the Golden Triangle. A bit south of Jaipur, Ranthambore National Park is the most popular and is where you are most likely to spot a tiger. It also has a beautiful old fort and plenty of other wildlife, so even those who don't end up seeing a wild tiger still find it worth their while. If you're headed from Delhi to Jaipur, you can opt to pass through Sariska Tiger Reserve, which is also home to a few tigers. Tiger sightings are much rarer here than in Ranthambore, but it's still an excellent place to see wild birds, mammals, and some beautiful trees, especially just after the monsoon when much of the park's flora is in full bloom. Bird lovers won't want to miss Keoladeo National Park on the road between Jaipur and Agra. This marshy sanctuary hosts hundreds of types of migratory birds throughout the year, and it's a great place for cycling.

◖ RANTHAMBORE NATIONAL PARK

India's best-known tiger sanctuary, Ranthambore National Park (Sawai Madhopur, tel. 7462/220-479, www.rajasthanwildlife.com) is one of the greenest spots in Rajasthan and makes for a perfect retreat from the noise and pollution of India's larger cities. The 392-square-kilometer park is home to over 35 tigers, and most people come with the hope of spotting the striped beasts. It's also home to leopards, jungle cats, hyenas, jackals, and sloth bears, not to mention a large variety of deer and antelope and over 300 types of birds. The park also has a wide variety of deciduous trees as well as numerous streams, lakes, and waterfalls.

Despite the variety of flora and fauna in Ranthambore, most people come with one major objective: to spot a tiger. Unfortunately, there's no way to guarantee that you'll see a tiger—they are wild, after all—and more often than not, safari participants do not spot one of the famous beasts. However, a safari is still worthwhile for all the amazing animals you'll end up seeing.

The park is divided into eight zones, five of which are used for safaris; the other three are buffer zones. During each safari session, a maximum number of four canters (open-top 20-seat minibuses) and four Gypsies (Indian-made jeeps) are allowed in each zone, and zone allocations are determined by government officials at the park's entry gate. Seats in jeeps sell out really fast, so if you prefer a jeep to a canter, it's best to book your seat well in advance, either through your hotel or on the Forest Department's website (www.rajasthanwildlife.in). Be aware that only 25 percent of the entry tickets are available in person; the remainder are reserved for online purchase. If you are absolutely dead-set on seeing a tiger, you can always up your chances by going on a couple of safaris in a day. March-April tends to have the highest number of sightings.

Safaris last 3.5 hours and start between 6 and 7 A.M., depending on the season, and in the afternoon between 2 and 3:30 P.M. A safari will set you back Rs. 783-914, and using a video camera costs an additional Rs. 400. Children under age five ride free. All visitors must carry some form of photo ID.

Ranthambore Fort

An often overlooked attraction inside the park is the massive Ranthambore Fort (sunrise-sunset daily, free), from which the park takes its name and which is believed to date back as early as the 5th century A.D. The fort has been ruled by a number of groups, including Rajputs, the Delhi Sultanate, and the Mughals, each of

© BOBBY SHEKHAWAT

Tiger sightings are common in Ranthambore National Park.

which added their own construction. Today, you'll find palaces, *chhatris* (canopies), Muslim shrines, a mosque, and plenty of Hindu temples. The most famous site within the fort is the Ganesh temple, home to a three-eyed version of the elephant-headed deity. It's believed that any wish you make here will come true, and it's also an auspicious place for the soon-to-be-married, who send thousands of wedding invitations to the god every year. The temple is surrounded by hordes of langurs, mostly friendly but who occasionally try to coerce snacks and flowers from visiting pilgrims.

Accommodations and Food

The bulk of Ranthambore's accommodations are in the midrange category, but if you just want something clean and basic, check out the **Hotel Dev Palace** (Ranthambore Rd., tel. 9983/053-968, bookings.devpalace@gmail.com, Rs. 400-500 d). This small guesthouse has basic guest rooms without much of a view

(the windows open up onto corridors), but there's a small terrace for eating and socializing with other travelers as well as 24-hour hot water. Some guest rooms are also air-conditioned, and there's Internet and a travel agent on-site. They serve cheap, spicy north Indian meals (Rs. 100), both vegetarian and nonvegetarian, that are cooked off-site. Because they don't have their own kitchen, allow plenty of time to get your food.

Ideal for groups or families on a budget, the spacious **Raj Palace Resort** (Ranthambore Rd., tel. 7462/221-331, www.rajpalaceranthambhore.com, Rs. 2,700-5,200 d) has spotless marble-floored guest rooms decorated with photos of tigers from the nearby park. There's also a clean swimming pool and plenty of garden space to roam around in. It is popular with tour groups, and group discounts are available. Note that the "suites" are actually just large guest rooms with big baths. Breakfast is included in the rates, and full-board plans that

SAVE THE TIGERS

Tiger conservation efforts are incredibly important to the species' survival.

India's national animal, the royal Bengal tiger, is on the verge of extinction, and only an estimated 1,411 of the beasts are alive in the wild today. Visitors to India's tiger reserves rarely spot them, and conservationists fear that populations will continue to decline. Not long ago, however, huge tiger populations were considered a threat to farm animals, and hunting parties were common–pay a visit to any royal hunting lodge in Rajasthan and you will likely see a trophy tiger head mounted on the wall.

Reuters reported in 1951 that the Indian government believed that 500-1,000 tigers could be killed in India annually "without affecting the general tiger population." In the 1950s, tiger hunting holidays were promoted as a way to increase American tourism to India and provide income to members of royal families whose livelihood had begun to diminish when their princedoms were incorporated into independent India. These initiatives also helped keep tiger numbers at bay, but after decades of poaching and modern encroachments on the big cats' traditional environment, tiger numbers are dwindling.

India's government passed the Wildlife Protection Act of 1972, which included a slew of new regulations and bans on hunting. It led to the establishment of Project Tiger, a tiger protection agency designed to increase sanctuary land and promote public awareness about wildlife conservation. While efforts to protect the tiger have been running for decades, it wasn't until late 2009, when the World Wide Fund for Nature (WWF) launched a major publicity campaign that featured images of an adorable baby tiger, that tiger protection was put back in the spotlight. Tiger conservation is currently a hot topic in India, although poaching is still reported. One can only hope that these efforts will prove fruitful and that tiger populations will once again be able to flourish in India.

EXCURSIONS

give you access to huge buffets are available. Even if you're not staying here, you're welcome to come to eat a meal (Rs. 140).

For the best views in town, head to the Rajasthan Tourism–run heritage property **❰ Castle Jhoomar Baori** (Ranthambore Rd., tel. 7462/220-495, cjb@rtdc.in, Rs. 4,900-6,900 d). The former hunting lodge of the Maharaja of Jaipur, this 150-year-old castle in the clouds is in the heart of leopard country, and the reclusive spotted beasts can sometimes be spotted from the rooftop. The road up to the hotel is a good place to catch a glimpse of nilgai (Asian antelope) and spotted deer. The guest rooms are decked out with old-fashioned furniture, and each floor has a common area with low seating and pretty furniture. Most guest rooms have a foyer, and the suites have separate baths and showers, which are ventilated through old rifle holes. The newly constructed guest rooms on the top floor are nice but not as charming as the old converted digs. Fresh Indian meals are included in the rates, and the restaurant is only open to guests.

The purpose-built **Nahar Haveli** (Village Khilichur, Ranthambore Rd., tel. 7462/252-281, www.alsisar.com, Rs. 6,000-8,000 d) is one of the quietest places in town. The guest rooms all have period furniture, and many also have colorful glass windows that make the property seem more Rajasthani than many of the simpler hotels around. The more expensive guest rooms also have window seats, and some come with balconies. There are plenty of spacious lawns as well as a pool and a small vegetable garden used to supply the kitchen, which serves up fresh vegetarian Rajasthani and North Indian cuisine (Rs. 120) to both guests and nonguests.

It's hard to compete with the luxurious personalized treatment you get at the **❰ Oberoi Vanyavilas** (Ranthambore Rd., tel. 7462/223-999, www.oberoihotels.com, Rs. 44,500-49,500). This beautiful property is spread over eight lush hectares that include mango, guava, and *amla* (Indian gooseberry) orchards, a large vegetable garden, and plenty of roaming peacocks. Each of the 25 tents has a claw-foot tub and a private patio, and even the fitness center is in a tent. On-site activities include nightly musical performances illuminated by a blazing bonfire, daily talks on the park by a local naturalist, and short safaris atop the two friendly elephants that live on-site. The spa is especially beautiful and opens onto a gorgeous lotus-filled pond. There's also a 16-meter observation tower offering panoramic views of Ranthambore. Both Indian and continental food are served, and much of it is prepared using fresh ingredients from the garden. Excellent continental breakfast options are available. Meals (Rs. 600-1,000 pp) are quite expensive by Indian standards, and the restaurant is only open to hotel guests.

You won't find many places in town quieter than the discreet, very peaceful **Aman-i-Khas** (Kushthala Village, just south of Sawai Madhopur, tel. 7462/252-052, www.amanresorts.com, Rs. 56,000 d). This small property has 10 enormous luxury tents made of canvas and cotton, which are packed up each year when the property closes during the hot summer season (July-Sept.). All guest rooms feature lovely sunken tubs, king beds, and elegant rustic-chic dark wood furniture. The swimming pool is naturally shaded, and there's a huge artificial lake that attracts a variety of colorful birds year-round. The restaurant is only open to hotel guests and serves fresh continental and Indian food. Menus can be specially arranged for guests, and there's a small à la carte selection.

Getting There and Around

Ranthambore is eight hours by road from Delhi, so if you are approaching from the capital, you are much better off taking a train to the nearby town of Sawai Madhopur. Around 10-12 trains connect the two cities on any

Tigers are more elusive at Sariska Tiger Reserve.

© MARGOT BIGG

with Dehradun (for Mussoorie, 20 hours), Haridwar (for Rishikesh, 18 hours), Delhi (8 hours), and Bharatpur (for Keoladeo, 4 hours).

Once in Ranthambore, the easiest way to get around is either by autorickshaw or by taxi. Most of the hotels can arrange transportation to the park entrance for a nominal fee.

SARISKA TIGER RESERVE

A visit to Sariska Tiger Reserve (State Hwy. 29A, south of Alwar, tel. 144/284-1333, 6:30-10 A.M. and 2:30 P.M.-sunset daily, Rs. 450 for eigners, Rs. 60 Indians, video Rs. 200) does not guarantee that you'll see an elusive tiger, but it's nevertheless an excellent place to clear your lungs of all the smog and dust of India's big cities. This deciduous forest at the edge of the Thar Desert was once the private hunting ground of the Maharaja of Alwar, and he used to invite dignitaries of the British Raj here on hunting trips. After independence, tiger populations began to drop quite dramatically, and by 1958 the area became a wildlife sanctuary. Sariska was declared a national park in 1982.

The park is home to a wide array of flora and fauna, and while there is supposedly a small number of tigers, don't expect to see one. You're more likely to encounter panthers, striped hyenas, jackals, wild boars, primates, and jungle cats. Visitors occasionally come across caracals, pointy-eared felines that are similar to lynxes but with longer legs and leaner bodies that can weigh up to 18 kilograms. Sariska also contains a large population of deer, including Indian species such as sambars and spotted deer as well as the ubiquitous nilgai (Asian antelope). The rainforest is thick with trees and plants ranging from bamboo to acacia. The most notable trees are the *dhok (Anogeissus pendula)*, which is barren most of the year but suddenly sprouts leaves within hours after the first downpour of the annual monsoon, and the *dhak (Butea monosperma)*, a sacred tree known as "the flame of the forest" for its brilliant orange buds.

given day. The fastest of these is the daily *Ag Kranti Rajdhani,* which shuttles passengers between New Delhi's Nizamuddin Railway Station and Sawai Madhopur in just over 3.5 hours. Tickets for this service sell out fast, so if you need something last-minute, book a seat in the air-conditioned Chair Car of the *Kota Janshatabdi,* which takes just under five hours. Trains can be booked at the railway station or online, although it's easiest to book through an agent, such as **Ranthambore Safaris & Tours** (Ranthambore National Park Rd., tel. 7462/220-769, www.ranthambhoresafaris.com).

It takes just under two hours to reach Sawai Madhopur from Jaipur by train, or about 3.5 hours by car via the Tonk Road. Anywhere from 12-15 trains run between the two cities on any given day. Three trains per day connect Sawai Madhopur with Agra Fort railway station and take 4-6 hours. The daily *Dehradun Express* connects Sawai Madhopur

the entry to Sariska Tiger Reserve

©RAJAT DEEP RANA

The best way to visit Sariska is to sign up for a guided safari in a Gypsy 4-by-4 (similar to a jeep). Safaris last four hours and cost Rs. 1,250 pp for foreigners, plus Rs. 250 for a guide. If you can, try to visit in the winter season (Nov.-Mar.). You'll likely see more wildlife during this time, and the temperatures will be much more pleasant.

Accommodations and Food

The Rajasthan Tourism–run **Tiger Den** (near Forest Rest House, Sariska, tel. 144/284-1342, www.rtdc.in, Rs. 2,250-4,300 d) is the sole accommodations option if you want to stay in the park (although it's actually just beyond the main parking lot). Although it admittedly lacks character, the property is well maintained, and there's a state tourism office on-site with very helpful staff. There's also a small restaurant on-site where you can have a simple Indian meal (around Rs. 100), or you can sign up for one of the hotel's meal plans.

About 16 kilometers from the park, just off the main road, 🎧 **Sariska Tiger Camp** (Village Dhawala, Jaipur Rd., tel. 144/288-5311, www.sariskatigercamp.com, Rs. 3,000-3,500 d) makes up for its distance from the park with amazing grounds and beautiful facilities set against a breathtaking backdrop of the craggy Aravalli Range. The guest rooms are made in the traditional village style, with mud—OK, manure—walls (it sounds disgusting, but it's perfectly hygienic and undoubtedly ecofriendly). Vegetarian meal plans are available. There's also a pool for hot summer days; in the winter, the hotel organizes bonfires.

Attractive yet unwarrantedly ostentatious, **The Sariska Palace** (Sariska, tel. 144/284-1323, www.thesariskapalace.in, Rs. 8,400) touts itself as a luxury heritage property, but it's more aptly described as middle-of-the-road. Nonguests are charged Rs. 500 to visit, considerably higher than the majority of sites in India and prohibitively expensive for most local visitors. It's best to save your money for something more worthwhile. That said, it's definitely the swankiest of the few hotels near Sariska, and the guest rooms are pretty, as is the swimming pool. Plus it's just across the street from the main gate of the reserve. There's an 80-seat restaurant on-site serving Indian, continental, and Chinese cuisine.

Getting There and Around

Whether you are approaching Sariska from Delhi or Jaipur, the easiest and best way to get here is by car. Reaching the park takes about three hours from Jaipur, 3.5 hours from Delhi. From Delhi, take National Highway 8 to Dharuhera, then State Highway 25 to Alwar. From Alwar, take State Highway 13 to State Highway 29A to the park. From Jaipur, take State Highway 55 to State Highway 29A.

You can also take a train from either Delhi or Jaipur to Alwar, the nearest city, some 40 kilometers away. The cheapest way to reach the park from Alwar is by taking a local bus—you'll be dropped just opposite the Forest Reception Centre—but the service is unreliable and has frequent stops, so it can take up to two hours. A taxi is a more comfortable option and will get you here in just over 30 minutes, but you'll be at the mercy of Alwar's hard-bargaining taxi drivers unless you book something ahead of time. A local taxi should cost about Rs. 700-1,000 each way.

KEOLADEO NATIONAL PARK

Even if you are not an avid bird-watcher, you should still pay a visit to **Keoladeo National Park** (Bharatpur, tel. 5644/222-777, sunrise-sunset daily, Rs. 200 foreigners, Rs. 25 Indians, video Rs. 200), which covers 47 square kilometers of wetland and forest just off the National Highway 11 between Jaipur and Agra. Often referred to as Bharatpur Bird Sanctuary, this World Heritage Site has existed since the mid-18th century, when Maharaja Suraj Mal of Bharatpur constructed Ajan Bund, a dam at the confluence of the nearby Gambhir and Banaganga Rivers, resulting in heavy flooding that turned the area into a marsh. Migratory birds began to flock here and at the turn of the 20th century, it was made into a shooting range, which it remained until the mid-1960s. It was declared a national park in 1981.

A total of 374 avian species have been recorded at the sanctuary. At any given time of year, hundreds of species of birds are present, including imposing storks, peacocks, crusted-pie cuckoos, and blue jays (which have tan backs, turquoise bodies, and look nothing like their North American and European counterparts). There are also tons of varieties of ducks, and if you're lucky, you may spot a long-tailed gray hornbill, with its distinctive double beak (the upper, apparently decorative, beak is actually a protective casque).

Plenty of mammals, amphibians, and reptiles call Keoladeo home, and rumor has it that a tigress ended up here, seemingly randomly, in 2010 and was later transferred to Ranthambore. There are also hyenas, porcupines, civets, wild cats, cows, primates, and *cheetals* (Indian spotted deer). The park is home to many *kadam* trees, known as Lord Krishna's favorite tree, as well as mimosa, datura, and wild bitter gourds that some locals collect and take home to cook.

Keoladeo National Park is accessed via one long road that stretches most of the length of the park. You can walk it, although most visitors choose to go by cycle rickshaw or bicycle. Cycle rickshaws charge a fixed Rs. 70 per hour, and authorized vehicles are identifiable by a large yellow sign at their helms. The biggest advantage of taking a cycle rickshaw is that most of the pullers have spent a lot of time in the park and are skilled at spotting and identifying wildlife.

There's actually quite a bit to do in Keoladeo besides bird-watching. On the way into the park is the large **Visitor Interpretation Centre,** which features a series of halls filled with

EXCURSIONS

a peacock in a tree in Keoladeo National Park

educational panels complete with poetic descriptions of India's seasons as well as molded plastic sculptures of the various animals that visit the park, a map of showcasing the origins of many of the migratory birds that come for winter, and a pair of life-size saras cranes studded in Swarovski crystals. At the opposite end of the park is a small lake for boating (Rs. 25 per hour), although there's not always water in it.

The park is worth a visit year-round, although the winter months (Oct.-Feb.) are more comfortable due to cooler temperatures. This is also the time of year when migratory birds quite literally flock to the park. Resident birds nest and breed March-June; waterfowl nest and breed July-September.

Accommodations and Food

The family-run **Jungle Lodge** (Gori Shankar Colony, tel. 5644/225-622, www.junglelodge. dk, Rs. 300-800 d) is by far the friendliest of the string of budget guesthouses behind the state tourism offices. All of the guest rooms are clean and open onto a small flower garden that doubles as the family Pomeranian's personal playpen. Reasonably priced home-cooked Indian meals (under Rs. 100) and snacks are also available.

The biggest draw of **Hotel Pratap Palace** (State Hwy. 1, near park entrance, tel. 5644/224-245, Rs. 600-800 d) is its medium-size outdoor swimming pool, accessible to foreign nonguests for Rs. 100 per hour, although even if there was no pool, the guest rooms would be a great deal. Unlike the majority of digs in this price range, all of the guest rooms are equipped with TVs. The on-site restaurant (entrées Rs. 160) serves a huge selection of Indian, Indo-Chinese, and continental dishes; beer is also served.

The reliable **Hotel Saras** (Saras Circle, tel. 5644/223-790, www.rtdc.in, Rs. 950-1,350 d), owned and operated by Rajasthan Tourism, is a bit more expensive than many of the guesthouses in the area, but it's consistently clean and well-staffed, with a decent restaurant serving up basic Indian fare. The staff are friendly and knowledgeable, and they go out of their way to help orient guests with sights and activities in the area. Buses to Fatehpur Sikri stop just in front of the hotel.

Hotel Sunbird (State Hwy. 1, near the park entrance, tel. 5644/225-701, www.hotel-sunbird.com, Rs. 2,000-2,500 d), is arguably the prettiest hotel in town, at least on the inside. The elegantly furnished guest rooms feature gilded ceilings, and some of the deluxe guest rooms even have fireplaces. The garden cottages, with cloth false ceilings, are cozy and are designed to give guests the impression of sleeping out in nature. The large garden welcomes birds from the nearby sanctuary, and every morning the property fills with birdsong. The restaurant (entrées Rs. 100) serves up an array of Indian food as well as a few Chinese dishes, and they keep the spice level to a minimum unless you request otherwise.

If you'd prefer to stay in the park, **Hotel Bharatpur Ashok** (inside Keoladeo National Park, tel. 5644/222-864, www.theashokgroup.com, Rs. 2,999 d), is the place to stay. The entire building is painted a rather off-putting shade of green to blend with the local environment, but the interiors are charming mixtures of wood and marble. All guest rooms come with air-conditioning, TVs, a bathtub, and a balcony. There's an on-site restaurant (entrées Rs. 150) and a small bar as well as a small library that includes some interesting guides to the birds of India.

The beautiful and reasonably priced **Laxmi Vilas Palace** (Kakaji ki Kothi, tel. 5644/231-199, www.laxmivilas.com, Rs. 5,500 d), Bharatpur's prime heritage property, is the most elegant of the accommodations options near Keoladeo National Park. The furnishings blend marble, hand-painted arches, and dark wood colonial furniture to give the property a classic Indo-colonial look. There's also an ayurvedic spa, a pool, and an outdoor jetted tub, perfect after a long winter's day in the bird sanctuary.

Getting There and Around

As Keoladeo is located on the fringe of Bharatpur, right on the main Agra-Jaipur highway, it's a very easy place to reach, with plenty of trains connecting Bharatpur to Delhi and Agra. The quickest way to reach Bharatpur from Delhi is on the *Kota Janshatabdi* train, which takes about 2.5 hours to link the two cities. Driving takes about 3.5 hours.

Bharatpur is a mere 53 kilometers from Agra, and trains between the two cities take around one hour. It's also quite convenient to take a taxi between the two, stopping in Fatehpur Sikri along the way. Note that this can be expensive by Indian standards (upward of Rs. 2,000) if you book your taxi in Bharatpur. Also, although the two cities are near each other, they are in separate states; therefore, if you approach Agra from Bharatpur, you have to pay a road tax to the state of Uttar Pradesh once you cross Fatehpur Sikri. If you're on a budget, you may find it better just to catch a bus from Bharatpur's Saras Circle (in front of the RTDC Hotel Saras); this takes about 1.5 hours.

If you want to go to Jaipur, about three hours by road, simply cross the street at Saras Circle and flag down a bus headed west. Alternatively, trains between Jaipur and Bharatpur take 2.5-3 hours. Bharatpur is also connected to Dehradun (for Mussoorie, 16.5 hours) and Haridwar (for Rishikesh, 14 hours) by the daily *Dehradun Express*. There are also plenty of trains between Bharatpur and Sawai Madhopur (for Ranthambore); these take 2-4 hours.

Bharatpur is a small city, and the easiest way to get around is by cycle or autorickshaw, both of which you'll have to bargain for. An autorickshaw from the train station to the national park area or to any of the hotels listed above should cost no more than Rs. 70 for two people with luggage. Cycle rickshaws can be hired by the day or part of the day, and most will charge you the official park rate (Rs. 70 per hour), even if you take the rickshaw into the city.

BACKGROUND

The Land

GEOGRAPHY

Delhi, Jaipur, and Agra all lie on North India's densely populated Indo-Gangetic Plain, which stretches across the northern expanse of the Indian subcontinent from Pakistan across into Bangladesh. This region is characterized by flat arid land that merges into the Thar Desert in the southwest and is flanked by the Himalayas to the north. The craggy Aravalli Range, one of the oldest mountain ranges in the world, cuts across this part of the country, insulating the plains from the Thar.

CLIMATE

North India has four distinct seasons: winter (mid-Dec.–mid-Mar.), summer (mid-Mar.–mid-June), monsoon (late June–Sept.), and postmonsoon (mid-Sept.–mid-Dec.). The seasons are extreme, and summers can get particularly uncomfortable, when temperatures in this region hover well over 40°C. Monsoons are not experienced as strongly in North India as they are in other parts of the country, and some years are devastatingly dry, much to the chagrin of farmers who rely on these rains for the success of their crops. Although this part of

© RAJAT DEEP RANA

© RAJAT DEEP RANA

Rajasthan becomes quite lush after the annual monsoon rains.

the world has relatively low humidity through most of the year, the postmonsoon period can get quite sticky. By the time November rolls around, temperatures start to fall at a dramatic rate through December. January is North India's coldest month, when temperatures often drop below freezing. The dry cold is exacerbated by the fact that most North Indian homes are meant to keep the heat out rather than retain it, so it's often colder inside than outside.

ENVIRONMENTAL ISSUES

With its constantly growing cities and booming economy, North India is at high risk of environmental degradation. Pollution is a major problem, and although regulations are in place, they are not very well enforced. On the plus side, initiatives such as a widespread switchover from diesel to compressed natural gas (CNG) have made the air a bit more breathable, most notably in Delhi.

Mining in the Aravalli mountains poses a threat to the region's increasingly delicate ecosystem, and although this practice was banned by the Indian Supreme Court in 2002, illegal operations continue to flourish in some remote parts of the range. Like everywhere in the world, global warming has had a noticeable impact on North India's climate, reducing the production of cash crops and pushing average annual temperatures in the region upward. There are now fears among scientists that if things continue at the current rate, the retreat of the Himalayan glaciers, which has been ongoing since the mid-19th century, will speed up significantly, causing rivers to flood and reducing the amount of irrigation water available throughout the northern subcontinent.

FLORA AND FAUNA
Flora

Most of the trees in Delhi, Jaipur, and Agra are deciduous, and some flower overnight after the first monsoon rains. Common species include

ECOTRAVELER

There are plenty of ways to minimize the impact of your stay in India. Here are a few:

- **Don't litter:** India can be a disheartening place for the ecoconscious, or even for people who learned from an early age not to litter. Multicolored garbage strewn across the side of a forested hill is a common sight, and people think nothing of throwing their litter out the windows of buses and trains. Don't join in. Carry a small bag with you to keep your garbage in (including cigarette butts, which take years to biodegrade). Leave no trace behind.

- **Reuse bottles:** Instead of buying 500-milliliter or one-liter bottles of water, buy a five-liter container to keep in your hotel room, and use it to refill a smaller bottle. When you're done with it, bring it back to the store where you purchased it for recycling. Some hotels and restaurants also offer free or inexpensive filtered-water refills to help minimize plastic bottle waste.

- **Avoid plastic bags:** Plastic bags have been officially banned in some places, such as Delhi and Rishikesh, but many people still use them. Reuse bags whenever possible, and don't let any plastic bags you do have get blown away in the wind—they can cause wild animals to choke, and they take ages to disintegrate.

- **Set your air conditioner to sleep mode:** Most air-conditioning units have sleep modes that automatically turn the cooling down or off when you go to sleep. This mode will help save an incredible amount of electricity.

- **Use cycle rickshaws:** Cycle rickshaws are a much more ecofriendly way of getting around and are usually a bit cheaper than cars and autorickshaws.

- **Keep your waste away from water:** India lacks toilets in certain areas, and sometimes, when traveling by road, your only option to relieve yourself will be "in the jungle." If you do end up using the great outdoor toilet, be sure to distance yourself from streams or bodies of water, and remember to dig a hole if you have to do more than urinate.

Butea monosperma, known as the "flame of the forest" for its fiery orange flowers; the bright red **gulmohar** (*Delonix regia*); **kadam** (*Neolamarckia cadamba*), the favorite tree of Lord Krishna; and various types of **acacia**. Other significant species include the **neem** (*Azadirachta indica*), the branches of which are often used as rather efficient makeshift toothbrushes, and **Alstonia scholaris,** a tropical evergreen that fills the air with its pungent scent as winter descends on the plains. India's national tree, the **banyan** (*Ficus benghalensis*), has exposed interconnected roots and is considered holy by some and the abode of *djinns* (high-level spirits or genies) by others. It is common to spot small shrines nestled in the roots of these massive trees. There aren't many flowers growing in this arid region, apart from those found on trees and shrubs. One of the most beautiful and noticeable flowering shrubs in the region is datura, a poisonous perennial with beautiful white flowers that bloom out of forebodingly spiky pods.

Fauna
MAMMALS

North India is home to a great variety of mammals, some native and others introduced. As in most of the country's major cities, you'll find plenty of cows wandering the streets, primarily belonging to the **Indian zebu** (*Bos indicus*) variety. This type of cattle, often referred to as a **Brahman cow** (which is actually a subspecies of zebu), is a bit smaller and has shorter hair than its European counterpart. It also has a hump at its withers, a dewlap hanging from its neck, and

langurs perched in a banyan tree

bunny-like floppy ears. Their owners often let them loose to forage for food every day; cows tend not to stray too far, and some have regular routes that they follow, visiting the same homes daily to beg for scraps of food.

You'll also spot plenty of other animals on India's urban streets, including stray dogs that pass their time chasing cars and playing, large wild pigs that eat up much of the garbage on the streets, and the odd feral cat (cats have a hard time in this part of the country, where many people believe they bring bad luck). North India's plains are also home to a wide variety of cloven-hoofed animals, including the *cheetal* (Indian spotted deer) and the **nilgai,** a South Asian breed of antelope.

You're also likely to cross paths with the occasional **Asian elephant.** Although there are some wild "tuskers," as they are often called locally, in the area around Rishikesh, you're much more likely to run into one in the cities along with its mahout (handler). If you stop to

take a picture, the mahout may ask for a donation. Because of their size, elephants are very expensive to feed, and it's common practice to give money to their owners—Rs. 100 is a reasonable offering.

Camels are known as "ships of the desert," and the single-humped dromedary variety are commonplace in India, particularly in Jaipur and other parts of Rajasthan. You'll likely spot one of these sturdy creatures pulling a cart at some point during your trip, and you may even get a chance to take one for a spin. Every November, an enormous camel fair is held in Pushkar, and the entire town fills up with herders and their beasts.

One of the most delightful aspects of a trip to India is getting to see **wild monkeys up** close and personal. There are two main varieties of primate in North India: the **rhesus macaque** (*Macaca mulatta*) and the **Hanuman langur** (*Semnopithecus* species). Most rhesus monkeys have a reddish coat and are comfortable

© MARGOT BIGG

Although not an everyday sight in urban areas, both elephants and camels are used as beasts of burden in India.

interacting with humans (particularly humans with food), but they can get a bit aggressive. Hanuman langurs are much larger and seem quite a bit more intelligent. They are often used to chase rhesus monkeys out of public spaces such as parks and college campuses. Langurs are large graceful animals, usually about 60–75 centimeters tall, with long tails, and they are generally fairly passive unless provoked. Both types of monkey frequent temples dedicated to Hanuman, the Hindu monkey god, where they are well fed by pilgrims.

BIRDS

North India is home to a wide variety of avian life. In Delhi, Jaipur, and Agra you'll spot plenty of pigeons as well as huge flocks of **green parrots, kites** (raptors), and quite a few **peacocks**, India's national bird. Get out into the countryside and the variety will increase

to include hornbills, cuckoos, and even storks and cranes.

REPTILES

You're likely to encounter a *chipkali* (house lizard) at some point during your stay in India. These geckos are normally no more than a few centimeters long, and they like to hide out behind tube lights, which are ideal places to catch the insects on which they feed. There are also a lot of snakes in India, especially in the rocky desert areas. Four of these are very dangerous and responsible for most of India's fatal snakebites: **Russell's viper,** the **saw-scaled viper,** the **krait,** and India's most famous (and feared) snake, the **king cobra.** In heavily touristed parts of India you'll spot the odd snake charmer; note that the cobras used for this cruel practice have had their fangs removed.

INSECTS AND ARACHNIDS

If you are horrified by insects, India might not be the best country for you. You'll probably spot a few bugs during your trip, and they may be considerably larger than what you have ever seen before. The peskiest insects are **mosquitoes,** which can spread diseases such as malaria and dengue. It's therefore important to use mosquito repellent and to keep windows and doors closed when you sleep. Common **houseflies** are all over the place too, especially in areas with a lot of livestock or where food has been left out. There are also plenty of **butterflies** and beetles, and if you're lucky, you may even spot a **praying mantis.** Unfortunately, you're much more likely to cross paths with a **cockroach.** These ancient creatures are ubiquitous in India, and their presence doesn't necessarily equate to low sanitation standards the way it would in many other countries. They can get quite big: A five-centimeter-long cockroach is pretty average. But don't be alarmed; they're just part of life, and although they are definitely one of the creepier creatures on this little planet of ours, they're completely harmless.

History

EARLY CIVILIZATIONS

India is believed to have been inhabited for some 9,000 years. The earliest records of flourishing civilizations in the region of Delhi, Jaipur, and Agra go back to the late Vedic Period, which started around 600 B.C. During this time, 16 kingdom-like polities known as Mahajanapadas were formed, and the primarily nomadic people of the region began to take up a settled lifestyle. It was in this period that the set of sacred texts known as the Upanishads was written.

One of the Mahajanapadas, Magadha, eventually expanded to encompass much of the northern part of the Indian subcontinent, and in 322 B.C. a ruler named Chandragupta Maurya usurped the king of Magadha's ruling Nanda Dynasty and founded the Maurya Empire. At one point, Chandragupta had control of most of present-day India and Pakistan, making him the leader of what was then the world's largest empire. His grandson Ashoka would later conquer the remaining southern kingdom of Kaling before converting to Buddhism and transforming himself from a warmonger to a spreader of peaceful ideas. The Maurya Empire began to decline after Ashoka's death, and it split into smaller kingdoms.

MIDDLE KINGDOMS

The next era in the region's history saw a more fragmented India as well as significant contact with outside forces, including the Persians and Greeks, who held power in parts of the subcontinent. It wasn't until the Gupta Empire was founded in the 4th century A.D. that North India would again be united under one ruler. Many historians consider this time to be the start of India's golden age, for it was under Gupta rule that Indian art, philosophy, and science really began to flourish. The decimal system and the concept of zero were invented in India in this era, and great works of literature, including the *Ramayana,* the *Mahabharata,* and the *Kama Sutra* were penned. Chess was also invented, and astronomers during the era began arguing—or at least exploring the possibility—that the earth was round.

Like all great empires, the Gupta Empire eventually fell in the 7th century A.D., largely due to an invasion by the Central Asian Huna people. The northern regions split up, and three new dynasties were formed: the Pala, the Gurjara Pratihara, and the Rashtrakuta. The Gurjara Pratiharas would rule over much of the northern part of the fallen Gupta Empire, and it is believed that the Tomar clan, whose leader Anangpal established Delhi in 736, were a subset of this group. The Rajputs would later emerge and take control over much of North India, including what is now Rajasthan, and would continue to rule the desert state, although sometimes under the auspices of other, indirect rulers, until India's independence from the British in the 20th century.

ISLAMIC SULTANATES

The 12th century A.D. marked the emergence of the Islamic Sultanates in India. Toward the end of that century, Muhammad of Ghor took over Delhi from Prithviraj III of the Rajput Chauhan Dynasty and declared himself sultan, a position he retained until his assassination in 1206. This marked the start of the Delhi Sultanate, a collective term used to describe the five sultanates, each relatively short-lived, that would rule Delhi and its environs until the Mughals took over in 1526. The first was the Mamluk Dynasty (1206–1290), which ended in a coup led by the Khiljis, who ruled for 30 years and successfully prevented the Mongols from invading. The next ruling dynasty was the Tughlaqs, who shifted India's capital to Daulatabad, Maharastra, for a couple of years, only to return to Delhi after realizing that their new capital didn't have enough water to sustain an entire city.

In 1398 the army of the Timurid Dynasty from Central Asia invaded Delhi, and their leader, Timur, ordered the extermination of Delhi's entire Hindu population. For a while there was no solid leadership in the weakened city, until 1414 when the Sayyid Dynasty, who claimed to be descendants of the Prophet Muhammad, took control of the city under the lead of Khizr Khan, the governor of Multan under Timur. The Lodi Dynasty was next and took over in 1451 after Sayyid ruler Bahlul Khan voluntarily abdicated and then skipped town. Sikandar Lodi founded Agra in 1504,

and his son Ibrahim ruled the sultanate from his seat in Agra until the Dynasty's last days. The Lodi reign ended in 1526, after they were defeated by Babur in the first Battle of Panipat.

THE MUGHAL EMPIRE

Babur defeated the Lodis and Maharana Sangram Singh of Mewar, in present-day Rajasthan, and the Mughal Empire was born. Babur died in 1531, and his son Humayun took over, lost the empire to the short-lived Sur Dynasty, won it back, and then died falling down a flight of stairs in 1555, leaving the Empire to his 13-year-old son Akbar, later called Akbar the Great. Akbar was instrumental in expanding the Mughal Empire to encompass much of what is now North India, and although he was cruel to Hindus in his earlier days, he later married a Hindu princess and appointed Hindus to high-ranking government positions. He was also a fond patron of the arts, which flourished under his reign. He left the throne to his alcoholic son Jahangir, who died in 1627. Next in line was Shahjahan, who built the Red Fort and the Jama Masjid in Delhi as well as the Taj Mahal. He also shifted the capital back to Delhi, founding Shahjahanabad in what is now called Old Delhi in 1649. Shahjahan fell ill in 1657, and his son Aurangzeb took full advantage of his father's malady, placing the old ruler under house arrest in Agra Fort. Shahjahan died 11 years later.

Aurangzeb was strict and purportedly strongly anti-Hindu, and he spent much of his time as emperor engaged in warfare and expansion campaigns, which cost the Empire fortunes. After he died in 1707, the Mughal Empire began a slow but steady decline, eventually falling under the indirect rule of the Marathas and the East India Company. It all came to an end following the 1858 Indian Rebellion, when the last Mughal Emperor, Shah Alam II, was exiled to Burma, and rule over India was transferred to the British.

© RAJAT DEEP RANA

Delhi's Red Fort was built by Shahjahan in the mid-17th century.

BRITISH INDIA

Britain had had a presence in India since the establishment of the East India Company in the early 17th century, and in the 18th century much of East India was under the company's rule. However, the Mughals had a stronghold over Delhi, Agra, and Jaipur until the 1857 rebellion, at which point the British took over. The British ruled India for almost a century, using divide-and-rule tactics that pitted members of different ethnic groups against each other to create disharmony and weaken the masses, along with indirect rule behind local figureheads, to keep the country under their control. They built India's massive railway system and began bringing Indians into the political process in 1909 through the creation of legislative councils. In 1911 the capital of India was shifted back to Delhi from Calcutta. When World War I broke out soon after, more than one million Indian soldiers were dispatched to fight around the world. After the war, the League of Nations, predecessor to the United Nations, was formed, and India was represented independently of Britain. This was one of many signs that India was on the path to independent statehood.

THE INDEPENDENCE MOVEMENT

An independence movement had been brewing since the Indian Rebellion in 1857, but it wasn't until the early 20th century that the struggle went mainstream. One of the key thinkers in the early stages of this movement was Bal Gangadhar Tilak, a journalist, activist, and strong advocate of the Swadeshi Movement, a boycott of British products that was influential in Gandhi's ideas. In 1919 the Government of India Act was passed, increasing India's autonomy through self-governance, although the British retained financial control. It was around this time that Mohandas Gandhi (who would later be referred to as Mahatma, meaning "great soul") became active in the movement. He advocated nonviolent civil disobedience as a form of rebellion and aligned himself with the Indian National Congress Party. After World War I the party, which had originally advocated an economically unified commerce zone rather than full-on independence, shifted its vision and began working toward complete autonomy. Gandhi promoted the party's vision, boycotting British goods such as textiles and teaching people how to spin khadi, a homespun alternative to British cotton. His most famous act of nonviolent civil disobedience was when he marched hundreds of kilometers from his ashram near Ahmedabad in Gujarat to the coast to harvest salt, symbolically opposing British-imposed salt taxes. Gandhi was later at the helm of the Quit India Movement, which threatened extensive civil disobedience if India were not given immediate independence. Although many Indian historians believe that Gandhi's protests didn't do much to convince the British to leave India—it has been argued that they were on their way out anyway—his actions helped unify the Indian people in a way that they never had been before.

The 1935 Government of India Act contained legislation that would establish an Indian Federation of elected provincial governments. These governments were formed two years later. Then, in 1939 Viceroy Victor Hope unilaterally declared that India would participate in World War II without first consulting the provincial governments. Subhas Chandra Bose, leader of the Azad Hind government in exile, sought alliances with the Axis powers during the war to help him overthrow the government. He eventually got support from the Japanese and organized the Indian National Army (INA) to overthrow British rule. His efforts failed, but he did send a strong message to the British. In 1946 India's naval forces staged a mutiny, considered by many to be the last straw. The British Empire was also quite weak at the time, having fought World War II for six years. This combination of factors led to India's freedom, which was granted in 1947. Gandhi was assassinated two years later.

Partition

India's independence from the British changed the landscape of the country in many ways. India would be united as a single democratically self-governed country for the first time in its history, but before this was to happen, the land that fell under British India would be divided into the largely Hindu Republic of India and the Muslim Dominion of Pakistan; East Pakistan would later become the sovereign Bangladesh.

Since the early 20th century, the All Indian Muslim League had been espousing the "two-nation theory," arguing that the differences in Hindu and Muslim worldviews meant that despite their common ancestry, the two groups intrinsically formed two nations and, therefore, in keeping with the prevalent Westphalian model of nation statehood, should be divided in two. Both the British and major leaders from both Hindu and Muslim backgrounds, including Gandhi, opposed the idea of a divided India, but because of a desire to get out of India quickly, coupled with fears of a civil war, the British eventually ceded. In July 1947, only five weeks before India was granted independence, an English barrister by the name of Cyril Radcliffe was brought to India and charged with dividing British India into separate states. It was his first trip to the subcontinent, but he was nonetheless given chairmanship of two boundary commissions, one for the Punjab region in the west and one for Bengal in the east. He went to work at splitting these two states in such a way that the land and resources would be redistributed fairly among Muslims and non-Muslims and farm plots would not be split. Unfortunately, the resulting boundaries were far from perfect. Some even went straight through people's houses—imagine inadvertently crossing into another country every time you went into your kitchen. The results were tragic. Millions of people fled from their homes overnight, leaving everything behind in order to escape possible religious persecution, and others continued to flee for years to come. Muslims moved to Pakistan, Hindus and Sikhs to India; a large percentage of Delhi's population can trace their roots back to this widespread displacement. Hundreds of thousands of people died on the journey.

CONTEMPORARY INDIA

India gained its independence on August 15, 1947, and its constitution took effect in 1950. The first prime minister was Jawaharlal Nehru, whose administration was marked by the nationalization of industries and significant investment in education. He also formed the Nonaligned Movement, which kept India out of the Cold War. After Nehru's death, Lal Bahadur Shastri took over, only to die two years later under mysterious circumstances during a state visit to Tashkent, where he'd signed a peace agreement between India and Pakistan following their second war.

The next prime minister was Indira Gandhi, Nehru's daughter, who devalued the rupee and went to war with Pakistan, which resulted in the establishment of Bangladesh. In 1975, following widespread protest spurred by allegations that Gandhi's Congress Party had committed electoral fraud, the president at the time, Fakhruddin Ali Ahmed, declared a national emergency, giving Gandhi the authority to rule by decree. The emergency lasted almost two years, and many Indians felt that their civil liberties were disregarded during this time. In 1977 Gandhi called an election and—not surprisingly—lost her seat, regaining it in 1980. In 1984 she launched Operation Blue Star, a campaign against Sikh separatists, and sent the military into India's most sacred site for Sikhs, Amritsar's Harmandir Sahib (the Golden Temple). She was then murdered by her Sikh bodyguards. Many Indians were angered by the assassination and took revenge on Sikhs, leading to a horrific massacre of Sikhs, especially in Delhi.

After Indira's assassination, her son Rajiv Gandhi took over as prime minister and used the position to try to reduce the thick bureaucracy for setting up new businesses, known as the license Raj, and to invest in science and technology infrastructure. He was followed by V. P. Singh, who resigned one year later, and then Chandra Shekhar Singh, who also resigned after a scandal. P. V. Narashima Rao became prime minister in 1991, and it was under his administration that India's economy was liberalized through privatization and regulatory reforms. These reforms were largely orchestrated by the administration's finance minister, Manmohan Singh, who is currently prime minister of India. These policies allowed India to open up to foreign investment and set the stage for India's economic landscape today.

Until the 1990s, India had a single television station, and most products sold were made in India. There were very few vehicles on the roads, and those that were available were the Indian-made Ambassador and, a bit later, Maruthis. Today, everything has changed. There are now over 400 TV stations, including local versions of MTV and VH1. Shopping malls have sprung up all over the country to sell U.S. and European brand-name goods. International companies have set up enormous outsourcing operations in India's big cities and are now beginning to expand into small cities and towns. Globalization has arrived, and it unabashedly declares its presence everywhere you look. But rather than whitewashing India with generics, turning the country into the carbon copy of a Nebraska strip mall, Globalization is simply adding to the country's diversity. In a part of the world as old as South Asia, where ancient traditions have withstood centuries of invasion, new influences are absorbed into the local culture without compromising local customs and traditions. Today's young urban Indian can carry off a Western business suit and a traditional kurta-pajama with equal pizzazz, switch from Hindi to English five times in one sentence, and feel equally at ease at a rock concert and a formal religious ceremony. This intrinsic ability to adapt to the new without compromising tradition has been key to the success of Indian civilization for millennia and will undoubtedly continue to keep the country's traditions alive for generations to come.

Government and Economy

GOVERNMENT

India is the world's largest democracy, and like the United States, its system of governance is based on that of the United Kingdom. India has a bicameral parliamentary legislature with two houses, the Lok Sabha (People's House), which is directly elected and comparable to the U.S. House of Representatives or the British House of Commons, and the Rajya Sabha (Council of States), the upper house that functions like the UK's House of Lords. The Lok Sabha is formed for a five-year period and has authority to pass motions of no confidence. They are also responsible for bills relating to taxes and government spending, and all new budget reforms are cleared through the Lok Sabha before moving into the Rajya Sabha.

India has a separate head of state (the president) and head of government (the prime minister). The president is elected by parliament and state legislatures using a system similar to the U.S. Electoral College and usually ends up being a member of the current majority party. He or she then appoints a prime minister to head the executive branch of government.

Governance also takes place at the state level in India. There are 28 states and 7 Union Territories, which are governed by state-level legislatures, a chief minister, and a presidentially appointed state governor who looks after federal affairs within his or her state. The Union Territories are directly controlled by the national government, with the exception of Delhi and Puducherry (Pondicherry), which have their own legislatures and councils of ministers (although their powers are limited compared to their counterparts at the state level). India also has a system for local-level governance known as the Panchayat Raj. Village-level councils (*gram panchayats*) look after issues relating to their villages, such as education and local infrastructure. These councils are part of larger blocks known as *panchayati samitis,* which deal with water sanitation and certain aspects of agriculture and education. These in turn convene at district level *zilla parishads* to deal with issues such as entrepreneurship and economic development.

POLITICAL PARTIES

There are hundreds of political parties in India, both at the local and national levels. The two most powerful are the nepotistic Indian National Congress Party, usually just referred to as "Congress," which was instrumental in India's independence movement, and the right-leaning Bharatiya Janata Party (BJP). Other smaller parties consistently win seats in the Lok Sabha, including the Communist Party of India (Marxist), Uttar Pradesh's Samajwadi Party, and Maharashtra's extreme-right Hindu nationalists, the reactionary Shiv Sena.

ELECTIONS

India's electorate exceeds 670 million people, and voter turnout is higher than in the United

States. Elections are a huge business that incur hundreds of millions of rupees in expenses every year. The largest chunk of the electorate is the rural poor, and this is where most campaigners focus their efforts.

BUREAUCRACY

In early 2012, India was ranked as having the worst bureaucracy in Asia in a study by a Hong Kong consulting firm. Getting even the simplest task accomplished requires days of standing in lines and shuffling back and forth among various government offices to get documents signed and approved with rubber stamps from various officials, who often go on long sabbaticals without getting a colleague to take over their duties. Few forms are available online, and processing times are often long. There is also a lot of corruption in the government, even at the low levels, which means offices are often understaffed: Some bosses take bribes from their employees in return for reduced hours. Moreover, it's very difficult to lose a government job once you have one, so there is little incentive for civil servants to do their jobs efficiently.

ECONOMY

India has an open-market economy, and just over half the country's 467 million–strong labor force is employed in the agriculture sector. The service industry is the second-largest contributor to the country's economy, accounting for an estimated 34 percent of the workforce, followed by industry at around 14 percent. India is one of the world's largest producers of key crops such as wheat, rice, legumes, jute, cotton, and oilseeds. The area around Delhi and Agra also has a large sugarcane industry, and sugarcane is the most significant cash crop in Uttar Pradesh, where Agra is located. Jaipur's state, Rajasthan, is also heavily reliant on agriculture, particularly wheat, barley, and oilseeds. The state is also a major producer of wool and milk and is a huge center for mining. Most of the country's

marble mines are in Rajasthan, which is also a major hub for cement production.

Both Uttar Pradesh and Rajasthan also have significant handicraft industries, and much of India's enormous leather industry is located in Agra—if you ever buy a pair of leather boots that have the words "Made in India" stamped on the tongue, they likely came from Agra. The tourism industry is a big part of what keeps Agra afloat; after all, it's home to the Taj Mahal, India's best-known attraction. Jaipur is also incredibly touristed, and the industry helps sustain not only hotels, restaurants, and souvenir shops but also transportation and infrastructure development. While tourism in Delhi does contribute to the economy, its role is naturally smaller than in Jaipur and Agra.

India has a large number of highly educated English-speaking professionals, and engineering is one of the most popular fields of study. The IT industry is huge, and many companies from around the world outsource their back-office work here. Due to concerns about low-quality output, however, many companies have shifted their operations to other countries, most notably the Philippines, or back to their home countries. Incentives for U.S. companies to reduce outsourcing following the global financial crisis in the late 2000s also led many U.S. companies to close their Indian offices. The financial crisis did not have as big an impact on India as it did on many other countries, partially because much of the Indian economy is fueled by domestic demand, but also because India maintains considerably more conservative banking policies. India's fast-growing economy is inducing noticeable inflation, and prices of everyday goods are rising rapidly. This is putting a strain not only on the poorest of the poor but also on India's burgeoning economic middle classes, and some economists speculate that it's only a matter of time before the Indian economy falters.

The gulf between rich and poor in India is

Handicrafts are big business in Agra.

extreme. The economic class system can be visualized like a wide-bottomed pyramid, with the very richest people occupying only a very tiny part of the top. The rich are incredibly rich, even by international standards, and the poor are incredibly poor. While liberalization and the ensuing increase in direct foreign investment have led to growth in the income of the middle classes, the country is still largely divided, with the rural poor making up the majority of the population.

People and Culture

DEMOGRAPHY

Delhi, Jaipur, and Agra are largely home to Hindi-speaking people, and the most educated people in these places also speak English with native-level fluency. The largest ethnic groups in the area include the Jaats, Gurjars, and Rajputs, all of whom trace their heritage back to the Gurjara Pratihara clans that ruled North India prior to the Islamic invasions. Delhi also has a large Punjabi community, many of whom migrated here in the aftermath of the 1947 partition.

One of the most salient features of India's social structure is the caste system. While caste plays a less significant role in the day-to-day lives of the urban educated elite, it is still very noticeable in smaller villages, where people often live on different streets based on their caste, just as they have for centuries (although it should be noted that this is often a relic of their ancestors' times, and they are simply living where their families have lived for generations). Caste comes up most often when it comes to marriage, and while nonarranged "love marriages" or

TRADITIONAL INDIAN DRESS

- **Choli:** A short midriff-baring blouse most commonly paired with a sari or *lengha*.

- **Churidar kameez:** Similar to a *salwar kameez*, except instead of a *salwar*, a *churidar*–trousers that are skin-tight and gathered at the ankle and lower calf–is worn.

- **Dhoti:** Sometimes called a *pancha*, dhotis are sarongs knotted and worn by some men in North India.

- **Dupatta** or **chunni:** A long lightweight scarf, normally worn draped across the chest and paired with a *salwar* or *churidar kameez*.

- **Gandhi topi:** Also called a Nehru topi, this is a white cap that's slightly pointed at the front and back. They are sometimes associated with politicians and activists.

- **Jutis:** Also known as *mojaris*, these traditional leather shoes are intricately embroidered, often with metallic thread, and sometimes adorned with sequins or beads. They are usually paired with formal wear.

- **Kurta:** A tunic. Men and women both wear these garments, which usually come down to about the mid-thigh. Shorter shirt-length kurtas are sometimes called *kurtis*.

- **Lengha:** A long skirt that's normally paired with a *choli* and *chunni*. Casual versions of this type of dress are popular in Rajasthan and Gujarat; in the rest of the country, *lenghas* are generally reserved for weddings and other formal occasions.

- **Lungi:** Sarongs stitched into a tube shape and most commonly worn by men in South India. The ends are often gathered and tucked into the waist to make them look more like shorts, although some men wear them long.

- **Salwar kameez:** Also referred to as a "Punjabi suit," these outfits combine kurtas with baggy drawstring trousers (*salwars*) and are normally worn with a *dupatta* draped over the chest. They're a popular, more comfortable alternative to the sari and can range from casual to quite formal, depending on the design and material used.

- **Sari:** The quintessential Indian women's dress, the sari is a length of fabric that is stylistically wrapped and draped over its wearer. Saris are usually around six meters long and paired with a short blouse, or *choli*.

- **Sherwani:** A long formal men's jacket often worn at weddings. A hip-length version of the *sherwani* is known as a Nehru jacket.

"caste-no-bar" arranged marriages are increasingly commonplace, some families are against the idea of intercaste matrimony.

RELIGION

Although India is a secular country, religion still plays a major role in the everyday lives of many of its people, and religion is a primary factor used in self-identification. The major religions in India are Hinduism, followed by Islam, Christianity, Sikhism, Buddhism, Jainism, and Zoroastrianism. Most of the people of Delhi, Jaipur, and Agra are Hindu, Muslim, or Sikh. Although tensions among groups (primarily between Hindus and Muslims) do occasionally flare up, most people live in harmony with each other, respecting the principle of unity in diversity that is so much the key to India's success.

Hinduism

The vast majority of Indians are Hindus, which is a widespread term used to encompass a vast array of practices and religious beliefs that are inspired by the teachings of the Vedas. Sometimes referred to as Sanatana Dharma, Hinduism is not so much a religion as a way of life. There's no central authority or governing body, and practices, deities, and beliefs vary drastically, not only from state to state but from household to household. There are a few central tenets, however, that most Hindus tend to ascribe to. The most notable is the concept of the eternal soul, or atman, which reincarnates through different lifetimes, accumulating and reaping its karma until it finally attains a state of *moksha* (liberation) from the seemingly endless cycle of rebirth and inherent suffering. Hindus also worship one or more of a pantheon of different gods, and most view these deities as different aspects of a supreme godhead known as Bhagwan, or God. The three main gods in Hinduism are Brahma (the creator), Vishnu (the preserver), and Shiva (the destroyer). People who are primarily devotees of Vishnu and his many incarnations (including Lord Krishna) are known as Vaishnavites. Those who have a stronger affinity toward Shiva are called Shaivites. Other popular deities include Ganesh, the elephant-headed son of Shiva and his consort, the goddess Parvati; Kali, the "terrific" form of Parvati who is worshiped widely in West Bengal; Lakshmi, the goddess of wealth; Saraswati, the goddess of music and education; and Hanuman, the monkey god who was the greatest devotee of Ram, another incarnation of Vishnu and the protagonist of the great Hindu epic the *Ramayana*.

Islam

Nearly 14 percent of Indians follow Islam, the majority of whom are Sunnis. India is also home to one of the largest Shia populations in the world, although this is partially attributable to the fact that India has a humungous population in general, second only to that of China. Islam first came to India's southern Malabar Coast in the 7th century, although it was through the Islamic Sultanates and, later, the Mughals that it really began to influence the culture of India's north. The Chishti order of mystic Sufis was instrumental in spreading the religion in India, and Sufi devotional music, Qawwali, developed here.

Sikhism

Sikhism was founded in 15th century Punjab by Guru Nanak Dev, the first in the lineage of the religion's 10 gurus. Their holy scripture is called the Guru Granth Sahib and is considered the final teacher in this lineage. Sikhs are monotheists, and their term for God is Waheguru. Their practices revolve primarily around meditation rather than on direct prayer or worship. For this reason, their temples, known as *gurudwaras,* do not contain idols. Sikhism also preaches equality, and unlike most other major religions, women and men are considered equal. Both men and women are expected to keep their hair covered while visiting *gurudwaras,* and many Sikh men keep their hair unshorn and tied in a turban; this is one of the five articles of faith introduced by Gobind Singh (1666–1708), the last guru of Sikhism.

The Arts

LITERATURE

India's literary tradition dates back to ancient times, when religious texts, such as the Vedas and the Upanishads, as well as epics that many believe to be a blend of myth and historical treatise, such as the *Mahabharata* and the *Ramayana,* were recorded. Reading modern English translations of these Sanskrit texts is challenging, especially for non-Indians who lack the context to understand the stories and sutras (verses).

India also has a huge modern literary tradition, and many of the country's most accessible novels and story collections are written in English. Major publishing houses, including Penguin and HarperCollins, have operations

The sitar is among India's best-known instruments.

here. Bengali Nobel laureate Rabindranath Tagore is among the most celebrated 20th-century Indian writers; he wrote in both English and Bengali. Other internationally popular writers working in English, often referred to as Indo-Anglian writers, include the incredibly witty Khushwant Singh, a master of both fictional humor and serious works of nonfiction; Vikram Seth; Kiran Desai; Salman Rushdie; Arundhati Roy; and Aravind Adiga. Some of India's most popular English-language writers today include Chetan Bhagat and Amish Tripathi, although they tend toward mass-market publications that are a bit less accessible to foreign readers.

VISUAL ARTS

The visual arts have been an important part of life in India for millennia, but for many centuries they were used primarily for worship and for the pleasure of the royals. Much of the older art traditions were inspired by practices introduced from Persia by the Mughals, including miniature painting. Sculpture and pottery have been around much longer, and bronze and stone pieces dating back to the Indus Valley civilization have been discovered by archaeologists. For a long time Indian art focused primarily on Hindu iconography, but the scene has witnessed a huge revival over the past half century thanks to contemporary artists of worldwide acclaim such as the recently deceased M. F. Husain. Other notable artists practicing today include Delhi's Subodh Gupta, known for making art from tiffin boxes (metal snack boxes), and his wife, Bharti Kher.

MUSIC AND DANCE

There are two major schools of Indian classical music: Hindustani classical from the North and Carnatic music from the South. Hindustani music is highly instrumental and uses rhythmic patterns known as talas that are maintained by percussion instruments (usually tablas). Carnatic music is composed to be sung, and the instruments used follow human voice patterns. Bollywood music, or *filmi,* is also incredibly popular in India, and although watching Bollywood films would lead you to believe that India's best actors are also talented vocalists, this music is actually recorded by a handful of playback singers and then lip-synched by actors. Over the past few decades, homegrown rock and, more recently, electronic music has caught on, and both are becoming increasingly mainstream in a country where Bollywood pop reigns supreme.

India also has a long tradition of classical dance forms that incorporate theatrics and tell stories. Many of the eight major forms trace their origins to temples and palaces. The most famous to originate in North India is Kathak, a storytelling form of dance that was once popular in North India's royal courts.

ESSENTIALS

Getting There and Around

AIR
International Flights

While you can enter India by land from Pakistan, Nepal, Bhutan, and Bangladesh, the vast majority of visitors to Northern India fly. The main airport is Delhi's Indira Gandhi International Airport (DEL). Delhi is served by most major international carriers, and there are direct flights from destinations around the world.

The quickest way to reach Delhi from the United States is by taking a direct flight. Air India and American Airlines operates direct routes between Chicago and Delhi; these take about 14.5 hours on the way to India, 15.5 hours on the way back. Air India has non-stop flights from New York's JFK, and United has nonstop flights from Newark, which are slightly shorter than the flight from Chicago.

Flights connecting in Europe are often a bit cheaper than direct flights. If you're on the U.S. West Coast and have more time than money, you may want to explore the option of buying two tickets: one to Bangkok or Kuala Lumpur and a second to Delhi. You can often get excellent deals to Southeast Asia from the West Coast, and once you're in Asia, it's relatively cheap and

© RAJAT DEEP RANA

easy to get to Delhi. Malaysian budget carrier Air Asia has direct flights from Bangkok and Kuala Lumpur, and if you book well ahead of time, you can get some amazing deals (although you have to pay extra for baggage).

Domestic Flights

Until the mid-2000s, domestic flights in India were quite expensive, and the country's airports were notoriously filthy and poorly maintained. Most people took trains, or buses for shorter distances. The bulk of flights were operated by the government-run Indian Airlines, which has since merged with Air India. Then, in the middle of the last decade, everything changed: A slew of new low-cost carriers started up, including SpiceJet, IndiGo, and GoAir. Larger airlines, namely national carrier Air India, Jet Airways, and Kingfisher, soon jumped on the bandwagon, launching Air India Express, Jet Lite, and Kingfisher Red (formerly Air Deccan), respectively. The first two are still operating, although Air India has been facing financial difficulties over the past few years. Kingfisher stopped operating their Red service in 2011, announcing that the budget leg of their airline was simply not fiscally viable.

India's airports have also undergone facelifts over the past few years, and most of the larger ones are on par, if not better than, the major air hubs in more developed nations. Some of the smaller domestic airports remain a bit on the basic side but are still cool and comfortable.

Note that it's often a lot cheaper to buy airline tickets in India or on Indian websites than it is through Orbitz or other non-Indian travel sites. Cleartrip.com is the most user-friendly of the lot, and they accept international credit cards. Makemytrip.com and Yatra.com are also excellent options. You can occasionally get even cheaper deals by buying directly from the airlines' websites, although some only accept Indian credit cards or use confusing and bureaucratic "payment gateways" instead of more straightforward secure payment systems.

Trains

Traveling by train gives you the opportunity to see parts of rural India that you wouldn't otherwise get to experience. It's also sometimes a bit quicker to get from point to point by train, especially if you take into account the amount of time it takes to get to the airport, check in, and board.

Trains in India range from the superfast *Shatabdi Express* and *Rajdhani Express* categories to "local trains" meant to shuttle people from cities to nearby villages. The latter tend to feature lower classes of carriage and usually travel at a snail's pace. The easiest way to reach many of the destinations listed in this book is via the various *Shatabdi* trains that link North India's key cities. *Shatabdi* trains generally travel during the daytime and have seats instead of the berths featured in most of India's long-distance trains. *Shatabdi Express* trains are air-conditioned (sometimes too much, so bring a shawl if you get cold easily) and food, tea, and water are included, along with newspapers if you travel in the morning. *Shatabdi Express* trains have two classes: First Class (1AC, sometimes called "Executive Chair Class") and a less-expensive Chair Car (CC). The main difference is that the First Class carriages have larger seats laid out on a two-by-two seating plan, and the Chair Cars usually have rows of three seats on one side and two on the other. The food is the same in both sections, although First Class passengers enjoy extra snacks (usually just a bag of chips) and get their tea served in china cups, rather than plastic. *Jan Shatabdis,* such as the *Kota Jan Shatabdi* that connects Delhi to Bharatpur (for Keoladeo Ghana) and Sawai Madhopur (for Ranthambore), do not have a First Class but have a Second Seating Class (2S), an unair-conditioned compartment. Food, water, and newspapers are not included on *Jan Shatabdi* trains.

Most other trains are designed for long journeys and are therefore furnished with berths or bunk beds. The cheapest type of carriage

DECODING INDIA'S TRAIN LINGO

1AC: First Class (air-conditioned). This code is used for the first or "executive class" seats on *Shatabdi Express* trains as well as the first-class berths on long-haul and overnight trains.

2AC: Second Class (air-conditioned). Two berths per wall partition, bedding included.

3AC: Third Class (air-conditioned). Three berths per wall partition, bedding included.

SL: Not air-conditioned. Three berths per wall partition, bedding not included.

CC: Chair Car (air-conditioned). Seated class.

2S: Second Seating (not air-conditioned). Seated class.

PNR: Passenger Name Record. This 10-digit number is assigned to all tickets, whether confirmed or on the waiting list, and can be used to track the status of tickets online or at automated booths at some railway stations.

RAC: Reservation Against Confirmation.

Tickets with this status are at the top of the waiting list and will likely get confirmed. You are allowed to board your train if your ticket has this code, but you have to ask the train conductor where to sit.

WL: Waiting list. Tickets with this status may or may not get confirmed. You are not allowed to board the train if your ticket has this code and is not confirmed. You can check the status of your ticket by using the PNR number online, or simply look for your name on the seating charts that are posted at the platform about 30 minutes before scheduled departure.

Tatkal: A set number of seats on each train are reserved for last-minute travelers under what is called the Tatkal Scheme. These tickets are released for purchase 24 hours before a train's departure and cost an additional 30 percent of the normal fare, or 10 percent of the fare for 2S tickets.

with this option, Sleeper Class, is not air-conditioned (although the windows in these carriages do open) and bedding is not provided. There are three levels of bunks in this compartment, arranged in small pods of six (the middle bunks fold up against the wall during the day so that passengers can sit comfortably on the bottom berths, which become de facto bench seats during the day). All other classes are air-conditioned and include bedding (two sheets, a pillow with a pillowcase, and a blanket). Of the air-conditioned classes, the cheapest is 3AC (this is basically the same as Sleeper Class, but with air-conditioning and bedding). The next level up is 2AC, with four berths per pod, and each pod has privacy curtains. First

Class (1AC) is, naturally, the most comfortable. The bunks in this class are wide and comfortable and are located in four-person pods with lockable doors.

Buses

Traveling by bus is another easy way to get around in India, and long-distance buses are a convenient way to get from city to city. Buses are not a recommended form of transportation within the cities, where they are generally jam-packed and routes are quite confusing.

Long-distance coaches range from the run-down government-operated variety to deluxe private buses with flat-screen TVs. The former usually pick up passengers anywhere along the

a cycle-rickshaw in Old Delhi

© MARGOT BIGG

route and don't cost much. They also move very slowly, and you aren't guaranteed a seat. Fancier buses are a lot faster and more comfortable and are usually air-conditioned. If you plan to read, sleep, or listen to music during your journey, you may want to avoid buses with TV or DVD service, which normally screen Hindi movies with the volume on full blast, often on repeat. Most buses in India do not have toilets and therefore stop every 2.5-3 hours so that passengers can stretch their legs and answer nature's call. They also stop for meals—cheaper buses usually at roadside eateries, or *dhabas,* whereas higher-end buses tend to take breaks at hotel restaurants or sprawling, hygienic "midway cafés" (essentially rest areas with decent diners). There are also sleeper buses available from private companies for longer routes (such as from Pushkar to Delhi). These come with single and double berths, although you'll generally need to bring your own sheets (sarongs and shawls can double quite nicely as bedding).

Taxis

Renting a self-drive car in most parts of India is difficult and expensive, and it is generally not a good idea. In fact, because traffic is chaotic, especially in Delhi and Jaipur, and roads are not clearly signposted, it is strongly discouraged. Hiring a car with a driver is a popular way to get from city to city, and many people rent a cab in Delhi and use it to travel to Jaipur, Agra, and the region. The cheapest types of car are dinky little Tata Indicas, basic cars that will get you from city to city but will be cramped if there are more than two people traveling. A more comfortable option is a Tata Indigo or Toyota Etios sedan. A three-night, four-day Golden Triangle trip from Delhi to Jaipur, Agra, and back in one of these costs around Rs. 11,000-12,000. This includes fuel, taxes, tolls, and up to 900 kilometers of travel (additional kilometers cost extra, of course). If you're traveling in a group, you can also rent a larger vehicle, such as a Qualis or a jeep-like Scorpio.

Many taxi stands and travel agents also rent cars by the kilometer (fuel included) and charge a daily "out-of-station" (out-of-town) fee to cover your driver's accommodations and food costs (although the kind thing to do is to pay for his meals or give him a bit of cash—maybe Rs. 50 per meal for food). Some hotels have complimentary drivers' quarters, which aren't always very nice; otherwise, drivers tend to sleep in their cars. Tolls and taxes are often paid separately if you're going about it this way. Note that a state tax is levied on all vehicles crossing into Uttar Pradesh, where Bharatpur and Agra are located.

Taxis are also quite useful for getting around larger cities, namely Jaipur and Agra. Both cities have radio cabs and private operators that can rent taxis for the day. You can occasionally hail metered cabs in Delhi too.

Rickshaws

There are two types of rickshaw in India:

human-powered cycle rickshaws and autorickshaws. Autorickshaws—sometimes called "autos" or "ricks" for short—are golf cart-like buggies that run on an engine similar to what you might find in a motorcycle. They aren't quite as fast as cars, although their small size makes them great for weaving in and out of traffic, and they often run on compressed natural gas (CNG), which makes them more cost-efficient and less polluting than a diesel- or gasoline-powered vehicle. In some cities, including Delhi, they have meters, but their drivers (called autowallahs) won't always use them. In Jaipur and Agra, you can hire an autorickshaw for a set period of time, even up to a whole day, but drivers usually try to coerce passengers into visiting shops; drivers generally get a commission for bringing passengers in, even if they don't by anything.

A cycle rickshaw is basically a three-wheeled cross between a bicycle and a cart, with a bike frame along with its front wheel at the helm and a two-wheeled cart—usually with a sun cover—big enough to carry two passengers in the back. Cycle rickshaws are usually used for short distances (up to few kilometers), and rates are negotiated in advance as they do not come equipped with meters. The men who pedal cycle rickshaws, called rickshaw pullers or rickshaw wallahs, are generally very poor migrants who have to do this incredibly arduous work just so their families can eat; be very generous to these people.

VISAS AND OFFICIALDOM
Visas

In most cases, you will need to obtain a visa prior to entering India. The Indian government has outsourced visa services in many countries, and now most visa applications are made through a third-party company, which then sends visa application materials on to the local Indian Embassy or High Commission for processing. In the United States, visa services are managed by Travisa Outsourcing (www.travisaoutsourcing.com), and you can apply either by mail or in person. They have offices, known as India Visa Centers, in San Francisco, Chicago, Houston, New York, and Washington DC, and where you apply depends on your state of residence.

VFS Global manages visa applications in many other countries, including Canada (www.in.vfsglobal.ca), the United Kingdom (http://in.vfsglobal.co.uk), Ireland (www.vfs-ireland.co.in), and Australia (www.vfs-in-au.net). In New Zealand, the Indian High Commission (www.hicomind.org.nz) in Wellington still processes visas.

There are separate visa categories depending on the purpose of your visit (tourism, employment, business, study, etc.). People of Indian origin and those married to Indians need to apply for an Entry Visa, also called an X Visa, regardless of the purpose of their journey.

If you don't have any family connection to India and you're just going to see the sites, you'll want to apply for a tourist visa—these are usually valid for six months and allow multiple entries. However, if you leave India at any point during your trip, you'll have to wait two months before reentering, unless you seek prior permission. If you plan to arrive in India and then head to Nepal, Sri Lanka, or another nearby country and then reenter India, you have to show your itinerary to the immigration officer when you first arrive in India. Alternatively, you can arrange for a Permit to Reenter India at the time you apply for your visa, although if you do this, you have to register your presence in India at Delhi's Foreign Regional Registration Office (FRRO, East Block VIII, Level II, Sector I, RK Puram, tel. 11/2671-1443) within 14 days of your arrival in the country.

India recently launched a visa-on-arrival pilot scheme for citizens of New Zealand, Luxembourg, Finland, Japan, Singapore,

EMBASSIES AND HIGH COMMISSIONS IN INDIA

U.S. Embassy
Shanti Path, Chanakyapuri
New Delhi 110021
tel. 11/2419-8000
http://newdelhi.usembassy.gov

Canadian High Commission
7/8 Shantipath, Chanakyapuri
New Delhi 110021
tel. 11/4178-2000
www.canadainternational.gc.ca

British High Commission
Chanakyapuri
New Delhi 110021
tel. 11/2419-2100
http://ukinindia.fco.gov.uk

Irish Embassy
230 Jor Bagh
New Delhi 110003
tel. 11/2462-6733
www.irelandinindia.com

Australian High Commission
1/50-G Shantipath, Chanakyapuri
New Delhi 110021
tel. 11/4139-9900
www.india.embassy.gov.au

New Zealand High Commission
Sir Edmund Hillary Marg
Chanakyapuri
New Delhi 110021
tel. 11/4688-3170
www.nzembassy.com/india

Cambodia, Laos, Vietnam, the Philippines, Burma, and Indonesia. These visas are issued only at the airports at Delhi, Mumbai, Kolkata, and Chennai and cost Rs. 3,000. They are valid for a period of 30 days and are only obtainable twice per calendar year. There must be a two-month gap between visits.

Note that visa rules and regulations can and do change without any notice. For the most up-to-date information, check with your local Indian consulate or contact the Bureau of Immigration of India's Ministry of Home Affairs (www.immigrationindia.nic.in).

CUSTOMS

The Indian customs process is pretty straightforward and similar to most other countries.

Before you land, flight attendants will pass out arrival cards that you need to fill out and present to immigration officials. You'll be asked to enter standard information (visa details, the address of your hotel in India, etc.) and sign the form. There's a small detachable tab at the bottom of the form—this is for customs. You have to note any dutiable items or currency you are bringing into the country and declare any agricultural products such as seeds and fruits as well as meat and dairy products that you are bringing in. When you go through passport control, the immigration officer will take the main part of the form and return the detachable customs tab to you. After you collect your checked luggage, you pass through customs, at which point you hand over this part of the form.

Accommodations

MAKING RESERVATIONS

It's getting increasingly easy to make reservations for Indian hotels online, either via email or directly on a hotel's website. Many hotels, especially cheaper guesthouses, will reserve a room without a deposit, simply because they don't have the online system to take one. Others will ask you to email or phone in credit card details to reserve your room—this is a common practice and nothing to be alarmed about. Some hotels also have reservation centers or corporate offices in major cities, such as Delhi, where you can make a reservation and put down a deposit in person.

HOMESTAYS

Homestays are a great way to experience local culture and are often a bit cheaper than traditional hotels. They are something like bed-and-breakfasts, but you'll generally live in slightly closer quarters with the proprietor than you would at a B&B. Most of the people hosting homestays are educated cosmopolitan types who have a good concept of the needs and interests of foreign visitors.

GUESTHOUSES

India doesn't have many youth hostels. Instead, most travelers on very restricted budgets stay in guesthouses, which are essentially cheap hotels without some of the standard frills (such as TVs and phones). Most have guest rooms with en suite baths. Guesthouses also often have room service and laundry, and they are popular with young people and backpackers.

HOTELS

Hotels in India range from luxurious five-star palaces to simple bare-bones accommodations. Note that the word *hotel* is sometimes used to mean "restaurant," primarily in South India and among South Indian people. While this can occasionally lead to confusion, it's normally pretty straightforward in North India, where a hotel is a place you do more sleeping than eating.

Food

India has an immense culinary repertoire, and no matter how many Indian restaurants you have visited overseas, you'll likely come across a lot of dishes you have never sampled, or even heard of, before. Many Indian dishes are very spicy, so make sure to ask your server if you want your food mild. If you do end up biting into a chili pepper, a good way of soothing your tongue is to suck on a piece of bread or eat a bit of yogurt. Drinking water only aggravates the pain.

Most North Indian meals consist of a vegetable dish or two, a meat dish (for nonvegetarians), and a side of stewed lentils, known as dal. A salad of cucumber, tomato, and red onion is often served as an accompaniment, as is *raita,* a cooling yogurt dish made with finely chopped vegetables, mint, and other light spices. Most Indian meals are served with either basmati rice or bread, and sometimes both. Popular breads include chapati, sometimes called roti, a more generic term; thick tandoor oven-baked naan; and *parantha,* pan-fried layered bread that is often stuffed with potatoes, cauliflower, and other vegetables.

REGIONAL FOODS
Mughalai Cuisine

Popular in North India and ubiquitous in Agra,

Mughalai food is rich, heavy, and delicious. This type of cuisine was inspired by the royal feasts introduced to India from Persia by the Mughal invaders, and it features lots of meat, especially mutton and chicken kebabs; creamy sauces; nuts; and thick breads such as naan.

Rajasthani Cuisine

As Rajasthan is a desert state, the cuisine is based less on fresh vegetables and more heavily on legumes, grains, and other items that can easily be stored in a hot climate. The food is also quite spicy: Many believe that chilies preserve food and keep those who eat them cool. Most restaurants in Jaipur and other parts of Rajasthan don't even serve Rajashtani food, partly because its fieriness makes it difficult for visitors—even those from other parts of India—to consume and partly because it's more a home-cooking tradition. If you do decide to go out for a typical Rajasthani meal,

however, you'll find a few key dishes. These include *lal maas* (mutton in spicy-hot red curry) and the quintessential *dal baati churma* (lentils served with flour dumplings and unleavened bread). Snack dishes such as *kachoris* (deep-fried disks stuffed with lentils or onions) and sweets such as *malpua* (pancake-like disks drenched in slightly rose-flavored sugar syrup) are also popular local delicacies.

Delhi *Chaat*

Given that Delhi's residents come from all over the place, there's an enormous variety of food choices, much of it influenced by the city's large food-loving Punjabi community. Delhi is known for stuffed *paranthas* and butter chicken (cooked in a sweetish mild tomato cream sauce), a dish invented at Delhi's Moti Mahal restaurant. What Delhi is best known for, however, is its huge variety of snacky street food, or *chaat*. Popular varieties include *aloo*

© MARGOT BIGG

Aloo tikki is a Delhi *chaat* favorite.

tikki (shallow-fried mashed-potato patties served with tamarind and coriander chutney), *papri chaat* (a mix of yogurt, tamarind, and coriander chutneys with deep-fried wafers made of all-purpose flour). *Panipuri,* also known as *golgappa,* is another popular type of *chaat.* This snack consists of thin hollow balls made of either wheat or semolina flour, stuffed with a mix of potato and legumes, and filled with spicy green water. They're bite-size in the way that sushi is bite-size, and you're expected to eat the whole thing at once; if you don't, the water will leak out all over the place. Because they contain water, it's best to get them from a clean restaurant and verify that they use bottled water—street vendors generally use whatever water is handy.

DRINKS

Although coffee is popular in South India, most people in the North are far fonder of tea, particularly masala *chai,* milky spiced tea made from boiling water, milk, sugar, tea leaves, and spices (usually cardamom, cloves, cinnamon, and sometimes ginger). This soothing hot drink is milky and sweet, and it's the inspiration for the redundantly named "chai tea latte" popular in Western coffee shops. North India has a great variety of special drinks, including *lassi,* the beloved Indian yogurt smoothie (served sweet, salted, or flavored with bananas or mangoes), *chaach* (buttermilk, often spiced), and *jaljeera* (a cooling spiced drink of cumin, mint, black salt, and lemon—most people agree that it's an acquired taste). Other popular libations include *thandai* (sweet milk and almond), *nimbu pani* (still lemonade, usually served sweet, salty, or a combination of both), and coconut water, usually sold at roadside stands and consumed through a straw inserted into a machete-hacked coconut.

Alcohol is also easily available in India. Popular lagers include the Indian brand Kingfisher as well as locally produce foreign beers, namely Tuborg, Carlsberg, Budweiser, and Heineken. High-end hotels and restaurants keep a good stock of liquor from around the world; the alternative is Indian-made Foreign Liquor, or IMFL—the name says it all. Locally produced Smirnoff, Bacardi, Teacher's, and Captain Morgan are popular. No visitor to India should leave without at least tasting Old Monk, a very sweet red rum that's usually mixed with cola. It's not to everyone's liking, but it is certainly the quintessential Indian spirit.

VEGETARIANS AND VEGANS

It's not uncommon to lose a few pounds while traveling in India due to the combination of hot weather, curry, and the relatively common stomach upset that many foreigners have to endure. Vegetarians tend to pack on the pounds, however, simply because India has so much delicious vegetarian food on offer (many Hindus follow strictly meat-free diets). You'll notice that food in India is referred to as "veg" and "non-veg." Most Indian vegetarians follow a "pure veg," or lacto-vegetarian regime, meaning they don't eat eggs. Vegetarians who eat eggs and dairy often refer to themselves as "egg-etarians" instead. Others will avoid omelets but might nibble on a cake containing "invisible eggs." Vegetarian food is normally marked with a green circle on menus and packaging, and food containing meat or eggs is indicated with a red circle. Even if you're not normally a vegetarian, giving up or reducing your consumption of meat during your India trip will greatly decrease your chances of falling ill.

Contrary to popular belief, it's easy to follow a strictly vegan diet in India, although many restaurant servers are not really familiar with the term *vegan,* so you may have to explain. Much of the vegetarian food you'll find in restaurants is cooked with oil rather than *ghee* (clarified butter) and is therefore vegan anyway. A typical North Indian black-lentil dish known as *dal makhani* is made with lots of butter, and the dumpling dish *khadi* is made from a yogurt base, as is *raita*. Always avoid *paneer* (a cheese), and check that dishes containing tofu are soy-based and don't use *paneer*, with a similar consistency, as a substitute. Most Indian sweets also use butter or condensed milk and are therefore best avoided by vegans, although *jalebis* are a vegan sweet-shop favorite, and Agra's famous *petha* is made from melon rather than milk, so it should be vegan (but double-check first).

Conduct and Customs

COMMUNICATION STYLES

Saving face, which often equates to fibbing to save embarrassment, plays a big role in Indian culture, and what might be perceived by Westerners as flat-out dishonesty is not viewed in the same way by everyone in India. For example, if you ask for directions somewhere, people will often point you in a random direction rather than admit that they don't know what you're talking about. While this might be perceived as a pretty nasty thing to do, it's actually just a way of preventing embarrassment. Of course, not everyone does this, and if you ask directions in a hotel, a nice shop, or from an educated person, you'll likely get a straightforward answer.

Also, keep in mind that being direct and forthright can come across as harsh to many Indian people, especially those not accustomed to dealing with Westerners. In business interactions, it's common to exchange pleasantries and engage in general chitchat, sometimes for hours, before getting down to business. As time in India is a lot more flexible than it is in the West, this is usually accepted as normal. However, it's perfectly acceptable to gently steer conversations back to the point when you're in professional situations—just do it gently.

Bargaining is important when shopping in markets and small shops in India, but it's very tacky to do it in upscale "fixed-price" boutiques. There's no real rule to bargaining, and contrary to popular belief, you won't necessarily get a better price if you bring an Indian person with you, especially if that person looks wealthy; you might in fact pay more, especially in backpacker areas where shopkeepers know that foreign visitors often travel on shoestring budgets, whereas Indian travelers generally don't. Another popular myth is that you should always offer half the price a shopkeeper quotes you. Merchants are expert hagglers and see through this formulaic approach right away—it makes it look like you don't know how much the item is actually worth. If you know the value, offer it; you can even be cheeky and just hand cash to the salesperson and be done with it—if he or she accepts, that is. Otherwise, decide how much you want to pay for something and then offer less. Smile, engage in a bit of banter, and work with your interlocutor to find a price that makes you both happy. And don't fight—have fun with it. Also, keep in mind that people in North India, particularly in Delhi, can come across as extremely aggressive at times. Don't let it upset you—it's not intentional. Some Delhiites speak in a way that sounds harsh because of the regional dialects and speaking patterns, which sound gruff to Indians from other parts of the country too.

BODY LANGUAGE

Body language plays a big role in communications, and there are a few gestures you should be aware of. The most famous is the great Indian head wobble, which ranges from a slight tilt of the head in the North to a full on gyration in the South. A sharp movement to the right or a shoulder-to-shoulder movement that looks a bit like a cross between a nod and a head shake usually means "OK" or "I understand." A wrist twist, in which a person extends the forearm out and then twists the wrist as if screwing in a light bulb, is a way to silently say "What is this?" or indicate bewilderment or confusion. A pinky wave means it's time to stop for a toilet break; taxi drivers often do this before pulling over to find the nearest wall.

TERMS OF ADDRESS

Family is incredibly important in India, and Indian languages have seemingly endless lists of words used to describe relationships with their relatives (imagine having a different word for your aunt depending on whether she was your father's sister versus your mother's). It's also polite to address strangers using family-member terms. You may call a man *bhaiya* or the slightly more formal *bhai sahib,* meaning "brother" or, roughly, "brother-sir." You can call a woman *didi* or, more formally, *behenji* (sister). If you are addressing the parent of one of your peers or someone who is significantly older than you, the terms "auntie" and "uncle" are appropriate (but be careful not to offend someone—if they are incredibly old and you aren't, the terms are always appropriate, but if you're not sure, it's better be charming and use a term for brother or sister instead). You can also call someone by their first name and add the suffix *-ji,* roughly translated to "sir" or "ma'am" to add respect. Because of this genderless term, Hindi speakers will sometimes call women "sir" to indicate respect. Don't take it the wrong way—it doesn't mean you are being mistaken for a man.

TABLE MANNERS

Table manners in India are different than in most other Western countries. First, food (even rice) is often eaten with the hands, especially at home, and there are no set rules for knife and fork use; in nice restaurants, do what you would do in your home country. Most curry and bread dishes are fairly easy to eat with your hands, and you might look odd eating a naan with a fork. However, eating rice with your hands is no easy feat and can be messy for the uninitiated. There's no shame in asking for a spoon if you're not given one. When eating with your hands, only use your right hand to bring food to your mouth (the left is traditionally reserved for toilet duties in India, and people usually don't even hand things to others with this hand). Indian people will often wash their hands and mouths after a meal. Some people, especially men, will let out a loud belch at the end of a meal, although this is considered incredibly rude in the higher strata of society.

When dining in an Indian home, you will be offered helpings of food over and over again, no matter how much you've eaten. If you're full, you will probably have to refuse profusely in order to get your point across, and then wait for your host to insist that you take just a little more. This is a common ritual of politeness—hosts insist to make sure that their guest really has had enough and is not too embarrassed to ask for more. If you can't eat another bite, say so with a smile. Also, try to finish everything on your plate if you can—if you don't, your host may worry that you didn't like the taste of what you were served.

TAKING PHOTOS

Always ask before taking photos—it's the polite thing to do anywhere in the world. Women may be a bit shy of having their photos taken by men, so don't be disheartened if you are refused. Some other people may ask for money in return for their photo, especially in touristed places. Other times, people will ask you to take their photo just for the experience (they often don't even ask to see the image after). Children are especially eager subjects, and you may encounter a horde of kids wanting their photos taken over and over again. It's nice to take at least one, but it's OK to refuse after the seven zillionth shot. Sometimes, people will want to have their photo taken with you, either on your camera or on theirs. Women are asked to be in photos much more than men are, and are often requested to hold babies or stand with the women of the family. Young men also often want their photos taken with foreign women. While agreeing to model for family shots is the nice thing to do, you have every right to refuse a photo with a young man.

Tips for Travelers

OPPORTUNITIES FOR VOLUNTEERING

There are plenty of opportunities for volunteering in India, especially if you have special skills such as water-resource management or medical training. Of course, even speaking English is enough, and many people come to India to volunteer at schools or orphanages, helping people improve their language skills. A good place to start researching organizations is www.idealist.org. This site has a comprehensive list of nonprofit organizations around the world as well as a number of volunteer opportunities. Just be aware that if you are coming to India to volunteer, you have to apply for an employment visa.

OPPORTUNITIES FOR STUDY AND EMPLOYMENT

India is becoming an increasingly popular spot to work and study, and you'll find a growing number of foreigners who have decided to make India home. If you're looking for a job, check out www.naukri.com and www.timesjobs.com. There's always a need for qualified professionals in India, although recent rules requiring foreigners to earn a minimum salary of US$25,000, a very high salary by Indian standards, has made it harder for Indian companies to afford to hire from overseas, even if they can't find qualified people in India.

Studying is also an interesting way to get firsthand exposure to life in India, and there are some excellent schools. The Indian Institutes of Technology (Delhi campus: www.iitd.ac.in)

are some of the most respected engineering colleges in the world. Delhi also has a few excellent universities, including Delhi University (www.du.ac.in), Jamia Milia Islamia (www.jmi.ac.in), and Jawaharlal Nehru University (www.jnu.ac.in). Note that employment visas and student visas can only be issued in your country of origin or residence.

ACCESS FOR TRAVELERS WITH DISABILITIES

India is not an easy place to travel if you have a disability, particularly if you use a wheelchair. A lot of hotels and older buildings don't have elevators, and the roads are often rocky and bumpy. Sidewalks do not always have ramps for wheelchairs. Blind people usually use white canes, and service dogs are uncommon. Some ATMs have audio options, however, although instructions on how to use these are rarely in braille, and the system is likely intended to help illiterate people rather than blind people. Deaf people in India have an easier time, as they can write things down. Indo-Pakistani sign language is somewhat different from ASL, although a lot of the signs are the same.

TRAVELING WITH CHILDREN

In many ways India is not an easy place to travel with children, and because of the health risks, it's better not to travel here with an infant. Diapers, baby food, and formula are also not easy to get outside of the upscale markets of Delhi, so come prepared. Also, no matter what your child's age, remember to take things very slowly—while a full day of running from historical site to historical site might be fascinating for an adult, it will likely be pretty boring for a kid and very tiring on short legs. Note that children will often struggle with the spicy food, hot climate, and long waits in line. On the upside, children are revered in India, and you will get a lot of loving attention if you travel with a foreign-looking child.

WOMEN TRAVELING ALONE

India is a perfectly safe place for solo female travelers, but there are a few things you should take into consideration. First, dress modestly. It's fine to wear jeans and even tank tops in most of India's most visited spots, although you'll need to cover your shoulders, and in some cases, your head, in religious places. Short skirts (above the knee) are generally not appropriate for sightseeing, although they are OK for going out to nightclubs in Delhi (just avoid walking down the street on your way out, if you can). Second, expect to be stared at. People in India stare at others a lot—sometimes out of boredom, sometimes out of curiosity, and sometimes just because they are spacing out, which is easy to do in a hot place. Many even stare unabashedly and may not stop even if you ask them to. If it's a woman staring at you, just stare back and smile—you're likely to get a smile back. If it's a man, just ignore it, as he may interpret a smile as an invitation for more staring, conversation, or even a romantic night out.

Sexual harassment (known locally by the dismissive term "Eve-teasing") and even groping are, unfortunately, pretty common in India. Both Indian and foreign women regularly have

to deal with unwanted advances and comments, at least to some extent; of course, most foreigners have the advantage of not understanding lewd remarks in Hindi. If you ever feel uncomfortable, look for other women or families, and go stand next to them or ask for help. Most Indians are incredibly warm and helpful and will do their level best to make sure you are kept out of harm's way.

SENIOR TRAVELERS

Plenty of seniors travel to India every year, and Indians' inherent respect for elders means that you will be treated with great respect if you are of the older generation. There are also special seats reserved for seniors on buses and on Delhi's Metro. If you have a hard time getting up stairs, you may have some difficulty in India, as elevators are not common, especially at historic sites.

GAY AND LESBIAN TRAVELERS

Although India is a fairly tolerant place, there's still a long way to go in terms of securing gay rights. Same-sex marriages are not recognized in India, and until 2009, homosexuality was illegal. While it's no longer a punishable offence, it's still heavily frowned upon. There's not much of a visible queer scene in Jaipur or Agra, but Delhi has a number of resources for LGBT people; check *Time Out Delhi* for full listings. There's also a gay pride parade every year at Delhi's Jantar Mantar as well as the annual Nigah Queer Fest (www.queerfest. com), which showcases LGBT art, film, and performances.

Health and Safety

VACCINATIONS

It's a good idea to make an appointment with your doctor or local travel clinic at least a month before you plan to depart for India to get advice about what vaccinations and preventative medicines you might need. Make sure you are up-to-date on routine vaccines, especially the one against tetanus. In the United States, tetanus vaccines are usually administered as part of the combined DPT vaccination, which also helps protect against diphtheria and whopping cough. You need a booster every 10 years. Also make sure you are up-to-date with your measles, mumps and rubella (MMR) vaccinations.

Most travelers to India are also advised to get inoculated against hepatitis A and B, typhoid, and polio. Hepatitis A is spread through contaminated food and water and is prevalent in India. This vaccine is given in two doses, an initial dose and a second dose after six months, although you are usually fine if you travel with just the initial dose, as long as you make sure to get the second one six months later. There's also a combined vaccine against hepatitis A and B if you haven't been inoculated against either. Hepatitis B vaccination is now routine in the United States, although people born before the mid-1980s may not have been vaccinated. Note that hepatitis B is only contractible through sexual contact and blood, but even if you don't plan to have sexual contact with the local population, it's a good idea to get vaccinated in case you need an emergency blood transfusion.

Typhoid is another common and easily preventable illness, and like hepatitis A it's spread through contaminated food. Vaccinations against typhoid are good for three years and can be administered orally or intramuscularly. Polio still exists in India, and even if you were vaccinated as a child, it's good to get a one-time adult booster. Tuberculosis (TB) is also prevalent, although the vaccine against TB, Bacillus Calmette-Guérin (BCG) is rarely administered in the United States. This vaccination has not proven very effective, and if you have had the vaccine, you can't be tested for TB using a tuberculin skin test as it provokes false positives. If you have had the BCG injection, you'll have a round scar on the upper part of your left arm. Some doctors may recommend inoculations against rabies and Japanese encephalitis if you are going to be working with animals or traveling in specific rural areas, although neither are commonplace.

If you don't get vaccinations, note that you are allowed to enter the country without proof of vaccination status, unless you come from a zone in South America or Africa where yellow fever is endemic, in which case you need a Yellow Card (international certificate of vaccination) to prove that you have been vaccinated. Remember that the public health situation in India is very different than in the United States, and you are far more likely to contract a disease here than in a developed country. If you do fall ill, the illness will cause far more damage to your body than a vaccine would have, and might even end up killing you.

FOOD AND WATER

Many of the illnesses travelers contract in India, from minor stomach upsets to hepatitis A and typhoid, can be traced to food and water, so it's very important to take a few precautions. First, be wary of eating meat-based food on the street and avoid street food altogether during the summer and monsoon months (approximately Apr.-Aug.), when bacteria have prime conditions to fester. Avoid ice and only drink bottled or filtered water, and while most people get away with brushing their teeth with

DEALING WITH POVERTY

No matter how hard you try, you will encounter a lot of poverty during your stay in India. You will be approached by beggars, some of whom will be only toddlers, barely old enough to speak but still able to extend a hand in search of alms. Others may be limbless or too deformed to walk. While India definitely has many people in need, a large fraction of beggars are actually working for criminal networks, and sadly, some of the disfigured people you see have actually been disfigured by the gangs they are enslaved to in order to increase their earnings. Oftentimes, women carry babies who are not their own and have been sold into begging by needy families. By giving them money, you may be contributing to their exploitation.

Whether or not you give is entirely up to you, and remember that if you do give to one person, you may attract a flock of others looking for money. As a rule of thumb, never give to children or to the able-bodied, although an elderly woman (who may have been kicked out of her home once she became a widow) may get my sympathies. Some people suggest giving money to charitable organizations, although you should verify an organization's reputation before donating, as many of them are corrupt. Alternatively, carry some fruit or nuts with you and pass these out when people ask. If they refuse, they are probably only interested in collecting money.

tap water, you may not want to take the risk, particularly if you're on a short visit. Salads in upscale restaurants are usually fine—they are often washed with filtered water, but if you're in doubt, just ask—and pretty much anything you get in a five-star hotel will be hygienic, even the ice.

Many visitors to India experience some sort of stomach problems, ranging from loss of appetite to full-fledged "Delhi belly" (severe traveler's diarrhea, sometimes accompanied by vomiting). Mild symptoms can normally be controlled with an over-the-counter medicine such as loperamide (Imodium), but you should seek a doctor if you have anything debilitating. Parasites such as giardia and, to a lesser extent, amoebic dysentery are common in India and need to be treated with antibiotics prescribed by a doctor, not a pharmacist.

MOSQUITOES

Aedes mosquitoes, common in India, are a major carrier of diseases, and the easiest way to avoid getting malaria, dengue, and *chikungunya* (CHIKV) is to avoid getting bitten. The best way to do this is by regularly applying mosquito

repellent (the stuff with DEET works best) and using mosquito coils (essentially antimosquito incense, widely available in India) or plug-in mosquito repellents (popular Indian brands include Good Knight and All Out). Keeping your ceiling fan on at night also helps by creating a whirl that mosquitos find difficult to fly through. Some people also choose to take antimalarial prophylactics; there are pros and cons to doing this, and they won't protect you against other illnesses, so it's best to discuss this option with your doctor.

ANIMALS

Animals are everywhere in India, and while you are unlikely to get attacked by an angry elephant or a ravenous tiger, there are a few things to keep in mind when dealing with India's more frequently spotted species. There are street dogs all over the place, and while a lot of them are friendly, you may not want to roughhouse with them: Rabies is still common, and if you get bitten, you'll have to face a series of painful shots in your buttocks—not exactly the best way to spend your vacation. The same goes for monkeys—if one bites you, rabies shots you

INDIAN BATHROOMS

TOILETS

If you're ever on a train in India, you'll notice that two types of toilets are available, "Indian Style" and "Western Style." Western just means that the latrines are of the seated variety, the same as you'll find at home. Indian-style toilets are of the squat variety and consist of two foot pads with a hole in the middle. There are also urinals for men and women that follow the same design but have a smaller hole, although these aren't very common.

Most, but certainly not all, hotels and guesthouses feature Western toilets. More upscale facilities have small spray hoses mounted to the wall used for post-business cleaning; others supply a jug for the same purpose. Nice hotels and guesthouses catering to foreigners often provide toilet paper, and public restrooms in shopping malls and restaurants are usually well stocked with it. However, if you are traveling by road, it's a good idea to carry a small pack of tissues with you, as the toilets in roadside eateries normally aren't well stocked. Hand sanitizer is also a must.

SHOWERS

High-end hotels usually have shower cubicles or shower-bath combos with shower curtains. However, many Indian bathrooms are essentially large rooms with drains on the floor and little demarcation between the shower and the main area. Central water heating is not yet the norm in India, and most houses have a separate boiler (known as a "geyser," pronounced "geezer"). Some ultrabudget guesthouses don't have geysers in the guest rooms, so you'll have to request a bucket of hot water to be brought to your room so that you can take a bucket bath. The easiest way to do this is to squat or kneel on the floor (some hotels also have very low stools to sit on while bathing) and use a jug (which will likely be provided) to pour water over your body.

---

must get. They might be cute, but they're fairly vicious, especially the reddish rhesus macaque variety. Avoid grinning at these creatures (remember, not all animals interpret bared teeth as a friendly gesture), don't mess with their babies, and don't withhold food from them if they are trying to get it from you—just give it to them and go. Errant bovines are usually pretty docile but can get spooked quickly, so give them a wide berth when passing. Remember that they are large and have horns.

HEAT AND SUN

The heat in India can get to you quickly, and it's important to adjust to it slowly, especially if you are coming from a colder climate. No matter how much you love extreme heat, a summer in Delhi with temperatures hovering in the mid-40s Celsius day and night will be challenging. Make sure to drink plenty of water (a minimum of three liters a day is appropriate for hot climates), wear sunscreen even if you have a dark complexion, and cover up. Loose light-colored clothing will actually keep you cooler than shorts and tank tops and are more culturally appropriate for India. Umbrellas, especially the ones with silver-colored interior linings that are sold all over India, provide excellent shade from the sun.

Keep Cool

Northern India can get very hot in the summer, and dealing with high temperatures becomes especially challenging when you add the dust and pollution of Delhi to the mix. Here are a few suggestions for beating the heat. Some may seem obvious, but they're often easily forgotten.

DRINK PLENTY OF LIQUIDS

Staying hydrated is the easiest way to keep your body cool and in proper form. Make sure you drink at least three liters of water or juice per day-and try to keep soft drinks such as cola to a minimum (they're very dehydrating). *Nimbu pani,* India's beloved sweet-and-salty still lemonade, is incredibly hydrating and will help keep your electrolytes in balance. If you start to feel really dehydrated, you can pick up a packet of rehydration salts from any pharmacy.

HAVE A CUPPA

Heat your insides to cool your outsides: It may sound like an urban legend, but it seems to work. Indians drink boiled tea on even the hottest of days, and many swear that it helps them deal with the heat.

COVER UP

Most people who grow up in cool climates assume that as temperatures increase, clothing should decrease. But have you ever noticed how the traditional dress in many of the planet's warmest countries tends to be body-covering? While this has a lot to do with the preservation of modesty in some places, it's also a practical way to stay cool. While shorts and tank tops are definitely better on hot days than woolen sweaters, you're better off wearing loose-fitting full-length cotton or linen clothing in light colors that will help protect you from the sun without trapping sweat in.

DITCH THE HIKING BOOTS

India's streets are dirty, and many people want to protect their feet from litter and the odd cowpat by wearing close-toed shoes. Others think that if they're going to do a lot of walking, they'd better get out the hiking boots. While these are perfectly logical arguments, it's sometimes more practical to head to your nearest outdoor store and pick up a pair of sturdy all-terrain sandals (such as Chacos or Tevas) for your India trip. Shoes and boots will keep your feet protected from the outside, but they also create the perfect environment for bacteria to breed. Moreover, many of India's religious

sites require visitors to remove their shoes (and sometimes socks) before entering, which means you'll spend a lot of time tying and untying your shoes. Finally, your body naturally loses a lot of heat through the feet, which is a blessing when temperatures pass 40°C. So wear sandals, and watch where you walk!

BREATHE

Breathing is our primary means for getting oxygen to our brains and other vital organs, which keeps us healthy and full of vitality. Unfortunately, many of us breathe shallowly and don't spend time focusing on deep inhalation. The Indian yogic practice of *pranayama,* extension of breath, is believed to increase the body's vital energy and thereby stamina. People who practice deep breathing regularly also tend to have better-adjusted internal radiators. Although pranayama encompasses a range of techniques, the easiest way to get yourself nicely oxygenated is by taking deep, full breaths into your abdomen and slowly releasing them. Just make sure you do this in a park or in your hotel room-there's nothing beneficial about deep whiffs of car exhaust.

PHARMACIES AND PRESCRIPTIONS

It's a good idea to bring all the prescription medicine you need with you during your visit to India, as not all medicines are available here. There are pharmacies all over the place, and most are happy to dole out medicines without a prescription; pharmacists are known for dispensing antibiotics like candy. Do not take antibiotics unless they were prescribed by a doctor, as taking the wrong antibiotic or following the wrong course can lead to multidrug-resistant and difficult-to-treat illnesses.

MEDICAL SERVICES

India has excellent medical services, as well as a growing medical tourism industry. If you are having a medical emergency, contact the front desk of your hotel or a hospital directly. You can also dial 102 for an ambulance.

Good hospitals in Delhi include: **Apollo Hospital** (Sarita Vihar, Delhi-Mathura Rd., tel. 11/2692-5858, www.apollohospdelhi.com), **Max Hospital** (2 Press Enclave Rd., Saket, tel. 11/2651-5050, www.maxhealthcare.in), **East West Medical Centre** (28 Greater Kailash I, tel. 11/2464-1494), and **Fortis Escorts Heart Institute** (Okhla Rd., tel. 11/4713-5000, www.fortisescorts.in). In Jaipur, **Fortis Hospital** (Jawahar Lal Nehru Marg, Malviya Nagar, tel. 141/254-7999) is your best bet. In Agra, **Asopa Hospital** (Gaicana Rd., By Pass, tel. 562/260-4606) has the best reputation.

INSURANCE

It's always a good idea to get traveler's insurance before any trip, which can protect you in case of illness and is especially handy if you need medical repatriation. You can sometimes get special travel coverage from your bank or insurance providers at a discount rate. When reviewing a policy, check whether it covers medical insurance, loss of possessions, or both. Also find out what the deductibles are and whether they pay hospitals upfront or simply reimburse you for medical expenses.

ILLEGAL DRUGS

Like everywhere in the world, illegal drugs are commonplace in India, and there are foreigners who have been sitting in Delhi's Tihar Jail for years awaiting trial for drug trafficking. The easiest way to avoid getting into trouble is not to bring them in or out of the country. Also, under no circumstances should you agree to carry suitcases or other items out of the country for anyone. Even if you check the luggage thoroughly, items inside may have false bottoms filled with drugs, weapons, undeclared gemstones, or even bombs.

Although you won't get the death sentence for drug possession in India the way you would in some neighboring countries, you can still get into a lot of trouble. Marijuana grows wild and in abundance here, but possessing any THC-containing products can still get you arrested. Bhang, an edible concoction made of cannabis and other plants, is legally sold in some government-authorized shops, particularly in Rajasthan, and it is acceptable during the annual Holi festival, but not much during the rest of the year.

CRIME

Violent crime against travelers in India is not common, but it is not unheard of either; the most likely scenario would be a bar fight rather than a random attack. Indian people are generally peaceful, and you're probably at greater risk of getting into a scuffle in your home country.

Crimes involving money and fraud are much more common, and foreign travelers make easy targets for pickpockets and scammers. Never carry all of your money in one place, keep an eye on your cell phone at all times, and don't let anybody convince you to carry gems (or anything else, for that matter) abroad. Always keep your luggage locked, and if traveling on overnight trains, it's not a bad idea to chain your luggage to your berth—there are special metal loops below the bottom berths for this purpose, and inexpensive chains and locks can be purchased at all major train stations. Women should be wary of walking alone after dark and, like anywhere in the world, should never accept rides from strangers. If you are a victim of a crime, you have to file a First Information Report (FIR) at the police station nearest where the crime took place. You'll receive a receipt of the FIR, which is evidence that the crime has been reported. You may also need this receipt to claim insurance refunds for crimes involving theft.

Information and Services

MONEY
Currency

India's currency is the rupee, abbreviated Rs., which is divisible into 100 paisa, although these are rarely used. There are rupee notes and coins; notes come in denominations of 5, 10, 20, 50, 100, 500, and 1,000, and get progressively larger with larger value. Coins come in denominations of 1, 2, 5, and 10. Coins in denominations of 10, 25, and 50 paisa are also still in circulation but are increasingly rare.

It's a good idea to always have a bit of small change on you. Due to a shortage of change in the country, breaking larger notes (especially Rs. 500 notes) is often very difficult. Also make sure not to accept worn or ripped notes, even if they've been taped together. Most merchants won't take them, and if you can't pass them off to someone else, you'll have to take them to a local State Bank of India branch to get them replaced.

CHANGING MONEY

It's easy to change hard cash in India, especially if you have U.S. dollars or euros; pounds sterling and Australian dollars are usually pretty easy to change too. There are government-authorized money changers in most touristed areas along with foreign-exchange bureaus that can also cash traveler's checks. Using an ATM directly is also an excellent way to get rupees—just check with your bank to make sure they don't levy heavy surcharges for this service.

TIPPING

Tipping is a customary in luxury hotels in India, as it is in most parts of the world. It's also a nice gesture to tip waitstaff, and although some upscale restaurants tack a service charge onto the bill, it doesn't necessarily go to the servers themselves. A tip of around 10 percent is customary in most restaurants, although rounding up to the nearest Rs. 100 is usually fine in cheaper places. Taxi drivers are not generally tipped for short trips, but a little something is always appreciated if you hire a taxi for an overnight journey.

COMMUNICATIONS AND MEDIA
Postal Services

There are post offices in all of the cities mentioned in this book, and the system is incredibly efficient. Letters weighing less than 20 grams cost Rs. 5 to send within India and Rs. 20 to send abroad. If you need to ship a parcel, you can choose the cheapest option, by surface, which takes about three months, but at Rs. 40 for the first 100 grams and Rs. 30 per additional 100 grams, you can't really expect speed. The next level up is Surface Air Lifted (SAL), a combination of air and surface mail. This costs Rs. 310 for the first 250 grams and Rs. 65 for each additional 250 grams to North America, Rs. 35 to Europe. Packages take about a month with this option. The fastest type of shipping—International Speed Post—takes just a couple of weeks at most and costs Rs. 425 for the first 250 grams and Rs. 100 for each additional 250 grams to North America; to Europe it costs Rs. 675 for the first 250 grams and Rs. 75 for each additional 250 grams.

You may be required to wrap larger parcels in white cloth and sew them shut before shipping. Write the address on the fabric with a black permanent marker. Most post offices in touristed areas have tailors who can do this for you for a small fee, and they'll supply the fabric.

Cell Phones

Most overseas cell phones will work in India, although they're often quite expensive to use. Alternatively, if you have an unlocked phone, you can buy a pay-as-you-go SIM card in India at most mobile phone shops. You have to bring your passport and a passport-size photograph with you at the time of purchase, and it's a good idea to have a local address; you can use your hotel's. Calling rates are some of the lowest in the world-expect to pay around Rs. 1 per minute for local calls or Rs. 1 per text message.

Internet

These days, most five-star hotels and an increasing number of midrange and budget hotels have Wi-Fi. Although Wi-Fi hotspots are becoming more common, they're nowhere near as commonplace as in the West. If you need to be online all the time, you can buy a USB modem or data card for around Rs. 3,000 from mobile telephony providers such as Reliance, Airtel, and Tata Indicom.

Newspapers and Magazines

India has the fastest-growing print media industry in the world, and English-language newspapers and magazines abound. Some of the most popular English-language dailies are *Times of India, Hindustan Times, The Hindu,* and *The Indian Express,* to name but a few. India also has a huge number of magazines, most of which are monthly or twice-monthly, including homegrown newsmagazines *Outlook, Tehelka,* and *India Today.* Indian versions of international titles include *Rolling Stone, Marie Claire,* and *Condé Nast Traveler.* In Delhi, *Time Out Delhi* and the local *First City* are excellent sources of local information and event listings.

Television and Radio

There are hundreds of TV channels in India, about 50 of which are broadcast exclusively in English. Local versions of National Geographic, Discovery, MTV, and VH1 are popular and contain a mix of international and India-specific programming. Radio is a little less exciting. Most radio stations play contemporary Indian pop songs, while a few play contemporary British and American music. The national radio station, All India Radio (AIR), has news broadcasts in both Hindi and English.

WEIGHTS AND MEASURES

The metric system is primarily used in India, with the exception of measuring height, where feet and inches are used. Fahrenheit is also used to measure body temperature, although most thermometers show both Fahrenheit and Celsius.

India also has its own unique terms for measuring weight and quantity that most visitors find confusing. The most common are lakhs and crores. A lakh is equivalent to 100,000 and is usually written as "1,00,000." A crore is equivalent to 10 million and is written as "1,00,00,000." A *crorepatti* is someone who has at least a crore in the bank, and the word has the same meaning in India as *millionaire* might elsewhere.

A *pao* usually refers to a 0.25 kilograms and is normally used when buying vegetables. A *tolah* is equivalent to 12 grams and is used frequently by jewelers, goldsmiths, and hashish dealers to measure their wares.

ELECTRICITY

Electricity in India runs on 220-240 volts AC, 50 hertz, so while British and European appliances will work, North American ones will not. There are two types of sockets (called "plug points"): smaller ones that have either two or three pins that will accept most European plugs, and larger M-type sockets used for larger appliances, such as refrigerators and space heaters.

TIME ZONES

There's a single time zone in India, and it is 5.5 hours later than Greenwich mean time. Daylight saving time is not observed.

RESOURCES

Glossary

aarti: prayer ceremony involving lighting of oil lamps

ADA: Agra Development Authority

ashram: Hindu hermitage, often focused on yoga or meditation

autorickshaw: a three-wheeled taxi built on top of a motor scooter chassis; known as a *tuk-tuk* in other parts of the world

autowallah: autorickshaw driver

ayah: nanny

ayurveda: India's traditional medicinal system

bazaar: market

Bhagwan: God, Godhead

bhakti: devotion

bhawan: house

biriyani: fragrant, slow-cooked rice dish

BJP: Bharatiya Janata Party, one of the two major political parties in India

Bollywood: Mumbai's Hindi film industry

canter: open-top minibus used for safaris

chai: tea

chappal: open-toed sandal

char bagh: quartered garden plan popular in Mughal times

cheetal: Indian spotted deer

chhatri: canopy or umbrella; also refers to cenotaphs, which often are capped with canopies in India

chipkali: gecko

CNG: compressed natural gas

Congress: short for Indian National Congress, one of the two major political parties in India

crore: 10,000,000

cycle rickshaw: three-wheeled combination of a bicycle and a cart used to ferry passengers short distances

dal: lentils

dargah: shrine

DDA: Delhi Development Authority

Devanagari: the script used to write Hindi and some other Indian languages

dhaba: roadside eatery

dhobi: person who irons and washes clothing

dickey: the trunk or boot of a car

diwan-i-aam: hall of public audiences

diwan-i-khas: hall of private audiences

djinn: genie

dosa: an eggless crepe (a *masala dosa* is stuffed with mildly-spiced potatoes)

dosha: bodily humor (in ayurveda)

filmi: Indian film music (lit. "of films"; can also refer to melodramatic behavior)

FIR: First Information Report (police report)

firang: foreigner

FRRO: Foreigners Regional Registration Office

ghar: fort

ghat: steps that lead into a river or lake

ghee: clarified butter

GOI: Government of India

gurudwara: Sikh place of worship

gurukul: residential school for spiritual aspirants

hammam: Turkish bath

haveli: large family townhouses, often built around open courtyards; common in Rajasthan

hawa mahal: palace of winds

idli: round spongy rice cake popular in South India

IMFL: Indian-made foreign liquor

INA: Indian National Army

ISBT: Interstate Bus Terminal

itar: essential oil

jali: screen; often refers to a carved marble screen

jharoka: decorative window or balcony common in Rajasthani architecture

jyotish: Indian astrology

kirtan: call-and-response devotional music

kund: water tank

kurta: tunic

lakh: 100,000

lassi: yogurt drink

Lok Sabha: lower house of the Indian parliament

mahout: elephant handler

mandir: Hindu or Jain temple

masala: spices

masjid: mosque

meenakari: a type of inlaid enamel jewelry from Jaipur

MHA: Ministry of Home Affairs

moksha: liberation from the cycle of rebirth

MRP: maximum retail price

nawab: ruler

NCR: National Capital Region

nilgai: South Asian antelope

NRI: Nonresident Indian; refers to Indians who no longer reside in India or have spent much of their lives overseas. Also sometimes used to describe Westerners of South Asian descent.

OCI: Overseas Citizen of India, the closest thing India has to dual citizenship

out of station: out of town

paan: a mix of herbs and spices wrapped in a betel leaf and chewed, especially after meals

paisa: 1/100th of a rupee; also the Hindi word for money

PAN card: Personal Account Number card, similar to a U.S. Social Security card or a British National Insurance number card

pandit: Hindu priest

paneer: soft Indian cheese similar in consistency to tofu; Indians often refer to it as "cottage cheese," but it's not at all comparable.

pao: 0.25 kilograms

parantha: fried flatbread, often stuffed with potatoes or other vegetables

petha: Agra's signature sugary pumpkin sweet

PIO: Person of Indian Origin, a legal status that allows right of abode to people whose spouse, parents, grandparents, or great-grandparents are from India

pol: gate (at a fort)

pranayama: yogic breathing

puja: ritual

Qawwali: Sufi devotional music

raita: cooling yogurt dish

Rajya Sabha: upper house of the Indian parliament

rickshawallah: rickshaw driver or puller; usually refers to a cycle rickshaw puller

RSRTC: Rajashtan State Road Transport Corporation

RTDC: Rajasthan Tourism Development Corporation, the state tourism board of Rajasthan

rupee: India's currency, often abbreviated to Rs. or INR

SAARC: South Asian Association for Regional Cooperation

SAL: Sea-Air-Land method of parcel shipping

Shaivite: devotee of the Hindu god Shiva, the destroyer

sheesh mahal: palace of mirrors

sutra: aphorism

Taktal: a special train quota for reserving last-minute seats

tala: rhythmic pattern

thali: platter of food; also a metal plate designed for serving a selection of different food items

tolah: 12 grams

UP: Uttar Pradesh, the state in which Agra is located

urs: death anniversary

Vaishnavite: devotee of the Hindu god Vishnu, the preserver, including his avatars, such as Lord Krishna

wallah: generic suffix used to imply "doer,"

"maker," or "seller"; for example, a *paan* wallah makes and sells *paan*.

zari: gold thread embroidery work popular in Agra
zenana: women's palace

Hindi Phrasebook

Hindi translations by Abhimanyu Singh Sisodia.

PRONUNCIATION GUIDE

Although Hindi is an Indo-European language that shares its early roots with English, there are many sounds that nonnative speakers find difficult to pronounce. Unlike English, Hindi is spelled phonetically when written in its official Devanagari alphabet. Some sounds don't exist in English or don't have an equivalent in the Roman alphabet. In this case, we've provided the closest possible English equivalent.

Note that a single *a* is used when transcribing Hindi into English to represent the vowel sound you hear in "sun" and "fun." The long 'a' as in "father" is represented with *aa*. In this guide, we've used *ay* to represent the hard 'a' sound as in "pay." Hindi also has a lot of aspirated consonants, which are represented by adding an *h* to the end of a consonant. So *th* in transliterated Hindi should not be pronounced like "the" but rather like "t-ha." You almost need to exhale the 'h' sound. Double consonants make the sound harder, so the consonant sound in *chhay* (the word for "six") is pronounced with much more stress on the *ch* than the softer word *chaar* (the word for "four").

Many English words have also made their way into Hindi. In some cases, the English word is used because there is no Hindi equivalent. Other times, a Hindi word exists but is rarely used and may sound at best archaic, at worst incoherent. In such cases, we have provided the English word, although bear in mind that to be understood, it's a good idea to Indianize the pronunciation of English words when using them in Hindi sentences.

NUMBERS

1 *ek*
2 *do*
3 *teen*
4 *chaar*
5 *paanch*
6 *chhay*
7 *saath*
8 *aath*
9 *nau*
10 *das*
50 *pachaas*
100 *so*
500 *paanch so*
1,000 *ek hazaar*
5,000 *paanch hazaar*
10,000 *das hazaar*
100,000 *ek laakh*
500,000 *paanch laakh*
1,000,000 *das laakh*
10,000,000 *ek crore*

DAYS OF THE WEEK

Sunday *Ravivaar*
Monday *Soamvaar*
Tuesday *Mangalvaar*
Wednesday *Brihaspativaar*
Thursday *Budhhvaar*
Friday *Shukravaar*
Saturday *Shanivaar*

TIME

today *aaj*
yesterday *kal*
tomorrow *kal*
the day before yesterday *parso*
the day after tomorrow *parso*
this week *is haftay*
last week *pichhlay haftay*
next week *aglay haftay*

this morning *aaj subah*

this afternoon *aaj dopaher*

this evening *aaj shaam*

tonight *aaj raat*

last night *kal raat*

one month *ek mahina*

six months *chhay mahinay*

late *der* (the word late is understood most of the time)

early *jaldi*

soon *jaldi*

later on *baad main*

now *abhi*

second *second*

minute *minute*

hour *ghanta*

one minute *ek minute*

five minutes *paanch minute*

quarter of an hour *pawnaa ghanta*

half an hour *aadha ghanta*

that day *uss din*

every day *har rose* (people often shorten it to *rose*)

all day *pooray din*

What time is it? *Kitnay budge rahay hain?*

It's (one) o'clock. *(Ek) budge raha hai.*

It's (one) in the afternoon/1 P.M. *Doh-paihar ka (ek) budge raha hai.*

(six)-thirty *saaday (chhay)*

a quarter till (one) *pawnay (ek)*

a quarter past (one) *sava (ek)*

one-thirty *dayrd*

two-thirty *dhaai*

USEFUL PHRASES

hello *namaste*

How are you? *Aap kaisay hain?*

fine *theek*

and you? *aur aap?*

so-so *theek thaak*

thank you *dhanyavaad*

thank you very much *bahut mehr baanee* (*dhanyavaad* is sufficient)

You're welcome. *welcome; koi baat nahin* ("no problem")

It's nothing. *Maamoolee baat hai.*

yes (correct) *haan* (*haanjee* is more formal)

no (incorrect) *nahin*

is *hai*

isn't *nahin hai*

I don't know. *Mujhe pata nahin.*

please *kripiya*

nice to meet you *aap se milkay khushee houee*

I'm sorry. *Mujhe maaf keejeeyay.*

good-bye/see you later *namaste/fir milainge*

one minute *ayk minute*

Excuse me, please (to get a man's attention) *zara suniye bhai sahib* (just *zara suniye* will suffice, but adding *bhai saab*, or "brother," is more polite)

Excuse me, please (to get a woman's attention) *zara suniye behenji* (just *zara suniye* will suffice, but adding *behenji*, or "sister," is more polite)

What is your name? *Aapka kya naam hai?*

My name is . . . *Mera naam...hai.*

How do you say...in English? *...ko Angrezi main kya bolte hain?*

Do you speak English? *Kya aap angrezi bolte hain?*

Do they speak English here? *Yahan angrezi boli jaati hai?*

Does anybody here speak English? *Yahan pay kisi ko angrezi aati hai?*

Would you like . . . ? *Kya aap...chahte hain?*

Would you like to have . . . ? (food) *Kya aap...layngay?*

Let's go. *Chalo.*

more *zyaada*

less *kam*

a little *thorda sa*

a lot *bahut zyaada*

hot (weather) *garmi*

hot (temperature) *garam*

cold (weather) *sardi; thankd*

cold (temperature) *thanda*

big *bara*
small *chhota*
better (than that) *uss say achha*
better (than this) *iss say achha*
best *sab say achha*
bad *bura*
quick, fast *tez*
slow *dheema*
easy *aasaan*
difficult *mushkil*
I don't speak Hindi well. *Main Hindi achhi nahin bolta* (if you are male); *Main Hindi achhi nahin bolti* (if you are female)
I don't understand. *Mujhhe samajhh nahin aa raha.*

TERMS OF ADDRESS

you (single or plural, formal) *aap*
you (single or plural, familiar) *tum*
he/him *voh*
she/her *voh*
my *mera*
his/hers *uusska*
we/us *hum*
they/them *woh, uun*
Mr., sir *shreemaan*
Mrs., Ms., ma'am *shreemati*
wife *patni*
husband *pati*
friend *dost*
son *beta*
daughter *beti*
brother *bhai*
sister *behen*
father *pita-ji; papa* (informal)
mother *maa*
grandfather (paternal) *dada*
grandfather (maternal) *nana*
grandmother (paternal) *dadi*
grandmother (maternal) *nani*
aunt *masi*
uncle (paternal, older than father) *taya; tau*
uncle (paternal, younger than father) *chacha*
uncle (maternal) *mama*

GETTING AROUND

Where is . . . ? *...kahaan hai?*
How far is it to . . . ? *...kitni door hai?*
How far is it from ...to . . . ? *...say...kitni door hai?*
highway *highway*
road *sardak*
north *uttar*
south *dakshin*
east *poorab*
west *pashchim*
straight ahead *seedha*
right *right* (*die* is the official word, but it's rarely used)
left *left* (*bye* is the official word, but it's rarely used)
next right/left *agla right/left*
driver *driver*
map *naksha*
toll *toll*
parking *parking*
Where is this bus going? *Yay bus kahan jaa rahi hai?*
What's the way to . . . ? *...ka rasta kaun sa hai?*
the bus stand (station) *bus stand*
the bus stop *bus stop*
the taxi stand *taxi stand*
the train station *railway station*
the boat *naav/kashti*
the dock *bandargah*
the airport *hawai adda, airport*
I'd like a ticket to . . . *Mujhe...ka ticket chahiye.*
first class *first class*
second class *second class*
round-trip *aana-jaana*
reservation *arakshan, reservation*
baggage *saamaan*
Stop here, please. *Kripya yahin rok deejeeyay.*
the entrance *pravesh*

the exit *nikaas/prasthan/baahar jaane ka rasta*
the ticket office *ticket ghar*
near *pass*
far *door* ('oo' as in "food")
to . . . *...ko*
toward . . . *...ki taraf/...ki ore*
by/through . . . *...say hotay huay*
from . . . *...say*
in front of . . . *...kay samnay*
beside . . . *...kay saath*
behind . . . *...kay peechhe*
the corner *kona*
the stoplight *lal batti*
a turn *mord*
right here *bus yahin*
somewhere around here *yahin kahin aas-paas*
right there *bus vahin*
somewhere around there *vahin kahin aas-paas*
street *gully*
block *block*
kilometer *kilometer*
bridge *pool*
toll *toll*
address *putta*

SHOPPING

I want . . . *mujhhe...chahiye*
money *paisa*
How much? *Kitna?*
May I see? *Kya main dekh sakta hoon?* (if you are male), *Kya main dekh sakti hoon?* (if you are female)
this one *yeh wallah*
that one *voh wallah*
expensive *mehenga*
cheap *sasta*
Can you go cheaper? *aur sasta ho sakta hai?*
foreign exchange bureau *paise badalne ki jagah, Forex*
I would like to exchange traveler's checks. *Main travelers cheque istemaal karna chahoonga* (if you are male), *Main travelers cheque istemaal karna chahoongi* (if you are female)
What is the exchange rate? *Exchange rate kitna hai?*
How much is the commission? *Commission kitna hai?* (The word for commission is *dalaali* but is not generally used in this context. *Aapka hissa* instead of commission would mean "your cut.")
Do you accept credit cards? *Aap credit card laytay hain?*

HOUSING

rent *kiraya*
apartment *kholi*
house/home *ghar*
kitchen *kitchen*
toilet *toilet*
shower *snaan* (verb), *snaan ghar* (noun)
heat *garam* (noun), *garmi* (verb)
water heater *geyser* ("GEE-zer")
fan *pankha*
deposit *deposit*
landlord *landlord*
insurance *insurance*
key *chaabi*
lock *taala*

AT THE HOTEL

hotel *hotel*
Is there a room available? *Kamra khalee hai?*
May we see it? *Kya hum dekh sakte hain?*
What is the rate? *Kitne ka hai?*
Is there something cheaper? *Aur sasta kamra hai?*
a single room *ek aadmi ke liye*
a double room *doh logon ke liye*
double bed *double bed*
twin beds *doh single bed*
with private bath *bath tub ke saath*
hot water *garam paani*
towels *tawliya*

soap *sabon*
toilet paper *toilet paper*
blanket *kambal* (rhymes with "humble")
bedsheets *chadurr*
air-conditioned *air-conditioned, AC ke saath*
manager *manager*

FOOD

I'm hungry. *Mujhe bhook luggey hai.*
I'm thirsty. *Mujhe pyaas luggey hai.*
menu *menu card*
order *order*
glass *glass* (often pronounced "gilass")
fork *kaanta*
spoon *chamach*
knife *chhoori*
napkin *tissue paper*
soft drink *cold drink*
coffee *coffee*
tea *chai*
sugar *cheeni*
salt *namak*
drinking water *peeney ka paani*
bottled carbonated water *soda*
bottled noncarbonated water *mineral water*
beer *beer*
wine *wine* (wine is also used to refer to alcohol in general)
milk *doodh*
juice *rass*
spicy *teekha*
not spicy *teekha nahin*
eggs *anday*
lemonade *nimbu pani*
papaya *papita*
watermelon *tarbooz*
sweet lime *mausambi*
apple *sayb*
orange *santra*
banana *kayla*
mango *aam*
chicken *murga* (chicken is understood most of the time)
fish *machlee*

mutton *mutton*
shrimp *jheenga*
beef *beef* (as the cow is sacred to Hindus, be careful when asking for this)
bacon/ham/pork *soovar* (literally, "pig"; be careful when ordering pork as it is prohibited in Islam, and this word is considered dirty. Most places that serve pork will understand the English word.)
shellfish *seepdaar machhli/ghongha* (most places that serve it will probably understand shellfish.)
rice *chawal*
nonvegetarian *maasahari*
vegetarian *shakaharee*
vegetables *sabzee*
fried *tadka maar key*
roasted *bhuna*
breakfast *naashta*
lunch *lunch*
dinner *dinner*
the check *bill*

HEALTH

I am sick. *May beemar hoon.*
doctor *doctor*
hospital *hospital* ("aspattaal")
pain *durrd*
fever *bukhaar*
stomachache *payt durrd*
headache *sir durrd*
burn *jala hua*
antibiotic *antibiotic*
ointment; cream *murrham*
bandage *patti*
gauze *saafi*
cotton *roowee*
sanitary napkins *use brand name, e.g. Kotex*
toothbrush *toothbrush*
dental floss *dental floss* (not stocked at a typical store)
toothpaste *toothpaste*
dentist *daant ka doctor*
toothache *daant main durrd*

Call a doctor. *Doctor ko bulao.*
Take me to . . . *Mujhe...leke jao.*
vomiting *ultee karna*
drugstore *chemist*
medicine *dawa*
pill, tablet *golee*
condom *condom*

POST OFFICE AND COMMUNICATION

Long-distance telephone *ISD*
(international)/*STD* (to a different city)
I would like to call . . . *Mujhe...ko phone karna hai.*
post office *daak ghar*
letter *chitthee*
stamp *stamp*
postcard *postcard*
registered mail *registered post*
money order *money order*

package; box *parcel; dabba*
string; tape *rassi; tape*

AT THE BORDER

visa *visa*
residence permit *residence permit*
embassy *doothaawaas; embassy*
customs agent *custom officer*

EMERGENCIES AND SAFETY

police *police*
ambulance *ambulance*
firefighter *fire brigade*
thief *chore*
Help! *bachaao!* (literally, "save me")
I'm lost. *Meh kho gaya hoon* (if you are male);
Meh kho gayee hoon (if you are female)
Fire! *Aag!*
Can you help me, please? *Meree madad keejeeyay?*

Suggested Reading

Adiga, Aravind. *White Tiger.* New York: Free Press, 2008. This best-selling novel shows readers life in India through the eyes of a villager working as a big-city driver.

Ali, Ahmed. *Twilight in Delhi.* New Delhi: Rupa & Co., 2008. Originally published in 1940, this novel tells of life for Muslim people in Old Delhi in the early 20th century.

Keay, John. *India: A History.* New York: Grove Press, 2011. A recently-updated edition of Keay's comprehensive guide to India's history from ancient times to present.

Miller, Sam. *Delhi: Adventures in a Megacity.* New York: St. Martin's, 2010. The musings of a longtime expat as he explores Delhi's many sides.

Mishra, Pankaj. *Temptations of the West: How to Be Modern in India, Pakistan, Tibet, and Beyond.* New York: Picador, 2007. An exploration of an increasingly globalized India from one of the country's most eminent essayists.

Murari, Timeri. *Taj: A Story of Mughal India.* New York: Penguin, 2005. A novel about the building of the Taj Mahal and the people behind it.

O'Reilly, James, and Larry Habegger, eds. *Travelers' Tales India.* Palo Alto, CA: Travelers' Tales, 2004. A selection of short stories based in India from well-known travel writers.

Sawhney, Hirsh, ed. *Delhi Noir.* New York: Akashic Books, 2009. A collection of short stories set in different Delhi neighborhoods, all written in the film noir style.

Sen, Amartya. *The Argumentative Indian: Writings on Indian History, Culture and Identity.* New York: Picador, 2006. A collection of essays on contemporary Indian society from Nobel Prize–winning Indian economist Amartya Sen.

Singh, Khushwant. *Delhi: A Novel.* New York: Penguin, 2000. Acclaimed author Singh explores Delhi past and present in this sometimes erotic, sometimes humorous novel.

Singh, Khushwant. *Train to Pakistan.* New York: Penguin, 2011. A moving and insightful tale set during the Indian Partition.

Sutcliffe, William. *Are You Experienced.* New York: Penguin, 1999. A hilarious account of a young man traveling around on India's backpacker circuit.

Tammata-Delgoda, Sinharaja. *A Traveller's History of India.* Northampton, UK: Interlink Books, 2007. This compact volume presents India's history from the Indus Valley civilization all the way up to the present century in an accessible, easy-to-read format.

Tharoor, Shashi. *The Elephant, the Tiger, and the Cell Phone: Reflections on India—The Emerging 21st Century Power.* New York: Arcade, 2008. Essays on change and diversity in India and what this means for the country's future.

Theroux, Paul. *The Elephanta Suite.* New York: Houghton Mifflin Harcourt, 2007. Three insightful novellas, each written from the perspective of different American visitors in India.

Tully, Mark. *No Full Stops in India.* New York: Penguin, 1991. Observations on India from the BBC's former New Delhi bureau chief.

Internet Resources

INDIA

Bureau of Immigration, Ministry of Home Affairs
www.immigrationindia.nic.in
The Government of India's immigration website; includes information about visas.

CDC India
www.nc.cdc.gov/travel/destinations/india.htm
Health advice for travelers to India from the U.S. Centers for Disease Control and Prevention.

CIA World Factbook: India
www.cia.gov
The U.S. Central Intelligence Agency's guide to India; includes statistics on demographics, economy, and more.

Eat and Dust
http://eatanddust.com
An expat foodie eats her way through India and chronicles her adventures on this blog.

Incredible India
www.incredibleindia.org
Nationwide visitor information from India's Ministry of Tourism.

India Mike
www.indiamike.com
A popular online forum devoted to travel in India.

Indian Railway Passenger Reservation Enquiry
www.indianrail.gov.in
Online database of train schedules and seat availability.

The India Tube
www.indiatube.com
Online magazine devoted to travel in India.

DELHI
Bring Home Stories
www.bringhomestories.com
Entertaining video guides to traveling in Delhi.

Buzzintown Delhi
www.buzzintown.com
Deals and events in and around Delhi.

Delhi Events
www.delhievents.com
Detailed listings of upcoming events in and around Delhi.

Delhi Tourism
http://delhitourism.nic.in
Delhi's tourism board.

The Delhi Walla
www.thedelhiwalla.com
Delhi as seen through the eyes of an insightful and knowledgeable local blogger.

Time Out Delhi
www.timeoutdelhi.net
Time Out Delhi's website. Not as information-packed as the print version of the magazine, but still has some useful reviews.

JAIPUR
Buzzintown Jaipur
www.buzzintown.com
Deals and events in Jaipur.

Rajasthan Tourism Development Corporation (RTDC)
www.rajasthantourism.gov.in
Rajasthan's tourism board, including information about Jaipur, Pushkar, Shekhawati, and Rajasthan's national parks.

AGRA
UP Tourism
www.up-tourism.com
Uttar Pradesh's tourism board, including information about Agra and vicinity.

Index

List of Maps

Acknowledgments

I'd like to extend my utmost gratitude to all the people who helped make this book a reality. I'm incredibly grateful for the patience and perseverance of Rajat Deep Rana, a brilliant photographer, super travel companion, and dear friend. I'm honored to have so many of his photos appear in the pages of this book.

I'm incredibly grateful to my dear friend Mohd Shafi Billo and everyone at Destination India Travel Centre in Delhi for their wealth of advice on how to best experience India's Golden Triangle.

I'm indebted to Abhimanyu Singh Sisodia for creating a top-notch phrasebook and for his research assistance on this book.

So many people helped in the making of this book, including Himmat Anand, Karan Arora, Robyn Bickford, Stephanie Borris, Holly Brown, Jyoti Chitkara, Dhruba Dutta, Aparupa Ray Ganguly, Mandi Gilroy, Becky Holloway, Ruchi Jain, Akshraj Jodha, Ashna Kapur, Suju Krishnan, Paritosh Ladhani, Ratna Malhotra, Tania Phillip, Maj. And Mrs. R.C. Rana, my little brother Pintu Rajoriya, Parveen Sayed, Richa Sharma, Bobby Shekhawat, and Ashima Sukhani.

Many thanks to the entire team at Avalon Travel, particularly my editor Elizabeth Hansen, with whom I've had the great fortune of working a second time. Big thanks to Grace Fujimoto, Lucie Ericksen, Sierra Machado, and Natalie Nicolson. I also want to extend a special thanks to Albert Angulo for putting in a ton of hard work to ensure the maps in this book are the best on the market.

Finally, as always, I'm thankful to my parents, Matthew and Carla Starrett-Bigg, for everything.

www.moon.com

DESTINATIONS | ACTIVITIES | BLOGS | MAPS | BOOKS

MOON.COM is ready to help plan your next trip! Filled with fresh trip ideas and strategies, author interviews, informative travel blogs, a detailed map library, and descriptions of all the Moon guidebooks, Moon.com is all you need to get out and explore the world—or even places in your own backyard. While at Moon.com, sign up for our monthly e-newsletter for updates on new releases, travel tips, and expert advice from our on-the-go Moon authors. As always, when you travel with Moon, expect an experience that is uncommon and truly unique.

KEEP UP WITH MOON ON FACEBOOK AND TWITTER
JOIN THE MOON PHOTO GROUP ON FLICKR